Will You *Sparkle* in the *Light*

An End-of-the-Age Crash Course in the Supernatural
and Spiritual Things of God

PROPHETIC INSIGHTS

LINDA L. EVANS

WESTBOW
PRESS®
A DIVISION OF THOMAS NELSON
& ZONDERVAN

WestBow Press books may be ordered through booksellers or by contacting:

WestBow Press
A Division of Thomas Nelson & Zondervan
1663 Liberty Drive
Bloomington, IN 47403
www.westbowpress.com
844-714-3454

ISBN: 978-1-4497-1959-3 (sc)
ISBN: 978-1-6642-4619-5 (hc)
ISBN: 978-1-4497-4597-4 (e)

Library of Congress Control Number: 2011931998

Print information available on the last page.

WestBow Press rev. date: 10/07/2021

CONTENTS

Dedications...v
Introduction vii

Chapter 1   A Timely Visit With, Jesus...1

        a.   1st, 2nd, and 3rd appearances
        b.   God's Time Table
        c.   Angel of the Harvest

Chapter 2   Supernatural, Understanding, Knowledge, and Wisdom (part 1).................23

        a.   How To Receive Power

Chapter 3   Supernatural, Understanding, Knowledge, and Wisdom (Part II)..............39

        a.   Biblical Supernatural Powers
        b.   The Power To Get Wealth

Chapter 4   Who Is Your Mirror Image?...59

        a.   Passed On To The Children
        b.   New Age Attemps

Chapter 5   Satan's New Age Minions 67

        a.   Unseen Predators Stalking the Children
        b.   New Age Umbrella Terms

Chapter 6   Voices of the Spirit 77

        a.   Four Steps In Recognizing Voices
        b.   Angel Appearance
        c.   Unknown Tongues
        d.   Prayer

Chapter 7   Satan In Person, and The Blood of Jesus.........................99

     a.   Healing from Cancer
     b.   Recognizing Demons
     c.   13 New Age Pillars Targeting Your Children

Chapter 8   My Moment in Heaven.........................115

     a.   Birthing of the Soul, and Spirit
        1.   Five Stages of Pregnancy
        2.   Blood Cries
        3.   Abortion

Chapter 9   Sex, The Devil's Advocate.........................141

     a.   Schizophrenia
     b.   Teen Sexuality
     c.   Depression, Emotional Distress
     d.   Sex, Marriage, Love
     e.   Restoration

Chapter 10   The Enemy's Camp of Fallen Angels.........................171

     a.   Discerning Spirits
     b.   Demonic activity in the Church
     c.   Bondage, Slavery, Danger
     d.   Error in the Church
     e.   Take the Good and Run With It

Chapter 11   Will You Sparkle in the Presence of God, or Burn?.........................195

     In The Presence of God
     a.   New Spiritual Body
     b.   Heaven and Eternity
     c.   Your White Robe
     d.   The Bride of Christ
     e.   Eternal Damnation

Chapter 12   Another Visit With Jesus.........................225

Thanks To God.........................235
Acknowledgments.........................237
Notes.........................239

DEDICATIONS

To my son Edward, daughter Patricia Leigh, and my 4 grandchildren, Zachery Joseph, Patrina Leigh, Montana, and DJ. My message to them is: Come to know the Lord Jesus Christ as your personal Savior with a heartfelt change. Don't accept Him into your life, and then forget about Him. He will love you when no one else will.

You must come to know Him personally, by a born-again experience. John chapter 3 says, "Ye must be born again." Read the Bible, know what it says, understand its message, and implement its values into your life. The Bible is your instructions to a happy and prosperous life. Then you must develop a prayer life, where you commune with God the Father daily. Do this through the name of Jesus, by the Holy Spirit.

Find a church that believes in the gifts of the spirit being in operation today and adhere to wise counsel. Come to know Jesus in a personal relationship and you will never be barren or unfruitful. Come to know the personal sacrifice Jesus made for each one in that He laid down His life for you because He first loved you.

Always remember I have loved you, prayed for you, and I give you, my blessings. I bless you going out, and I bless you coming in. Use the Bible to guide you and do the work of the ministry. If you do, you will never be barren or unfruitful in the promises of God, and you will be successful in all you do. I have given my life, and service to the Lord, not only because I love Him, but also because I love you, and that you may live in the heritage, and blessings of the Lord.

I give a special dedication to my aunt Mary who has been an inspiration to me since my childhood, and through my adult life. Thank you for being more like an older sister, and for loving me unconditionally. Thank you for believing in me when no one else did. Thank you for not turning your back on me when the world, and family walked away. Thanks for all your support when I had none. Most of all thank you for your prayers, your enthusiasm in this project, and your love. I AGAPE Love you.

I love you all unconditionally by the heart of God. When you all grow old in the word you'll understand.

INTRODUCTION
Prophetic Insights

The contents of this book are true, based on personal experiences of the Author, and others. It is a book teaching how to step out of the natural, and into the supernatural realm of the Spirit of Truth.

You can possess the most powerful weapon on earth for performing Spiritual warfare. The weapons of our warfare are not carnal but mighty through God to the pulling down of strongholds (2 Corinth. 10:4). For we wrestle not against flesh and blood, but against principalities, against powers, against the rulers of darkness of this world, against spiritual wickedness in high places (Eph. 6:12).

No matter the challenges life brings you can be an over comer. God is the same yesterday, today, and tomorrow. He is alive, and He will still manifest Himself to you the same as He did to the Patriarchs of the Old Testament, and the Apostles of the New Testament. Our forefathers laid a foundation by God for which all generations may live.

There is no viable reason why people today can't know God in His Omnipresence, Omniscience, and Omnipotence. Take this journey in simple truths passed down through the ages, so you can know your Creator in the way He has provided.

I will begin with a vision the Lord gave me one evening while in prayer, and Bible Study. The Holy Spirit took me in the Spirit to the edge of a vast wheat field. It was night, yet a bright light shone on the field lighting every blade of wheat swaying in the breeze. The wheat mimicked soft, golden, rolling waves of the sea. As I watched, my heart pounding, a fine mist resembling a black fog came rolling toward me. It hovered over the field in midair like a blanket. The fog was a foot thick as it hovered about a foot over the top of the field. It was such a dense fog that it appeared more like a cloud.

In the distance there was a storage shack, aged and about to fall, sitting in the middle of the field. Suddenly, out of the darkness of the left of heaven came a huge flash of light, accompanied by the terrifying sound of crackling lightning so loud it sounded like an electrical stage production backed up with the roar of thunder. The lightning struck the shack, and it began to burn. As the flames roared, and crackled I was speechless. I didn't know where I was and didn't know what was happening.

Then something in the right of heaven caught my attention. In the Bible days of old, it would have been described as a wheel turned on its side, rotating counterclockwise. It had emerald, colored stars outlining its circumference. I had never seen anything like it. It resembled a spacecraft much like those as seen in the movies. I watched as it slowly glided across the darkness of the universe. There was no noise as the supernatural forces of the spirit were entertaining, and the universe was its stage.

Suddenly, the entire heavens began to descend to the earth. In total amazement, not knowing what to do, I felt powerless. My thoughts were, "When the sky begins falling there is nowhere to run."

There was complete silence now as the heaven came closer to the ground. It looked like the heaven but turned out to be a vast grayish white cloud large enough to appear as heaven. It lowered itself down, covering the black fog, and the field of wheat. The spacecraft likewise disappeared into the cloud. Once the cloud was resting atop the fog, and wheat field, it began to unfold like a scroll, and stopped at my feet. I waited with anticipation as one would wait for a gift to be unwrapped. Once the cloud stopped unfolding there in the far distance, in plain sight, stood the City New Jerusalem.

Even though I had no real knowledge of this city, in an instant I knew in my heart its name and origin. I knew that it was my home came down from God. From where I was standing, I couldn't see the fine details of its architect, but could see it was made of white glittering crystal clear like glass. I saw the tops of buildings protruding above the walls, and they too glittered like crystal. The entire structure was translucent, as it sparkled, and twinkled like the stars in the universe.

There were no colored stones evident at that moment, and I didn't see the color as in diverse kinds of stones like John the Revelator had seen. It was surely a city came down from God, hovering in midair, adorned like a bride in white apparel. As I continued to watch I saw hints of color in the sparkles from the city, but the city was too far away to see what made the color. It would be revealed later.

Ready to go into the city, I proceeded to step into the cloud. As I raised my foot the Holy Spirit spoke, and said, "Not yet." Quickly pulling my foot back, the Holy Spirit continued to speak, "You can go into the city, but not now. I have work for you to do. Are you willing to give your all to me? If you do, this is your inheritance."

No sooner had I formed the thought "Yes" I was back in the natural realm. I was frantic for a moment but soon calmed by the realization of what I had just encountered. My intimacy with the spiritual things of God immediately gave way to peace as God then revealed His passion for the work, He had called the Church to do.

The field of wheat swaying in the breeze represented unstable souls in the Church being swayed by every wind of doctrine. The black fog represented Satan's snare as it covered the earth with gross darkness. The lightning bolt was the word of God coming down from heaven as the two-edge sword setting on fire everything that wasn't built upon His word. The shack represents the broken down, deteriorating condition of the Church unsuitable for threshing, and overcome by the conditions of the age of this world. There was much wheat ready for harvest, but no suitable threshing floor was found on which to fan the chaff. God then set the shack (The Church) on fire with His breath as in burning the impurities out by His judgement.

Meaning of the wheel. The stars on the wheel represented the church of today as being divided and holding different doctrines much like the seven churches in the book of Revelation. The rotating of the wheel represented the church in its present state of apostasy spinning counterclockwise searching for signs and wonders instead of focusing on the harvest of Christ. There was an inner wheel, representing the true Church going around in a flat circle, and moving very slowly in a clockwise motion. The true Church was being stripped of her weights and being moved into position to receive her reward.

The Church of today has two legs. One leg is made of true believers, and the other is made up by those who have forsaken their faith, and beliefs. While there are those who make up the body of the true Church, many others have become corrupt. In their endeavor to put the promises of God into effect by their own selfish attempt at righteousness they reject knowledge. They are the apostate Papacy, and the other is the Church of Jesus Christ continuing in the faith without fail.

For the most part The Church of today lives according to the flesh, and outward appearance instead of living in the Spirit, and the circumcision of the heart. Yet God has a remnant that belongs to Him. They are known as the body of Christ. In this body there is neither Jew nor Greek, Male nor Female, Bond nor Free, but one in Spirit with God. Galatians 3:28-29 KJV

Like the wheel the shack holds a double meaning. The shack is where the threshing floor is supposed to be but has become the enemy's camp. The burning of the shack is illustrative of the enemy's camp in the true Church where Satan has made his abode. He and those like him will be in torment and will go up in flames.

The separation of the tares from the wheat has begun in the lives of Christians. It is Judgment on the house of God. This book is about how to recognize the tares in your Christian walk, what changes you may need in your life, how to change, and what you will receive once the changes are made. The New City Jerusalem is the reward for the true believer if they remain faithful, and true believing God, and in the work of the ministry bringing in the harvest of Christ.

However, ready or not, the time is at hand, and the end time events have begun. It is time for the Church to restore their soul and spirit, and to trim their lamps for the return of the bridegroom. Jesus is coming for His Church, one that is spotless, and without wrinkle. When the earth begins to move, and the heavens begin to descend, there will be no place to go accept with Jesus, and only those He knows will He take with Him.

The time is soon where there will be no turning back to do the first works over. That time will come suddenly, like a thief in the night, overtaking those who are not watching, and those who don't know the signs of the times. Like John the Baptist, one crying in the wilderness, "Prepare ye the way of the Lord", the same cry is being heralded to the Church and the people of the earth in modern time. The trump of warning is sounding, and the cry of Moses can be heard above the roaring of the lion, that ole Satan, "Let my people go".

The following is a prophetic word to the Church given to me by the Holy Spirit on January 25TH, 2010:

PROPHETIC WORD FOR BELIEVERS IN 2010, BASED ON VISION WHILE IN INTERCESSORY PRAYER JANUARY 25TH, 2010, WASHINGTON, NC

THE COUNTERFEIT HAS COME AND IS NOW OPERATING, LEADING, AND TURNING THE WORLD EVENTS TO COME IN A COUNTERCLOCKWISE DIRECTION. KINGDOMS, NATIONS, CITIES, STATES, COMMONWEALTHS, AND COUNTRIES ARE ESCALATING FASTER, AND FASTER INTO DESTRUCTION AS THIS IMPOSTER-DECEIVER LEADS THE WORLD BACKWARDS. EVENTS WILL BEGIN TO HAPPEN SO FAST THAT IT WILL BE SPINNING LIKE A WHEEL UNTIL IT BECOMES A BLURRED VISION TO THE NATURAL EYE. THIS IS THE DEFRAUDING OF THE PEOPLE. THIS BACKWARD MOTION IS AN UNNATURAL MOTION AND WILL CAUSE MUCH DESTRUCTION. THINK OF A MECHANISM LIKE THE CLOCK. THE WORLD IS THE SECOND HAND THAT MOVES SWIFTLY, AND AS IT MOVES IT PUSHES THE HOUR HAND CLOSER TO THE HOUR. IN THIS CASE THE SECOND HAND IS MOVING IN THE WRONG DIRECTION AND IS MOVING BACKWARDS FASTER, AND FASTER, OUT OF CONTROL. AS IT WINDS BACKWARDS, IT CAUSES A CENTRIPETAL FORCE TO OCCUR AND BEGINS TO CAUSE ANOTHER WHEEL TO EMERGE, GRAVITATING TO THE CENTER, OF THE OUTER WHEEL'S REVOLUTION. THIS INNER WHEEL APPEARS TO HAVE NO MOTION BUT IS MOVING AT THE PACE OF

THE HOUR HAND ON THE CLOCK, IN A CLOCKWISE DIRECTION. IT SEEMS IMPOSSIBLE BECAUSE THE INNER WHEEL IS ROTATING ON THE SAME AXLE AS THE OUTER WHEEL. IT'S LIKE THE SECOND HAND MOVING IN THE WRONG DIRECTION, BUT THE HOUR HAND IS STILL MOVING IN THE RIGHT DIRECTION. THIS SEEMS IMPOSSIBLE, BUT IS POSSIBLE, BASED ON THE HOUR HAND BEING CONNECTED TO THE AXLE IN A DIFFERENT WAY, AND IS RAN BY A DIFFERENT TIME MOVEMENT THAN THE SECOND HAND (the Spiritual Realm versus the natural realm). THE CENTRIPETAL FORCE IS WHAT CAUSES THE INNER WHEEL TO EVOLVE AND GRAVITATE TO THE INNER CIRCLE OF THE OUTER WHEEL. BECAUSE THE INNER WHEEL IS TURNING IN THE RIGHT DIRECTION FORWARD, IT IS MOVED INTO THE CENTER, AND IS OUT OF LINE WITH THE DESTRUCTION WHICH IS GOING TO OCCUR FROM THE SECOND HAND GOING IN THE WRONG DIRECTION. THIS UNNATURAL BACKWARD MOVEMENT WILL CAUSE THE MECHANISM TO SELF-DESTRUCT. ON THE INNER WHEEL I SAW PEOPLE REPRESENTING THE TRUE CHURCH BODY GOING ON AS USUAL, BUT THEY WERE NAKED. NOT IN AN OBSCENE WAY BUT STRIPPED OF THEIR CLOTHING (WEIGHTS). THE OUTER WHEEL WAS LIKE A MOTION PICTURE FILM CLIP, OR NEWS REEL SPINNING COUNTER CLOCKWISE. IN THE FIRST FILM CLIP I SAW THE WORLD LEADER GLARING BACK OVER HIS SHOULDER AT THE EVENTS FOLLOWING HIM, SUGGESTING THEY HAD BETTER BE FOLLOWING HIM. IN THE NEXT CLIP I SAW A CATHEDRAL, AND THEN CITIES, STATES, KINGDOMS, NATIONS, COUNTRIES, COMMONWEALTHS, ETC FILLED THE OTHER CLIPS. THERE WAS NO CERTAIN ORDER, BECAUSE THE FASTER THE EVENTS OCCURRED THE MORE BLURRED THE PICTURES BECAME. THE ONLY FILM CLIP VERY VISIBLE WAS THE FIRST ONE THAT CONTAINED THE IMPOSTER-COUNTERFEIT LEADER BARAK OBAMA (NOT SAYING HE IS THE ANTICHRIST) AND PART OF THE SECOND FILM CLIP, WITH THE VISIBLE TOWER OF A CATHEDRAL REPRESENTING THE TWO LEGS, THE APOSTATE CHURCH AND THE TRUE CHURCH. AFTER THE SECOND FILM CLIP I COULDN'T SEE THE INDIVIDUAL THINGS, BUT I KNEW WHAT THEY WERE. THE CATHEDRAL HAS A DOUBLE MEANING. IT REPRESENTS THE APOSTATE CATHOLIC CHURCH, AND THE TRUE CHURCH COMING OUT FROM AMONG THEM. THE TRUE CHURCH WILL BE THE ONLY THING THAT WILL BE PULLED OUT OF HARMS WAY.

THE FATHER SAYS, "AS THE LEADER LEADS THE WORLD BACKWARDS IT WILL SELF-DESTRUCT. THESE DEVASTATING EVENTS WILL MOVE THE CHURCH, THE TRUE BELIEVERS, INTO THE RIGHT DIRECTION. THE CHURCH BODY BY CENTRIPETAL FORCE WILL BE PUSHED INTO THE CENTER OF THE OUTER WHEEL, AND OUT OF HARMS WAY". THE FATHER SAYS TO THE BODY OF TRUE BELIEVERS, "I HAVE SHAKEN ALL THAT CAN BE SHAKEN, AND NOW I WILL STRIP THOSE OF MY BODY, OF THEIR WORLDLY GARMENTS WHO ARE WILLING TO STAND NAKED BEFORE ME, IN SPIRIT AND IN TRUTH. DO NOT BE AFRAID OF THE THINGS HAPPENING AROUND YOU, AND BE NOT ALARMED, FOR I AM THE LORD THY GOD WHO WILL DELIVER YOU FROM MY WRATH. I WILL SET YOU APART FROM THE WORLD BY A CENTRIPETAL FORCE, LIKE THE SEPARATION OF THE WHEAT FROM THE TARES. IT WILL BE A SEEMINGLY SLOW MOTION, SO THAT THE WHEAT WILL NOT BE HARMED. CONTINUE TO WALK BEFORE ME AND BE THOU PERFECT. CONTINUE TO LIVE, SET APART FROM THE WORLD AND DO NOT LOOK BACK FOR ANY REASON. LOOK NOT TO THE LEFT, NOR TO THE RIGHT, AND I WILL TAKE YOU OUT OF HARMS WAY. STAY ON THE STRAIGHT AND NARROW. IT WILL APPEAR THAT THE BODY IS NOT MOVING FORWARD, BUT LIKE THE HOUR HAND ON THE CLOCK, MY BODY WILL MOVE, WILL PROSPER, WILL BE FRUITFUL, AND WILL MULTIPLY. THE GREAT TRANSFER IS HAPPENING. BE PATIENT, UNAFRAID, DILIGENT AND FAITHFUL. LIVE FROM DAY TO DAY SEEKING FIRST THE KINGDOM OF HEAVEN, AND YOU WILL SEE THE SALVATION OF THY GOD. THE TIME IS VERY SHORT. THAT YOU MAY BE DELIVERED, THESE THINGS MUST COME TO PASS IF YOU DO NOT LOOK BACK. IF YOU LOOK BACK YOU WILL BE CAUGHT IN THE CENTRIFUGAL FORCE OF THE SECOND HAND-THE WORLD, WHICH LIKE AN F-5 TORNADO WILL PULL YOU BACK INTO THE PATH OF DESTRUCTION. WHEN YOU HAVE DONE ALL TO STAND, CONTINUE TO STAND, FOR I THE LORD GOD SHALL DO THE WORK. I HAVE SET INTO MOTION THOSE THINGS THAT CANNOT BE REVERSED, BEGINNING WITH THE DAY MY SON DIED ON THE CROSS. HIS DEATH WAS VICTORY, A MASTER PLAN FROM THE BEGINNING, BUT NOT UNDERSTOOD BY THE ENEMY. SO LIKEWISE, THE TIME IS NOW FOR THE MASTER PLAN OF SALVATION TO BE FULFILLED. THE TIME OF THE GENTILES IS FAST COMING TO ITS END. THOUGH IT SEEM TO TARRY, IT WILL NOT", SAITH THE LORD.

- In addition: All the while I was seeing the clock, the hour hand was pointing at 2 minutes to 12, the midnight hour. I don't know for sure what this means, but I believe it could mean 2 minutes as the next 2 years, and the 12 means 2012. Calculate from Feb. 1st, 2010. Or it could mean when the doomsday clock is set to 2 minutes to midnight these things will begin to happen.
- On the evening of Feb. 9th, this vision was brought to remembrance, and I realized the film clip containing the cathedral represents the false religion-religious leader (Revived Roman Catholic Church), or system that is already in place, working with the counterfeit leader. The apostate church.
- On Feb 10th, I was in Honey Baked Hams in Rocky Mount North Carolina, for lunch and to visit a friend. A young woman came in to pick up her order. She said she had just returned from Italy and had seen some of the most awesome cathedrals. St Mark's Cathedral had stood out to her. As she was describing it to me, I realized its description fit the one I had seen in the vision. I later found a picture on the Internet of St Mark's Cathedral in Venice, and it was exactly as I had seen in the vision. This was a confirmation from a total stranger without her even knowing it must have been a Divine appointment. I felt she must have been sent by God. She suddenly appeared, no one in the establishment had ever seen her before, she struck up a conversation with me, then suddenly she was gone.

Until this prophecy I didn't fully understand the wheel turned on its side. Having this prophecy in this time assures me the time is at hand for these things to begin to come to pass.

Will You Sparkle in the Light is a trump of warning for the people of earth, believers, and unbelievers alike. It gives information concerning the things Christians have adopted into their lives leading them in the wrong way: things of which to be aware, and the way to overcome them. Hope deferred makes the heart grow sick (Proverbs 13:12) best describes the condition of the Church in the times in which we live. Many Christians have been watching, and waiting a long time, for the return of Christ. According to the current calendar He should have already come in the Rapture, therefore we are living on borrowed time.

My hope is to encourage the Church that Jesus is just around the corner from coming back. Each chapter is filled with instruction that will steer the Christian from heading in the wrong direction and steer the unbeliever into the right direction. There are many diversions in the world against the righteous, and the sinner, causing each group to wander further from God. These diversions have blinded the eyes of understanding and are the cause of people choosing the ways of the world as the natural course for their lives. We have chosen the kingdoms of the world Jesus refused. Satan flashes the world before us that we will bow to worship him.

The chapters of this book are designed to show the power of the Holy Spirit, the presence of God, and the principles by which we are to live. Things that are coming and how to get through them. I pray Christians will come to see some of the major ways they have allowed Satan to enter their faith walk, and how he has led them off the path of righteousness a little at a time. Then suddenly one day, they wake up in the middle of great turmoil, and tribulation, and ask, where is God, their spiritual eyes blinded once more? This same thing happened to the children in the wilderness. So long as Moses was with them, they kept their eyes on the ways of God. When Moses went up on the mountain the children looked back to the idols of Egypt, falling back into idol worship, from which they had been delivered.

My desire is to introduce the one true God by discussing some of His supernatural and spiritual attributes available to everyone, and to help people know Him in a personal way, even when you can't feel His presence. God is a spirit, and to know Him in spirit and in truth He must be approached in spirit, and truth. God hates a lie and the pride of life, yet these are the areas of downfall the believer has adopted as their lifestyle, having little or no knowledge, and no understanding of where they have gone wrong.

We are without doubt living in the end of the Church age. God wants a people who will worship and praise Him. In these last days people must move in the supernatural realm if they want to meet God and come to know Him as He is. I pray this book will shed light on the supernatural, and spiritual things of God. To help others come to know Him in the way that they can relate, and experience God in their lives. He is a God that honors faith and gives us a way, to understand the hope in Jesus Christ is the solid foundation. Amen!

Chapter 1
A Timely Visit With, Jesus

In 1973 I rededicated my life to God, married a Baptist Minister of Music, and by all appearances, we were a couple dedicated to Jesus Christ. We went to church, and lived a decent life, but neither of us really knew Jesus. In fact, we didn't know anyone who knew Him.

I was saved but had no true knowledge of who God is until January 4th, 1984. This was the day I was healed of breast cancer, and through this healing I met a God I didn't know existed. I remember thinking how long I had been a Christian and had never heard that God is a healing God.

I read my Bible a little, and witnessed, but like most young people, I didn't know the importance of learning the word of God. Once I met the Great Physician, there was no stopping. In the days to come, up to three years, I had an intense devotion to learning about the God that heals. I spent endless hours devouring His word, praying, and communing with Him. The relationship I now have with God is my most valued treasure.

Approximately one year after the cancer healing, I asked God for over two months to allow me to see Jesus. I had heard that others had seen Him, talked with Him and He had been seen of five hundred directly after His resurrection. In my way of reasoning, I thought it only fair and right that God allow me, also to see Him: Not that I thought myself special, I just didn't know any better. I had received Jesus into my heart at age 6, and I wanted to see Him with my eyes, as had others. In that moment I thought I was supposed to see Him.

I found we must stay in persistent prayer day and night asking Jesus to manifest Himself to us. In John 14:21, it reads that Jesus will manifest Himself, and I believed He would. Later I learned the scripture was in reference to another kind of manifestation, but I also learned that it means exactly what it says. Everywhere I went and in everything I did I was looking for Jesus to get a glimpse of Him – to see His face. Jesus was the only thing on my mind upon waking in the morning and going to sleep at night.

Linda L. Evans

My brother and I in 1985 were driving back, from a weekend in Palm Springs, to Los Angeles where we both lived. The day was beautiful. It was the kind of day rare for southern California. Usually, the sky is so thick with smog that white clouds, or any clouds, would have to be in the imagination. The day was a perfect spring day. The sun was shining, there was a gentle breeze, the sky was a deep blue, and there were white, fluffy clouds gliding across the sky. The grass on the hillside was greener than I had ever seen in this part of California. It was at the end of the rainy season, and everything looked fresh, new, and green. In a few weeks, the little rain that had fallen would no longer be evident, and the land would return to its dreary, dried-out state of desert.

It is about a two-hour drive from Palm Springs to Los Angeles, so I relaxed in the beauty of the moment. Leaning the car seat back I thought how long it would be before I see this scene again. My brother was driving, and I was looking out the window basking in the freshness of the day. Suddenly there appeared a man walking up the hillside in the far distance to my right front. Behind Him followed a large herd of sheep stretched out for what looked like miles. The man was a great distance away, and yet, he appeared very tall. I didn't understand why He looked so tall at such a long distance away. By my estimation, He would have been 700 to 900 feet tall or greater. He had shoulder length hair golden, chestnut in color. I could see the glistening of His hair, as the sunshine seemed to light up each strand. It shone like gold. He wore a long white garment tied at the waist with a cord belt made of strands of gold, and he carried a staff, I think, in his right hand. I can't remember for sure in which hand he held the staff.

Understand I was taken off guard by the scene. As fast as I sat up to get a better look, the man, and His sheep vanished into thin air. It wasn't until he vanished that I realized I had just seen Jesus. Excited I said to my brother, "I just saw Jesus". My brother had seen nothing. I was disappointed he hadn't seen Jesus. I felt privileged, and honored, and all I could do was humble myself before the Lord.

It was difficult to contain myself. Had I been driving I would have pulled over, gotten out, and would have ran, and shouted for joy. It was all so new to me. The joy, and excitement of seeing Jesus was a bit much to process. I did the next best thing. I rejoiced silently, with soft tears, and reverence. My brother may have been a little skeptical of the moment, he didn't say. He seemed to believe me in asking what Jesus looked like. One thing I've learned. If I tell someone I saw Jesus, and they don't ask what He looked like, I know they don't believe.

When I first saw the man in the distance, I really wasn't sure at first what I was seeing. For only a few seconds, I thought it was just a man with sheep. I did wonder for a moment whether sheep were common in that part of the country. I have since learned that according to Sheep 101.info, the 2007 Census of Agriculture, that California raises the second largest number of sheep in America.

I didn't know I was having a vision. As soon as my heart knew the man as Jesus, He, and the sheep vanished. Sometime soon after that day I came across the scripture in Jeremiah 24:7, "And I will give them a heart to know me, that I am the Lord: and they shall be my people, and I will be their God: for they shall return unto me with their whole heart." One of the best things about the Lord is His confirmation. Every time He gives a vision, or He speaks a revelation, He will always lead us to the scripture, confirming what He has said, or of what He wants us to know.

Since the vision of Jesus my Theological friends have asked, "Did you see His nail scarred hands?" People like to dispute any claims to seeing Jesus with the natural eye. It isn't necessary to see His scars, or his pierced side, unless there is doubt of His resurrection. Mary Magdalene, after His resurrection didn't see these abrasions, but knew Him when He spoke to her. She didn't recognize Him until He called her name. She recognized His voice. When Jesus appeared to the disciples, He showed them His scars, and they were glad. Cleopas, and another on their way to Emaus met up with Jesus, but they didn't recognize Him right away either by His scars, or His voice. It wasn't until Jesus went His own way that they recognized Him by the words He had spoken.

John Hagee, a Television Preacher and advocate of Israel, said in one of his sermons, "If anyone tells you they have seen Jesus go not there and don't believe them". He is referring to the verse Matthew 24:26 where Jesus is speaking to the Jews about His second coming. I am not telling you Jesus is in a particular place for you to go and see. I am telling you about His appearance to me.

I believe Jesus will appear to anyone in the manner they are most likely to believe. Thomas, one of the disciples, had already made up his mind he wouldn't believe until he saw, and touched the nail scars, and Jesus' pierced side. Thomas had doubt in his heart of the resurrection and couldn't have recognized Jesus in any other way. Doubt, and unbelief are blind, and needs proof, whereas faith, need only a heart to know Him. Most people can't see Him because they don't believe He is a real person and alive.

After arriving back home and unpacked from my trip I went onto the balcony and gazed up at the sky. The weather had changed from being sunny, to dark grey rain clouds, and a big wind had begun to blow. Rain was always welcomed in southern California being as even in the rainy season it hardly ever rained.

My mind reflected to earlier in the day when I had seen my Lord. Tears of Joy overwhelmed me. As I stood there reminiscing, singing a song of praise, soaking in the reflection of seeing Jesus, He appeared again. I blinked my eyes to clear the tears, and there He was. He was in the clouds looking at me. He stretched out His hands to me as if He were going to pick me up and hug me. This time I saw Him from the waist up. He stood far into the heavens, and His height didn't appear to be measurable. I can only determine His height stretched as high in the sky, if not higher, than where planes fly. He was extremely close to me, and seemed to be somewhat transparent, yet I couldn't see through Him. I couldn't get over the vastness of His size, and the fact He was translucent.

He looked at me with great compassion, and love. The nearest description to the look in His eyes were ones of a mother as she looks at her child in awe. His eyes spoke of great care, and comfort. As He reached out His arms toward me, He began to slowly fade into the clouds, and soon out of sight. I now realize the largeness of His stature, the closer He came to me, caused me to see less of Him. He didn't disappear rather my eyes could not distinguish His figure from the surrounding heavens because of His size. The closer He came to me the more He became the heavens. His size blocked out all space as far as I could see with the human eye. I was being nestled in the bosom of Jesus. I felt a warmth, love, and security I had not ever felt. The peace, and tranquility in that moment deleted all fear, confusion, and frustration. I became instantly filled with His love.

My emotions went from a state of extreme gladness to extreme sorrow. I stood there searching the heavens for another glimpse of my Lord. "Please come back," I cried. Over and over I called out to Him.

but He had left. I felt lonely, and desperate to be with Him again, yet very fulfilled to have seen Him.

Standing there with the wind blowing through my hair, tears of joy in my eyes, I began praising and thanking Jesus for coming to visit me. Though He was gone from my natural sight I realized He was still there. He had left His love with me. A love of trust, loyalty, honor, kindness, and oneness surpassing anything I've ever known. Love as I had known was shallow, empty, and void of what is real love. In that moment, I saw in the spirit realm the world walking in the deception of lust and pride and searching for a love existing only in Christ.

It was getting late, and before the rain began again, I needed to go into town. Driving to town I finished my chores and started driving toward home. Reflecting on the events of the day, I could hardly keep my mind on driving. I was making a left turn, when suddenly, there He was again. He was standing in the street, in the middle of the intersection. This time I could only see His feet, and ankles, and a small portion of his legs. I leaned my head out the car window to look up at Him, but He was too tall to see more of Him at that close range. Being pretty good at judging height, if I had to guess how tall He was, I couldn't do it. I used to say He stood around 700 to 900 feet tall, but that isn't even close to how tall He appeared here. His sandals were golden, as was His cord belt hanging nearly to the ground. His garment of white had a sky-blue panel down its front. Here again, He appeared to be transparent, but I couldn't see through Him.

I completed my turn, and for the third time, He seemed to have vanished again. I was so overwhelmed at this point I could hardly keep my composure. Never in my wildest dreams would I have thought to see Jesus three times in one day. In His third appearance downtown, I realized I was at His feet. This was significant, in that, I somehow knew He had placed me there. The first time I had seen Him that morning He was far away. The second time He appeared closer and the third time I was at His feet.

While driving home in a daze and recalling the appearances, I wasn't on cloud nine, I was on clouds so high it would be impossible to count. Not only had my prayers been answered in seeing Jesus, but I had seen Him three times over a period of about eight hours. Looking back, I wish I had looked at the time of each appearance. Time was the last thing on my mind while all this was happening. Two months passed before I had another visit with Jesus, and He revealed to me what these three appearances meant. I'll share His second visit in chapter 12 "Another Visit With, Jesus."

"First Appearance on the Hillside"

He explained the first time I saw Him I was a sheep in His flock. Seeing Him to my front right herding His sheep, positioned me on the corner, at the end of the far left, back row.

"Second Appearance on the Balcony"

While standing on my balcony, He heard me call out to Him, and He appeared in the clouds, reached over, picked me up, and drew me to His bosom.

"Third Appearance downtown"

In town, He placed me at His feet. Now instead of being far away in the flock, I was now right behind Him. He had placed me beside another sheep, and we were leading the herd. I later learned the bell sheep is positioned right behind the shepherd. Being placed in a lead position, leading the flock, is the same as being a minister. I don't know whom the other sheep is, but I'm sure if I'm meant to know, Jesus will show me. We were both right behind Jesus, following Him, and the sheep were following us. No matter what position we hold in the flock we are only a heart's cry away from our shepherd.

Not only was Jesus giving me a new place in the flock, He also revealed important knowledge about "time" in the spirit realm. His time isn't the same, as we know time in the natural. There is no time in the spirit realm. Its eternal. 2nd Peter 3:8 reads, "But beloved, be not ignorant of this one thing, that one day is with the Lord as a thousand years, and a thousand years as one day."

This scripture is self-explanatory, yet we really have no perception of its meaning. Time as we know time is different depending on who we are, what we are doing, and where it is being done. For example: A mother leaves her baby in day care for several hours, or ten minutes. The baby has no concept of the time passed when she returns for him. To a student in Junior High, seven hours in class may seem more like ten, or twelve. Some days in the office eight hours seem to pass quickly, or they can drag out, seemingly forever. In each of these examples, the hands of the clock move at the same pace – sixty seconds make a minute, sixty minutes an hour, and twenty-four hours make a day.

Consider the size of people. It will take a person of six feet tall less time to walk a mile than it would a person three feet tall, moving at the same pace. The taller a person the more distance he can cover with one step than that of the shorter person. The taller persons stride is usually wider, and one of his steps can make two or three of the shorter person's step.

I believe animals have a perception of time, but of the seasons rather than hours, or days. When you go away, and leave your dog with a sitter, the dog may miss you, but doesn't really know how long you've been away. The dog has no perception of hours from days, but the dog's chemical makeup discerns the seasons. Dog's shed their coat of hair in the summer and grow new hair in winter.

In the example Jesus gave me, He used the ant. The ant is referred to in scripture twice as being a wise people preparing their meat in summer and gathering in harvest (Proverbs 6:8, 30: 25). The ant is tiny and will take at least a minute to crawl the distance of three feet. This is not exact time, but close, based on trying to time an ant going this distance. An adult of medium height 5'3" to 6' can take one step, and in less than 2 or 3 seconds, has covered this same three feet. I found, by this experiment, size can determine the time span in which we live and move. It is all pertinent information to the times I saw Jesus.

I have always thought that driving, flying, or any mode of transportation at high speeds influences our bodies in some way; possibly moving us into the future. I believe this is what happens when a jet breaks the sound barrier. I never learned physics but am sure this is common knowledge.

However, compared to Jesus, as I saw Him, too tall to measure, I am in size to Him as the ant is in size to me. From the time I saw Jesus on the hillside until I was placed at His feet approximately eight hours had passed. For Jesus it took only a matter of seconds to turn around, bend over, pick me up, nestle me in His bosom, and place me at His feet. It is the same as if I were to bend over, pick up the ant, snuggle it in my bosom, and place it back on the ground at my feet, in one continuous motion. The ant is lifted to a height of at least four feet, nestled in my bosom, then, another four feet back down to the ground at my feet. The ant was at least two feet away from me when I picked it up covering approximately another two feet in its journey. To cover these distances for me was a simple movement and took only a few seconds of my time. To the ant, it probably took approximately two hundred seconds of its time.

Eight hours of my time being only a few seconds in Jesus' time stirred my interest. I have, for twenty-eight years, tried to solve this equation. I am good with numbers, but every time I tried to calculate this, my mind would go completely blank. It was as if I weren't supposed to know the answer and it wasn't until I started writing this book that I was able to come up with a formula. I'm not a date setter, however this conclusion was astonishing to me.

Jack Van Impe, Christian TV News host, Evangelist, Author calculated a generation to be fifty-two years. He based this on the number of generations recorded in the Bible from Abraham to Jesus. You'll have to purchase his product to see how he discovered his conclusion.

One evening in January 2011, I was thinking, and writing the things the Lord put in my heart. Suddenly, out of the blue, I decided to again try to work this equation. If I could find an answer, I could come close to finding the season when Jesus might return. He said we couldn't know the day or the hour, but we can know the generation or season. The signs of the times point to His soon coming, now more than ever. In fact, the signs ushering in the return of Christ, spoken in Matthew 24 are beginning to happen as I write.

It took only minutes to come up with a formula. I was completely caught off guard due to the many years I struggled with it. The following is a guess, not an exact formula, but it sure caught my attention. Based on eight hours of my time being only a few seconds of Jesus' time the following formula is my finding. Based on the time it took to bend over, pick up the ant, bring the ant to my chest, then place the ant at my feet, I used 3 seconds for this motion.

Jesus		Us
1 minute	=	24 hours or 1 day
1 hour	=	60 days
24 hours	=	1,440 days
1 week	=	28 years (actually 27 225/365 rounded off to 28)
70 weeks	=	1,960 years

According to Daniel chapter 9, Daniel's prophecy of 70 weeks until Messiah comes, (end of days – end of tribulation), and Jack Van Impe's calculation of a generation being 52 years, I came up with the following: In past years everything in Bible prophecy being fulfilled was based on 1948, when Israel became a Nation. Jack Van Impe recently declared on his broadcast, in January 2011, to calculate from the time Israel gained control of Jerusalem, in the 6-day war of 1967. Next add 52 years bringing us to the year 2019. According to Bible prophecy all prophecies needing to be fulfilled before Jesus said He would return met their fulfillment with the 6-day war of 1967, not Israel becoming a nation in 1948 although that was one of the prophecies.

Jesus said in Matthew 24, the generation who sees this fulfillment would not pass before the coming of the Son of Man (Jesus). Jesus also said this generation would see all the signs He mentioned in Matthew 24 come to pass converging at the same time. Everyone can see we are that generation. Subtract the 7 years of Jacob's Trouble from Jack Van Impe's 2019, and we get the year 2012. Add a generation of 52 years to my calculation of the year 1960, and we get 2012. This would put us in the first part of the 71st week of Daniel's 70 weeks, meaning we are on borrowed time. (Daniels 70th week has not yet happened).

However, because there is no 71st week, and our calendars, and timelines are not correct, or right on the money, we can bet we are at the brink of the 70th week of Daniels Prophecy. Meaning, I believe the tribulation is so near beginning we need to look up, because Jesus is that close in coming.

In my calculations, not having the exact times of Jesus' appearances beginning to end, I rounded off my figures to simplify the process. How much more amazing is this, when considering the simplicity of it I arrived at the same date as Jack Van Impe's 2012? I'm not saying Jesus is coming in 2012, but a number of things pointing to the year 2012, makes that year clearly a year to watch as the beginning of prophetic events. I believe the table is being set for the finish.

Another clue: Based on the scripture reference of Christ return in Hosea 6:2, "After two days shall He revive us: in the third day He will raise us up, and we shall live in His sight." This scripture came to mind, shortly after my calculations. The year now is 2011, and according to this scripture, and many Bible scholars, two days have passed, and we are now living on borrowed time in the third day.

Since each day represents 1000 years, we know that 2000 years (2 days) have passed from Jesus' resurrection, until the present, thus the year is now 2011. The 3rd 1000-year represents the 3rd day, of Hosea's prophecy, or the Millennium. The Millennial reign of Christ, for those who don't know is a 1000 years.

The pre-Millennial rapture has been calculated to happen before the 7-year tribulation begins, in a twinkling of an eye (1st Corinthians 15:52). A twinkling of an eye is computed to be 11/100th (one hundredth) of a second. You will see in chapter 8 why this is so exciting to me, and hopefully will be for you. We are in the 11/1000th (one thousandth) of the third day. I will say that in my calculation we would need to subtract a week of years to make it right. If we do that the year would be 2005 not 2012. By this we can see that there are no calculations that will tell us when the rapture is to happen. That it indeed is imminent.

I know we can't calculate when Jesus will return. My calculations are more for seeing how close we are to His return, knowing this could be the year; and in taking the 11/1000th (a bonus revelation) into consideration, sent shivers down my back at my findings. Now I wonder how many people live their lives looking up for their redemption drawing nigh or have they forgotten God?

Continuing my studies on this subject, the Holy Spirit gave me a few more scriptures, which lead to another point of discovery. Jesus in speaking of His return said in Matthew 24:36, "But of that day, and hour knoweth no man, no, not the angels of heaven, but my Father only." Jesus goes on to say in Matthew 24:33-34, the generation seeing all the signs He declared announcing His coming, shall not pass away till all these things be fulfilled. In Matthew 16:3 Jesus said, "O ye hypocrites, ye can discern the face of the sky; but can ye not discern the signs of the times." We are to live daily with the anticipation of Christ return. There are end time signs all around us, and they are ramping up.

"Now learn a parable of the fig tree; When his branch is yet tender, and putteth forth leaves, ye know that summer is nigh (Matthew 24:32) (the fig tree is Israel, and the budding of the leaves is her becoming a Nation)." Proverbs 30:25, "The ants are a people not strong, yet they prepareth their meat in the summer (virgins trimmed their lamps). Proverbs 6:6-8, "Go to the ant thou sluggard, and consider her ways and be wise. Which having no guide, overseer, or ruler, provideth her meat in the summer, and gathereth her food in the harvest." The budding takes place in summer, and then the Harvest. It stands to reason God's people are to be watching and waiting for His return at all times but especially at summer's end when Harvest is due. Especially when all the signs He spoke are being fulfilled all at once like we are beginning to see. I will mention here that there is reason to believe Jesus could return in spring Harvest to rapture His Church

Another scripture that has captivated my attention for many years, is Matthew 24:30, "But pray ye that your flight be not in the winter, neither on the Sabbath day." For years I have tried to find an answer for what this last scripture means. I've not found a satisfactory answer to this day. The meaning I see is, "pray Jesus doesn't come back before you are ready, having no works unto righteousness. Winter is considered barren months of no planting, sowing, etc, and the Sabbath day is a day of rest, when no work is performed." Stands to reason, the winter represents an absence of work, or works. We are not saved by works. Just a thought!

Humans are the only ones of all God's creation living by the hands of a clock. We are not to calculate time in minutes, hours, days, weeks, etc., but by the seasons. While I was pondering the 11/1000th theory, and the scriptures above, the Lord began to drop other scriptures into my spirit. Along with Matthew 24:31-51, the others are Proverbs 10:5, Jeremiah 8:20, "The harvest is past the summer is ended, and we are not saved", Amos 3:15, 8:1-14, and Daniel 2:35, "Then was the iron, the clay, the brass, the silver, and the gold, broken to pieces together, and became like the chaff of the summer threshing floors. Remember the vision in the introduction? It is clear the vision was at the end of summer because the wheat was ready for harvest, and the lightning was like that of summer storms; and the wind carried them away that no place was found for them; and the stone that smote the image became a great mountain and filled the whole earth."

After all this, everything came together, and this is what I have. The three days of which Hosea speaks: first day is first quarter winter, and the second day is second quarter spring. The third day is third quarter summer. The first two days represent a time of breaking the ground, planting and sowing, building the Church, the third day is Harvest, the return of the Lord in the rapture. The fourth day, fourth quarter, not mentioned by Hosea is fall, and represents the fall of the wicked in the 7 year tribulation represented by the statue of Daniels vision of the clay, brass, silver, and the gold, broken to pieces; meaning Satan's apostate church, the false prophet, and all those who take the mark of the beast will be broken to pieces, and blown away like the chaff of the summer threshing floor. When Jeremiah said the harvest is ended, and we are not saved (Jer.8: 20), appears to be those who are left behind after the rapture. The stone, the great mountain that rises up and smote the great image and became the great ruler in all the earth is Jesus Christ. Those not yet saved are the Jews, though they will be saved once they see who their true Messiah is.

Having said all that to say this. We are living in the 11th year (2011) (11/1000th) of the third day and in the 3rd day we will be raised up, which could be the twinkling of an eye, only faster. The first two days having passed, we are nearing the summer Harvest, of the third day, and the 11/1000th could be a sign that this is the year announcing the Rapture. Since there is only 70 weeks in Daniel's prophecy we must assume Harvest is at the end of the season of planting, growing, and reaping. This will put us in the same time frame of Teshuvah, which includes, Yom Kippur (Day of Atonement, holiest day on the Jewish calendar), Rosh Hashanah (Feast of Trumpets, the first Fall feast), and Feast of Tabernacles (Booths, or Season of our Joy). Then in tribulation in the winter months makes sense. A barren time having no works unto righteousness because the Holy Spirit has returned to heaven and is not here to guide into all truth.

These Feast Days play an important role in what I'm writing, but I'm limited to writing only the material I have planned, and not to include the teaching on the Feast days of Israel. However, it would behoove you to do your own research to see just how it all fits. I will tell you this, I, and others believe Jesus will come back during the Feast of Trumpets (Rosh Hashanah). Feast of Trumpets is determined by the New Moon, and no one knows the day or hour the New Moon will appear to start this feast in the month of Tishri and must be witnessed by TWO WITNESSES. Could it be the rapture will happen at the twinkling of the first sight of the new moon that begins the feast of Trumpets, and at the sound of the last trump the dead in Christ shall rise first, then those who remain, and are alive will be caught up to meet Jesus in the air? Could it be the two witnesses may be the two witnesses who will be here during the tribulation walking in all power of the Holy Spirit? It could be just a pattern to remind us how it will happen.

After the rapture we have the Feast of Tabernacles when, we the Saints will tabernacle with the Lord in heaven at the marriage supper of the Lamb while the tribulation is happening on earth for seven years.

The next feast is the Feast of Booths, season of our joy. Could this season of our joy be when we will become married to the bridegroom, Jesus Christ, and will honeymoon with Him for an entire year? In a Jewish wedding, the couple takes a year, no work, just getting acquainted, and enjoying each other as a newly married couple. Could this mean the season of our joy, our honeymoon with Christ, will be the 1000 years in the Millennium, where we will rule, and reign with Jesus?

Jesus was referring to Matthew 24:36 when He said no one knows not even the angels the day or hour only His Father in heaven. Jesus was saying what the groom in a Jewish wedding says when asked when will be his wedding day? In a Jewish betrothal, no one, but the father of the groom knows when it is time for the groom to go get his future bride and bring her home as his wife. The groom once betrothed, goes home to prepare a place for his coming bride. When the father of the groom thinks the preparations are done, he tells his son to go get his bride. The groom, and the bride could be away from each other during betrothal for as long as a year. No one knows but the groom's father.

Getting back to the equation of time, it has been a great challenge in putting it all together. I didn't want it to be too long and drawn out, but just enough information to spark your interest, and make it as interesting to you as it is for me. If you will read the scriptures mentioned you will find a deluge of information about the end times, the condition of the people, what is to happen, and why.

I know the return of Jesus will be based on His schedule, and not ours. I believe Jesus was trying to illustrate how, in the spiritual realm, time is different than we know time. He said He will come in and hour we think not. Jesus cautioned us to be ready when He comes. The hour, of which He speaks, according to my chart is a 60-day period. On my chart 60 days of our time is one hour of Jesus' time. I believe somewhere in a 60-day period surrounding certain events that precede the rapture is when He will come. Most will not be looking for His return because they will be focused on the events happening in the world. That is why it is important not to be distracted by the things of the world, like the news, terrorist, economy, weather, political things, pestilence, wars and rumors of wars etc. We need to know these things, but don't lose sight of where you are on the Father's timetable.

In Jesus' illustration, and from the equation, I realized that on the other side of eternity, time has no beginning, and no end. In the illustration of 1000 years is as a day, and a day is as a 1000 years Jesus may be saying, that it makes no difference how we gage time, because where He is, time is nonexistent. He instructed us to discern the signs of the times, which would point more to signs of the seasons, than to a clock. If we do this, we will see our redemption draws nigh, and is even at the door. Praise God.

Bible scholars have determined that the Old Testament covers 4000 years. If it is so, and I believe it is, we have entered the 3000-year period, beginning from the death of Christ. This is determined in the book of Genesis, by the seven days of creation. Each day represents 1000 years, 6-days equals 6000 years, and the 7th day is the Sabbath rest of 1000 years, compared to the millennial reign of Christ for 1000 years. This age will end with Jesus coming for His church in what is known as the rapture at the end of 6000 years (Acts 1:11, John 14:3, 1

Corinthians 15 and 1 Thessalonians 4:16-18).

Assuming our calendar is more right than wrong, we have moved slightly past the 6000 years into the 3000 years period by 11/1000th of the year. Do I believe this could be the year Jesus returns? I certainly do. The Feast of Trumpets begins September 29-30 of 2011. Am I a date setter? No, but if I were, I would say the rapture could happen by the end of the year 2012. If it doesn't, I will look for Jesus in 2013 and so on. God doesn't do anything without warning His prophets first. God Himself is a date setter that we do not need to be. The Old Testament is full of times and seasons set by God. All the Jewish feast days come at a set time, or season, and were set by God. The date isn't important, and we don't know the date, but we are commanded by Christ to know the signs, and season of His return.

After this there will be a seven-year period at the end of the 6000th year known as the tribulation, ruled by the anti- Christ. His rule will be for seven years, after which Jesus will return with His saints (those who were caught up in the rapture) to set up His Kingdom on the earth. He will usher in the Millennial Kingdom and will rule and reign for 1000 years.

At this time there will be peace on earth for the 1000 years, as Satan will be bound for the same 1000 years. (Book of Revelation-all)

Based on the seventy years, and seventy weeks of Daniel, the book of Revelation, and the Bible prophecies that have been fulfilled, we know we are living in the end of the age of Grace, and the rapture is about to occur. Many factors play a role in the time system of the world. The Jewish calendar, for instance, is based on a three hundred, and sixty day-year.

The United States uses the Gregorian calendar, a three hundred and sixty-five day year, as does many other countries. In the book of Joshua 10:12-13, the sun, and moon stood still for a whole day. Thus, the rotation of the earth, flat or globe has affected the time in which we live. There is no possible way to know the exact time of the day, or night. We can only look at our watch and assume that it is reasonably close to the real time, give or take a few minutes, days, or months. By this, I don't believe we need to concern ourselves with the time, but the season is a different matter. The season points to the Imminent return of Christ any day now. "Therefore, be ye ready: for in such an hour ye think not, the Son of Man cometh." However, concerning the Rapture we have a compass of sorts.

1st Thessalonians 5:1-4, if we are in Christ, this scripture is our consolation, "But of the times, and the seasons, brethren ye have no need that I write unto you. For yourselves know perfectly that the day of the Lord so cometh as a thief in the night. For when they shall say, peace, and safety; then sudden destruction cometh upon them, as travail upon a woman with child; and they shall not escape. But ye, brethren, are not in darkness, that that day should overtake you as a thief." Jesus has truly given us signs to announce His coming. If you do not read the Bible, accept Jesus as your Savior, the only way of escape, you will be ignorant of these signs of destruction coming on the whole earth. You will be overtaken as a thief in the night.

To emphasize how near the Lord's return is, let us read Hosea 6:1-2, "Come and let us return unto the Lord: for He hath torn, and He will heal us; He hath smitten and He will bind us up. After TWO days (emphasis mine) will He revive us: in the THIRD (emphasis mine) day He will raise us up and we shall live in His sight." People, two days have passed, and we are living in the third day when our Lord will return, and we will live in His sight. No one knows when the Lord will come, but we know He is coming. No matter when He returns, we need to be ready, and be equipped to go through some difficult times, should He tarry. We don't know how many hours of our time is left but one thing is certain; the Lord's return in His dimension is only a few seconds away.

I've heard many people make the remark, "I've got plenty of time." Friends, we don't have plenty of time anymore. Time has nearly run out, and it is time to make a decision. The Bible tells us, "Seek the Lord while He can be found, for the time is at hand, even at the door." (Isaiah 55:6, Matt. 24:33, Rev. 1:3, and 22:10)

While I was writing the book, the Lord gave me a scripture that explains where we are in Bible prophecy. The year 1991 was a devastating year for all Americans. In 1990 George H. Bush had made his new world order speech. America had fallen into a recession, The Persian Gulf war happened, and America was engulfed by unemployment, hunger, and pestilence, such as the country had not seen since the great depression of the 1940's. The year 1992 did not start out any better but seemed to grow worse as the months passed. More people were losing their jobs, homes, and lives than I had ever seen in my lifetime. The Church body was under much persecution, and even the believers were suffering from the loss of lives, possessions, and finances. Renowned women, and men of God, Ministers of the Gospel had fallen from Grace, businesses, were lost, inflation, and the list goes on.

I spent much time in prayer asking God what has happened to cause so much destruction. As I was leafing through the Bible, searching for a certain scripture, the Holy Spirit led me to read Revelation 3:10-11. This scripture had nothing to do with the one for which I was searching. As I read the verse, I heard the voice of God saying, "The world is now living in an hour of temptation. Not THE hour of temptation in reference to Jacobs Trouble that will come upon the whole earth. It is a time that Christians will either stand up for what they believe or will fall back into the ways of the world by compromising their relationship with God." The verse closes with, "Behold I come quickly: hold that fast, which thou hast received that no man takes thy crown."

In the early 1980's America experienced a similar time of an economic crisis, involving job loss, business failure, and the like. In the year 2001 the twin towers incident happened and caused another devastation to America. In 2007, an economic downfall was evident, as the whole world began a recession. This is the time we are in now. The world, not just America is experiencing one of the most prophetic events of our time. It is 2011, and we have been in recession since 2007. It began long before 2007 but wasn't evident to the people.

You may ask how this time is different than the times before? The times before were the beginning of trouble, birth pangs if you will. The world has had many warnings of the coming present times. We are living in a time where we know a delivery is coming. Today's economic distress is not something that just happened. It has been happening for many years. It has been coming like a tsunami sweeping across the face of the earth and has finally hit.

The world has never seen such destruction, corruption, and devastation. Wars, rumors of wars, uprisings around the world, terrorist attacks, suicide bombings, plagues, famine, pestilence, nations rising against nations, and kingdoms against kingdoms, false prophets (false religions) rising, deceiving many, and people saying they are Christ (calling themselves Christian, but believing something entirely different, coming in the name of Christianity), many being offended, betraying one another (the banks, and the government have betrayed us), iniquity is abounding, and the love of many has waxed cold.

Politicians in the same country fighting against each other (Matthew 12:25), banks foreclosing on homes, calling for balances on loans, no lending, business loss, inflation, mortgage insurance at unaffordable rates, gasoline prices so high most can't afford to drive, millions out of work with no unemployment benefits left, millions still on unemployment, and still millions more to come, loss of stocks, The DOW, and NASDAQ have hit bottom, an ounce of gold at higher prices than ever before, outrageous tuition for college students, banks failing, health care prices sky rocketing, social security broken, wages so low one can't support their family, seven applicants to any available job, natural disasters like floods, tornado's, hurricane's, torrential rains, snow, mud slides, earthquakes in divers places, loss of life in unprecedented temperatures, tsunamis, erupting volcanoes, and signs in the heavens in preparing for a galactic lineup in December of the year 2012. I could go on naming the signs happening now, but this should be enough to get your attention, and for you to discern the signs of the times.

These things are converging across the world back-to-back. These are the signs Jesus spoke of in Matthew 24. He warns that the generation who sees all these things happening at once will be the generation to see His return. There are too many signs to go into detail. Listen to the News for more information on these events and do your homework. You will be glad you did. But understand the News media is biased to government party affiliation. The truth only comes from the Holy Ghost.

Isaiah 13:6-16 gives a full description of the birth pangs spoken of in Matthew 24. Verse 10-13 gives a description of the heavens being shaken, and the earth removing out of her place. Could this moving of the earth out of her place be the galactic line up in December 2012 when a polar shift could take place? Most do not believe anything of a cataclysmic proportion will happen as predicted by the Mayan calendar ending, but the possibilities are phenomenal. If you are a flat earth believer, you know there could be no polar shift.

The good news is, Jesus said in Matthew 24:6, "See that you be not troubled; for all these things must come to pass, but the end is not yet." 24:14, "And this gospel will be preached in all the world as a witness unto all nations and then the end will come." The gospel has been and is being preached throughout the world. People we have ran out of time.

These are the signs of a country going bankrupt, and its destruction by evil. The American government has no money, the American people have no money, and there is just of matter of a short time before this world economy will collapse for good. America is in debt to China, and America is now servant to the lender. America has become the tail and not the head. (Proverbs 22:7, Deuteronomy 28:13) Larry Bates, banker, United Nations Speaker, and Economist, has been the guest speaker on many of the Christian Television Broadcast. He announced in the end of 2008 that in two years, 5 years at best, the entire system would collapse. If you are in debt, get out of debt that you will not suffer loss.

The first, and foremost action as Christians in times such as these is being in constant guard of our faith. When we go through trials, and tribulations we can easily fall from our faith if we don't continually seek the Lord in their midst. Through troubled times is when many Christians fall back into the world. The reason they fall is they don't know the word of God and do not have a right relationship with Him enough to carry them through these valley experiences. The hour of temptation coming upon the whole world has come into view but is not yet. This is the reason so many Christians are experiencing extremely difficult times. The Church is being purged by God and conditioned by government. Whatever there is in you, unbecoming a Christian, is being purged from you. If you will submit to God, and let Him do His perfect work in you, you will be saved. If on the other hand you are not a believer having not had a born-again experience, you will not have a place of safety. The government will continue to lead you by your cognitive dissonance. Do not be deceived, Christians can be stuck in their cognitive dissonance too. Unwilling to wake up to the corruption.

This is the time for Christians to be aware of what is happening in the world, and to make your election sure. We have a double portion happening here. We not only have the judgment of God upon the Church, but we have a last, and final attempt by Satan, in trying to make us fall.

It is apparent Jesus is coming soon. Satan is firing all his weapons at the Christians, God is purging us, and we are like a Yo-Yo being slung in many directions. Our stability, and to have a sound mind rest solely in our personal relationship with Jesus, having knowledge of the truth, and hearing the voice of God. Taking no part in the evil doings in the world but doing what we know to be right. Living a holy life unto God, author, and finisher of our faith.

Satan is out to destroy the Church. Be not deceived, nor offended. Jesus was preaching in the synagogue, when an unclean spirit spoke to Him saying, "Let us alone, what have we to do with thee, thou Jesus of Nazareth? Art thou come to destroy us? I know thee who thou art the holy one of God." And Jesus rebuked Him saying, "Hold thy peace, and come out of him." The unclean spirits know who Jesus is. They also, know there is no evil thing in Jesus, giving them no place in Him.

I believe this is one reason the Church doesn't see the miracles they desire to see. There are too many things like the world in us, that the demons know we have no power. We have power in the name of Jesus, but if we are walking in disobedience to God, bad intents of the heart, the ways of the world working in us, and having no knowledge of the word working in us, our power of authority is going to be hindered. Not by Christ but by our own subconscious condemnation of ourselves causing us to quench the Holy Spirit.

There are people afraid to dance before the Lord. They like to say they don't dance because that is not their style of worship. When in fact, it is usually because they are embarrassed, or shy. Being embarrassed to dance before the Lord sounds like a need to die to the flesh. Even this will offend someone, I'm sure. However, it is not my intent to offend, but to say wake up, and get with the program. There's a place in the Lord you need to move into. Embarrassment, shyness, timidity, bashfulness, all is flesh. It is selfishness. One way to know if these things are in you is by your anger level when someone talks about them to you. If these things are in you, you are none of His, and you need to get rid of them. It doesn't mean you aren't saved, if you have accepted Jesus as Savior, but it does border being ashamed of Him. You don't have to dance before the Lord, but will you dance before the Lord? You be your judge. Until you have danced in the Spirit, I promise you, you don't know true freedom. King David knew this freedom.

The unclean spirit showing up in the synagogue proves there is no ground Satan will not travel to get to us. I was in a Wednesday night service listening to a dynamic sermon on when Jesus comes and being ready to meet Him. Suddenly out of nowhere came a voice saying, "That preacher is not telling you the truth. He is lying to you. The gospel is a lie, and they that believe it are fools. If God is real and is love, then why are you going through such trials and terrible things?" I knew instantly this was the voice of Satan. God would not say these things and only Satan would call God a liar. Had I not been rooted and grounded in the word of God, having tasted of the goodness of the Lord, I may have allowed Satan's words to take root in my mind. Then doubt and unbelief would have prevailed. Had I not recognized the voice, I may have entertained the words as my own thoughts. This is how deception begins.

I was in a vulnerable state of mind, Satan knew it, and boldly came into the house of the Lord to lay a snare for me. I didn't entertain Satan's accusation, and rebuked him immediately. When his message didn't compute, he quickly fled. Submit to God, resist the devil and he will flee from you.

Church, we are embarking on the brink of the greatest event in history called the rapture. If we are living in deceit, partaking of the forbidden fruit of the world, we will not be ready to stand during the things happening in this time. The Father is preparing His Bride for the coming of the Bride Groom. Are your lamps trimmed, and do you have enough oil to wait for His appearing? The Lord gave me the following prophecy for the end time Church:

"How graciously I have adorned thee with riches. Riches such as the world has never known. Fret not in despair of the circumstances for haven't I fed you in times past? And have I not ministered to you those things that have fed your spirit? Come hither unto me even in this time when all seems lost, and souls are lonely. Draw closer to your God, even I, the I Am of all who are: for I have come to give you light that you may see where time does lie. Lie in the sense of an untruth: for time would seem to go on as before, but time is time forgotten; for in a short time, I shall call thee home and you will ascend into the Kingdom as an eagle climbs the very heights of the air. It will be soon as you have viewed the particulars of the world, and the status of its system. You will surely see in days to come the time of my appearing. The time not remembered by those that long for the worldly things, but a time not forgotten by those who hear my voice. Time, which was forgotten, now remembered; time, which was, and was not, and now is: time that has passed, but time that will be again; time forevermore. A time of love which is the time of your God. For isn't your God love. Then surely your God is time, and the time is love; for God is love, and the time is now time to love. Love your God with all your heart for that time shall stand still for eternity and shall not pass away; for your God has always been, and forever will be, and will not pass away. Therefore, because the word is God, and God is love, and the time is time to love; then know, that if the word does not pass away, time will not pass away; thereby being with God in love for all time to come; for all is love in time."

I believe 2011 the time we are in is spoken of in 1st and 2nd Peter. The Father would like you to read these two books and pay close attention to what Peter is saying. One thing I would like to insert here is the passage of scripture in 2nd Peter 3:9-13. I prophesied in Church one Sunday, and the Lord spoke of these verses. He said, "There is no such thing as global warming. Global warming is of the world. He said, "What man is seeing happen is the heavens are making ready for the coming of the Son of Man." Verse 10 –12 of 2nd Peter 3, "But the day of the Lord will come as a thief in the night; in the which the heavens shall pass away with a great noise, and the elements shall melt with fervent heat, the earth also and the works that are therein shall be burned up. Seeing then that all these things shall be dissolved, what manner of persons ought ye to be in all holy conversation, and godliness?

Looking for and hasting unto the coming of the day of God, wherein the heavens being on fire shall be dissolved, and the elements shall "melt" with fervent heat." Verse 14, "Wherefore, beloved, seeing that ye look for such things, be diligent that ye may be found of Him in peace, without spot, and blameless."

The Lord has used the two books of Peter in several prophecies during the last two years in showing the importance in knowing the time in which we live. I want to share a vision, and prophetic message The Father gave in 2009.

The picture on the cover of this book is a painting I painted of an open-eye vision I had on August 21st, 2009. I was sitting on my deck at 6:15 am, when suddenly the glory of God bordered by royal bluish, purple lights appeared in the distance. A portal of heaven had opened, and the Father began to speak. He told me this was the ascending of the prayers from our church, into heaven. Our church was having a week of prayer and fasting, as we do every year. The following is the prophecy the Lord gave me that morning for the Church.

HE INSTRUCTED ME TO READ ISAIAH 58:1-14. ALONG WITH VERSES 3-7, THE FATHER EMPHASIZED VS 1-2, 8-11, AND HEAVILY EMPHASIZED VS 13 –14. THE FATHER THEN INSTRUCTED ME TO READ LEVITICUS 19:30-31, ISAIAH 56: 1-2, JOB 22:21 –29, DEUT 32:13, ISAIAH 1: 18-20, (REFERENCE VERSES FOR VS. 13-14 ARE LEVITICUS 19:30, ISAIAH 56: 1, JOB 22:26, DUET 32:13, ISAIAH 1:20, THE OTHER VERSES WERE ADDED BY THE FATHER)

THE FATHER WANTS US TO KNOW HE HAS HEARD OUR PRAYERS FOR THEY HAVE ASCENDED UP TO HEAVEN INTO HIS EARS. THE LIGHT IS THE GLORY OF GOD PRODUCED BY THE PRAYERS OF THE CHURCH. THE FATHER SAYS, "THIS IS A TIME WE MAY ASK ACCORDING TO OUR FAITH WHAT WE WILL, AND WE SHALL HAVE IT, SUDDENLY. HE WANTS US TO KNOW WE ARE TO BE A HOLY PEOPLE, AS HE IS HOLY, AND TO KEEP THE SABBATH DAY HOLY UNTO HIM. THERE WILL BE FAMILIAR SPIRITS, AND FALSE PROPHETS COMING INTO OUR CHURCH, AND ARE EVEN IN THE MIDST OF US NOW TO CAUSE DIVISION. HE WANTS US TO NOT FOLLOW AFTER THESE SEDUCING SPIRITS, NOT TO TURN TO FAMILIAR SPIRITS FOR ANSWERS, AND TO TRUST IN HIM FULLY. HE LOVES US, AND WILL TAKE CARE OF US, AND WE ARE TO BE CAREFUL ABOUT NOTHING, CASTING OUR CARE UPON HIM, NOT LETTING OUR FAITH WAIVER. GOD IS GOD AND HE WANTS US TO KNOW THAT WE ARE TO TRUST IN HIM COMPLETELY."

HE IS GIVING US THE OPPORTUNITY TO PROVE AND TRY HIM.

"FROM THE DAY OF FASTING, AUG. 21ST, THROUGH SEPTEMBER 29TH, 40 DAYS, I WILL GRANT YOUR PETITIONS THAT YOU MAY KNOW I AM GOD AND

THAT I NEVER SLEEP, NOR SLUMBER. MY EYES ARE CONTINUOUSLY ON MY CHILDREN. I SEE THE DESPERATION OF MANY, AND MY HEART BREAKS. ASK FOR WHAT YOU WILL, AND YOU SHALL HAVE IT ACCORDING TO YOUR FAITH. LET THE STAR OF THE MORNING ARISE IN YOUR HEARTS, AND TURN FROM THE WICKED INTENTS OF THE HEART. YOU WORSHIP ME WITH YOUR MOUTH, YOU ATTEND MY HOUSE OF PRAYER, AND ON THE OUTSIDE, YOU APPEAR TO HAVE FRUIT, BUT INSIDE YOU ARE STILL CHILDREN OF WRATH, OUT FOR YOURSELF. YOU HAVE BEEN TAKEN CAPTIVE BY YOUR ENEMIES, AND NOW IS THE TIME FOR THE BONDAGES TO BE BROKEN. YOU SAY TO ME, BUT LORD, I HAVE NO ENEMIES, AND I SAY TO YOU, YOUR ENEMIES ARE THOSE OF YOUR OWN HOUSE, EVEN SICKNESS, DISEASE, LACK OF FINANCES, STRIFE AND DEBATE, GREED, AND THE LOVE OF MONEY. THE LIST GOES ON. I THE LORD GOD HAVE PROSPERED MY PEOPLE NOT FOR THEIR OWN PERSONAL GAIN, BUT TO GIVE TO THOSE WHO HAVE NOT, THAT ALL MY CHILDREN MAY LIVE IN UNISON OF SPIRIT, HAVING NO TROUBLE, AND ABLE TO RECEIVE MY JOY WITHOUT OPPRESSION. WHERE YOUR TREASURE IS, THERE WILL BE YOUR HEART ALSO. DO NOT WORRY, OR FRET OVER FINANCES. I KNOW WHO GIVES AND WHO DOES NOT GIVE. GIVING UNLOCKS THE FAVOR OF HEAVEN INTO A LIFE. WHEN I GAVE MY ONLY BEGOTTEN SON, DID NOT THE HEAVENS OPEN AND RECEIVE HIM? THE CHURCH WILL PROSPER IN THIS TIME, AND IT SHALL FLOURISH IN MUCH SILVER. THEREFORE, DO NOT FRET IN MAKING THE MOVE INTO THE NEW PLACE, BECAUSE AS YOU MOVE INTO THE NEW PLACE, SO SHALL MY PEOPLE MOVE INTO A NEW SPIRITUAL PLACE OF UNDERSTANDING. THOSE WHO DO NOT GIVE NOW WILL BEGIN TO GIVE THEN. BE CAREFUL TO FOLLOW IN MY WAYS, AND TO NOT DOUBT IN YOUR HEART, NOR BE DOUBLE MINDED, NOR WAIVER IN YOUR FAITH. I THE LORD GOD HAVE SPOKEN, AND IT SHALL BE DONE ACCORDING TO MY WILL, AND ACCORDING TO YOUR FAITH. REMEMBER THE FAITH OF ABRAHAM, AND HOW HE BELIEVED ME IN A TIME OF GREAT DISTRESS. DID I NOT SPARE, SUPPLY, AND PROVIDE, IN THAT TIME? I AM THE LORD, AND I AM THE SAME YESTERDAY, TODAY, AND TOMORROW. DO YOU BELIEVE ME? TRY ME AND PROVE ME, SAITH THE LORD OF HOST. YOU HAVE ONLY TO ASK, AND YOU SHALL HAVE WHAT YOU SAY."

THE FATHER WANTS US TO NOT TAKE THIS LIGHTLY, AND TO BE CAREFUL IN WHAT WE ASK. SOMETIMES WE ASK FOR THINGS WITHOUT WEIGHING THE CONSEQUENCES OF THE ANSWER. DO NOT ASK AMISS, BUT TRULY, FROM THE HEART, ASK FOR WHAT YOU NEED. TURN YOUR FACE TOWARD YOUR FATHER GOD, AND HE WILL TURN HIS FACE TO YOU. THIS IS A SPECIAL TIME ORDAINED TO RECEIVE WHAT THE FATHER HAS LAID UP FOR HIS CHILDREN, THAT WE MAY KNOW THE GOODNESS OF HIM, AND THAT HE IS NOT A GOD AFAR OFF, BUT A GOD AT HAND. A PORTAL OF HEAVEN IS OPEN. AMEN

The Father spoke from 6:15 am until 6:40 am. He also told me to call the leader of our Intercessors and tell her about the vision. I called Alice, and humbly explained to her what I had just encountered. She was reading a book by Perry Stone about the feast of Teshuvah. I knew nothing about Teshuvah, but later learned the entire word of prophecy from the Father was an invitation to take part in the feast of Teshuvah. Teshuvah that year began on August 21st, the day of the vision.

SATURDAY MORNING AUGUST 22ND, THE FATHER INSTRUCTED ME TO READ THE TWO BOOKS OF PETER, AND STUDY THEM AGAIN. IN THEM, THE LORD SHOWED ME WE ARE LIVING IN THE TIME OF WHICH PETER SPOKE. WE ALL KNOW THIS, BUT GOD IS TELLING US NOW. HE SAID HIS SHEEP WILL HEAR HIS VOICE, AND THAT THIS TIME WILL NOT OVERTAKE US WITHOUT WARNING: THAT WE WILL KNOW THE SIGNS OF THE TIMES IN WHICH WE LIVE. THIS MAY BE THE BEGINNING OF SORRORS. It will behoove you to read these two books in their entirety. Amen.

The Father continued to minister through the entire month while Teshuvah was in progress. On the morning of September 25, I was suddenly awakened in time to see The Lord of the Harvest standing by my bed. I was still in a state of slumber when he opened my right hand, and in it placed a head of golden bearded wheat. With my hand in his, he then closed my hand tightly around the wheat, as a mighty wind began to blow. The wind was getting stronger when the Lord said, "Hold tightly for this is your Harvest." I wasn't fully awake until the Lord had left.

When I got up, and dressed, I immediately called bill, a wheat farmer, to find out more about the wheat. I described the size of the wheat to him, and he said a head of wheat that size could have as many as 50 seeds in it. He went on to explain that once planted, those seeds could bring forth double heads on one stalk. I won't go into the entire process of learning what this message is about, but I can't help but go back to the beginning of the introduction of this book where I wrote about the vast field of wheat; it is like seeing the end before the beginning. God is so amazing, mere words can't describe Him. He does love symbolism. I think He enjoys watching us try to figure it all out like a baby working their first puzzle.

Judging by this vision, and the prophecy, I believe more than ever God wants us to recognize what the foreshadows of the feast days are. Teshuvah is a feast celebrated each year by the Jews. It is a time of repentance, prayer, restoration, and asking God for special things, and favor as we return to Him. It is a time set aside each year by God to demonstrate His goodness, His power, His favor, His omnipotence, and a time for the people to repent, and try God.

Some of the people to whom I shared this word had trouble with the part where God said this is a season that He will give us what we ask according to our faith. Alice our church intercessor leader brought out the fact that we have this privilege every day. Archie, an intercessor explained, "yes we do have this privilege every day, but God was offering a special time of fulfilling our request." She gave the analogy of Christmas, "We celebrate the birth of Christ year-round, but Christmas is the time we honor His birth with special flair and adoration."

This was a great analogy, and no doubt from the Holy Spirit. Of course, we know Christmas is not the time of Christ birth.

Did you ever dream the day would come when the name of Jesus would not be allowed spoken in America? Did you ever dream the day would come when a Christian prayer recognizing Jesus could not be recited in public? The day has come when Christians are being slaughtered in Egypt, Pakistan, and other countries, and announcements of the same happening in America. Churches are closing at the rate of 4000 per year according to Perry Stone (Bible Scholar, having a fivefold ministry), and only 1000 rising in their place. According to Grant Jefferies, (Bible Scholar of end time prophecy) in his telecast of January 19th, 2011, Christianity is growing worldwide as fast as 4.9% per year. This is an amazing increase, and proves the gospel is being preached across the world, and God is pouring out His Spirit for the end time gathering of the Gentiles.

(Prophetic Visions for the Future)

1. Around the year 1987 I had a vision of churches being boarded up and closed. I saw multitudes of people crawling over each other on the ground in a futile attempt to get to God. I saw the famine of the Word of God coming to America. About the same time period I had another vision of large green water trucks parked and people standing in line with empty milk jugs, and other containers to get fresh water. This is a water shortage coming to America, and probably the world. I also saw America under a martial law, with military units, and soldiers on every street corner with high-powered weapons, guarding the streets. The streets were empty of people. I had these visions between1985 to 1987. They were future tense, and I know they are for this season. The season we are in now may last several more years. They could be for the time of tribulation. It could be they will happen before the rapture of the Church. Perhaps it is a warning to the Church to be prepared for difficult times.

2. In 1989, I had just moved to Rocky Mount, North Carolina. I attended a July 4th, town celebration in City Park on July 3rd. The town officials, the Chamber of Commerce, and a great turn out of people were there. Peoples Bank hosted the event. It was almost nine pm as we all began to sing patriotic songs. The stage was set for the speakers, having a large, approximately 16' X 20' American flag backdrop. As we sang the Stars Spangled Banner, our national anthem, the Lord took me into a vision into the future.

"I gazed around at the faces of the people gathered there. As I observed I saw the American Flag as it is but meaning something different. Its meaning had been changed. It no longer stood for freedom.

I saw the faces of the people no longer holding sacred honor for our nation as in God we trust. The people were walking in deception, turned over into the hands of a one-world government, known as communism, or socialism, under the religion of the New Age movement. They believe in spirit guides, channeling, lord Maitreya, and such. There was neither a pride in being an American, nor was there a spiritual air among the people, meaning no honor for God Jehovah, the one, and only true God. Instead, there was a no concern attitude for the moment. I saw the spirit of self-love surrounding the people, government, and the officials.

The flag with the stars, and stripes looked the same in appearance but represented a nation in captivity. The people were unaware of what it meant behind the scenes. It appeared the flag had embedded subliminal suggestions."

The overall view I saw was this: The flag no longer stood for freedom, the people no longer believed in God, and Satan's deception ran rampant in destroying souls. The people were all brain washed through a false religion giving higher power to the government willingly, and without reservation. I remember thinking, "God help us, anti-Christ spirit is in the world, and the people are falling fast.

Having come out of the vision, I began to cry before the Lord praying for His forgiveness, for my country, and the times just ahead. May God forgive us. America was founded on the name of God, and now has taken the name of God out of its midst. The decline of this great country is here."

3. Another vision I had around the year 1994 happened while I was sitting at a stop light on the way to church one Sunday. While waiting for the light to change, a man dressed in a suit, tie, white shirt, very dapper, appeared in the sky. It was a huge silhouette, and his face was not so I could see who it was. He held out his arms to each side like a bird spreading his wings, threw up his hands in a defeated gesture, and said, "That's it, that's all we can do". I didn't see his face and I wouldn't have recognized him then. Now I know it was President George W. Bush. I was thinking about this vision in 2008, and I suddenly recognized the silhouette.

Jesus is just before coming to receive His Church unto Himself. He is preparing us in this time of temptation in the separation of the tares from the wheat (Matt. 13:25). Jesus promised to do this just before He returns to gather the wheat into His barn. The separation of the tares from the wheat is not only symbolic of the dividing of the nonbelievers, from the believers, but also the bad intents in our hearts, from the good intents in our hearts. It is a purification process the believer must experience to make ready for the Lord's return. We spend our entire Christian life preparing. This separation of the tares from the wheat is an end of the age attempt by God to purge His Church. The separation is not pleasant, and there will be many who will not make it through by falling back into the world. If we are not rooted and grounded in the word of God, we will be uprooted from the very foundation of the truth. Jesus' declaration after this separation is, "behold I come quickly." (Some believe this division takes place at the end of the Tribulation and still others believe at the end of the millennium.)

The day is coming in which there will be a famine of the word of God. Bibles are already taken from public places, not allowed in the workplace, schools, universities, and clothing depicting anything related to Christianity is banned. What more does one need to see that we are indeed living in the time of which Christ spoke? When a country leaves God and His image out of the equation of government rule that country will not stand. Look in the mirror of God's word to see where you stand in this equation: whether you are truly in the faith and able to stand in this time of separation? What image do you see?

This book is a book of visions, dreams, and visits from Jesus, angel appearances, being caught up in the spirit, prophetic messages for the future, revelation knowledge, and supernatural occurrences. It is a book of teachings learned from these experiences and information straight from the voice of God. It will take you from where you are to where you should be as a Christian and is scriptural.

Watch for the nuggets of revelation as you read. Enjoy the words of the Holy Spirit as He speaks to the generation who will see the coming of the Son of Man. Look for Jesus to visit you and ask Him for His Knowledge, Understanding, and Wisdom. He will visit you and He will equip you to be ready for the end of the age. Amen!

CHAPTER 2

Supernatural, Understanding, Knowledge, and Wisdom (part 1)

Hebrews 5:11-14, "Of whom we have many things to say, and hard to be uttered, seeing ye are dull of hearing. For when for the time ye ought to be teachers, ye have need that one teaches you again which be the first principles of the oracles of God; and are become such as have need of milk, and not of strong meat. For everyone that useth milk is unskillful in the word of righteousness, for he is a babe, but strong meat belongeth to them that are of full age, even those who by reason of use have their senses exercised to discern both good and evil."

"So that thou incline thine ear unto wisdom, and apply thine heart to understanding; yea, if thou criest after knowledge, and liftest up thy voice for understanding; if thou seekest her as silver, and searchest for her as for hid treasure; then shalt thou understand the fear of the Lord and find the knowledge of God. FOR THE LORD GIVETH WISDOM: OUT OF HIS MOUTH COMETH KNOWLEDGE, AND UNDERSTANDING (emphasis mine). He layeth sound wisdom for the righteous; He is a buckler to them that walk uprightly. He keepeth the paths of judgment, and preserveth the way of His saints. Then shalt thou understand righteousness, and judgment, and equity: yea, every good path. When wisdom entereth into thine heart, and knowledge is pleasant unto thy soul; discretion shall preserve thee, understanding shall keep thee: to deliver thee from the way of the evil man, from the man that speaketh forward things." (Proverbs 2:2-12)

Being a Christian is like digging a well. Each layer of dirt we dig out brings us closer to the water beneath the ground. If we don't quit, and our hope isn't deferred (Proverbs 13:4), we will hit pay dirt. The mother lode treasure is when we finally reach the place where rivers of water flow mightily. To find the treasure we must dig and search with diligence never giving up.

In spiritual truth, to obtain the treasure we must make the search our soul's ambition, to reach the engrafted, in depth, word of God, made manifest by our faith. Until we make God our hearts desire, heaven our treasure, Jesus our gateway to the Father, and the Holy Spirit our guide, we will never move into the depths of the spiritual things of God. To find the treasure of heaven, we must dig deep into the word of God. In digging deeper, and deeper, we will someday reach the rivers of living water, flowing mightily in us.

It is imperative to come to the place of falling on our face, crying out to the Father for justice before we can experience the ecstasy of intimacy with the Him. Unless we walk in true righteousness, and holiness we can't go into the Holy of Holies. Yes, we are allowed to go to the throne of grace boldly, the outer court if you will, but to move into the bridal chamber we must be pure in heart, like a chaste virgin. We become pure by the word of God changing the intents of our hearts, in esteeming others more highly than ourselves in all our ways. Jesus did this very thing, and by His servitude He opened the gates of heaven for all. Jesus said in 1st John 3:2-3, "He who hath this hope of His appearing purifies himself, even as He is pure."

To become like Jesus means we can't get offended, we can't get puffed up, and we must bear the fruits of the Spirit. The Fruits of the Spirit is the power of God. This is Wisdom, and truly the Supernatural things of God. Let him who has an ear hear what the Spirit is saying.

In experiencing dealings with God, we can't lean toward our own understanding (Proverbs 3:5). There must be an understanding that spiritual things are of the supernatural, and carnal (means relating to bodily appetites, sensual, sexual, not spiritual) things are of the natural, or earthly. Having no understanding of the supernatural is why most people can't or won't come to the knowledge of God. People try to relate to God in the natural realm, and it can't be done. Several denominations won't admit the supernatural wasn't just for the early Church but is also for the Church in this present time. God is a spirit, and they that worship Him must worship Him in Spirit and Truth (John 4:24).

A large portion of the unbelieving world today is dabbling in the supernatural, but to most, the supernatural automatically means astrology, witchcraft, tarot cards, Satanism, and the like. The reason some people seek the supernatural is for the intriguing, interesting, alluring, effects of the unknown. They even seek direction in these carnal things. There is something about the unknown forces of the universe that draws people into its grasp. What is this unknown force? The world labels this force a higher power through which they can contact the spirit realm. The problem is, in which spirit realm are they contacting?

It doesn't take an intellectual to experience the unknown. This will surprise many Christians in that interest in the supernatural is a natural God given desire. The Christian has become afraid of the supernatural because they connect it with evil. This is one of the numerous reasons why so few Christians ever come to have a personal relationship with God: that, and a lack of knowledge in the scriptures. By turning away from the supernatural, God cannot be reached. God put a desire of the supernatural in man's heart that man can reach into the spirit realm, and commune with Him. The drawing force in this case has a name. It is the drawing force of the Holy Spirit. He is the third part of the Godhead, or Trinity that woos, and beckons us to come to Jesus. Christians know the higher power as God the Father, Jesus as the gateway and the Holy Spirit as the force or power.

Satan has taken many things intended for use by God's Church, and uses them, for himself, under a different label. One of the things is the ability to experience what lies beyond the natural realm. Séances, satanic rituals, astrology, to name a few are popular among the unbelievers. Persons able to administer these techniques are said to have a sixth sense, or higher power, and are in many cases referred to as spiritual advisors, or psychics. The higher power, in this case, is referred to as Extra Sensory Perception, or ESP. ESP covers several types of psychic phenomenon. The higher power referenced here is the rulers of darkness of this world, and wickedness in high places.

To foster the powers of Telepathy, Precognition, or Clairvoyance, is considered unlawful, or taboo by Christians, and rightfully so. A Christian can experience a type, of these kinds of powers, but only through the Holy Spirit. The difference in using these powers for God than for Satan, is for God's will to be done. A Christian can demonstrate these powers but must first understand the origin from which they come, how to receive them, and the wisdom in how to use them. As we will see, these powers in the Bible are not known by their worldly name, but by spiritual names given by God, through Jesus Christ, and administered by the Holy Spirit. They are not practiced, sought after, or demonstrated by any other than the Holy Spirit.

Practicing, or seeking after these powers, proves to be for selfish, or wrong motives, and is foolish. When selfishness is present, a natural breeding ground for Satan, and his demons has been cultivated. To fulfill God's will, should be the intent of a true Christian heart. To fulfill God's will, or purpose to its highest potential, the power of the Holy Spirit must be present. Selfishness is fulfilling the will of self, or the flesh, is of the world, and carnal.

It is a natural human desire to possess power. Jesus told his disciples, that in His absence, after receiving the Holy Ghost, they would receive power (Acts 1:8). Jesus said in Luke 10:19-20, "Behold I give unto you power to tread on serpents, and scorpions, and over all the power of the enemy, and nothing by any means will harm you. Notwithstanding in this, rejoice not that the spirits are subject unto you, but rather rejoice, because your names are written in heaven". Jesus is saying don't rejoice because you have the power, but rather that you were counted worthy to receive the power.

Power, if desired for the wrong reasons can result in self-destruction. While dying to self is a main goal in Christian growth, self-destruction is not dying to self. Self-destruction is destroying the body, soul, and spirit. If a Christian possesses supernatural powers, and uses them negligently he is condemning his body, soul, and spirit. It is the same as witchcraft, idolatry, astrology, etc., and is of a wrong spirit. God will not give this kind of power to someone He can't trust to use it for righteousness.

When we look back over the characters in the Bible, we need to see them in perspective. In today's time, we tend to spiritualize people in the Bible. They were real people just like you, and me. God will use us the same way He used them if we will allow Him. When reading about the supernatural things of God don't get hung up on the ways of the world. Try to see, and think the way God sees, and thinks. He is the same yesterday, today, and tomorrow. Though some of the things in this book may seem frightening to you, I assure you they are spiritual, and from God the Father. Keep in mind the way God dealt with people of ancient times. He is no different today.

The following example of a word of knowledge may differ from what you are accustomed to, however natural, when God chooses to work this way. He must first have a willing vessel.

Some years ago, while in college, the cast, after a night's performance, all went to a cast party. The party was being held at one of the cast member's apartment. She was the female lead in the play we were currently performing. I, and a few of my friends were sitting on the stairs that led to the upstairs rooms. We were discussing the evening performance, and how well Rita had sung that night. Rita, and I both were in our early twenties. I was a Christian, and I was to be married that following September. She being a young married girl was helping me with my wedding plans. She loved her husband, but something had happened to hurt her tremendously. She felt alone, and forsaken, and really had no one with whom to share her problems.

Suddenly, and without warning, the spirit of my mind was transferred to Rita's mind. It was as though her pain drew me to her. She was sitting in another section of the apartment, out of my sight. For one moment in time, we were as one in the spirit of our minds. I knew what she was thinking, and she knew that I knew. The spirit of my mind had entered Rita's thoughts long enough to find she was having marital problems. I was accustomed to experiencing supernatural phenomenon, but I had never read someone's thoughts, at least not in such a supernatural way. Our minds being knit together, separated us from our earthly bodies, and we were standing in a large museum type room in another dimension. We were standing facing each other discussing her situation in the Spirit.

Then as suddenly as this happened, it ended just as sudden, and the spirit of my mind was back in my head. I immediately went down the stairs, and peaked around the wall that separated Rita, and me. She was looking toward where I came to stand. We looked at each other for a moment, waiting to see if the other knew what had just happened. She stared at me, and I her, and we both knew it had happened. I went to her, and we immediately began sharing about the experience. I began to tell her what she had been thinking. It was exciting, and thrilling, but at the same time humbling. Neither of us was frightened by the experience, though most would have been. It just seemed so naturally supernatural. The unusual thing was, I could read her thoughts, but she wasn't able to read mine. This made a lasting impression with me, in learning of God's infinite power in us.

The experience allowed me to feel the great pain, and hurt Rita was feeling, and allowed me to introduce her to God's infinite love. My arms were an extension of the Holy Spirit's arms, as He used me to comfort Rita. Who knows, maybe she needed a dramatic demonstration to provoke her interest in knowing God. I couldn't see any other reason why this mind mingling happened except to reveal how the Holy Spirit administers the gifts of the spirit. It was bazaar to say the least. The Father did reveal His reason for this mind mingling, as I will try to explain.

I've never told anyone about Rita's problem. I continued to pray, and console her until there was a release. I later realized this was a true test of whether God could trust me with the secrets of another. It is humbling to know the thoughts of others. Think about it. If you knew the thoughts others have of you weren't flattering, could you keep quiet, and still love that person? I believe most people would be offended if they knew others have unflattering thoughts about them. Some may feel this is an invasion of privacy. Thoughts are not private to the Holy Spirit, and He will reveal as He sees fit. Thoughts for the most part on earth are in secret. However, there are times the Holy Spirit will reveal your secrets to another, but only for the purpose of prayer, or ministry. He will never reveal your innermost secrets to someone who will harm you. Revealing secrets is called word of knowledge. There are no secrets from God. In heaven, thoughts will not be in secret. Everyone will know as they are known. We will communicate by our thoughts. The Holy Ghost does read our mail.

Satan realizes the world's desire to harness the powers of the universe, and he preys upon this desire for his own benefit. His first step is to capture the soul by trickery. When people begin to take interest in the supernatural, Satan automatically sends his fallen angels, or demons to lead the unsuspecting souls astray, unsuspecting in the lack of knowledge of spiritual entities. Therefore, it is important to teach children about God in their infancy. If the word of God is taught to children at an early age, Satan may try to take their soul captive, but God's word will not come back void.

What most Christians don't understand is that Satan can, and will capture the thoughts of a born again, Christian, but only if the person allows. Since the living, breathing, decision-making part of man is the soul; the thoughts are where Satan begins his tricks. If Satan's attempts at captivity are successful, in the case of a born again, Christian it will only be for a season. If the Christian is in good standing in relationship with the Father, having knowledge in the word of God, this season will be short lived, however not isolated from future attempts.

Abstaining from the lust of the flesh is a necessary change in the lifestyle of a child of God. Romans 12:2 reads, "And being not conformed to this world: but being transformed by the renewing of the mind, and proving what is that good, acceptable, and perfect will of God." A Christian must have a mind change. Paul wrote in Galatians 5:16-17, "Walk in the Spirit, and ye shall not fulfill the lust of the flesh: for the flesh lusteth against the Spirit, and the Spirit against the flesh: and these are contrary the one to the other: so that ye cannot do the things that ye would." Here Paul is explaining walking in the spiritual eliminates the works of the flesh. The Spirit can't do the works of the flesh and is in constant conflict with the flesh.

According to the above scriptures, there is a way to walk apart, and beyond the way we walk in the natural. "There is a way that seemeth right unto a man, but the end thereof are the ways of death (Proverbs 16:25)". Jesus said in Matthew 7:13-14, "Enter ye in at the straight gate: for wide is the gate, and broad is the way, that leadeth to destruction, and many there be which go in thereof: because straight is the gate, and narrow is the way, which leadeth unto life, and few there be that find it."

Like many in the Church, some have head knowledge, but not heart knowledge. They can recite psalms 23 but they have not met the Shepherd. They do not know the true meaning of sin, and the spiritual things of God. If they had, they wouldn't be judging by the outer appearance, but by the fruits of the Spirit. Holiness is a heart (mind) condition, not a law of the flesh working in the members of the physical body.

Once we have come to the knowledge of God, we must begin to seek the things of God. If we allow self-will to control us, we can't be in constant communion with God. Adam, and Eve submitted to their will instead of to the will of God, and they were cast out of the garden. Satan deceived them into the thought of possessing a higher power making them like God, in giving them all knowledge, understanding and wisdom. It was their will, their soul's choice to disobey God, and follow Satan. One sad aspect of their disobedience is they didn't become like God as Satan said they would. They were already like God, before they disobeyed. What they became by Satan's lie was separated from God.

Submitting to our own will is the same as yielding to Satan, being used by him as he pleases. Submitting to our own will is walking in disobedience to God. Our mission is to yield ourselves to God, not to Satan. The choice we make will be the master we will serve, and the master that will direct our path in life. Remember it is the soul that decides to follow righteousness, or sin, and carry out the action of its choice. (Matt. 6:24)

Christians are fascinated with the supernatural, yet they shy away, and are fearful of the source from which it comes. God created the supernatural, and it is exactly what it implies. It is the natural in a super form. In other words, the supernatural is knowledge beyond the knowledge we have in the natural (world, or normal).

Experiencing the supernatural should come natural to the Christian. After all, Jesus instructed us to walk in the spirit, and truth. However, this is difficult for a Christian to comprehend. Lack of knowledge in the paranormal causes the Christian to automatically look to Satan when they experience a super-normal happening. It is by a lack of knowledge and understanding of the supernatural, and fear of the unknown, that keeps us from seeing and walking in the Spirit.

Satan's power is a false power, copying the real power of God, and has no substance, or validity in its diversion. As we experience psychic phenomena, we assume we have tapped into the forbidden forces of evil. This assumption in one respect is right, while on the other hand is wrong. I'll explain.

If we believe the spiritual realm belongs to Satan, we have truly stepped beyond reality into a world having no power unless we give it power. Satan has a kingdom, and it may appear to exist, but it only becomes real when activated by our belief. His very existence is based on a lie. Everything built on the foundation of a lie, and untruth, a false foundation, can't stand. Satan's kingdom is a lie, and will be cast with Satan, into the lake of fire in the Day of Judgment. Satan has no power of his own. Believing Satan's lies, is allowing the forces of evil to control our minds. These forces can take us down extraordinary avenues of the paranormal in mind control, but only if we allow.

Allowing Satan to take complete control of our minds is a practice in demonology, and satanic worship. To understand, let us say a poisonous snake that can't open its mouth has no power. It still has fangs, venom, a mouth, and in all appearance is deadly. Since the snake can't open its mouth, it can do no harm. Satan gets his power from the thoughts he puts in our minds. If we dwell on these thoughts, exercise them, and put them into action, we have made Satan's power real, and applicable. Satan's thoughts, like the mouth of the snake are bound unless we unlock them, and activate them, otherwise they lay dormant.

Any power that isn't used for God in fulfilling His purpose of righteousness is a false power here today, gone tomorrow. If a power must be practiced with chants, weird guttural sounds, abnormal body positions, drinking blood, urine, or use other than the natural use of a thing, sexual performance, and/or practiced often to retain the power, it is a false power of evil. Satan is the source of evil, and he wants to destroy you by allowing you to experience the paranormal his way. He loves to put on a show in demonstrating his supposed power. When people involve themselves in the cruel acts of satanic ritual, they are opening the door for Satan to act. These acts demonstrated with such flair will distract you from the real power in the gifts of the Spirit given by God. If Satan had power of his own, he wouldn't have been cast down from heaven as a defeated foe. Not saying he would have been more powerful than God, but merely demonstrating he has no power on his own.

The only real power Satan has is the power of suggestion. That is how he tempted Eve. He suggested that she would become like God, and she believed him. He had no power over her until she partook of the forbidden fruit. She activated the thoughts Satan projected to her. She was already like God, but Satan planted a thought that suggested she wasn't like God. Since she didn't realize she was already like God she was tricked by Satan's suggestion. Satan did this to Jesus. Satan posed the question to Jesus, "If you are the Son of God, cast yourself down and God will give His angels charge over you". Jesus knew who He is, and He didn't fall for Satan's trickery. Satan didn't know Jesus was God in the flesh, so the trick was on Satan. This is what Satan does. He comes in a subtle way, and unless we know who we are in Christ, we can be deceived. He doesn't want you to know who you are in Christ. He knows if you know who you are he will never gain power over you. Allowing Satan to tempt us by using the power of suggestion, allows our mental faculties to become sensitive to the occult. Satan can't read our thoughts, but he is fully aware when we act on his thought suggestions.

Ordinary people do this to each other without even knowing by whom they are being influenced. I've heard husbands call their wives stupid in trying to make them think they aren't intelligent. I've heard others say things like, "You're not who you think you are", or "Who do you think you are?" People who say things to each other like, "You aren't saved, you just think you are", "You don't have the Holy Ghost", "You're nothing without me". These are examples of the power of suggestion people use when influenced by the wrong spirit. It is an attempt to make another feel incompetent, degraded, and powerless. If a husband can make his wife think she is stupid, she will be stupid in her mind, and controlled by the husband or wrong spirit, unless she knows she isn't stupid. These are examples of how psychic phenomena, or power of suggestion is used in a wrong way. One of the worst and most often used is, "IF YOU LOVE ME, YOU WILL DO WHAT I'M ASKING, ETC". That is a complete lie. If they love you, they would, not use that manipulation.

The power of God comes to us by the Holy Spirit. The power of the Holy Spirit is found in the fruits of the Spirit. Access to these fruits is free to a born again, believer in Jesus Christ. The fruits of the Spirit are assets in the Christian lifestyle, in performing that good and acceptable will of God. Like any other fruit bearing tree, the fruits of the Spirit take time to mature. From groundbreaking to fruit bearing is a process. At Salvation we receive the seeds of the fruit, which contains the life of the fruit, but the seed first must be planted, cultivated, pruned, etc., before the perfect fruit can emerge on the tree. The Fruits of the Spirit are not the source of our power but is the power of our source.

There are nine fruits of the Spirit listed in Galatians 5:22-24, and they are, "Love, joy, peace, longsuffering, gentleness, goodness, faith, meekness, and temperance". In possessing these character traits, the enemy, in coming against us is stopped dead in his tracks. He has no power over these fruits in trying to deceive, kill, steal, or destroy. Jesus said in St. John 19:11, "Thou couldest have no power at all against me, except it were given thee from above: therefore, he that delivered me unto thee hath the greatest sin." Jesus has the fruits therefore there is no power that can overcome Him. He laid down His life to atone for our sins. It was taken from Him.

When Jesus came against the demon of Gadara, the demon spirit knew there was nothing in Jesus in common with him. That is one reason why the demons (legions) had no power over Jesus. They knew Jesus by name, and that He is the power. They knew they could not stay in the man they had possessed, because Jesus came by to cast them out. They even asked Jesus to let them be cast into the swine standing nearby. All Jesus said to the demons was, "Go", and they went. When we possess the fruits of the Spirit, they are our spiritual armor. When these fruits are operating in our life, with little effort on our part, demons must flee. I believe this is why in Acts 5:15 the sick were brought to where Peter would pass by in the hope his shadow would land on them. If the fruits of the spirit are operating in our lives, even our shadow will manifest healing.

It is not a good idea to try and cast demons out of people if you lack the fruits of the spirit. I saw a preacher pray for a man that had a limp. While the preacher was praying, I saw a skeleton walk out of the man and go into the preacher. The name of this skeleton was limping spirit. Before the service was over the preacher was limping and limped for at least two weeks. I didn't tell the preacher what I had seen, but I did ask him if when he prayed for the man could that limping spirit have come into him. The preacher said no it couldn't. Even he wasn't aware of the impartation. We need to be careful when laying hands on the sick, diseased, and demon possessed. We need to make sure we are in right standing with Jesus, having the fruits of the spirit, especially love in our heart. (Repeated in the chapter The Enemy's Camp)

Fruits of the Spirit are contrary to the fleshly character traits called works of the flesh, like fear, hate, rebellion, stubbornness, drunkenness, envying, reveling, strife, seditions, heresies, variance, idolatry, witchcraft, and murders. The works of the flesh are Satan's fruits. That is how he gains his strength, and power. If he can cause you to walk in the flesh in one or all these character traits, he can control you. There is only one way to walk in the spirit, and that is to not fulfill the lust of the flesh in continuing in carnal thinking and speaking.

Possessing the love of God is the only way to achieve the fruits of the Spirit. You must possess the fruits of the Spirit, or you will be subject to Satan. In the case of the husband calling his wife stupid, if she believes him, she has given him power over her. On the other hand, if she has the love of God in her heart, she is going to know she isn't stupid, and will not fall prey to Satan's attempt through her husband to trick her. If a person does these things to another it is called manipulation, or witchcraft).

For psychic phenomena to work in the right way, the love of God must be present in one's heart. If the love of God is in the heart, the fruits of the spirit will be present, and there will be nothing in a person like Satan, in giving him ground. If the wife has the love of God in her heart, she will not receive the lie of Satan, will not get puffed up, angry, and bent out of shape. She will be confident having a meek spirit. When the husband can't get her puffed up, or in a corner, he will see she is not surrendering to his power play and will back off. This is when psychic phenomena are used in activating who we are in Christ.

"There is no power but of God (Romans 13:1)." We are given authority in the name of Jesus, but the power is in the Love of God, shed abroad in our hearts by the Holy Spirit. Without the Holy Spirit we have no teacher to teach us how to be obedient, or about the Love of God. We can hear about it, talk about it, read about it, and write about it, but we can't live it if it isn't in our hearts. In our daily Christian walk we practice at right living, but if the Love of God is not in our hearts, our sin nature will eventually manifest by the works of the flesh. The devil can't always hide his pernicious ways. He exposes himself automatically through deeds, attitudes, and words. Without the Love of God in our hearts it is impossible to live the life of Christ.

We are naturally the children of wrath, and under the influence of Satan if we don't know God's love, and how to obey Him. People under the influence of Satan are not law-abiding citizens, and aren't subject to doing good, keeping the ordinances of God. Without God's law of love, humans aren't capable of loving God, Jesus, the Holy Spirit, self as the temple of God, family, friends, neighbors, and enemies. They are living a life concentrated upon self-gratification. When self-gratification is the primary motivation to success, there is no true love for others, and self. To love others, and self, God's love must be present in our hearts, for God is love. The Holy Spirit establishes God's love, and without Him there is no love. Without the Holy Spirit, power that is practiced, or sought after is a lower, destructive form of false power. It is used solely for the purpose of evil, or self-gratification, against others, and against our self under the influence of Satan. This is a false power and may be why we do not see miracles today.

Power in the hands of people without God is extremely dangerous. It would be used for selfish greed, and gain, breaking the law, doing evil against others, and fulfilling the lust of the flesh in selfish desires. If we haven't learned to love our enemy, the Holy Spirit is not going to give us the power to know what someone is thinking (the ability to read minds or discern spirits - Matthew 9:4). Most Christians have not matured in living the life of Christ to the extent that they can use this power to the Glory of God. If people could see what others think of them, there would probably be countless numbers of murder committed several times over, without end. This is one reason why we must be renewed in the spirit of our minds, and not be affected by what others think about us individually.

Our need is to learn to focus our attention on the condition of the heart, whether it is evil, or good, and not on what people say, and think of us. In getting offended by what people say, do, or think, is a clue that we have not crucified the flesh, have not renewed the spirit of our minds, and the love of God is not present in our heart.

According to Jesus, we don't know what we are doing. Those are the words He spoke as He was dying on The Cross at Calvary. You see, He can read our thoughts, and He knows how simple, hateful, and rebellious our thoughts can be. He could see from the cross, as He sees today, that there was no hope for mankind in the evil state of man's heart, or mind. He saw we needed a Savior from ourselves. That is primary in why He gave His life for us. There was no other recompense by which we could be saved.

God left the splendor of heaven, where He has everything mankind desires. He came to earth to lay down His life that we too can live with Him in the same splendor in heaven. The only way He could do that was by destroying the works of the devil. (John 3:8) When Satan saw Jesus fully man and fully God, laid down His life to death, and rose from the grave, Satan knew he was in trouble. Death being his only reason for taking souls, Jesus took that reason away from him. Now he has no reason, no mission, except to deceive us into thinking he still has power.

If you are afraid of death Satan will have a stronghold in your life. Fearing death can, also indicate how far from knowing God we are. Jesus conquered death. There is no more death. When sinners die, they are in for a rude awakening when they wake up in hell's fire. "Oh, grave where is thy sting? Oh, death where is thy victory?" (1 Cor. 15:55) When true believers pass over the great gulf they wake up in heaven. The first death has no power over the believer, for they simply move on to the next level of life in the resurrection. The sinner moves to the next level too, only it isn't a level of resurrected life, but eternal damnation.

To be a Christian in right standing with God, we must first learn how to look beyond the faults of others and see their need. If we aren't dead to our flesh, we can't see the need others have in needing Jesus in their life. To love in this manner, we need the Agape love of God. We must die to self before the agape love of God can be perfected in us. Agape love is the highest form of love. It is a self-sacrificing love, one that is giving, not taking. Agape means having the highest admiration, or holding to highest esteem someone, or something, and giving such honor, as to die for, or lay down your life.

Without the agape love of God, we are going to see the faults of others, instead of their needs. We are to strive to see through the eyes of Jesus, having compassion on a dying world in their lack of knowledge of truth. Caring only about oneself, and our feelings will not allow the love of God to operate in our heart. There must be unconditional Agape love. I don't think we are there yet.

The Bible tells us the tongue is the unruliest member of the body. It has the power to kill or give life. If we can tame the tongue, we can walk in perfection, and bridle the whole body. Show me a person who can't control what he says, and I'll show you that person is still operating in the flesh. (James 1:26, 3:5,6,8) Do a research on all the scriptures about the tongue and see how important it is in our life. It will be an eye opener to your heart if you'll be honest with yourself.

Another way Satan uses his influence is through our words. When an unkind word is spoken to us, how do we react? Do we get puffed up, and angry in our flesh, and react with unkind words, or a fist in their mouth? If we do, we have not died to self. When we get offended, or hurt by what others say, it is because their words have attacked the state of perfection in which we think ourselves to be (Thinking our way is the only way, and that we are always right). We feel that by their words they have succeeded in exposing our true character to not only others, but to oneself.

In most cases, hateful words will confirm how we think about ourselves. If we get offended, or hurt by what others say to us, it is because, what they said is the truth, or we think it to be the truth. If it were not the truth, we would know it in our spirit, and would not get offended. If you can be easily hurt by the words of others you are in need of knowing God's love. Don't turn away from Him but turn to Him that the Holy Spirit may teach you who you are in Christ and bring to light how precious you are to and in Him.

Another kind of offense happens when we misinterpret what someone has said. In other words, we hear what we want to hear. Sometimes we hear what we have been taught to hear by our lifestyle. Other times we hear something totally different from what was said. A good rule to follow is, "To the pure all things are pure (Titus 1:15)." Don't always assume the worst. Getting offended is only hurting yourself. You will become bitter, anxious, angry, stubborn, rebellious, sick in body, and in general having a restless spirit. When someone speaks truth to you in love, be mature enough to receive it, and consider your ways. Take it to God, He will reveal to you the truth about yourself if you allow it.

On the other hand, when others speak unkind words to us, and we have the love of God in our heart, we are going to recognize their words as a lie. Since the tongue has the power to kill, or give life, then unkind words are meant to kill. In this case we will see through the eyes of compassion, and see the need of the speaker, in that they are being used of Satan, and need deliverance. Therefore, they need our undivided intercession for their soul. What they don't need is rejection. They need love.

For demonstration, I'll use a personal experience. Many years ago, as a young Christian, I was given charge over a holiday program at church. It was a week before the program, and I had laid the format plans in my mind. A few of the ladies in my group, my elders, began coming up with ideas for me to use. I immediately proclaimed, "Who is overseeing this program anyway? I don't mean to offend anyone, but I have the program lined up, and I don't really need any suggestions at this point." I immediately saw expressions of rejection and hurt in their faces. I had not intended to hurt them, in their intention to help me.

My reaction was uncalled for. What I had said, and what they heard were two different things. I was trying to let them know that they need not concern themselves over the program; that I had it all worked out. What they heard was, "Mind your own business, I don't need any help". Not only was this a sign of pride in me but is how Satan gains ground. He disguised my true feelings with a false thought. I should have listened to their suggestions, and secondly, I should have kept my mouth shut. It would have been so much easier to have said nothing and allowed them to voice their ideas. This circumstance also revealed the condition of my heart. There was still that self-element working inside me, better known as vanity.

In one way I was telling the truth, and they got offended. I oversaw the program, and they didn't need to be concerned. On the other hand, I was wrong in my attitude. My attitude said, "Mind your own business". How many of you can see we place ourselves in the devil's playground when we act selfishly or in pride? Though it was not my intention to hurt anyone, I had reacted to what they had said, in the wrong way. I took their suggestions to mean, "You don't know what you are doing, so let us help you." Right then I saw I had a wounded heart in much need of repair. The way we interpret things depends on whether our heart is right.

At the time, I didn't know this was how I felt inside. I took their attempt to help, as an attack against my ability to perform. The reason my words were received differently than the way I thought I had meant them was, in my heart I meant exactly what they had heard. I had been triggered by what I thought I had heard. The tone of the voice can also be an alert to the issues of the heart.

It is the same as when a baby cries, and a mother knows by the tone of the cry whether the baby is hurting, hungry, needs a diaper change, or is agitated. The same applies when we speak. If I say, "I love you," but my attitude isn't right, the recipient may hear the words "I love you, but I don't really love you with my whole heart." We can't operate in the gifts of the Spirit, fulfilling the great commission if Jesus is not in us. In this example, I should have listened, if for no other reason, because they were my elders. I apologized with deepest regrets, repented, and asked theirs, and God's forgiveness.

When we have the love of God in our hearts, our choice of words, and our attitudes are going to change. The way we receive what others say is also going to change. If the words we speak do not give life, regardless of whether we think ourselves to be right, or wrong, we are wrong. Even if we speak the truth, if the attitude is wrong, or the choice of words are wrong, we are still wrong. Get the picture? It takes a lot of change, and a lot of God's words operating in us to get it right and walk in the righteousness of Christ. Our main goal should be to allow Jesus to live His life through us, and the Holy Spirit to speak expressly through us.

Another challenge we face in the spoken word is correction. The Bible says a wise man loves correction. If we are being corrected in a way that will make us better in our walk with God, by someone who cares for us, has the rule over us, and loves us, we should not get offended, or hurt.

When a Pastor, an elder, or any person who knows God, corrects us in love by the word of God, we should be grateful for their concern, and not angry. Even if we don't believe they are right at that moment, we should not disregard their words of truth. Take into consideration the person doing the correcting. Ask yourself, is this person in right standing with God? Knowing someone is in right standing with God should make taking correction a little easier. Instead of becoming instantly angry, or rebellious ask God to show you the error of your ways.

If we are truly abiding in Christ, and His word truly abides in us, we will be open to God, and His Spirit, allowing ourselves to see the state in which is our own heart. Most often than not, we are going to find they were right, and we did need correction. Knowing the scriptures and having a personal relationship with God is vital for these reasons. If someone corrects us, and they are not in right standing with God, but they have the rule over us, take the correction in peace. If they are wrong, God will deal with them, and we stay in right standing with God. The alternative is to confront that person in love, and make peace turning what Satan meant for harm, into good.

There are times when there is a genuine concern for someone, and it is received wrong. I knew a lady, and her daughter that became estranged by what the mother thought she heard the daughter say. The Mother had many medical problems. She also had a mindset of thinking with every symptom she experienced, she was getting another disorder. The Mother was elaborating about her medical problems to the daughter, and the mother said, "And next I'll have Alzheimer's". This statement triggered the daughter because the daughter knew how important the spoken word is. The Mother on the other hand didn't know what the Bible says about the words we speak. The daughter responded with, "Mother don't say that." The Mother claimed the daughter had yelled at her, and took this to mean, the daughter was showing disrespect, and trying to control her. In fact, the daughter was concerned that her mother was speaking death to herself.

The two didn't speak with one another for months. The daughter tried to make peace with the mother, but the mother stayed in her stubbornness for a long time. The daughter could see the mother had taken the daughters concern and treated it as a control issue. The daughter kept praying for the Lord to show her mother the truth.

The daughter in this case could see her mother didn't know the truth in what had happened, so she just turned it over to God. She could see her mother's reaction was one of pride, in that the mother knew she had made a ridiculous remark. Upon seeing the foolishness in making that statement, a self-protection mechanism came on, and she yelled at the daughter, and hung up the phone. The crashing sound of the phone sounded like an explosion in the daughter's ears. In yelling at the daughter, and hanging up the phone, the mother was venting her feelings of anger, and being selfish onto the daughter.

When the mother said the daughter yelled at her, I happen to know the daughter did not yell, however in the mother's anger, she heard something that didn't happen. Satan can play tricks on people, and they don't realize his manipulation. The mother's response was to the daughter like a slap in the face. At first the daughter became angry, but after a day or two, she repented, and began asking God to take charge. The daughter through the love of God could see the spiritual condition of her mother's heart and didn't stay angry. The daughter knew that in time the mother would come around, it was just a matter of waiting on the Lord to correct the problem.

Had the daughter not known the word of God, had not the love of God in her heart, she would have reacted in a rebellious way, and Satan would have had his way in this division. The Mother would have not been set free of her offense, and the house divided would have fallen. Not so in this case. The prayer of the daughter was, "Father show me how to bring this situation to light." The Father did just that. He showed the daughter a way out, and it brought restoration to both mother, and daughter. The daughter had the right attitude, and motive. The Father took that right attitude, and turned what Satan meant for harm, into good. (Romans 8:28)

Motives, and attitudes must be changed for the flesh to die. Otherwise, instead of what God is saying we will continue to hear what Satan wants us to hear. If our hearts are not changed, and our mouths speak forward things, it is best to keep our mouths shut, and ask God to forgive us for our selfish thoughts. Ask Him to create within us a clean heart and renew within us a right spirit. If we allow our evil thoughts to manifest in word, or deed, we are not justifying our actions, but are condemning ourselves. If our hearts are filled with the word of God, our mouths will only speak life-giving words. Wrong words, actions, thoughts of evil do not glorify the Father, and they don't glorify us.

Voice of the Prophet:

Let us discuss the role of a prophet regarding the spoken word. Prophets are people who bring messages from God to the people. Prophets have a good insight when it comes to the Christian lifestyle, and they usually are ones who know the word of God in depth. When they speak, they speak truth. Prophets, for this reason, are often misunderstood. The truth in general conversation, with friends and relatives, can sound harsh to the listener. To the prophet the word he, or she speaks isn't intended to offend, but to speak honestly. However, most people get offended at the truth.

This is to no fault of the prophet. To the prophet there are no grey areas. It is either truth, or nothing. Prophets can't help but speak the word of God in spirit, and in truth. That is why it is not wise for prophets to engage in general conversation, because most people can't take this kind of honesty. First, prophets are in constant fellowship with Father, and are going to speak what they hear God say in love. Prophets are directed by the Holy Spirit what to say, and the Holy Spirit speaks expressly through the prophet.

If you don't want to know the truth about something don't ask a prophet. Prophets have few friends, which is sad, because everyone needs friends. However, most prophets are content in their relationship with the Father. They have no need for friends on the level other people do.

If we don't see the error of our ways, we need to ask God to teach us to see them. If we ask with a repentant heart, The Holy Spirit of truth will teach us. This is usually where trials and tribulations begin. Show me a person who has come to the light, and is going through affliction, after affliction, and I will show you the affliction of the righteous. I'm not saying that all afflictions, and tribulations are spiritual growing pains. I'm saying our, understanding, knowledge, and wisdom in the word of God will teach us the difference.

If a person is seeking God, searching, and studying the scriptures, they will indeed change by the daily renewing of their mind. As change occurs, we will still walk in error in learning the right way to go. The point is to continue seeking God with a repentant heart even in our error. Doing this is a sign we are growing in God's Grace, and knowledge. Little by little, our errors will evolve into holiness as the nature of Christ is formed in us (Galatians 4:19). For as long as we are on this earth in the natural body, we will have error, until Jesus comes. Continue to ask God to teach you the error of your ways, especially if you don't think you are in error.

On the other hand, if we are faced with afflictions often, and there seems to be no change in our spirits, this is a clue that these afflictions are self-inflicted by disobedience (sin). If sin is present in our lives, we are going to have to ride the consequences until it has run its course (Matt. 5:25-26). If sin is allowed to persist with no restitution, or repentance, there will be no baptism in the love of God, by the Holy Spirit of truth. Staying in this condition will produce bitterness, hardheartedness, and un-forgiveness. These blemishes will govern our lives and hinder our relationship with Father.

If we don't change, it is a sign, we don't know the Savior, Jesus. If we don't know Jesus, we can't know the Holy Spirit, and if we don't know the Holy Spirit, we can't know God. If we don't know God, we are not saved, and do not possess the ability to do anything for good. There is none good but God. If we don't possess God's love in our hearts, we have nothing good in us. We will be powerless against the supernatural forces, having given all power to the enemy.

It is not possible without God to possess powers of good. If a person says they are using their power for good, but possesses not the Spirit of God, the truth is not in them. If a confessed Christian claiming to be Spirit filled, gets puffed up, speaks unkind words, and does not seek God in repentance, he is not walking in the power of the Holy Spirit.

Therefore, there is no need for him to even lay hands on the sick and expect to see a miracle. For the miracle of healing, or any other gift from God to manifest, the love of God must be evident in the heart of the one administering the gift. Evidence of God's love in a heart produces evidence of Jesus in that life through their words, deeds, attitudes, and actions.

God can perform the miracle without us, but should God use us to exercise the laying on of hands, and our hearts are not right, God cannot use us.

It is God's love that has the power to conquer evil and perform miracles. Power from the Holy Spirit is given to all that will come to God with a repentant heart, being not conformed to this world, but being renewed in the spirit of their mind, rightly dividing the word of truth.

As you are laying hands on the sick, the blind, the lame, etc., and miracles are not occurring, you might want to examine yourselves. 2nd Corinthians 13:5, "Examine yourselves, whether ye be in the faith; prove your own selves. Know ye not your own selves, how that Jesus Christ is in you, except ye be reprobates?" Reprobate means having lost all sense of duty. (Funk & Wagnall's standard desk dictionary).

Where God's love is, there is all power; Power over serpents, scorpions, over all power of the enemy, and all manner of evil (Luke 10:19). God's power is freely given to whom God can trust, and he can only trust those who have received knowledge of the truth, with understanding, and wisdom. Make sure your sin nature is changing into the nature of Christ, bearing the fruits of the Spirit, and wisdom in how to use them.

CHAPTER 3

Supernatural, Understanding, Knowledge, and Wisdom (Part II)

Supernatural powers used without the direction of the Holy Spirit is dangerous, uncontrolled, and directed by Satan, and will give him a stronghold in your life. The stronghold may not be evident right away, but will at some point in time be tested, and brought to light. Though these powers may be used for seemingly good causes, there will come a time when Satan, will demand payment. For this cause, it is wise not to fear the supernatural, but to understand it, and know how to use it properly. Most often, people used by Satan are Christians that know not the word of God in all truth, having no understanding of the scriptures in depth, and can't rightly apply them to their lives.

The Bible tells us that God's perfect love cast out all fear (1 John 4:18). It also tells us to fear the one (God) that not only has power to kill, but has power to cast both body, and soul into hell after He has killed. Having this kind of fear means to reverence God for who He is. To fear God is the first step in getting wisdom. God will, in turn, give you His knowledge, understanding, and direction for your life. The way to get the fear of God is to hate evil (Proverbs 8:2 - (13) 31).

Proverbs 3: 6, 7, 13 reads, "In all thy ways acknowledge the Lord, and He shall direct thy paths. Be not wise in thine own eyes: fear the Lord and depart from evil. Happy is the man that findeth wisdom, and the man that getteth understanding. Do not cease to pray that ye might be filled with the knowledge of His will in all wisdom, and spiritual understanding (Wisdom is more precious than rubies, and all the things thou canst desire are not to be compared unto her (Proverbs 3:15); that ye might walk worthy of the Lord unto all pleasing, being fruitful in every good work, and increasing in the knowledge of God (Colossians 1:9-10)." Until we die to self, and our opinion, we can't use the powers, and gifts of the Spirit wisely, and without negligence. They will be harnessed by a lack of knowledge in who we are in Christ, instead of released by knowing who Christ is in us.

Linda L. Evans

There are numerous accounts of supernatural happenings in the Bible. In reading through the Old, and New Testaments, the paranormal is displayed in various kinds of ways. Para" means "Beside; nearby, along with, beyond, aside from." The word "normal" means "Conforming to, or consisting of a pattern, process, or standard regarded as usual, or typical." Combine the two, "Para normal", and you have "Beside nearby, along with a pattern, process, or standard regarded as usual, or typical." Because the word paranormal, or psychic phenomenon is used frequently in association with the occult, or the evil side of the supernatural, most people think these two words are on the eerie side of the spiritual things. The difference between Satan's terminology, and the Bible's terminology in psychic phenomenon is as follows:

1. (Satan) Telepathy – the ability to read minds and transmit thoughts.
   (Bible) this same power is referred to as having a discerning of spirits. Discernment allows one to know of what spirit a man is. There are times that the Holy Spirit will allow one to know someone's thoughts, as was the case of Ananias, and Sapphira in Acts 5, and Jesus in (Luke 9:47) perceiving their thoughts.......... God speaks to mankind by transmitting thoughts to us, and in many cases revealing the thoughts of others. Also, known as Word of Knowledge.

2. (Satan) Precognition – the ability to perceive future events
   (Bible) Prophecy/Foretelling. The Old Testament is a testament, or prophecy of future events, whereas the New Testament is the fulfillment of those foretold events. The Book of Revelation is a prophecy for the end times. John the Revelator saw past, and future events, beginning with the birth of Christ already past when he saw them written in the constellations, and ending with the return of Jesus Christ in the second advent, and the City New Jerusalem coming down from heaven.

3. (Satan) Retro cognition/Forthtelling – the ability to see into the past and the future.
   (Bible) also referred to as prophecy. There are many cases when prophets were told by God of something someone else had done. Then the prophet was sent to the person with a prophetic message directly from God. Examples are between, Nathan, and King David, Samuel, and Eli, Peter, and Cornelius, and Annanias, and Saul (on Strait Street), and John the Revelator. As you will read later in this book, I had an experience where God took me in the spirit back to Mt Sinai, or Horeb when the children of Israel were in the wilderness. Ananias was told of a man name Saul/Paul would be coming. That Ananias should lay hands on Saul/Paul to heal him of his blindness.

4. (Satan) Clairvoyance – the ability to see objects, or events beyond the range of physical vision.
   (Bible) having visions. All prophets in the Bible, and of today experience this kind of phenomenon. A vision is a faculty of natural sight that is given as a foresight, or insight through the spiritual, or supernatural realm. It means that the Holy Spirit shows a sort of film in the mind, allowing a person to view things to come. While this film is being shown, the person viewing is in the film in the Spirit and taking part in the things that transpire. The actual participation gives understanding

to the message of which God is giving the person in vision. While in vision, a person is, in essence, transported to another time, place, and dimension, not the physical man, but the spirit man. Daniel, Isaiah, Jeremiah, Ezekiel, Zachariah, and other major, and minor prophet's experienced spiritual travel. Unless you have experienced this phenomenon there is no way to completely understand (in 2nd Cor. 12, Paul was taken to heaven).

This phenomenon may, also be labeled by the World as "Astro projection. The difference being Astro-projection is self-willed. Some Hollywood actors have been known to have this experience. Shirley McClain in her book "Out on a Limb" speaks of her experience. Astro projection, according to her requires a silver cord attached to your body as you float around in space with no mention of the Holy Spirit. Spiritual travel performed, by the Holy Spirit, requires no cord, and you don't just float around in space. The Holy Spirit holds your hand and takes you to a specific place giving you knowledge and understanding of why you are there. You will gain better understanding as you continue to read.

In the spring of 2010 while at intercessors I had a vision. In this vision the Lord, and I were standing outside a hospital. The hospital building was white. It was night, and there were blue, and green landscape lights shining on the building, and there were palm trees casting their shadows on the building. As the Lord and I stood there, He showed me multitudes of the sick getting out of their hospital beds, and walking, completely healed, out of the hospital. The Lord spoke to me and said, "The day is coming when the world will see this happen, and even the Christians will gasp in awe when they see it." Once my spirit returned to the present, I began to tell the others in the group what I had just seen. My voice, as I spoke, gasped from loss of breath in awe and amazement as a demonstration of how people will react when they witness this tsunami of healing. It was an amazing sight.

In this vision, the Lord took me in the spirit, and we both went to a hospital. My body didn't go anywhere, but my spirit did. This is spiritual travel. It isn't evil, and it isn't unlawful. It is a spiritual phenomenon consistent with the spiritual, and supernatural things of God.

It is difficult for Christians to understand, and accept the supernatural, but most nonbelievers seem to have no problem accepting it. Therefore, is why Satan has an open door to most people, Christians because they don't believe, and nonbelievers because they do believe. On the other hand, it should be that the Holy Spirit have an open door to the Christian because they do believe, and an open door to the nonbeliever because they don't believe. In other words, if a Christian doesn't believe in the supernatural, they will be void of the power they need to turn their battles over to Jesus; letting Him combat the powers, and principalities of the air, and the rulers of darkness of this world. They will have a difficult time seeing the things of God in the way God views them.

Becoming a Christian, and never receiving the power of the Holy Spirit is like going to first grade and staying there for life, never completing high school, or going to college. If Christians will believe, they will be more submissive to the Holy Spirit in allowing Him to complete His perfect work in them. Nonbelievers who seem to find it easy to believe in the supernatural are open for Satan to misguide them into the paths of darkness, because they have no knowledge of God. Whereas, the believer, having no knowledge of the supernatural, can be wooed and beckoned by Satan in drawing them into his web of deceit. Before people come to the knowledge of the Holy Spirit, Satan tries to contaminate their minds before drawn into God's saving grace by the power of the word. Nonbelievers may have experienced the evils of the world, but once they are saved, God then turns the bad experiences into good by the power of His love, and grace. The things we did before we were saved will be avenues of strength in our walk as a believer.

I believe this is the difference between people that have lived a Christian lifestyle, never having partaken of the worldly things, and people that have lived in the world before coming to the saving knowledge of Christ. I have found that people who have always lived the Christian lifestyle cannot understand the things of the world. For the most part they have less understanding, and compassion for the sinner's circumstances than does a sinner out in the world after salvation. This is not a detriment of character, or rule of thumb, in the always-was-Christian. It is my observation over the years. If you haven't walked through it, you aren't going to understand the journey.

Take for example a major flood. You can see it on TV, you can read about it, and you can hear about it, but until you are in a flood like that, you can't understand the devastation, and what it does to your mind. I've experienced a major 500-year flood. I saw people killed, homes were under water, people were being rescued off tops of major department stores, and people lost everything overnight. It isn't a pretty sight. Seeing it on TV is nothing like a first-hand experience. The journey makes a difference. It becomes up close, and personal.

Most often the always-was-Christian tends to live by tradition instead of what the word of God declares. In living by tradition instead of searching the scriptures one can fall into deception very easily. Traditions are for the most part based on myths, and personal convictions rather than the truth of God's word. When living by tradition based on what one has been told, renewing of the mind doesn't take place, and knowledge of the whole truth never develops. We often find this kind of tradition in Pentecostal Holiness churches. I have first-hand experience in this. There are genuine believers in the PH movement, but their ancestors were more under law, not grace, and continue to teach their traditions, and personal convictions instead of understanding the truth of God's grace.

Most always-was-Christians, are more likely to be slothful in their Bible reading, and study, and tend to live solely on Sunday sermons, and what seems right. This is not the case with PH, but they seem to spiritualize many scriptures when they should take them literally. I believe in spiritualizing scripture, if the Holy Spirit gives the spiritual meaning, as part of the translation. Spiritualizing scripture in many cases is the deeper meaning of scripture 2, or 3 times removed. However, the literal translation is far more consistent.

If there were one scripture that caused me to leave the PH church, it was 1st Samuel 16:7, "God looks on the heart, not the outer appearance". The PH church lives under law in their dress code. For me, wearing my hair in a bun doesn't make me holy. I'm not trying to offend, but hopefully to break bondages. If the PH members want to love Jesus, and wear their hair in a bun, they are allowed to do so. However, don't put personal convictions onto other people. Scriptural convictions yes, but not personal.

Some always-was-Christians have developed an all-knowing attitude in thinking they have all knowledge of God; never realizing the Bible is a never-ending source of knowledge in teaching them how to apply the word to their lives daily; evidenced by those who spend more time watching TV, reading a book, taking vacations, etc., than time spent in the word of God. These people tend to stick to their traditions, and can't look beyond the fault, and see the need of the sinner. They also can't look beyond themselves and see the need. If you want to follow tradition, make sure it is the tradition of the Gospel, and not that of man.

Some Christians, older in the faith, in the Church for 30 plus years sometimes continue to use slang words without compassion such as nigger, dope-head, drunks, bum, foreigner (as a derogatory remark), whore, queer, (homosexual), redneck white cracker, etc. These are the words they learned as children and carried into their adult years. These kinds of remarks reveal the condition of their hearts. "Out of the abundance of the mouth the heart speaks." One denomination likes to say, "We don't smoke, and we don't chew, and we don't hang with those who do". It's the same denomination that I've seen throw people out of the Church because they raised their hands in worship to God.

It is obvious that a renewing of the mind, and a changed heart hasn't yet happened, leaving their heart void of compassion for the sinner. If the heart is not changed, the carnal nature remains, and all one can see is the color of another's skin, the slant of the eyes, the accents in language, habits, or the act of the sin instead of seeing the soul, and spirit of the sinner. We as Christians are to hate sin, not the sinner.

A sinner made righteous through Christ, can see a marked difference in the sin nature, and the Christ nature. Where the sinner once used slang words, he now uses the word sinner with compassion, and understanding. Salvation to him becomes an eye-opening experience, in knowing good from evil. He develops a hunger, and thirst for truth that most always-was-Christians lack. Always was Christians often rely on their good works as a profession of Holiness.

Because he experienced Satan in his cruelest form, God's word becomes a fountain of life to the out in the world sinner made righteous. The Apostle Paul had this kind of experience. He was a Christian killer. By his own admission he was the chiefest of sinners. We can't change if we don't know we need to change. That is why we need the word of God. It is a mirror reflecting what we are, the kind of spirit in us.

I'm not type casting the always-was-Christian. There are many always-was-Christians who have served the Lord for many years and are considered saints. I'm trying to distinguish between someone who thinks being a member of the Church through their good works certifies their Christianity compared to someone who received a life-changing experience when they met Jesus.

Multitudes followed Jesus in His day. These people listened to Jesus preach, they saw Him perform miracles, they marveled at His teaching, yet when they had a chance to free Him from crucifixion, they didn't. They acted as if they never knew Him. These same multitudes cried out the name Barabbas, a murderer, and thief, to be released in Jesus' stead. It happened in Pilate's courtyard over 2000 years ago. These had no change of heart even in their time spent with the Savior.

The disciples, on the other hand, had a life changing experience. They continued to serve Jesus even after His resurrection, and ascension to heaven. Judas having served, and ministered with Jesus, and the other disciples was the only disciple not having a life changing experience, and he fell back into the world. Condemned to die, he committed suicide. Judas is a picture of one who comes to Christ, and a change of heart didn't take place. Jesus said, "Depart from me ye workers of iniquity, for I never knew you." (Luke 13:27).

To prove that always was Christians, and sinners made righteous are not altogether different, we will mention Peter the disciple closest to Jesus, the leader of the early church. Peter knew Jesus was the Son of God, revealed to him by the Father. Jesus called Peter the rock. Yet, at the last supper Jesus told Peter he would deny Him three times before the cock crowed twice. No way would Peter believe this. He loved Jesus with his whole heart and would not accept this saying as truth. It wasn't long after that in the same night that Jesus was arrested and taken to Pilates court. Peter looked on from the courtyard where others recognized him as a disciple. Peter being afraid denied knowing Jesus. He denied Jesus three times before the cock crowed twice, just as Jesus said he would. Peter demonstrated the reason Jesus came, why Jesus had to die, and why Jesus would rise from the dead.

No matter what walk in life one has had, there are none so righteous that they can't fall. Peter in his righteousness was as filthy rags and needed a Savior. No matter how much we love Jesus, we still have the capability of falling in sin. There is none righteous, no not one.

If we were to take a count, we would find that most Prophets, Evangelist, Pastors, and Teachers of the Gospel are converted sinners having once lived in the ruddy elements of the world. These are the ones having been delivered from the depths of hell and received a life changing experience. They are the ones walking in the power, and gifts of the Holy Spirit from the dynamic change in their heart after meeting Jesus.

I've never met a dynamic minister of the Gospel who walks in the gifts, and calling of God, in all power, that hasn't lived in the world, and converted by God's saving Grace. I'm sure there probably are many who came from a solid background, walking in the gifts of the Spirit, unmarred by the world. I just haven't met one in over thirty-five years.

I am speaking of the people who have always been Christians, never having dealt with the evils of the worldly things, thinking more highly of themselves than they ought; people who think because they haven't fallen prey to the worldly elements of sin, they are more righteous than others. These things ought not be. Jesus is the one righteous, and if He abides in us, we can be no more righteous than the next person who receives Jesus.

No one person's understanding of God is the same. That is why there's so much confusion, and jealousy in the body of Christ. The body of Christ is not made perfect overnight. There are going to be Christians that have not yet come to the knowledge of truth but are on their way. A daily renewing of the mind is necessary to grow in God's grace, and knowledge. Growing in grace means coming to recognize the errors in one's nature, and the Holy Spirit replacing them with God's holiness, by renewing the spirit of their mind. Sanctification is a process.

The natural man can't see the totality of his error all at once, because he can't receive the vast knowledge of God all at once. The vastness of God's knowledge can only come through much prayer, daily repentance, diligent Bible study, applying the principles of the scriptures to daily living, seeking God daily, having a relationship with Jesus, and on goes the list. Even then, we can't receive the vastness of God's knowledge in our finite minds. We may be a speck of sand on the beach but that is about as far as anyone is going to get.

As revelation knowledge comes, along with it comes the knowledge of our evil ways. Revelation comes one by one, and then comes the knowledge of how great our God is and how undeserving we are of His grace. Until we fully understand how undeserving we are of God's Grace, we can't fully understand the totality, and wondrous beauty in the nature of salvation.

At the altar of salvation, we receive God's grace, unmerited favor. The benefits of God are not manifested until we apply ourselves to understanding, and the fear of God. If someone thinks they got it all at the altar of salvation, it is like expecting a college degree the same day of enrollment in first grade. Enrolling in first grade is the first step in earning a college degree but doesn't guarantee a degree unless we finish the course of sixteen years, or more of education.

After sixteen years of education there are various levels of knowledge. One person may have a grade point average of C, and another a grade point average of A. These two letters represent the level of knowledge a person gained about the subject of study. The difference is in the understanding of knowledge. One's level of knowledge and understanding determines one's ability to administer his authority in a subject. If a person thinks he can become a doctor with a first-grade education, this thinking hinders him in becoming a doctor. He will never make it. With a first-grade education he will not have learned how to administer healing by his lack of knowledge of the various kinds of sickness, and disease. He will have no recognition of the symptoms and won't be able to make a correct diagnosis.

I think you get the point. This is what happens to many Christians. There are too many avenues of the sin nature to list them all. If we become a born, again Christian, and don't continue daily for the rest of our lives, in the renewing of the spirit of our minds, feeding our spirit with fresh manna daily, we will never come to knowledge, and understanding seeing the error of our ways. If we don't see the error of our ways, a change will not take place, and we will never graduate from wrath to meekness (Matt. 6:5). Contrary to this we will live for self and will strive to exalt ourselves in thinking we are the "Cat's Meow". Thinking all the while because we got saved, that I'm okay, you're okay. This too is deception. You're not okay, and I'm not either if we don't apply ourselves to the truth.

Without full knowledge, and understanding of the word of God, how will you be able to stand against the wiles of the devil? You can't. Satan is flinging his darts at you, causing you to tremble through sickness, disease, trials, and tribulations, and you don't recognize what is causing the problems. You don't know because you have not educated yourself by the word of God, and in your ignorance, you yield yourself to Satan. "Know ye not you are subject to whom ye yield your members (paraphrased Romans 6:16." We are all guilty of this.

If Satan can make you think you have a disease, and you believe him, you are going to have that disease. Satan can work disease in other ways too. If he can convince us to abuse our bodies through eating, alcohol, drugs, and the like, we will reap physical decay by our own choice. Reaping what we sow. These things aren't necessarily sin, but physical decay will most likely be the result.

Not learning to be all you can be in Christ Jesus is a selfish act. You are not supplying the body of Christ with that portion God gave you to give. If you stay ignorant of the word of God you will never walk in the power of God, coming to realize God's purpose for you. You will never learn to be a servant to others, and in submission to God. Meekness, submission, and servant hood are keys to the Kingdom.

Jesus never used His power for His own purpose. He only used His power for the benefit of others in fulfilling God's purpose. This may be why Jesus didn't want to turn the water into wine at the marriage feast. His mother told Him to do it, and He responded that His time had not yet come. But then He obeyed His mother, and He turned the water into wine as His first miracle. I believe He was able to perform the miracle as a symbol of the new wine and the new wine skins to come. 1 Corinthians 15:46 KJV. Philippians 2:5-7 reads, "Let this mind be in you, which was also in Christ Jesus, who being in the form of God thought it not robbery to be equal with God; but made Himself of no reputation, and took upon Him the form of a servant, and was made in the likeness of man."

Therefore, the power of the Holy Spirit is given to those that have come to the knowledge, and understanding of Jesus Christ, born in His likeness. Becoming like Jesus means dying to self, crucified in the flesh (dead to the works of the flesh), and resurrected as a new creature through the resurrection of Christ Jesus. In Jesus' resurrection is found the mystery of power. It is resurrection power, which is God's love, that the Holy Spirit administers in one's life after a born, again conversion. In a born, again conversion, life has overcome death, and takes away the only possible power Satan has, the power of death. The only way Satan gains this power is in submitting of oneself to him. In submitting to the ways of Satan, power, and authority, is given to him to take your life. In this case, Satan has the power to do the only thing he came to do, kill, steal, and destroy.

It is time Christians must learn to be servants to one another, seeking no reputation, so the powers of the Holy Spirit can be fully exercised. This has been preached for over 2000 years, and many Christians still don't get it. Jesus washed the feet of His disciples, and said in Mark 10:44-45, "But whosoever of you will be the chiefest, shall be servant of all. For even the Son of man (Jesus) came not to be ministered unto, but to minister, and to give His life a ransom for many." In Matthew 23:11-12 Jesus said, "But he that is greatest among you shall be your servant. And whosoever shall exalt himself shall be abased; and he that shall humble himself shall be exalted." Stop thinking you are better than someone else and stop thinking you know everything. This is an abomination before God.

If Christians would seek servitude there would be no confusion, and spiritual jealousy in the body of Christ. Instead, there would be love, caring, compassion, and never being able to do enough for each other. Thus, fulfilling God's purpose, and not one's own. This is difficult and can't be achieved without a genuine born, again experience, and the renewing of the spirit of the mind. To be a servant is contrary to the very nature of mankind. Humans, by nature, are selfish, and inclined to fulfill the lust of the flesh by exalting oneself above the other. That is how Satan gets a stronghold in one's life. This can happen before, and after becoming a Christian.

Jealousy is an extreme stronghold. That is why it is called the Green-eyed Monster. Miriam, the sister of Moses, was stricken with leprosy after becoming jealous over Moses' relationship with the Father. When we become jealous, we are stricken with a form of spiritual leprosy. It eats away in the inward man until the spirit is completely consumed with decay. Stop being jealous and get delivered. Get prayer immediately and have this demonic python of jealousy cast out before it squeezes the life out of you and you die in your sin.

I sympathize with people who have a jealous spirit. It is the most defiling spirit in the way of causing pain and hurt. It not only causes pain in the jealous person, but in others to whom the jealousy is directed. Jealousy is selfishness. Jealousy exalts itself above another. Jealousy is a suicidal, and murdering spirit. I curse the spirit of jealousy in Jesus' name in those reading this book that may have a jealous spirit. Amen! People who have jealousy need love, and understanding, not rejection. However, they need deliverance from the controlling spirit dominating their life, and others through them.

To become a humble servant after a lifetime doctrine of self-exaltation is not easy and is impossible without the Holy Spirit. However, this is the key to success in life. When a born, again experience takes place, Satan goes to war. His armies take position at the front line, and fights with full force to keep the new babe in Christ from growing in God's knowledge. Before coming to Christ, Satan has each person captive, and does not have to fight for what he already has. Jesus came, and gave us the key to the prison door. We no longer have to be a POW, held captive by Satan. One of the first, and foremost keys to the kingdom is becoming a servant.

The world teaches us that being a servant is something bad. Here is another lie of Satan. He has tricked us into believing that servitude is something menial. Here again, we can't go by what seems right. It seems being a servant is bad. The meaning of the word servitude is bondage, or slavery. Satan has been busy persuading us that servitude is bondage, slavery, and degrading. In our blindness, we don't see he has captured us by our lack of understanding, lust, and greed. A bond servant to Christ is top of the line in humility.

The truth is, servitude IS bondage, and slavery. If we are in bondage, and slavery to the right master, it becomes power, and freedom, not degradation. Jesus teaches, "Love your enemy," Proverbs 25:21-22 reads, "If thine enemy be hungry, give him bread to eat; and if he be thirsty, give him water to drink: for thou shalt heap coals of fire upon his head, and the Lord shall reward thee." In loving our enemy, we destroy the forces of evil, and bring many to the Gospel of Jesus Christ. Christ said the gates of hell can't prevail against us; and therefore, has no power over us. In turn it gives us all power over evil.

In serving others instead of ourselves, we begin to take on the life of Christ through His love. In serving others we are demonstrating the love of Jesus to the world. When we are servants to Christ, He is our master. While we are in His care and working His labor of love, we have His divine protection. It is the manifested love of God that defeats the enemy. If the enemy can't get us puffed up, and angry, it defeats him, and he has no power over us. In submitting to anger, wrath, or malice, and the like, we have given power to Satan, and we become the defeated foe, becoming like him. The state of being puffed up, and angry allows Satan to control us, and manifest his deeds through us. Therefore, we must be diligent in learning to do all things to the glory of God, that we may prosper as our soul prospers, and be in health. Having life more abundant, by the name above all names: Jesus. (3rd John 2)

Jesus said that a workman is worthy of his hire (Luke 10:7). He will reward us for all we do for Him. If we become laborers for Christ, united in one spirit with Him, having love for one another, there is no power, principality, ruler of darkness, or any evil force that can come against us, and win.

When we accept Jesus into our hearts, He comes in as a warrior, and begins to conquer the enemy for us. He doesn't end the battle until in our mind the enemy is defeated. In yielding ourselves to Christ, as His servant, we are allowing Him to fight our battles. While we are busy about our Father's (God) business, we can rest in the knowledge that Jesus knows full well what He is doing, and that He, and us through Him are already the victors. If we jump ahead of Christ, using our own wills, it is the same as standing on the front line of the war without a gun, and barricade; it is spiritual suicide.

Continuing in the word of God, even during our trials, we gain power, and great authority over the enemy, through Christ. As the prisoner of the Lord for the Gospel's sake, we are made free. Paul said in Philippians 1:27, "Only let your conversation be as it becometh the gospel of Christ; that whether I come, and see you, or else be absent, I may hear of your affairs, that ye stand fast in one spirit, with one mind striving together for the faith of the gospel." This, also, holds true for the church of today. If we would get our spiritual jealousies, backbiting, gossiping, and our feelings out of the way, develop the mind of Christ, and strive TOGETHER for the faith of the gospel, in becoming servants to each other, we would see the power of the Holy Spirit moving in phenomenal measures. The Church is lacking in power because exaltation is not given to God, and who He is, but to whom we think ourselves to be with, and without Him. Wake up Church, and see the light, Jesus Christ. Why will you labor in vain? If we can get self out of the way, Christ will work through us.

"The Power to Get Wealth" (Deut. 8:18)

There are many roads to take on this subject, however in staying with the subject of servitude I want to demonstrate how to have success, and possess great wealth through love, and servitude. The well-known Bible scripture, "Do unto to others as you would have them do unto you" (paraphrased-Luke 6:31) is the GOLDEN RULE. The reason it is labeled "golden" is because of the wealth of gold found in its meaning.

In Matthew 5 there are eight verses, 3-10, known as the beatitudes (Be Attitudes) In verses 3-5 is the key to receiving wealth, and success.

Vs. 3 "Blessed are the poor in Spirit for theirs is the kingdom of heaven." This verse doesn't mean what it seems to mean. It reads as if it is telling us that we are blessed if we are poor. This is not so. Poor in spirit does not mean that we can't possess small, or great wealth. Neither does it mean that we are to lack in our spiritual needs. Being poor in spirit means to be happy, or content in whatsoever state we find ourselves, being fruitful in the work of the ministry in love, always desiring the meat of the word.

Paul said in Philippians 4:11-12, "Not that I speak in respect of want; for I have learned, in whatsoever state I am, therewith to be content. I know how to be abased (poor), and I know how to abound (rich): everywhere, and in all things, I am instructed both to be full, and to be hungry, both to abound, and to suffer need."

Being poor in spirit can be defined as, "When possessing great wealth, we should not consume it on our lust, but prepare for being poor. In other words, do not spend money foolishly, but in a way if there should come a time the money is gone, we will not suffer. Learn to be content in the Spiritual things of God, and His love whether, or not we have money.

The greatest treasure is the kingdom of God. Matthew 13:44 reads, "Again, the kingdom of heaven is like unto treasure hid in a field; the which when a man hath found, he hideth, and for joy thereof goeth and selleth all that he hath, and buyeth that field." Jesus is explaining how we are to seek the treasure of heaven, and when we find it, sell all we have, do whatever it takes, to possess this treasure. Without this treasure there is no other. In the end, this is the only treasure that will not pass away. You can carry this treasure with you when you leave this world, and what you can take with you will be what you will have in heaven.

We are to sympathize with the poor, and needy, helping them in every way possible. We are to use our resources in serving others first, meeting their needs as we would our own. The Bible tells us that if we see our brother in need, and have it to give, we should fulfill that need by giving. Whether we have riches, or whether we are poor in material wealth, we can be content in the knowledge of our Lord, Jesus Christ. If we are poor in spirit, the kingdom of heaven is ours not only in the world to come, but also in this life. Being poor in spirit allows us to experience heaven on earth in our hearts. This doesn't mean our pockets will always be full, but that we will never lack what we need.

Vs. 4 "Blessed are they that mourn for they shall be comforted." As a servant of Christ, working His labor of love, we will be comforted in times of need. If we are not serving Christ, we are going to mourn over the many troubles that life brings. By not abiding in Christ, and His word abiding in us, we will not find comfort for our sorrows. Most people, regardless of their belief, mourn over their lack of worldly possessions, or over menial trials, and tribulations. Many people try to buy happiness with their riches. Material gain, and spending money can divert sorrow for a season, and give a momentary supply of relief, but eternal comfort is only found in the arms of Jesus. To be blessed in our mourning it must be godly mourning, mourning for the sins of the world, afflictions of others, and our self. Only a Godly mourning, or sorrow will be comforted, not spiritual crybabies having no victory, living in self-pity. Throwing pity parties is not of God. They are Satan's attempt at causing you to be depressed, and depression as we will learn is lack of prayer, and wisdom.

The comfort comes in knowing we shall be comforted, and rewarded for our sincere concern, and dedication to the Lord's work. A Godly mourning can only come through possessing the love of God in our hearts. It is an unselfish love in caring for others above our own needs. Therefore, in our servanthood, we are blessed in knowing we shall be comforted for any, and all discomforts we might endure in our task. In serving God we will experience the abundance of His riches in Glory through Christ Jesus (Philippians 4:19), and our light afflictions, or sufferings of this world are not to be compared to the glory that will be revealed in us (Romans 8:18).

The world, or sinner does not have this consolation, and will never find comfort for its sorrow in the things of the world. Whether we have power, or riches, without the love of God, and a servant's heart, it will all be consumed upon our lust, and will vanish away.

Vs. 5 "Blessed are the meek for they shall inherit the earth." The world considers meekness:

1. a flaw in human character
2. teaches to flee from meekness
3. sees meekness as a weakness

This couldn't be farther from the truth. Meekness is a necessary character trait in being like Jesus: for Jesus is the epitome of meekness; being meek is His nature and is the power of God. It simply means to "submit self to God." Having an attitude of meekness is being patient in all things, enduring affliction, ridicule, and persecution for the Gospel's sake, while remaining in an undisturbed frame of mind (not becoming angry when everyone else is). We are made in the image of Christ by having this trait. Meekness is displayed by a humble attitude in whatsoever state we are, and especially when in trials, and tribulation.

The second part of vs. 5, "For they shall inherit the earth." Since the Christian is going to leave this earth, and go to be with the Lord, it stands to reason we have no need of the earth while in heaven. Therefore, we can only suspect that this portion of verse 5 means we shall inherit the earth while we are here on the earth. The earth contains all the resources needed to supply us with our every need. Jesus is telling us that if we are meek the whole earth will belong to us. Having a meek, and humble attitude is the only way to take possession of the earth. If we are not meek, we are allowing Satan to keep the earth, and all its resources for himself, and his followers.

Jesus, by His death, burial, and resurrection took back the earth man had lost to Satan while in the Garden of Eden. Jesus gave the earth back to mankind. We have dominion over the earth if we don't give it away. By not submitting to God, being crucified with Christ, and resurrected in His resurrection, we have no power to take what is rightfully ours. Therefore, it is the resurrection (in dying to self, being raised in Christ, walking with His love in our hearts) power that gives us our wealth in this world, and in the Kingdom to come.

We can take possession of the earth, full of God's glory, all its resources, producing great wealth in monetary value. There is one catch. We must be prosperous in our soul. When our soul prospers in coming to the knowledge of the love of God, being meek in spirit, we will be blessed, and shall inherit the earth. You can say it like this, "When our soul becomes rich, we will be rich and will have access to all the riches of the world." This is a spiritual law.

If the church would pull together, and strive together "for the perfecting of the saints, for the work of the ministry, for the edifying of the body of Christ, and all come in the unity of the faith, and of the knowledge of the Son of God, unto a perfect man, unto the measure of the stature of the fullness of Christ (Eph. 4:12-13)," we could see the wealth of the world turned over to God's people. God said that the wealth of the sinner is laid up for the righteous. This wealth can be gotten in this day, and time by the Church (the rightful owners), but not until we are "joined together, and compacted by that which every joint supplieth, according to the effectual working in the measure of every part, maketh increase of the body unto the edifying of itself in love (Eph. 4:16)."

The church body is supposed to be the manifestation of God's love here on earth. Love is the result of the chastening of the Lord; for God only chastens those He loves. The way to manifest that love is to develop a servant heart by following the rules, and regulations of God's law of grace. In other words, the Church needs to get it's act together, or we will never see the manifestation of the sons and daughters of God in its fullness.

If we, the Church, would walk by faith, loving each other as Christ loves the Church (laying down our lives for each other, even our enemies for the Gospel's sake), God will see that the riches of this world would be turned over to His people (Church). This means that goodness, and mercy will follow us wherever we go. The Church is not a building. I, and you are the Church.

The Church of today is lacking in spiritual understanding to the point that God will not act where He is not known. For God to act through us, we must come to know who He is, to understand by His wisdom, and knowledge His authority, and the way He has made for us; thus, receiving His power. In Joshua 1:7-8 God said, "Only be thou strong, and of a good courage, that thou mayest observe to do according to ALL THE LAW (emphasis mine), which Moses my SERVANT (emphasis mine) commanded thee; turn not from it to the right hand, or to the left, that thou mayest prosper whithersoever thou goest. This book of the law shall not depart out of thy mouth; but thou shalt meditate therein day, and night, that thou mayest observe to do according to ALL that is written therein; for then thou shalt make thy way prosperous, and then thou shalt have good success." It is saying to obey our covenant relationship with God.

When we acknowledge God's authority, and keep His laws (Jesus fulfilled the law, but did not do away with the law), His rules, His power of love prevails. Spiritual understanding is the key to life in this world, and the kingdom to come. If we do not have understanding we have nothing. If we have nothing, we are acting in ignorance. Acting in ignorance is dangerous. In ignorance we allow ourselves to be controlled by the wrong master, condemning ourselves to death, and damnation without knowing what we are doing.

If we are not keeping God's law of love, we are walking in disobedience. While walking in disobedience everything we do will fall apart and we will not prosper in the things that will not pass away. If we were to obey God by His word, (you need to KNOW the word first) everything we apply our hands to do would result in a fashion of spiritual prosperity. For example: when we break the laws of the land, we are walking in disobedience. If we don't abide by the speed limits in traffic law, we will pay the price. Grace does not cover speeding. If you speed you will get a ticket, and you will pay for that ticket. Wisdom is in not speeding. Not obeying the law of the land, we are working against ourselves. We are bringing harsher penalties upon ourselves, and others when we break the law: For then our laws become stricter, making them more difficult for all of us by which to live.

The same applies to the Church body. When we don't keep the law of love, we are bringing God's wrath upon us. The Bible says that it rains upon the just, and the unjust alike (Matt. 5:45). This is evident in ministries that have not operated in a Godly fashion. In their attempt to lead people to Christ they have fallen into error through their vainglory, and abounding lifestyles. In the end they lose all their gain and will bring God's wrath upon themselves. They have caused many to fall away. Then, God's wrath falls upon those that fall away for following man instead of God. This is idolatry.

While it isn't wrong for God's people to prosper, it is wrong for them to live an unbalanced lifestyle. If Christians would use their financial gain for helping others in the body (not the slothful) for the Bible teaches, "If you don't work, you don't eat" (2nd Thes. 3:10). Those that can't work due to physical problems, sickness, and the like are excluded. For example: If I had a million dollars, instead of building myself a mansion, I should build myself a modest home. God said He would supply our needs. We don't need a mansion here on earth. Having a mansion on earth is not balanced living. The world says get all you can, and God says, in balance. The tithe was set up to help us live a balanced lifestyle.

Jesus has told us that there are many mansions in heaven, and someday we will have our own mansion. While on earth we are supposed to take care of our family and Church family as we would ourselves. If we can build five modest homes for the price of one mansion, providing shelter for the homeless in the body, this is fulfilling God's law of love. God is no respecter of persons. It is foolishness to God, for us to live in a mansion, and say, "Look what Jesus did for me." By these kinds of remarks, we are casting a stumbling block before the brethren. There are millions of people that love God with all their heart, living in the slums of life. We are saying to them, "God doesn't love you as much as He loves me." This causes the poor to think that God's love is measured by what He gives us. Purchased love is lust, found in the world, not in the love of God. We are bought with a price, but Jesus paid the same price for us all. In covenant we are all of equal value.

People can't change the environment from which they came. Some came from a poor environment, and will always be poor, unless someone teaches them how to prosper, and helps them get started. Many people could be prosperous if the government would stop knocking them down every time they get up.

There are other people that are victims of natural disasters, losing everything, and can't build again. Still others with unavoidable circumstances are struggling to keep their homes, and feed their families caused by a bad economy. Not everyone who lacks in the world is slothful. Sometimes bad things happen to good people.

Here is where the Church is supposed to be in the Spirit enough to know, and to help. It is great for people to give the right hand of fellowship handshake with five, ten, twenty, and sometimes a hundred dollars, but sometimes people need a car, a home, a job, medical expenses paid, a new roof, a visit to the dentist, and so many other things. Of course, this kind of money is tied up in the mansions, and such, and is not available to give. I am not knocking the right hand of fellowship handshake. Without them some people couldn't even put gas in their car if they have a car.

I'm talking about the funds that are tied up in stocks, and other investments, and isn't available. In fact, the Church is so not in the Spirit that many don't even hear the prompting of the Holy Spirit telling them to give finances to those in need. See James 2:116 KJV

I'm trying to make the point that the Church has gotten so far into left field they can't see the batter hitting the ball. What's the point of being the left fielder, a key player, if you don't know the ball has been hit, and coming your way? When someone is in need, they are to ask Father God to meet that need. They are not to ask the people. God does the asking from those He wants to use in supplying that need. The Father speaks to the heart of a person, or persons prompting them to supply the need. Supply for the needy shouldn't have to be prompted. We should always give when we see a need. The problem is that people are not looking beyond themselves.

Don't judge the needy in whether they are worthy or not, don't assume they have resources of their own, and don't hesitate to fulfill a need. I'm sorry if some disagree with this, but this is the raw truth, and one of the most basic Christian duties, however one forgotten, never learned, or selfishly rejected, by turning a deaf ear to the voice of God. (It is proper to ask others to supply a need, especially in offerings, etc., but it is fitting to ask the Father first since He is our provider)

I believe therefore, is why Jesus said that it would be nearly impossible for a rich man to enter heaven. If a rich Christian can live in a mansion while others in his Church family are living in poverty through no fault of their own, he can't be abiding by God's law of abasing, and abounding.

This takes us back to being poor in spirit. If we are not seeing to the needs of others even before our own needs, we are breaking the law of God's love. When the rich can live in comfort while his brethren are living in lack, his heart is not in the right place, and he has missed the whole point of Christian love. He will never be prosperous and stay prosperous; he either will lose all he has, or he has his reward. Why? He isn't poor in spirit, living modestly, and supplying the needs of others before himself. He can't be meek in his attitude, and does not have Godly sorrow, or mourning. That is a bible fact.

The tree may have green leaves on it, but upon closer inspection the fruit is missing, because he can't part from his money. If we can't be as happy living in a modest home, as living in a two-story house having 3,000 or more square feet of living space, then we have not learned to be abased, and how to abound. That is the law of prosperity.

In the Old Testament days, Abraham, Isaac, and Jacob, as well as many other people, lived in what we would call today, Communes. Communal living is a great way to live, and I'm most certain it is God's way. Not so much all living in the same place but looking after the needs of others and making sure there is a balance for everyone. For example: America is a commune. We should look after our own in this country before trying to take care of the other countries in the world. In taking care of our own, we will be more able, and apt to care for others. Taking care of our own, meaning the household of God, we increase our own wealth. As individuals succeeds the more wealth there is for the body. Assuming everyone is giving back to God in tithes, offerings, time, and work of the Ministry.

I know everyone is probably angry at this point, crying socialism, but just bear with me. If you don't like the thought of communal living, and taking care of each other, you aren't going to like living in the City New Jerusalem.

If Jesus is living in us, we are going to do unto others, as we would have others do unto us if we were to find ourselves in a state of poverty. This is the law of God's love in operation, to give unto others, if we have it to give. Jesus didn't say get all you want first, and if there is any left give to the poor. Mark 8:36 reads, "For what shall it profit a man, if he shall gain the whole world, and lose his own soul?" It doesn't stop here. Jesus said to love your enemy as well. Therefore, to have great success, we must love everyone with no exceptions to the rule;

learning to be content in who we are in Christ, and who Christ is in us, not in our material possessions; always abounding with thanksgiving, and in the love of God. This is the law of love, and a key to the kingdom of heaven.

Colossians 2:2-7 reads, "That your hearts might be comforted, being knit together in love, and unto all riches of the full assurance of understanding, to the acknowledgement of the mystery of God, and of the Father, and of Christ; in whom are hid all the treasures of wisdom, and knowledge. As ye have therefore received Christ Jesus the Lord, so walk ye in Him. Rooted, and built up in Him, and established, in the faith, as ye have been taught, abounding therein with thanksgiving."

When we learn to be happy in the prospering of our souls, instead of personal wealth, and gain, we have fulfilled God's law of prosperity, and have the power to get wealth. By seeking God's kingdom, and His righteousness, through His word, making this our daily objection, and heart's desire, we will receive power to get wealth, and have great success. Therefore, live by the gold in (golden) rule, and it will produce gold in (golden) return.

The next time you look at your brethren, look beyond their fault, and see their need. In looking for the Jesus in them, they will see Jesus in you. By living the life of Christ wealth will automatically follow.

People in the world have learned this spiritual law better than most Christians. Hollywood performers for example give to charities, as does large corporations, and such. They just keep getting richer, and richer. Giving to the poor is a spiritual law that automatically works. If you are a good steward in giving, finances will find you.

I had a vision in Sunday service during praise, and worship. I saw the floor of a room in heaven covered with a white sheet. It was bulging from the weight of what was on, or in the sheet. Looking closer I saw blessings beyond measure. The Lord spoke saying, "These are the blessings for my children. If they would begin to give, these blessings would automatically flow into their lives. Some do give, but not with a cheerful heart." I paraphrased the quote, but in essence God is saying in order to walk in abundance we must give that the body will have abundance. There is a difference in trying to buy a blessing and giving a blessing.

I can't remember a time when I didn't walk in abundance. I was out of work for over 2 years, from having been laid off, and every need was met, and still is. For example: I have given clothes away by the truck loads, and I just can't give them away fast enough. My house is so full of clothes others have given me, that I don't have a place to store them all. I keep giving, and I get more, and more. Sometimes I'm tempted to not give the clothes to not have this issue. However, I can't move the clothes out of my house without giving them, and then the cycle starts over again. The same happens with food, and finances.

It's amazing. 2nd Corinthians 8:8-15, "I speak not by commandment, but by occasion of the forwardness of others, and to prove the sincerity of your love. For ye know the grace of our Lord Jesus Christ, that, though he was rich, yet for your sakes he became poor, that ye through his poverty might be rich. And herein I give my advice: for this is expedient for you who have begun before, not only to do, but also to be forward a year ago. Now therefore perform the doing of it; that as there was a readiness to will, so there may be a PERFORMANCE (emphasis mine) also out of that which ye have. For if there be first a willing mind, it is accepted according to that a man hath, and not according to that he hath not. For I mean not those other men be EASED, and ye be BURDENED; But by an EQUALITY, that now at this time your ABUNDANCE may be a SUPPLY for their want; that their ABUNDANCE may be a SUPPLY for your want: that there may be EQUALITY: As it is written, He that had gathered much had nothing over; and he that had gathered little had no lack." (Emphasis mine) The power to get wealth isn't directed just to the rich. The poor have an obligation too. Remember the widow's mite that gave all she had (Luke 21:1-4)?

The supernatural things of God are not only found in the visions, dreams, prophetic words, mind reading, and such. I think this is where the Church has gotten off the path a little, or a lot, you are the judge. We look for things in the spiritual realm to take the form of angels, Jesus, and demons, when in fact the supernatural is found as much in the word of God, as anywhere. To find the hidden treasures of life is about as supernatural as one can get. Jesus said, "Search the scriptures for in them you think you have eternal life, and they are they which testify of me." (John 5:39) Proverbs 23:23 reads, "Buy the truth, and sell it not; also, wisdom, and instruction, and understanding." "The fear of the Lord is the beginning of knowledge: but fools despise wisdom, and instruction (Proverbs 1:7)."

Wisdom is not only spiritual insight, and discretion, but is an art form as in workmanship. When the children of Israel came out of Egypt, and after receiving the law, God instructed them to build a tabernacle. The Hebrews had been slaves in Egypt for 400 years, and only knew how to make bricks. They had no other trade. They didn't know how to build a tabernacle. Exodus 31:3-5 reads, "And I have filled him with the spirit of God, in wisdom, and in understanding, and in knowledge. And all manner of workmanship, to devise cunning works, to work in gold, and in sliver, and in brass, And, in cutting of stones to set them, and in carving of timber, to work all manner of workmanship." Exodus 35:26, & 35 reads, "And all the women who stirred them up in wisdom spun goats' hair. Them hath he filled with wisdom of heart, to work all manner of work, of the engraver, and of the cunning workman, and of the embroiderer, in blue, and in purple, in scarlet, and in fine linen, and of the weaver, even of them that do any work, and of those that devise cunning work."

The wisdom of God is found in the ability He gives in performing a task. It is a talent. We can never say we don't know how to do a thing, because God will supply the knowledge, and understanding of how to perform His perfect will. He just needs a willing vessel. The parable of the talents in Matthew is letting us know that God has not only purposed in our lives the work of the ministry, but He has also given us the ability to perform His perfect will. If we don't complete our mission, we will have nothing to take with us to heaven that will not pass away. I'm not talking about material things, but things of wisdom, knowledge, and understanding.

The Church is lacking partly, because people are not seeking God in their talents (Money and abilities) and using them for the building of the Church. Most of the people hide their talent, never bringing it to full fruition. Matthew 25:14-30 is the parable of the talents. It speaks of servants having received talents from their Lord, and what they did with them. Go read this parable that you may understand and apply knowledge to your soul. The servant who had been given one talent hid his talent in the earth. He was supposed to gain other talents but didn't. Jesus said in verse 30, "And cast ye the unprofitable servant into outer darkness: there shall be weeping and gnashing of teeth".

The wisdom of God is given to us in talents, and along with the talents, the knowledge, and understanding of how to gain increase. In Ephesians 4:16 is the clearest definition of the will of God to those who don't know God's will for their life. It reads, "From whom the whole body fitly joined together, and compacted by that which every joint supplieth, according to the effectual working in the measure of every part, maketh increase of the body unto the edifying of itself in love." We, the Church body are supposed to be supplying that part, or that talent to the body, making increase in the body by love.

The only thing you can take with you to heaven is that which you have gained in knowledge, wisdom, and understanding. The increase you gain in these things will be your portion in heaven. Only in heaven the knowledge, understanding, and wisdom will manifest into rewards, even your mansion. "Wisdom is more precious than rubies, and all things thou canst desire are not to be compared to her" Proverbs 3:15.

The supernatural things of God have their place in serving God, and they are benefits to the minister. However, we are not to seek these things, but seek the Lord while He can be found. Seek the kingdom of God and His righteousness before all things, and all these things (clothing, food, shelter) will be added to you (Matthew 6). Will behoove you to read 2 Corinthians 13:1-13KJV

"Faith worketh by love (Gal. 5:6)". "Without faith we cannot please God (Hebrews 11:6)". Spiritual Understanding, Knowledge, and Wisdom come from the mouth of God, and the supernatural powers of His Word, His Spirit – His Love. Amen!

CHAPTER 4

Who Is Your Mirror Image?

After the fall of man in the garden, Cain and Abel were the first recorded sons of Adam and Eve. God accepted Abel's sacrifice, but not Cain's. Cain, out of jealousy, murdered Abel, and is the first murder to be recorded in the Bible. Violence, and crime has since been on the rise. Once sin had entered the world it began to grow rapidly, one acts of sin, begat another act of sin, and so on.

Parents can appreciate how God must have felt when man first sinned. God tried to protect His creation from knowledge of evil by forbidding him to eat of the tree of knowledge of good, and evil (Gen. 2:17). God told Adam, if he were to eat of this tree, he would surely die. As the story continues, Adam, and Eve did eat, and by this act of disobedience sin (death) was ushered into the world. Because of their disobedience (sin) man was cast out of the Garden of Eden - Paradise.

We, as parents try to protect our children in the same manner God tried to protect mankind. We know the things harmful to our children, and we try to dissuade them with warnings of the outcome, should they persist in disobedience. We warn them against alcohol, drugs, premarital sex, crime, violence, etc.

By nature, we are subject to do that which we are taught not to do. According to the word of God, it is the nature of humans to do wrong. For example: Parents warn against the use of alcohol. The time comes when friends begin to drink the alcohol, and thus, begins the peer pressure. They guzzle their first beer, and once done, the world didn't come to an end, and the devil didn't jump out to devour them as they had been told; at least not at that moment. Satan has, however staked a claim as soon as the first step of disobedience to the parent was taken. After being told not to drink the beer, the harm isn't in drinking it, but in being disobedient to the parents. Adam and Eve weren't cast out of the garden from the action of eating the fruit. They were cast out because they didn't follow God's instructions. Sin began in their mind as soon as the thought of partaking of the wrong tree was conceived. God is serious about obedience to His word. Obedience is better than sacrifice.

If the taste of alcohol is pleasing, we most likely will continue to drink. This is the beginning of bondage to sin. Beer leads to liquor, liquor to drugs, and acts of sin, to more acts of sin. Ephesians 2:3 reads, "Among whom we, also had our conversation in times past in the lusts of our flesh, fulfilling the desires of the flesh, and of the mind; and were by nature the children of wrath." There are people who will disagree with me about the process of drinking leads to drugs, etc. Hear me out, so you can make an informed decision.

I'm not trying to be legalistic, but truthful. I believe the mindset of the Church about legalism presents a grave problem. There is a fine line between what is legalism, and what is viewed as acceptable sin. Paul writes in 1 Corinthians 6:12, "All things are lawful unto me, but all things are not expedient; all things are lawful for me, but I will not be bought under the power of any." Paul is saying, Christians should not merely consider what is lawful to be done but whether it is fit for them. They should be careful not to carry these maxims too far, that they be not brought into bondage (Matthew Henry commentary).

I'm not saying one can't drink a beer, or glass of wine. However, teenagers cannot usually judge what is fit for them. Today's society, pressures to excel are vast. Alcohol will most likely become the first step to a dependency of some kind, leading to a long line of curiosity. Avoiding all appearance of evil is the best thing, so as not to be a stumbling block to others. Most people believe alcohol to any degree is a sin. Here again we have misinterpreted the word.

I hear comments everyday about how terrible our world has become. The crime ratings are up, abortions are unlimited, divorces are out of control. Drugs, alcohol, child abuse, Satanism, witchcraft, pestilence, famine, wars, pedophilia, and many other dangers have swept our world into a corner of self-destruction. The world is on the broad path.

What happened to the days when honesty, integrity, love, respect, honor, caring, helping, and goodness prevailed? The days when children could feel safe walking alone, or playing in public parks, and playgrounds; the days when we didn't even lock our doors, and cars? The days when families stayed together in a committed love, providing family security? The days when helping our neighbor was as important as helping ourselves? The days when trusting each other was never a question? Where did those days go? Did they die with our ancestors, or are they still here hidden in our heart?

There is a generation referred to as the "baby boomers" that remember the days of which I'm speaking. I am a member of this generation, and I remember those days so long ago as though it were yesterday. The "baby boomers," are now the leaders of our country. We are presidents of multimillion-dollar corporations, senators, governors, congressman, teachers, professors, doctors, lawyers, pastors, and filling many more of the white, and blue-collar positions in the workplace of America, and the world.

We are the examples for the up-coming youth of today. We are the moms, and dads, of (and in some cases are) the illiterates, drug addicts, alcoholics, pornographers, child abusers, rapist, and criminals of all types. Yes, there are exceptions, and not all of America's youth are on the streets. The ones who are on the streets, are the ones involved in these acts of disobedience, are the focus of attention in our everyday news media. These are the ones of whom we must be aware.

Why are there millions of our young people, the future leaders of America, sitting on street corners, alleyways, bars, massage parlors, in prisons, and other institutions? Why do our daughters jump at the chance to wear clothing exposing their nearly naked bodies, or pose naked in front of a camera, while our sons run from their obligation of manhood? Why are our children disobedient to us, and the values in which we believe? Why is the teen suicide rate out of sight, and tipping the scales? Why do mothers push their daughters into the ungodly world of modeling, and fathers pat their sons on the back when they experience their first lust for girls?

It was the "baby boomer" generation that changed the world in music, ideas, tradition, religion, politics, and education. The "baby boomers' wanted more for their children than the common poverty of their own childhood. Poverty meant doing without, sacrificing, a degree of suffering, and in many families, and lifestyles, much suffering. On a higher income level, it meant driving last years model. The goal of the "baby boomers" was to give their children more, and better than they had in their youth.

Working harder, and longer to succeed financially has been the primary goal of the "baby boomers", while neglecting our children was the result. The "baby boomers" may have been deprived in the way of material wealth, but what they did receive is overlooked, disregarded, forgotten, and lost on the pages of history.

Upon closer examination of the youth of today, we are seeing a mirror image of ourselves. Our youth have become exactly what parents, and leaders, have given them. Each one has played a part in assisting the minds of our youth in becoming the wasteland it is today. Here again, let me say, I'm not talking about you in particular. If the shoe fits, be wise enough to see it.

The youth have no direction, no purpose, no desires, no challenges, no virtues, no self-esteem, no reason, no honesty, no trust, no security, and no love. The unity of friends, and family has been replaced with boats, cars, clothes, movies, trips, education, money, cell phones, ipads, computers, video games, HD television, and self-love (2 Tim. 3:2-5). If you don't believe it, try taking these things away from your kids and see what happens.

There is a need for love within a person to be satisfied. Children need love, but don't know where to find it. To give a son, or daughter a new bike, both mom, and dad have to work. There was a time when mothers stayed home with their children giving them love, and security, while dad went to work. If dad didn't earn enough to get a new bike, the bike wasn't purchased. The child may have been deprived without, by not getting the bike, but not within. Chances are the new bike would have been purchased eventually. Maybe not at the exact time of the want but later.

Most often than not we get our wants mixed up with our needs. Many times, our wants are fulfilled, but not our needs. Love in today's world is measured by what money can buy, and not by what is important. God loved Adam, and Eve. He gave them everything they could possibly want, and they were still disobedient. Apparently getting a everything we want is not the answer in growing up and becoming responsible adults.

Let us look at one example of deprivation. A boy, or girl comes home from school, and mom, and dad are at work. Who does the child in question talk with about his problems, or his day at school? With whom do they share their successes, and defeats? If the home is empty when they arrive from school, they become lonely. They have been told not to have friends over in the absence of mom, and dad, and not to open the door to anyone, including friends. Who, or what do they turn to in their time after school void of family, and friends, and hearing the voice of another human being? Of course, the solution is simple. They tune in to face book, twitter, blogging, and the like. With the push of a button, a click of the mouse, presto, out come voices, music, and stories of all kinds. Television, and the Internet are the worst. With television, they become couch potatoes, and with the Internet, unless blocked, they learn about everything from sex to drugs. While viewing television programs, or sites on the Internet filled with crime, sex, and violence, the seeds of destruction are being planted in the fertile ground of your child's mind.

Without parental supervision, children are going to view things that will mold, and shape them into what they are viewing. It is only natural they are interested in sex, crime, violence, and the like, because by nature, from the beginning, they are children of wrath (Eph. 2). When children are exposed to the popularity of drugs, rock, and rap with the bad lyrics, presented on television, or the Internet, this opens the door for every drug dealer on the street to invade the purity of your child's inner most being.

Drug dealers, and pushers are on every street corner, schoolyards, shopping malls, and parking lots, lurking in the shadows, waiting for your child to ride by on that bike that is so important. There are children that attend grade school who deal in drugs, so you can imagine the junior, and senior high level of drug trafficking, and use; not to mention our young adults in colleges, and during the jobs after school.

While living in California I ministered to drug dealers, and addicts that began their life of addiction at the ages of eight, and nine years old. Some of these young people in their teenage years engaged in the use of drugs with their own parents. The evils of this world are without boundaries in gender, age, race, creed, and color. It is like a scud missile, zoned into its target, and only knows destruction.

The next step in the plight of the children is being seduced into thinking how cool it is to use and sell drugs. They are introduced to the money to be made in dealing. When approached by a dealer, what is going to stop them from getting involved? Once they have experienced the togetherness of friends, and good times along with the company of drugs, and money, they are unlikely to turn away.

In the comfort of friends, the children have found a way to fill their loneliness, and despair. In filling their emotional desires, they think they are doing the right thing. Sure mom, and dad, has told them not to become involved in these things, but if Adam, and Eve didn't listen to God, why would children listen to their parents?

In supplying the wants, above the needs, love, attention, affection, supervision, and direction goes lacking. When children are lacking in these things, they are going without within. They have paid for the big house, nice clothes, new family car, better schools, and bicycles, with their security. What the children need is love, security, and family unity. It turns out the children have paid for all these things with their emotional instability, lack of respect for their self, their parents, and others, and lack of direction for their life (2 Thess. 2:7-17).

Many times, as parents, we tend to overlook, in our children, the problem areas of their lives by declaring, "Well, at least they aren't on drugs, alcohol, and the like." While this is commendable, what about the problems they do have? Do we overlook attitudes of slothfulness, disobedience, disrespect, and selfishness just because they aren't on drugs? Thats the same as saying, "I know my child is involved in teen sex, but at least he/she isn't homosexual." Two wrongs don't make a right.

Our world is a result of our greed, whether we want to admit it or not. Now in our elder years hopefully we can see where we went wrong in raising our children. How can they lead based on what we have given them? The values are gone, and an entire generation is lost. We have finally destroyed ourselves. Our destination was foretold, by Hitler when he said, "To destroy a country destroy one generation of that country's youth" (paraphrased).

When I look in a mirror, I see the hard work of my youth: work that taught me discipline, and the value of having a heater in winter. I see the honesty of a little girl who collected money, door to door, for her Sunday school class; food on the table I helped grow and pick from the garden. I see the desire for a candy bar, and the gratefulness of a chance to earn it. I see the diligence of my grandparents in supplying me shelter, clothing, and food: the unity of a family pulling together in hard times, and neighbors reaching out a helping hand to others. I see the worthlessness of a new bike compared to a mother's love, and emotional needs being met.

I know what I'm talking about. I didn't have much in material wealth while growing up. I grew up in the deep, south where money seemed to always be scarce. Though feeling deprived at times, I now cry out for the return of those days when nothing was everything. Now as an adult, society has made me to need material gain to be a functioning member of the world. Unfortunately, material possessions can't take the place of grandma's arms of security, the loving words of a mother, the wisdom of a dad, and the love of God.

Like many of you probably do, I remember my grandma taking care of her five children, working an eight-hour, second shift job in a cotton mill. She worked from four o'clock pm to midnight. She made sure her family's needs were met before going to work. She was up by five, or six a.m. each morning, prepared breakfast, continuing through the day with lunch, and dinner, did all the household chores, gardening in summer, worked a fulltime job, and still found time to spend with me, and teach me about God, by showing me His love. She was there for her children when they arrived home from school, and provided for their emotional, and physical needs. Her enthusiasm, strength, goodness, happiness, values, and love are the things I remember.

I do remember her sweeping, and mopping the floors, along with cooking, working a garden to put food on the table, and seeing to all the other necessities of running a household. I don't remember the color of my clothes, or the meals that may have been beans and cornbread. While I do recall these things along with the lack of toys, candy, and heat in winter, my memories are made up from the love my grandma so freely gave, even when she didn't feel like it. I don't know that she didn't feel like it, but no one feels like giving all the time. I suspect she didn't either. I never saw her sick or complaining about anything. She demonstrated the selfless kind of love Jesus gave. She chose to work a second shift job so she would be there for her kids during the day and working while they slept. She didn't work to have more, but to help feed, and clothe the family. Now I have a few possessions, but I don't have my grandma. What I do have of her is our love for each other in my heart.

I could look back on my past and see it as a bad memory. I could hate in my heart from having to earn money at the age of four years old to buy candy. I could hate not having enough heat in winter, and not having the best clothes. In fact, there was a time when I did look back, and see the bad. Once I really came to know Jesus my blinded eyes were opened, and I could see the good in those days. Now when I look back, I see Jesus there in all we had, and I see no reason to escape the lifestyle of my youth. I see the successes instead of the defeats, and I like myself, and what I have become because of those days. When I look in the mirror, I see what the world is lacking.

We as a nation are beginning to see our world as the pit of corruption that it has become. If we look deep into our hearts, we will see the values of days gone by, and how different they are from what we see around us now. We are beginning to recognize that which has been disguised, and covered up by our greed, and desire to obtain more than what our parents had. We are seeing the results of what we considered "giving our children more" than we had.

Much of the world can't understand what has gone wrong, or where we have failed our youth. We are all too ready to criticize and put the blame on each other when in fact the fault lies with us all. We have not passed on the moral values taught to us by our parents, school systems, and our churches. Most of us learned about God not only at home, and church, but also in school. We were taught to have pride in our country, by the pledge of allegiance, and patriotism by the national anthem. We learned to love and be secure in the goodness of a great God, in that good prevails. We were given a goal, and purpose through our prayer time at school, church, and home. These were the foundational rules that gave us stability, direction, security, and a purpose of achievement – a reason to live. These were the rules of all Americans.

The schools of today have eliminated God from the textbook, and the classroom, as well as the inspiring songs, and stories of heroism of our country's history. Instead of Christianity, and patriotism, our educational system is teaching witchcraft, visualization, and basically doctrines of devils (1 Tim. 4:1). There are many books on this subject including and oldie but goodie, "Lambs to the Slaughter" by Johanna Michaelson. She gives detailed information on what your child is being taught in today's classrooms across America. Our fault is we have been too busy to notice what our children are learning in school. We have assumed they are getting the same values taught to them as was to us. We have even gone so far as to not teach our children at home because we have assumed our school system is doing it for us.

Thank God for parents who choose to home school their children. They are making a difference. Thank God for School Teachers, some of whom I know personally, who go on Saturdays, their day off, and lay hands on the children's chairs, and pray over them. Teachers who ride around the school praying Holy Spirit filled prayers over the school. These same teachers take the time to do spiritual warfare over the children, even when they are not present. God's word will not come back void.

People in general are concerned with the wars, famines, natural resources, save the animals, and such, but no one seems to be concerned about the youth in our world. Who is going to save the children? I know there are organizations, state funds, Christian Ministries, and the like, who are making a difference. I'm talking about in our everyday lives, in our neighborhoods, and homes that are lacking in the care needed. Could it be we are afraid to face the problem of neglect because we are too busy, or afraid to admit that we have made a mess of the world? Could it be we are afraid we don't have the answers, and just don't know how to clean up the mess we've made? By doing our own thing in our own way, we have destroyed the values, and the morality our parents had before us. If we would take time to stop, look, and see, we would see the results of giving our children more than we had. Our children have no sacrifices, and no sufferings from lack of material gain, and the results are a world without order; wanting everything, and not regarding the way everything is obtained.

The children are committing suicide at alarming rates, because of peer pressure, lack of purpose, or fulfillment in life. The needs of their flesh have been well provided, but the needs of their soul, and spirit have gone dangerously neglected. Our youth are dying not only in body, but also in spirit, and mind too. The ones that remain living are as walking zombies, caused from lack of direction in their lives.

It is no wonder multiple sex partners are sought after in a half-witted attempt to find the love, and acceptance so desperately needed. People are so starved in their heart that they will fulfill their need for love in homosexuality, or wherever they can find love. To them, any love, and understanding, even the wrong kind is better than none at all. After all, no one has taught them the Bible speaks against these things, but through the worldly influences they have instead been encouraged to experience free love. Proof is in the prison systems, half-way houses, juvenile hall, boys, and girl's camps for correction, schools (Christian, private, and public), Church, and the streets of our cities.

Until we get back to the basic principles of God's laws of love, and the Holy order of the family, our world will continue as Sodom and Gomorrah: A city filled with witchcraft, sorcery (drugs), astrology, homosexuality, adulterers, whoremongers, and murderers (Gal. 5:19-22). Sound familiar?

It will finally get to a point when God will say, "I've had enough of this iniquity," and He will destroy the world as He did Sodom, and Gomorrah (Gen. 13:10, 19:24, Jude 5-8), or He will have to apologize to Sodom and Gomorrah. He isn't going to do that.

I know it is difficult to hear all these disgusting things associated with children, and possibly with your own. Don't get me wrong, there are multitudes of our youth in ministry, in Church every Sunday, participating in youth programs, and spiritual movements, as well as going on mission trips. Praise God for the spiritual youth movements of praise, and worship flooding states, and countries in our world. I'm not saying all the youth of the world is going to hell in a hand basket. I am only trying to make people more aware of the snares, and traps the devil uses in deceiving us, and our children.

There is a way to correct what we have done, through the grace of God, His love, and prayer. The change has to begin in the leaders of today, you, and me. We can keep placing the blame on Adam, and Eve, saying, "They started all this by sinning against God in the first place", or we can take the chance God has given us to start over through Jesus Christ. The world can only be changed through Him, and His teachings. Unless we accept Him and learn of Him, destruction is our end, whether by Satan, by our own hand, or by God Himself.

Look in the mirror and try to see beyond your reflection. What do you see looking back? Do you see what you have become, or what you were in your youth? Is there a difference? Is there a part of you that is covered up, and hidden in your heart? If you can't see what you are, or have become by looking in the mirror, look instead, at your mirror image found in the face of America's youth. There you will see that the mirror doesn't lie.

CHAPTER 5
Satan's New Age Minions

S atan and his demons are on the job twenty-four hours a day, to harass you, and your family. They seek to rob, kill, and destroy you. "Be sober, be vigilant; because your adversary the devil, as a roaring lion, walketh about, seeking whom he may devour." (1 Peter 5:8)

The existence of Satan, and demons is a subject most believers hesitate to discuss. Giving no acclaim to the enemy, we must still be aware of the existence of evil. The biggest drawback in a Christian concerning the underworld is fear of acknowledgement. The powers, and principalities of the air, and the rulers of darkness of this world, and wickedness in high places that Paul speaks of in Ephesians 6, are real. Christians come in constant contact with these entities twenty-four hours a day. Awareness of their presence, and influence, and recognizing their mission is most important.

The mission of a Christian is to overcome evil with good. Christians know the difference between evil, and good, but do not always recognize evil when it comes. Satan comes in like an angel of light. If Christians don't know how to discern his light from the light of Christ, they will be deceived. A commander in the military would never go to battle without first knowing the strategies of the enemy.

I find in Christians a frightening lack of knowledge when it comes to protecting themselves, and especially their children. Children aren't immune from the attacks of Satan, and in fact are his main target. An unsuspecting child is easily influenced and led captive by Satan's tricks. I'll give an example.

At the age of six, I made my public profession of faith. I knew, full well, what this meant. I had met Jesus, received Him into my heart, and I was saved. In my child like faith, I knew my conversion as a Divine, and Holy ordinance. Even at the age of six, evil wasn't a stranger.

Not long after my conversion, I had an encounter with a demon spirit. I was at my grandparent's home in South Carolina. They were wonderful Christians and lived what they preached. I lived with them in summer, and most holidays. Their house was a small mill town house standing on uneven ground and was at least three feet off the ground on the low side. I used to play under the house, with friends. It was not underpinned, making it a prefect play area.

Inside the home, the windows on the low side were too high to see in from outside. One evening, just after dark, I came in from playing. During the fifties children could play outside after dark, and still be safe. I was hungry, and my grandma was busy, so I went to the kitchen to make a sandwich. We usually had a full course meal, but I had missed dinner. To me, a sandwich was a luxury item because I could make it myself. Back then, sandwiches weren't often offered. Considering our meals came from a garden, having to be prepared, sandwiches were a treat of sorts.

The refrigerator was in line with the dining table, and they both were in line with a kitchen window. I was taking items out of the refrigerator, turning, and placing them on the table. Something moved and caught my attention. At first, I saw my reflection in the window, and was not alarmed, but then I saw something else. I couldn't move from fright as I looked at what seemed to be the shape of a person. There were no details, like a face, hair on the head, or having arms. It was more like the outline of a person draped with a sheet.

The inside of the outline was filled with white, swirly smoke. It looked like thick, heavy, cigarette smoke floating in the air when no wind is blowing. I could still see my reflection inside the image. Thinking back to that time, I remember feeling paralyzed, and manipulated by this image. Suddenly it vanished, releasing its grip on me. Screaming uncontrollably out of fear, I tried to close myself into the refrigerator. I was about 6 or 7 years old when fear gripped me.

My grandma heard my screams and came running. She tried to calm, and comfort me as I explained, the best I could, what had happened. I'm sure she didn't know what really happened that night. Though my grandparents had seen various supernatural phenomena, they weren't sure of what I had seen. They dismissed it by saying, "It was an angel". In their sainthood, they didn't think of this as demonic. They thought it to be a vivid imagination though knew I had seen something.

In the fifties, and probably today, people believed children were, and are protected by God, and immune to evil forces. While children are in one sense protected, they are not immune to the unseen forces of evil. Satan knows no age barrier in his schemes to take a soul.

As the years went by, I could not forget that incident. I felt the image I had seen had somehow became a part of me. I wondered about this encounter until I was twenty-three years old. I was working in sales. The manager, and the sales team, met at a restaurant for the weekly sales meetings. On that night after the meeting had ended, we all lingered over dinner.

My sales manager had just become a Christian, and I had just rededicated my life to Christ. As we talked, religion became the topic of discussion. There were some nonbelievers there, and a few Christians. My manager made a reference to God, how God was working in his life, when suddenly I responded in anger, "I don't want to hear about your God". When these words left my mouth, I heard their echo, and was able to see my face without a mirror. I could feel the contortion in my face, and it was no longer me sitting there.

As soon as this happened my manager pleaded the blood of Christ over me. In that instance my co-workers saw a smoke, filled haze ascend from my body, and vanish. Needless, to say the unbelievers didn't hang around after that. In that moment I felt a presence of peace. At that time, I wasn't aware of the blood of Christ as a protector, or the demonic forces of evil.

The voice I had heard, the face I saw, was not mine. It was the voice, and face of a demon spirit, having oppressed me for seventeen years. It was her face, her personality, her voice, her image, her feelings, her beliefs, and her life, lived through me. It was the image in the window. I later learned there are spirits of a goddess nature that influence and try to possess women. Wanda Marrs book, "New Age Lies to Women" is worth the read.

From that day of deliverance, I can look back over my life, and see the demon influence. I had accepted Jesus into my heart, filled with the Holy Spirit, and yet this demon could influence my life. She could not take complete control, but in my lack of knowledge of Satan, I didn't recognize his presence. Though I had the Holy Spirit, I still opened myself to the evil around me. When faced with good, and evil, I had no problem choosing the evil. I didn't want to do wrong, but I was weak in giving into wrong. In all my decisions, I could hear that still small voice saying no, but I still yielded to the acts of sin. I didn't recognize that voice. There was a battle going on, for my soul, inside me. If this she-devil could get me to renounce Christ, it seems that Satan would have won my soul.

In the time just prior to my rededication to Christ, I had become an atheist. I don't think I was a true atheist, as much as I wanted the attention over being one. Despite the demonic experience, I was on the brink of becoming an agnostic. I thought it was a cool thing to go to Sunday school, and ask questions the teachers, and others could not answer. By their not knowing the answers, I began to think there was no God. I was reaching out to the church, however in rebellion, but no one recognized my plight.

Though I walked a path of sin in those years, it was that still small voice echoing loudly in my ear that began to keep me from harm's way. In its softness, and gentleness, it was a voice of thunder, and great wisdom. In being weary, and confused in my life, this persistent voice of power kept me from going down for the third time. Once this voice got my attention, I realized it was God calling out to me each time I started to fall.

After rededicating my life to Christ in May, I was delivered from this she-devil in June. God surely is a God at hand, and not afar off.

Satan thought if he could possess me when I was a child, he could take my soul. Thank God I had a grandma who had taught me about Jesus since the time of my birth. Had I not been saved this she-devil would have taken residence in my body forever. Though she had power in my life, she had no power to rule my life. She only had the power I gave her, but I didn't know how to resist her. When she had nearly driven me to the point of no return, in my desperation, I opened the door to God.

At the age of four I knew even then the call on my life. I wanted to be a missionary after growing up. In a Baptist church, women were not to become preachers. The next best thing was a missionary. To all who would ask what I wanted to be when I grew up, my answer was "to be a missionary". What I meant was, I wanted to serve God.

Satan knows everyone has a call on his/her life. If he can get to them before they realize that call, he can take their purpose. Upon receiving salvation, the demons of hell went to war for my soul. Satan's mission was to destroy an unsuspecting child before she could realize God's call in her life. 1 John 4:4 said it best, "Ye are of God, little children, and have overcome them; because greater is He that is in you, than he that is in the world."

This testimony is to encourage parents, grandparents, and church leaders how important it is to train up a child in the way he should go. Get the children to the altar of salvation at as early an age as possible. Had I not been saved, the she-devil could have possessed me, instead of oppressing me. Possession is the act of ownership. A possessed person is the property of the possessor.

Oppression is a sense of weight, or constriction, mental depression. You might ask what is the difference? The difference is Jesus Christ in our salvation. God is in control, upon our yielding to Him. Many people possessed or oppressed become depressed. Depression is withdrawal, and a lack of response to stimulation. In depression there will be a lack of response to the voice of God. In the withdrawal state of mind, one may not even hear the still small voice.

In oppression, they hear the voice but do not recognize whom they are hearing. Most under the influence of depression believes the voice to be their sub conscious speaking, or their own thoughts. Consider this, you have no thoughts except God, or Satan gives them to you. You choose to whom you will listen. Unfortunately, a depressed person depending on the type of depression loses all their care for anything. Be encouraged God can fix this.

While praying one evening, and communing with the Father, He told me what depression is. Just before someone goes into depression, they are beginning to feel a sense of loneliness. Loneliness will turn into rejection of self, or an "I don't care" attitude if left untreated.

People in general have a need in their spirit man to commune with their life source or be connected. At the first signs of what we call depression if we would begin to talk with our Creator depression would not manifest. Depression only becomes depression in our need to talk to the Father, or He with us, and then not follow through in prayer. If in this need, we don't turn to the Father in Prayer, the need will be taken over by oppressing spirits turning the need to communicate with our creator into depression.

The feelings we define as depression is really our need to commune with Father, and Father tugging at our heart, letting us know He wants to commune with us. There must be a split-second decision when we feel Father tugging at our heart. If we delay prayer, the demonic spirits of oppression, and depression will take over immediately.

I can truly say I haven't been depressed in over twenty years. I'm not saying I haven't had times when I cry, hurt, or don't understand something right away. Tears were given as a release for the varied emotions in our heart. I cry when I'm happy, I cry when I'm sad, I cry when the spirit of the Lord is upon me, and I cry when I see the pain, and sorrow of others. When I walked in fear, I cried in being afraid. However, in our tears, no matter what kind of tears they are, if we will turn to Jesus, the Holy Spirit will either cry with us, or He will dry our tears.

The Holy Spirit is our Comforter. He will share your tears of Joy, and He will dry your tears of sorrow. The first encounter I had with the Holy Spirit in a vision, happened one night while I was praying. During my prayer a spirit of laughter filled my soul. Laughter is the best medicine in getting rid of the stresses of this world. While laughing hysterically, and rolling on my bed, laughing out loud I heard the audible laughter of the Holy Spirit. It was amazing. We just laughed, and laughed, until my eyes were filled with tears of Joy.

The way to fill a child's spirit with the word of God, when they are too young to understand, is to read the word of God out loud. In the womb is not to soon to begin teaching a child the word of God. Back in the late 60's, or early 70's, studies showed that babies, once they were born would show signs of response, while in the womb, to the things taught to them. I tried this with my own child. She began to crawl, sit up, and pick up toys at 3 months old. She drank from a baby cup, fed herself with her hands, and she spoke her first word "mama" just as she had turned 4 months. She walked as early as 7 months old and climbed the high sliding board ladder at the nursery at the age of 9 months. She, using phonics, with my help, taught herself to read before she was two.

While in the womb, she loved the music at Church. Inside of me, I could feel her move each time the music played, or her daddy would sing. She was just an amazing little girl and has become an amazing woman. I don't worry or fret over her life. I dedicated my daughter to the Lord when she was born. She was saved at an early age, baptized, and filled with the Holy Spirit, with evidence, at age eleven. She hasn't always done everything right, but I know God is in control of her life, and I believe she, also knows this. I know my prayers, and God's word in her, over her, and with her will not come back void. My confidence and trust are in God.

The times we are living in are extremely perplexed. Every form of false doctrine is sweeping rapacious across the world. The New Age doctrine is one we don't hear of as much as we should. People inside, and outside this movement are unacquainted with the intentions of its doctrine, whereas the leaders are much aware of its goal set by Satan.

The New Agers claim is enlightenment saying every individual is a god and can control his/her own destiny through reincarnation, or some other false higher authority, other than Jehovah God. Isn't this what Satan did to cause his fall from heaven? He tried to exalt himself above the throne of God (Isaiah 14, Ezekiel 28). In choosing to live a life without God, we are, also exalting ourselves above God. Trying to live without God, is detaching us from our life source, bringing death to our souls, not life. God is a Spirit, He created us in His image, and we are spirit. In disconnecting from God, we are disconnecting from our life source. Just as a seed planted in the ground becomes the fruit of the seed, once it is plucked from the ground, it dies. If we are detached from God, we can't know the truth in His word, and the evils lurking in the false doctrines of the world.

The goal of the New Age movement is to secure world peace, and tranquility. To obtain this goal they practice techniques deriving from eastern mysticism, and religious practices like yoga, chanting, meditation, channeling, drugs, witchcraft, Satanism, astrology, mind control, imagery, and visualization. Their objection is that every person has an individual spirit guide, to be contacted through one or more of the above religious practices. After contact has been made, the spirit guide will function as a spiritual advisor for the person who summoned it. The spirit will now guide them through all of life in all things. Satan is jealous over the Holy Spirit. Christians have their Spirit Guide the Holy Spirit, so Satan had to invent spirit guides for his followers. He tries to steal everything God does in providing a counterfeit.

I want to mention yoga at this point. Many Christian women, and men take yoga classes. These classes may seem harmless enough but in reality, yoga is derived from eastern mysticism, in the worship of Buddha. Some of the exercise positions mean different things in the worship of the spirit world. Yoga is a huge New Age pass time. Search yoga on the web and do your own study. It is largely a Kundalini spirit which dwells in the base of the tail bone. No kidding. Search it.

The persons converting to the New Age movement doesn't realize they are giving heed to seducing spirits warned against in 1 Timothy 4:1-2. This doctrine is a doctrine of devils.

Regarded members are as a race of superior human beings, much like the Aryan race of blond blue-eyed people which Hitler tried to create. The New Ager considers a Christian, or anyone outside its doctrine to be weak, undesirable, and believes they should not be allowed to live. New Age doctrine believes in killing those who do not belong to their movement. This will allow through reincarnation, another chance for the convert to make a wise decision and join the movement. A do over if you will. Keep doing it until you get it right. They believe that through the reincarnated new life one can correct what they previously lacked in the old life, and become a superior human being, or a god. The New Age sees no harm in killing. They see killing as the way the weak ones achieve another chance at life the right way. (Notes at end of book list detail material, and research used)

There is a motion in this time for New Agers to control the world. This motion begins with a one-world-government, already in place, their doctrine being taught in the public, and private schools, seminars of large business, in international governments, government agencies, like the United Nations, and Federal Reserve, The Round Table, organizations in Free Masonry, The Bilderberg Group, Trilateral Commission, The Brotherhood, and high, ranking politicians across the world. Famous personalities such as Ted Turner of TBS, Oprah Winfrey, and Kissinger are among the elites of these names.

Oprah Winfrey, a once renowned Television Show Host, denied Jesus Christ, and His being the only way to heaven on one of her last televised programs in 2010, or could have been early 2011. The video of that show was posted on Face Book, and still many Christians like to promote her by watching her shows. Promoting people like these does not reflect right thinking in a Christian, but lack of knowledge in the word of God. Jesus said to be separate and set apart from the world.

There are many more recognizable names associated with the New Age. We aren't safe, even in many Church organizations, in which this doctrine is becoming more prevalent than the gospel of Jesus Christ. Fox News, in 2008 before Obama was elected reported, 57% of evangelicals do not believe Jesus Christ is the only way to God. Jesus said in John 14:6, "I am the way, the truth, and the life: No man cometh unto the Father but by me." In Matthew 16:18 Jesus said, "And I say unto thee, thou art Peter, and upon this rock I will build my Church, and the gates of hell shall not prevail against it." Jesus was referring to the actual gates of hell on Mt Hermon where the transfiguration took place. Most people have been taught Peter was the rock but not so.

The majority of the true Christian Church is unaware of the popularity, and large degree of support the New Age doctrine holds. The number of church members, and other people involved range in the millions, in America alone, and billions worldwide. Churches teaching this doctrine fall under the umbrella of the New Age order in which many doctrines are developed but are all based on the foundation of the New Age beliefs. The New Age holds a belief system developed from Eastern Religions, and its practices from 19th century Western occultism.

Occult is derived from Latin, meaning "hidden", any attempt to gain supernatural power or knowledge apart from the God of the Bible. (Watchman Fellowship 2001 index of cults, and religions) The word Cult is also derived from Latin, meaning, in modern use to describe strange, or dangerous religious groups. (Notes: same as occult) The Watchman Fellowship is a Mormon expositor of nearly every religion from A-Z, with brief but detailed information of a religious view, and beliefs. Considering my beliefs on the Mormon religion, I wouldn't ordinarily shop this site on the web. However, the information provided is worthy for research on religions of the world.

Christians not well versed in the word of God can be easily deceived by the New Age movement. Much of the words, and concepts in their belief system, and doctrine is nearly a mirror image to those found in true Christian doctrine found in the King James Bible, but with a twist.

Below I have listed some of the beliefs in the New Age doctrine.

1. Belief in Christ, but his name is Lord Maitreya, not Jesus. New Agers believe Jesus was a real man, and did, indeed have the Christ spirit, but lost it by committing a

wrong. They believe the Christ spirit now belongs to Lord Maitreya, their superior, and Lord of all.

2. We are to be enlightened or illuminated. These are familiar words to the average pew warmer, but the concept is not the gospel of Jesus when used by the New Age doctrine.

3. Believes there is no such culprit as sin, and that each person can live according to the way that seems right. In other words, to each his own. (Rev. 3:14-22)

New Age umbrella terms for organizations exhibiting:

1. All is one. All reality is a part of the whole
2. Everything is God, and God is everything
3. Man is God or a part of God
4. Man, never dies, but continues to live through reincarnations

These are just a few beliefs to give you some idea of their doctrinal beliefs.

The New Age movement is the very attempt by Satan to overtake the world, and to destroy God's children. Satan is taking advantage of the Christian's lack of knowledge. Scriptures for study are Matthew 24:24, 1 Timothy 4:1-2, 2 Peter 2:1-2, 1 John 3:7) To further study the New Age doctrine, I suggest books by Texe Marrs, his wife Wanda Marrs. These books are written plain, and simple for reading. They are oldies but goodies. Wanda Marrs book; "New Age Lies to Women" is a great book for women to read. She writes about the Goddess Spirits, which are evil female spirits that seek to empower women. Texe, and Wanda Marrs are Christian people who have researched the New Age movement, and for what it stands. Their books will make you aware of the evil motives of the New Age.

You've heard this before, but bears repeating. Hitler said in order to destroy a nation, take one generation of that nations young people. This has already happened in America by abortion, drugs, and socialistic ideas in the classroom. If everyone could live in, not just visit, New York, Los Angeles, and other large cities in America, they would not believe the difference. The evil that has become so prevalent in the world it is no longer a hidden secret, but is found on the streets of these, and most cities in masses.

Life in the southeastern United States has its share of crime, violence, drugs, and such, but can't be compared to what I've seen in the larger cities across America. On one of my trips from California to North Carolina, I could see in each state I drove through, a difference in the people. In leaving California after ten years, it was like leaving hell, and coming to heaven in North Carolina. I'm not saying all people in California are devils, and all in North Carolina are angels, there are some of both in each location. I'm saying there is a vast contrast in the cultures of these two North American States. Although, evil is spreading like a wildfire, and it is getting difficult to anymore see a difference in any State.

The future, and some present leaders of America are the drug addicts, illiterates, homosexuals, prostitutes, child molesters, and other victims of Satan. These people are far more widespread than any could imagine, and they are all searching for their way in life. The New Age doctrine seemingly has that way. I would have to write a book entirely on the New Age to list all the acclaimed assets they think they employ in appealing to the world. The glittering, gleaming, glow of evil is pleasant to the eye, but death to the soul.

Drugs are extremely predominant in our society at every level of life. A form of drugs is being used by every age, sex, education level, occupation (blue, and white collar), government, military, law enforcement, prisons, and religion. They are used socially, to enhance demonic activity, and to introduce the angel of light. (2 Corinthians 11:14) These demons are then used as spirit guides, and are the very powers, principalities, wickedness in high places, and rulers of darkness of this world (Eph. 6:12).

Most believers, and nonbelievers are ignorant to the fact that unseen forces are at work in the world. We become victims of these faculties by lack of meditation in the word of God, staying in fervent prayer, abiding in Jesus, and He in us. The position of the Christian should be forgetting the petty trials of this life, focusing on how to do spiritual warfare in warding off the darts of the enemy in yours, and your family's life. We are at war with an enemy who can do more harm, than any terrorist.

The information, instructions, weapons, shelter, knowledge, and wisdom to do spiritual warfare are given in the word of God. We stand idly by and are captives through our own ignorance. God's people are destroyed from lack of knowledge. (Hosea 4:6) This verse is so important to the Christians daily walk that it will be repeated more than once in this book.

Christians are destroying themselves within the body of the Church. God said we should be separate, and set apart from the world, not each other (2 Cor. 6:17). Yet Christians are set apart from each other by denominational walls, racism, and pride of life. There will be no unity, or one accord of the spirit until all Christians come to a personal relationship with Jesus and learn to walk in the Spirit as one with God.

If God is not in your waking thoughts, continuously throughout the day, and the last on your mind upon retiring for the night, you have not begun to walk in the spirit. God said we should examine ourselves. Until the body of Christ gets serious about God, and who He is, the fullness of God will not be experienced.

God is pouring out His Spirit but for His Spirit to move in your life, it must be received. God said, "He inhabits the PRAISES of His people (Psalms 22:3)." In praising God, we find His JOY in His PRESENCE (Psalms 16:11), and in His JOY we find His STRENGTH (Nehemiah 8:10 emphases mine). Once you know Jesus as your Savior, ask God to give you His Holy Spirit, and then believe by faith you have received Him. Begin to praise, and worship God in song, and prayer. Open yourself up to receive. When the hands are up in total submission to God victory prevails, as was in the case of Moses in the battle between Amalek, and the children of Israel. (Ex 17:11) It's a spiritual law that automatically happens.

Linda L. Evans

Be in tune with God's still small voice and be able to recognize the enemy. Learn to recognize what is not expedient and turn away from the weights that so easily beset you. Draw near to the Holy Spirit. He is the third person of the Godhead. He is your power, comforter, and guide into all truth. Look into the mirror of the word of God daily and behold your image in the face of today's youth. Pray for your children and bless them daily. When your children leave the house, you can rest assured the Holy Spirit will lead, guide, and direct their steps.

The only spirit guide you need is the Holy Spirit. All others are demons from which you are to turn away. Do not yield to the New Age doctrine of Devils, but to the New Testament of Jesus Christ. (2 Cor. 3:18, James 1:23-25)

CHAPTER 6

Voices of the Spirit

(Tune in to God's Voice)

In May 1987 I moved from California and enrolled in an Evangelism Missionary Training School. I packed my car with all I needed and started on my journey. It was a good day yet a sad one. Finally, I was getting to do what God had called me to do. All my life, I had known I was to serve God, but just never knew how, or when Had I been a man, I could have realized my calling sooner. In my younger days, women didn't go into the ministry like they do today, so I was confused about what to do. I later learned women like Katherine Kuhlman, had blazed the frontier trail for women in ministry, but other than she I wasn't aware of others.

I was sad because I had to leave my little girl. Her father and I were divorced, and she mainly lived with him and his wife. We lived very close to each other, so we could visit anytime we wanted. My trip to the East coast was just going to be for a short time. My dad was in North Carolina, and ill, so I thought this to be a chance to be near him and go to school. After school my plans were to return to California. Our plans are not always God's plans.

It had been prophesied in the beginning of the semester that during the school year there would be an angelic visitation. After the prophetic word, I never heard anyone comment concerning the visitation. I don't think anyone gave it much thought. On the other hand, I believed, and watched daily for angels to appear. My daughter when she was 11 and I had seen angels together, and I was excited at the thought of seeing them again.

It was early morning in October of 1988. I was on my way to class. I decided to skip my first class, and drive into town for coffee. I had driven about two miles when I had a strange feeling, I shouldn't miss class that day. Having learned to listen to that still small voice within, I turned the car around, and went back. Entering the classroom, I took a seat near the back and proceeded to get my homework out. There came a noise in the background. It sounded as though it were coming from outside right above the building. As the noise came closer, it appeared to be the flutter of bird wings as they flew over, only the noise grew louder, and louder. It now sounded like thousands of birds, and the sound was coming closer overhead. In fact, it was so close I ducked down because I couldn't determine from what direction it was coming. I thought it was coming into the building. It all happened fast.

Suddenly, there appeared an angel in the front of the classroom. It appeared as a male gender having wings, with a wingspan of at least twenty feet. When I saw his two wings, I knew the span of the wings were the exact span needed to make the noise I had heard. (Ezekiel 1:34) In the spiritual realm we have knowledge we don't have in the natural. This was a matter of Physics, and in the natural I know nothing about Physics. I did a search after this and found that a large human would need 21.9816 wingspan to fly. Incredible.

Sitting there amazed, I looked around the classroom to see if anyone else could see the angel. It was apparent that no one besides me saw him. He had flown down through the ceiling, and was standing between me, and the professor. He was carrying a stack of papers, which he placed on the floor, and then he disappeared. I was astonished at his size, and the grandeur of his appearance.

His hair was short, very curly, and white in color. He was wearing what looked to be a gown of sorts. The gown was white with panels of Emerald green. His wings were, also white. He stood at least eight feet tall, and he was huge in stature: very fit. He was extremely beautiful. The oddest thing was, he seemed to be transparent. I should have been able to see through him, but I couldn't see the professor sitting on the other side of him. I'm beginning to learn that celestial bodies are translucent. Each time I see one it is just as amazing as the first time. They are so beautiful, unlike anything on earth.

After he had gone, I looked to see the papers he had placed on the floor. They too had disappeared. I have wondered for years of what importance the stack of papers played. I was sharing this vision with a friend recently, and I commented about having no knowledge of what the papers were. She knows I'm writing this book, and without hesitation she said, "It's your manuscript." When she said this my spirit bear witness to it. The notes, journals, and research I've collected over the years when stacked looks just like that stack of papers. It even included paper enough to write more books.

After seeing the angel, I wasn't able to speak while all this was happening. During other encounters with celestial bodies, I recall not being able to speak. It could be, that one is so overcome by the presence of heavenly beings, that one is rendered speechless. In either case I couldn't talk. When the people in the Old Testament saw celestial bodies, they fall prostrate on the ground as was in the case of Abraham.

Some might say I had a vivid imagination that day, or that it was from a lack of caffeine. By hearing the noise first, I knew I was seeing the angel, and it wasn't my imagination in play. Encounters with the supernatural often begin, and end so quickly that it would be easy to write them off as one's imagination. In this case, I couldn't have written it off, because I heard the noise of the wings first. Truly, once you have seen celestial beings, there is no question when seeing them again.

If we are in tune with the spiritual realm, we can believe what we see. This is not to say we should walk around in a daze looking for angels. It simply means if we have a gift of discernment, we can see into the spiritual realm at any given moment. I never know when it is going to happen. Experiences happen without notice.

I've thought many times about that day the angel appeared, and I can see no apparent reason why the angel had come. Could it be he came to bring me the manuscript, and that's why only I saw him? I wonder if God allowed me to see the angel because I believed the prophetic word announcing his coming.

People who have never seen celestial beings probably have a difficult time in believing to see them. I don't know why I have this gift, but I have been able to see into the spiritual realm as far back as I can remember. I saw things when I was a child, though too young to know what I was then seeing. Because of this I grew up accustomed to spiritual sightings.

As time went by, I soon became a sign seeker. Instead of seeking God for who He is I began to look for the supernatural. After a while I felt God had left me because it had been a long time since I had an encounter with Him. The supernatural is a benefit of living the Christian lifestyle. If we are graced with this gift, we need to learn how to understand it, and not leave God out of it.

When I realized my condition, I sought God for who He is. In late 1990, a prophet of God prophesied to me that I would come to know God as He is. This was an answer to prayer, and proof that God had heard my prayer.

It wasn't long before God reestablished His relationship with me. Once I was back on the right track, I knew not to seek the signs, but to seek God, and the signs, and wonders will automatically follow. On the other hand, if I never see another sign, I will still believe God in His Omniscience, Omnipresence, and Omnipotence.

Spiritual sightings are not the reason for walking in the spirit. However, they are tools for our trade in the ministry. Having a discerning of spirits means you can perceive things by sight, or mind. Being able to discern spirits is most helpful in ministry. Jesus encountered this in His ministry (Matthew 17:15-21, Luke 8:26-39, Matt. 22:18, Mark 2:8, Luke 5:22, 20:23).

One example I recall happened when I was two years old. My grandparents were my legal guardians, and I had been living with them. My mother was divorced from their son and had remarried. Now that she had a home to offer, she wanted me to come live with her. On one of her visits with me, she decided to keep me with her. In those days, a mother in keeping her children had rights over anyone, and anything.

I remember the day my grandparents came to visit me. I didn't suspect what was going to happen. Having arrived at my mother's home, my grandparents visited for a short while, and then the time came for them to leave. I automatically prepared to leave with them, to go home. My mother seeing this told me to go and get my teddy bear to show my grandparents. I began to cry and refused to leave the room. Somehow, I knew if I left that room, my grandma would be gone when I returned. I told my mother I knew my grandma was going to leave. She assured me this would not happen.

To this day the expression on my grandma's face is etched in my memory. It was one of hurt, and heartbreak. She wasn't accustomed to not telling the truth, and she didn't like that I was being deceived. She took no part in the deception, other than not saying anything. She could not go against my mother's wishes. After a few minutes of persuasion, I could see I had no choice but to leave the room. I hurried to get the bear in hopes I could return before my grandma left. Upon returning to the room, it was just as I had expected, they were gone. In this case I was able to discern the presence of a lying spirit. The Holy Spirit of truth resided in me even then. He knows no age barrier. It's important to discover that still small voice of God. He will lead us into all truth.

How was it, that a two-year old knows the difference between a lie and a truth, and when someone is lying to them? There was a supernatural power at work. The spirit of truth (the Holy Spirit) within was the Spirit who recognized the lie and knew the truth. Had the Spirit of truth not resided in me, I would have believed the lie as the truth. Then a relationship between mother, and daughter would have been built on the lie. Relationships built on a lie will not stand causing the entire structure to collapse. Though I didn't make my public profession of faith until I was six, I believed in Jesus in my heart at the age of two. My grandma made sure I knew Jesus. I, also believe the Holy Spirit resided in me at that early age.

This is the reason it is important to accept Jesus. In His presence, Him being truth, our spiritual eyes, and ears will open to the truth, and will recognize a lie. If we don't know the truth, even those we trust can deceive us. When the Holy Spirit lives in us, and if we listen to Him, He will lead us into all truth, and protect us from deception. We may still have to encounter the situation, but with the Spirit of Truth working in us, we can go into it with our eyes open.

In thinking back over my life, as many do, I can clearly see the mistakes I made, and evidence of the Holy Spirit's attempts to guide me in truth. If I could have recognized Him, I could have saved myself much anguish. He attempted to help me in all I did, but the older I got, the less I knew His voice. Which I suspect happens to most of us for a period.

Like the children of Israel, we wander aimlessly in the wilderness, seeking the Promised Land. Without the Spirit of God leading us, we will never find it. We aren't going to be led by a cloud by day, and a pillar of fire by night, as they were. We will be led directly by the voice of the Holy Spirit. "The steps of a good man are order by the Lord, and he delighteth in His way. Though he falls, he shall not be utterly cast down: for the Lord upholdeth him with His hand (Psalms 37:23-24)." When we fall, we need the Holy Spirit to get us back on that path that leads to righteousness.

I didn't get on this path overnight. It took many years of suffering, pain, confusion, depression, and continuous searching for my place in the world. I found the path when I realized that I didn't belong in this world. I realized I live here, but it isn't my home. The scripture tells us we are pilgrims passing through. The Spirit kept telling me this, but through my carnal way of thinking I couldn't accept it. I thought it was a fantasy that gave me moments of escape from reality. Until I began to listen to the right Spirit, it never occurred to me that I really wasn't of this world but had come from another place. (John 15:19, also see the chapter "My Moment In Heaven"). As in all things, learning to listen to the Spirit takes time, effort, dedication, and desire. I propose four steps in learning to listen to the right spirit of truth.

Step One

Looking back on the day I made my public profession of Christ I can see a bubble of fire surrounding me. It wasn't a fire that hurt me, but one that seem to bath me in its flames. Not all people experience this kind of phenomena. Most people experience only a good feeling in that they have received Christ as Savior. I believe they experience more but can't recognize the supernatural side of the experience.

I am not a denominationalist, but I must reveal that my profession of Christ was made in a Southern Baptist Church. The Southern Baptist in those days didn't teach the significance of receiving the Holy Spirit, and speaking in other tongues, and to my knowledge still don't (Acts 2). However, having no prior knowledge of speaking in tongues, I received the baptism of this gift in full force.

As I grew into adulthood, my life became a mass of disorder, and confusion. In my thirties, I had a career, and dabbled in social drugs, and alcohol, along with friends. At the age of thirty-four God healed me of breast cancer. After that, I gave my life to God in a commitment to serve Him forever. I had been saved since I was six but had not committed my life to serving God.

Once I had made my commitment, a friend prayed for me to receive the Holy Spirit. Neither of us knew I had received the Holy Spirit twenty-eight years earlier. As she was praying, I opened my mouth, feeling somewhat awkward, and I began to speak in another tongue fluently. My friend got excited thinking I had just received the baptism of the Holy Spirit. She then informed me of my infilling, and I in turn informed her I had been speaking in tongues since I was a child.

I had no knowledge of what speaking in tongues was but had been doing this nearly all my life. I thought I had been speaking in a language I had made up between me, and God. This is how I know speaking in tongues is evidence of being filled with the Holy Spirit.

As a child I used to play at making mud pies and singing to God in my new language. I didn't know until my friend identified it for me, that it was the language of the Holy Spirit. I find it extremely difficult to believe I spoke in tongues for twenty-eight years without knowing what I was doing. Where was the church? I didn't even know there were others who possessed this gift.

During my college years, I remember driving to class one evening, and singing to God in my prayer language. I remember thinking that if anyone had heard me, they would think I was out of my mind. On the contrary, I had found my mind in the mind of Christ, by the Holy Spirit. It is disturbing to me, to know I had this gift nearly my whole life and didn't know anything about it. I only knew that when I spoke to God, my prayer language initiated. I did remember visiting my neighbors Church of God when I was young. They spoke in tongues, but I had no idea at that time that it was the Holy Spirit nor what they were doing.

Many church denominations think and believe that speaking in tongues is an unnecessary gift. They don't even believe the gift is in operation today. They teach it was a onetime gift to the Apostles in the day the Holy Spirit was sent to the upper room in tongues of fire. Outside of being taught against receiving it, I believe many people do not receive this gift because they are hindered by their pride. Nevertheless, it is a gift from God, and refusing to accept it is refusing to accept an essential tool for persistent, and fervent prayer and power of God.

The people who argue against the validity of speaking in tongues are the very ones who are afraid of the gift. I believe one reason people argue against it is in not possessing the gift, threatens their claim to having the Holy Spirit. They use their pride, and fear as an excuse for not yielding to the Spirit. Remember the foolish things are used to confound the wise (1 Corinthians 1:27).

People who say, "I will not accept speaking in tongues," certainly will never receive the gift. Jesus said, "If we want the Holy Spirit, after believing, we have only to ask, and He shall be given", with fire. (Acts 2, Luke 11:10-13, Matt. 3:11, Matt. 7:9-11) We can't receive the Holy Spirit unless we submit ourselves to God, forgetting our foolish pride.

It isn't necessary to be with any one when you ask for this gift. My suggestion is to be with a Spirit filled Christian when you ask for the infilling that you may know you received. Most often than not, a person receives, but doesn't know how to release their guard, and let it happen. Being with a spirit filled Christian gives you support. I'm not one to try to force someone to receive. When the time is right for you, and if you so desire, it will happen.

It is important to understand what is happening in being baptized in the Holy Ghost. The reason most do not receive with the evidence of other tongues is they are afraid to do what the Spirit is prompting them to do. While a person is praying to receive with evidence, they hear words, in their spirit. They are not accustomed to the language of the Holy Spirit, having not heard His voice, so the words are not familiar words to them. In their natural way of thinking they won't allow themselves to acknowledge the words and voice them out. It is a prime example of hearing the voice of the Holy Spirit but not recognizing Him.

The importance of being filled with the Spirit with fire, is this: If you can die to yourself in the flesh enough to overcome fear of the unknown, embarrassment, pride, and trust God to do what He said He will do you can receive the Holy Spirit evidenced by other tongues. It is simply a matter of opening your mouth; letting words you think you have made up in your own mind, flow out. These words may seem to be made up, and to some degree they are, but not by you. They are the words of the Holy Spirit and can only come out your mouth if you submit yourself to Him.

Speaking in an unknown tongue is proof a person is submitted to God in giving Him complete control, giving no care to his own flesh, and what others might think. We can't receive anything from God if we aren't willing to die to self and submit to God. If we can't receive the Holy Spirit evidenced by the gift of tongues, we will know we are not dead to self, and pride is in our way. Speaking in tongues doesn't mean we are completely dead to self but is proof we are on our way because it is proof one is filled with the spirit of Truth.

Children are very open, and uninhibited, and are more likely to receive the gift of tongues, than are adults. Jesus said in Luke 18:17, "Verily I say unto you. Whosoever shall not receive the kingdom of God as a little child shall in no wise enter therein." Becoming as a child is difficult for most adults, because they have become conditioned by the world, and life in general. Things are not as innocent to adults, as they are to children. Becoming as a child is the key factor to receiving the Holy Spirit with fire, with the evidence of an unknown tongue. In fact, it is essential to become as a child. Most children trust, they don't get embarrassed, neither are they inhibited, nor intimidated by anything. Everything to them is an adventure.

In becoming as, a child one must rid himself of the way that SEEMS right and enter by faith to the knowledge and gifts of God through Jesus. Before we become adults, doubt is not a part of our vocabulary. As we grow into adulthood, we begin to learn how to doubt, by the ways of the world letting us down. Doubt fosters unbelief and is why coming to Jesus, and receiving the Holy Spirit is difficult for some people. Becoming as a child by faith is the first step in hearing the voice of the Spirit of Truth, that our spiritual ears will be opened.

Step Two

Once salvation is obtained, one must receive the baptism of the Holy Spirit with the evidence of other tongues. Then it must, be practiced daily, that a prayer language can be perfected. It is the same as when a baby is learning to talk. If it doesn't practice its vocabulary daily, it will never learn to communicate effectively. Prayer works by the same principle. Prayer is the way we talk with God.

In the days of Jesus, the Pharisees could be seen standing in the square reciting prayers for all to hear and see. Much prayer was a common practice in those days: but when they prayed, their prayers were mere words, repeated daily as a habit. Their aim wasn't to get closer to God, but to appear as holiness to their friends, and townspeople. When Jesus prayed, it was obvious He had a personal relationship with the Father. This is what prayer is. It is to develop a person's relationship with God by talking to Him daily from the heart.

The Jews are criticized for their repetition in reciting certain prayers, and psalms in their worship of God, especially during feast days. I personally see nothing wrong with this kind of repetition if it is from the heart. Reciting certain prayers, psalms, and the Lord's Prayer is not synonymous with repetition, in that it can be a heartfelt prayer recited unto God as a preliminary introduction to prayer time. These kinds of prayers move our spirits into the halls of worship. If these kinds of prayers are repetition, so likewise, are the hymns sung in worship services repeated time, and again; only these repetitions are applied with music.

If worship songs are sung as a repetition, and not a heartfelt voicing of words, leading into communion with God, they too are vain repetitions. Unless our words of any kind when worshipping, or praying comes from the heart, they are considered habitual formality rather than for the purpose of ascending into the heights of glory.

The disciples could see that Jesus prayed differently than they had ever before heard. When Jesus talked to the Father, He prayed with desire, reverence, and with an intense expectancy that assured an answer. They could see the close relationship Jesus had with God, and they wanted the same. They then asked Jesus to teach them to pray as He prayed. Jesus answered, "When you pray, say, "Our Father which art in heaven, hallowed be thy name. Thy kingdom come thy will be done on earth as it is in heaven. Give us this day our daily bread. Forgive us our sins, as we forgive those who sin against us. Lead us not into temptation but deliver us from evil: for thine is the kingdom, and the power, and the glory forever." This prayer is illustrative of the pattern we are to follow in how to pray. (Matt: 6:9-13) Have you ever heard someone pray, and wondered how they can pray the way they do? It is in their relationship with God that makes the difference.

I believe the Lord's Prayer is a key unlocking heaven's door, allowing prayers to ascend into the very presence of God. I intentionally pray this prayer as the prolog to my prayer time. Figuratively speaking, I believe it is like a password on the computer when trying to enter a certain program. The Lord's Prayer sets our heart in the right mode, or condition to enter the presence of God, and to be heard by Him. It announces the arrival of our prayer.

Most people have heard these steps before, but it bears repeating:

1. Our Father: In calling Him our Father, we show we have confidence in Him as His children, and we have assurance that He will hear us, and supply our needs (we know to whom we are speaking).
2. Hallowed be thy name: Hallowed shows reverence meaning that we recognize His name as Holy. It describes His never ending, love for us, His unchanging character, and His acceptance of us (we recognize who He is and respect Him).
3. Thy kingdom come, thy will be done: This expresses our submission to God in His control of the events in our lives, and that we do not want our own will to be done (we want Him to control our lives).

4. Give us this day, our daily bread: We are asking Him to meet our physical needs daily by showing we give no thought for the morrow (Matt. 6:34), God is a spirit, and we must worship Him in spirit and in truth. Remember, we must learn to recognize God's hand in our lives. For example: In asking God for finances, a friend comes along, and pays back a loan he has owed for many years, take the money. It is an answer to prayer. Just because the money didn't fall out of a tree, or some other supernatural way, doesn't mean it isn't from God. Learn to recognize God's way of supplying our daily needs (letting our needs be known).

5. Forgive us our sins, as we forgive those who sin against us: We must be careful when making this request. We are asking God to forgive us the same way we forgive others. In short, if we do not forgive others, God will not forgive us. If we forgive little, we will be forgiven little, and so on (what we expect from God acts according to how we line up with His word).

6. Lead us not into temptation: God does not tempt His people (James 1), but He does allow us to be faced with temptation. However, 1 Corinthians 10:13 reads, "There hath no temptation taken you, but such as is common to man; but God is faithful, who will not suffer you to be tempted above that you are able; but will, with the temptation, also make a way for you to escape, that ye may be able to bear it." God is our source of deliverance from a temptation. The sooner we turn to Him in our trials, the sooner our trials, and temptations will end (we know He wants the best for us).

7. Deliver us from evil: We are asking God to keep us safe when in the face of trouble. We are to trust God when our faith is challenged. He will give us spiritual protection (we can trust Him to protect us from harm).

8. For thine is the kingdom, the power, and glory forever: In this prayer, we recognize God in all His power, glory, and majesty in giving Him the honor due Him (we recognize His authority over our lives).

Pray using the Lord's Prayer as a prelude to your daily talks with the Father. Some people don't know how to start praying. If you are one of these people, the Lord's Prayer will get you started. It is like writing a book. If you can ever get the first words on the paper, the others will come.

As you pray often, you will begin to develop a personal relationship with God and will begin to know His character. Praying the Lord's Prayer is praying with the understanding in the natural. Praying in the Spirit, using your new prayer language, is putting you in touch with the Holy Spirit. The more you pray, the more you will begin to know the Holy Spirit, and eventually you will be aware of His presence in your prayer life, and daily living. Through prayer you will be able to see who the Holy Spirit is, what He is, and the part He plays in the Trinity, and in your life. The Holy Spirit is the intercessor of our prayers. He takes them to heaven. Don't quench the Holy Spirit by not using your prayer language. (Eph. 4:30, 1 Thess. 5:19)

The purpose of the prayer language varies. It is a way to pray to God when the need to pray arises, but what to pray isn't known. It is a way to testify of Jesus to someone of a foreign tongue, like Peter did on the day of Pentecost (Acts 2). For example: If you meet a person of another language other than your own, and you have the faith to speak in tongues to Him to testify of Christ, I believe he will hear you in his own language. That's exactly what happened on the day of Pentecost and has even happened to missionaries on mission trips.

It isn't that we are necessarily speaking the other language. Although there have been reports of ministers doing this, and the language they spoke was recognized by others as an authentic language.

When we speak in tongues, we are speaking the universal language of the Spirit allowing each nationality to hear in his, or her own language. The Holy Spirit translates the words of the unknown tongue into the tongue of understanding to the recipient. This is why speaking in tongues are referred to as speaking in an unknown tongue. No one knows what tongue it is except for whom it is meant, and of course, God.

I once had an experience while in Sunday service. My Pastor spoke something from the pulpit that I knew he would never have spoken in front of the congregation. The Pastor didn't record his sermons, so I couldn't rewind, and listen. I heard him announce, by name, a couple in the church was having marital problems. I know the Pastor would have never divulged the couple's name, but I heard him say the name. It wasn't him saying the name, but was the Holy Spirit saying it. Howbeit, the Pastor was speaking in an unknown tongue, and I heard with the understanding. The congregation heard tongues, and I heard the translation. No one else heard it. I later verified this with the Pastor, and he knew the Holy Spirit had revealed this to me.

Speaking in an unknown tongue is not to edify the church, but to edify oneself (1 Corinthians 14:4). Speaking to the Father without understanding gives God a clear picture of the need of one's heart. Praying with understanding sometimes hinders one's heart in trying to get the words right. God wants prayer from the heart. If one prays from the heart words unfamiliar to oneself, God is glorified when the prayer is answered, thus proving God knows the desire of the heart. A prayer language isn't to replace praying with the understanding. It is to aid one's prayer in never ceasing to pray and praying with power.

I often hear others say, "God has not yet answered my prayer". When you pray believe God has heard and will answer. Then wait for the manifestation of the answer. God sees the needs of His people and answers their prayers even before they pray. I personally believe God answers our prayers in the time when the answer will bring results. Sometimes the answer is immediate, and other times the answer seems delayed. This is when our faith and trust must be put into action. Some of my prayer answers didn't show up for twenty years, and some are immediate. In either case, God is right on time. Some of my grandmother's prayers weren't answered until she had left this world. I am a witness to this. In fact, my life is an answer to her prayers.

Step Three

Once a prayer language has been perfected through much use, hearing the voice of God is the next step. This involves knowledge of the scriptures. Having the Spirit and having learned to talk to God as the Spirit gives utterance, you now must learn to recognize God's voice. God can speak to you in different ways. He can speak to you by people through words of prophecy, through events, scripture, visions, dreams, the inner ear (which will be discussed in step four), by signs, and wonders, and by an audible voice. More often than not God will not speak in an audible voice. Don't be disappointed if He doesn't.

No one can come to the altar of salvation unless the Spirit of God draws him or her. The fact that you came to God in the first place proves you hear His voice. Now you must learn to recognize it. The Bible is data to be fed into our minds. The laws of God are written in our hearts, but we don't know His laws, as we should. They are locked away in our heart, or the memory bank of our mind. Each word of God we feed into our mind (by reading, hearing, studying) is a password that will begin to unlock the memory bank of our spirit.

After much searching in the scriptures for the hidden truths, and by prayer, our mind will begin to store new information or having new thoughts. Not new, as having never been heard before, but new to us. As this new program replaces the old information programmed by the world, the new information will be keyed into our mind. If we will push the save key, a whole new file of data will flash on the terminal of the mind's eye, which is the spirit of our mind, or heart (Jeremiah 31:33, Hebrews 10:16), revealing the truths that were locked away. This new information is referred to as revelation knowledge. The more scriptures we feed into our heart, the more of God's knowledge we receive. As this knowledge increases it develops into God's understanding and wisdom.

To develop the mind of Christ, having wisdom, and understanding, we must become hearers, and doers of the word of God. The more wisdom and understanding we have the more our actions will reflect God's knowledge in us.

As we take on the mind of Christ, we will begin to hear God's voice more clearly. Proverbs 2:6 reads, "The Lord giveth wisdom, and out of His mouth cometh knowledge, and understanding." He has always spoken to us, but our recognition of his voice has been clouded by our sin nature, and the words of the world (the old program). By being familiar with God's words, we will, more readily recognize His voice by the words He uses when He speaks. As He speaks His words, our minds, will receive them, and will transmit them to the spirit of our minds. If the words spoken match the laws in our heart, or the spirit of our mind, we will know that it is God speaking, and not a stranger. Then, when Satan tries to speak to us, we will recognize him by the words he uses. His words will be different from those of God. His words will not compute, thereby exposing him for who he is.

Satan uses the words of the world, in which we are more familiar, before salvation. This doesn't rule out words of cursing but includes the way the words are transformed in meaning. After salvation, and knowledge of God's word, Satan will try to confuse us by twisting their meaning. Therefore, we must not only hear the word, but also have knowledge of the word. Satan used the words God had spoken to Adam, to deceive Eve, by twisting their meaning. It all seemed harmless enough to Eve, though she was in the very act of deception. That is why we must be careful to know God's word, and program it into our heart to be compared to the laws in our heart. The more we know of God's word the more the light of Jesus will shine on Satan, and reveal to us his darkness.

In your walk with God, Satan will come to you, and try to rob you of what you have received from God. He will try to make your life miserable. When this happens to you, do not become discouraged, but be encouraged that you must be on the right path. In your afflictions, and sufferings in this world, become more determined to follow Jesus.

If you will stay on the highway to heaven, and not turn back regardless of Satan's attacks, you will find the Promised Land. It is how you walk through the trials, temptation, and tribulations that determines how, when, and where you come out of them. To stand against the wiles of Satan, we must put on the full armor of God (Eph. 6:11-19). One of the weapons that we have is the sword of the Spirit, the word of God. Once you learn God's word you will be able to detect Satan as he speaks, and you can use your sword against him. Isaiah 54:17 reads, "No weapon formed against me shall prosper; and every tongue that shall rise against me in judgment I shalt condemn. This is the heritage of the SERVANTS of the Lord." If you do not know God's word, every weapon formed against you will prosper.

Step Four

How does one hear God? Does He speak with an audible voice? Yes, God can, and will at times speak with an audible voice. Most people will never have this experience mainly because they don't believe it can happen, and they are not listening. Have you ever thought you heard your named called, but no one admits to calling it? This could be God calling you. I used to hear my name called a lot, but I never realized it could be God until I read about Samuel in 1st Samuel 3. God called Samuel 3 times, but each time Samuel thought it was Eli calling him. After the third time of Samuel responding to what he thought to be Eli calling him, Eli told Samuel if it happens again answer, "Here I am Lord". Samuel was hearing the audible voice of God before he even knew there was a God, but he didn't recognize Him.

Another illustration is in Acts 9, when Jesus spoke to Saul (Paul) on the road to Damascus. He was a murderer of Christians, and God wanted him to be a follower of Jesus Christ. Suddenly a great light shone round about them, and The Lord called out to Saul, "Saul, Saul, why persecutest thou me?" Saul answered saying, "Who art thou Lord?" Saul didn't say Lord, because he knew it was Jesus, he called out Lord because it was a proper title used in those days. Jesus' answer, "I am Jesus whom thou persecutest: it is hard for thee to kick against the pricks." Saul's traveling companions heard the voice but saw no man.

In the same chapter, Jesus spoke to a man called Ananias in a vision. The Lord called out, "Ananias." Ananias" replied, "Behold, I am here Lord." Then Jesus gave him instruction to follow regarding Saul. Since Ananias had the word in his heart, he recognized Jesus by His voice, and the words He used. Jesus said, "My sheep will know my voice." (John 10:3,4,27)

Here are three circumstances in which Jesus spoke in an audible voice. Ananias was the only one out of Samuel, Saul (Paul), and Saul's traveling companions who recognized the voice as Jesus. Ananias knew the word of God, and the others did not. So even if God were to speak to you in an audible voice unless you know His word you may not know it is He.

One can hear God by knowing His words, and the sound of His voice. Here is where walking in the spirit begins. Each person that receives the spirit of God will be transformed. The Bible tells us there is a spiritual, and natural realm. There are things seen, and unseen in these two realms. Through the reading of the Bible the spiritual part of man will begin to develop just as a baby develops in the womb.

First the eyes of your understanding, your heart, will begin to open (Eph. 1:18), and you will begin to understand things in a different way than you did before salvation. You will begin to see things with spiritual eyes and hear with spiritual ears. In other words, you will begin to have thoughts that will cause you to understand the ways of God, and how they differ from your ways before you knew His word. You will begin to understand life.

Hearing with the spiritual ear is like hearing with the natural ear. Like the natural ear, the spiritual ear needs to be trained. The natural ear, in infancy can hear voices, but it needs to be trained to distinguish between the voices of its family members. The same is true of the spiritual ear. As we feed the words of God into our mind, our spiritual ear begins to tune into these words when they are heard. The spiritual ear is like an inner ear that is plugged into the spiritual realm. It is like radio and television frequencies. Radiant energy in the form of electromagnetic waves is transmitted through the atmosphere, and received by radio, producing sound. Television receives waves that produce audio, and visual effects.

Each wave of energy transmitted is to be received to produce an effect. These waves of energy are flowing through our atmosphere, and each one has its own target receiver. It is a wonder that things don't get all confused, and television would receive radio transmissions, and radio would receive television transmissions. Things would be a real problem if this should happen. The reason it doesn't happen is, a receiver having its own frequency, is programmed to pick up its own significant wave, and is equipped with the right tools in which to produce the desired result. For instance: radio is programmed to receive sound, and not visual frequency waves.

The natural ear hears all the sounds of the world around us. The inner ear, however, is programmed to receive the spiritual sounds. Before salvation the inner ear is trained to hear the voice of Satan. Satan's vocabulary consists of words we hear in the natural world. Therefore, when we hear his voice with the inner ear, we do not recognize it as his voice, because we have been programmed to receive it. His voice is transmitted to our mind as a thought, which we in turn receive, storing the thought in the spirit of our mind, and manifesting them by our actions. His voice is so much like that with which we are familiar that we automatically respond without question. I attribute this to being born into sin.

An example is a serial killer who kills and claims that God told him to kill. First, only a believer would know for sure he is hearing the voice of God, and a true believer would not be a serial killer. Aside from that, God does not tell people to do things contrary to His word, and His word tells us, "Thou shalt not kill". The killer was hearing the voice of Satan but could not distinguish it from that of God because he did not know God's word. Satan may have introduced himself as God to the killer, but had the killer known God's law of "Thou shalt not kill", he would have known it was Satan, not God, speaking. Then the action of murder would not have been manifested. Though the laws of God were written in the heart of the killer, he had not unlocked these laws through The Blood of Jesus, by salvation. The killer could not see them, hear them, or know them.

More examples of hearing the voice of Satan are in committing the works of the flesh. When a person decides to commit an act against God's laws, his thoughts are the driving force behind the action. If a person thinks, "I am going to rob a bank", this is a thought produced by the voice of Satan, heard by the inner ear, transmitted to the receptor of the mind, stored in the spirit of the mind, and fulfilled by the physical act of robbing a bank; thus, planting a seed of destruction, and allowing it to take root, thus producing the action, self-will.

The spiritual inner ear is a receiver that receives the spiritual waves transmitted by sounds in the spiritual realm. We must become familiar with the sound of God's words to hear God speak. Then when He speaks, we will recognize his voice. Jesus said He only says what He hears the Father say.

The devil is a mocker, and master of disguise. We must become so familiar with the word of God that we completely reprogram our way of thinking to God's way of thinking. We must train our inner ears to receive only the word of God that we may produce that good, and acceptable will of God in our thoughts, and deeds. Paul said in Philippians 4:8, "Finally brethren, whatsoever things are true, whatsoever things are honest whatsoever things are just, whatsoever things are pure, whatsoever things are lovely, whatsoever things are of good report; if there be any virtue, and if there be any praise, think on these things." It is impossible to think on these things if we are not programmed with God's word.

If we are programmed to receive only the word of God, we will be unlikely to receive the evil words of Satan when we hear them. Even if Satan's words sound like those of God's we will know the difference and reject them. We will automatically disperse them the same as we would a bad taste in our mouths from eating spoiled food. Radio receives sound waves but rejects the sound waves intended for television.

Now that we have the word of God programmed in us, and we hear Satan's words, we will become confused. His words will go against what we have learned as the real words of God. The Bible tells us that God is not the author of confusion. In this confusion we will know that it is Satan transmitting, and we are not to receive his voice, and carry out his commands. When you are confused by a decision be still and wait on God. Where there is confusion, Satan is talking to you, and he is the author of confusion.

Compare hearing the voice of God to retrieving data from a computer program. To retrieve any one document, there is a title under which this data is filed. If the title is not entered correctly the program will display the words, insufficient data, or no files recorded. The file will not be retrieved; and the work will not be done. If our mind has been renewed, Satan's words will produce insufficient data, and we will not respond.

When God speaks to our inner ear, and we receive His commands, they will be transmitted to our mind, or heart. The words in our minds will become thoughts of virtue. If these thoughts match up with the laws in the heart of our spirits, and are in line with the Bible scriptures, we will know that it is God's voice, and that it is safe to carry out the command. When we receive the command of God, there will be perfect peace, and harmony, instead of confusion. We must stay in perfect communion with God, speaking to Him, and listening for His voice. Without peace and holiness no man shall see the Lord.

We have learned that we cannot recognize God's voice if we don't know His word. In the case of a believer, and a nonbeliever a common phrase is used. "That's your opinion." This phrase when used in reference to what the word of God means, is the most ridiculous phrase anyone could use. Before I had knowledge of the truth, I would use this phrase to defend my interpretation of the scripture, when someone didn't agree with me. Now I realize how ignorant I appeared in the eyes of those who had more knowledge than I.

The phrase is most often used when the word is given, but not received by the recipient. Let us use for example a conversation between two Christians. One being a converted sinner, having much knowledge through endless study, and preparation in the word, and the other being an always was Christian, living by his traditions, and lacking in study, and knowledge of the truth. When I say an always was Christian, I am describing someone who thinks they are Christian because they were born in America to Christian parents, but never had a conversion experience, or someone who received salvation but stays on the milk of the word, and not the meat, never growing in the knowledge of truth. Let us call these two Bob, and Bill.

As the story begins, we find Bob arguing with Bill about a scripture, and its meaning. The Holy Spirit is given as our teacher to teach us how to rightly divide, or understand the scriptures, and apply them to our lives. Different individuals can interpret Scripture and can make them to fit any given situation. However, the Bible tells us that there is no private interpretation of the scriptures. The Holy Spirit teaches us to understand and to use God's word in the right context of the meaning by building precept upon precept, precept upon precept, line upon line, here a little there a little.

In the case of Bob and Bill, Bob often violates the scriptures. He doesn't read, and study, he has no real knowledge of the scriptures, and no foundation of precept on which to build. Having little knowledge can bring big deception, or destruction. It can be like knowing a car needs gas to make it run, but not knowing where to put the gas. If the gas is put in the wrong place the car could explode. In Bob, and Bill's relationship, everything seems to explode instead of running smoothly. Bob, in his little knowledge of the truth, tends to manage his life according to his own opinion. The meaning of opinion is "standing firmly by a belief but having no knowledge of what is believed" (Funk and Wagnall's standard desk dictionary).

Linda L. Evans

When Bill tries to direct Bob in the way of truth, Bob gets rebellious. His response is, "That's your opinion". Bob gives this response because he has read enough of the word to get on the right track, but not enough to rightly divide it. When Bill gives Bob a truth, it is a truth that has come through much study, and teaching by the Holy Spirit. It is usually a truth that is in general, common knowledge to Bible Scholars, and Theologians alike. Instead of receiving the truth, Bob sees Bill's attempts as manipulative, and controlling, and rejects what Bill is telling him. Bill does not have this kind of spirit, but Satan translates Bill's words into the words he wants Bob to hear knowing full well that Bob will not know the difference because of his lack of knowledge in the scriptures.

Like the Jews, the Word became flesh, and dwelt among them, and they recognized Him not. They had been looking for Messiah/deliverer for 100's of years, and when He came, they didn't recognize Him. Their scriptures were full of information about what to expect from the Messiah, what to look for, and they still didn't recognize Him. This is what I'm talking about. Unless we have head knowledge, AND heart knowledge, we can't know the scriptures with understanding, and Wisdom.

Did you know that you are quenching the Spirit if, through the lack of study, you do not recognize, or know the truth? If you do not know the truth because you are slothful in your study, you are not allowing the spirit to perform in you God's purpose for your life. This is the same as rejecting the Spirit, which is blasphemy. Blasphemy is the only unforgivable sin. This is the reason God said that His people perish from lack of knowledge. What does perish mean to you? To me it means I don't hit the mark for the prize of the high calling of God. (Philippians 3:13)

Satan knows the word in its entirety, and he knows who does, and does not have knowledge of the truth. In Acts 19, an evil spirit spoke to the vagabond, and said, "Jesus I know, and Paul I know; but who are you?" If we don't learn the truth in its entirety, we will have no power against Satan.

Reading a little of the Bible now and then instead of every day can harm a person more than it can help them. Without the daily manna, (guidance by the word), building precept upon precept, we are going to grow weak in our spirit. In this weakness, we find ourselves like a weak battery in a car, unable to receive, or transmit. The energy becomes less, and less, as we turn the ignition, and pump the gas, until finally there is no juice left in the battery, and it dies completely. Even if we leave the car alone, and only try to start it once in a while, it will die all the same. Without our daily bread, we become weaker, and weaker, just like the battery. By not partaking of fresh bread each day, we become undernourished. The word of God is our manna, our daily bread.

The manna received yesterday will not last, but will spoil, breed worms, and stink if held over (Exodus 16:15-31). This is what happens to the word if it is read on occasion instead of daily. It will not be held over to the next day without becoming spoiled. The only way to preserve what was taken in the day before is to read more the next day, and the next, and so on. In doing this we are charging our minds (battery) to produce the wisdom, and knowledge of

God with the understanding needed to continue to drive out the enemy. To build precept, upon precept line upon line (Remember the Lord's Prayer, "Give us this day, our daily bread).

In reading the Bible daily, concentrating on its message, even if you think you don't understand it, you are receiving truth into your spirit. The truth is feeding you. Think of the benefits you will receive if you read out loud. In reading out loud, you are thinking the word, and hearing the word. This is a double portion blessing.

Without precept upon precept, line upon line, here a little and there a little we are not going to come to the knowledge of the truth and will be led by the voice of Satan instead of God in our daily walk. Satan controls us by giving the basic words of scripture with which we are familiar, and then adds his own twisted meaning to them. If we are not well versed in the scriptures, we are going to do what Satan says because it seems right. He will use the little bit of scripture we know, and will tag his meaning to it, causing us to follow him. "There is a way that seemeth right to a man, but the end thereof is death (Proverbs 14:12, 16:25).

Having little knowledge, the meaning of this knowledge can be used wrong and is the same as knowing nothing. Then when we try to walk in the spirit, we can't seem to get there. Everything we do will be wrong, and destruction will result.

When we know the word of God, we will not go by what seems right, but will go by what we know to be right. The first sign that we are lacking in knowledge is when we use the phrase, "That's your opinion". If you are one to use this phrase when addressing the word of God, you need to examine yourself closely. If you use this phrase often, when you hear the word of God, it is because you are being controlled by the voice of Satan, not wanting to accept the truth. The person that uses the phrase regarding the word of God is the very one that lives by his own opinion and does not have knowledge of the truth; he is set in his ways and will not allow Jesus to change him; he is ever learning, but never able to come to the knowledge of the truth; being fruitless, and destitute of reality; laboring in vain.

Another example is someone young in the Lord, whether adult or younger, having little knowledge, unable to submit, and thinking he/she knows it all. There is no need of arguing over the scriptures, for there is one sure way of knowing the truth. Begin to study, and if your understanding doesn't line up with what the Spirit of God is saying, examine yourself, whether you are in the faith, and seek wise counsel. The word of God is not based on opinion, but rather fact, and is a reference for all who will desire the truth and take the time to search for it.

Some of the character traits listed below are made manifest in people who will not listen to wise counsel and cannot hear the Spirit of truth.

1. Stubbornness – following their pernicious ways.
2. Rebellion – choosing not to hear the truth if it sounds different from what they think they know the truth to be.
3. A forgetful hearer – twisting the scripture to satisfy their own interpretation.
4. Lack of daily prayer, and Bible study – hearing Satan's voice instead of God's.

5. Lack of witnessing, or testifying – never coming to know Jesus, and how to abide in Him. Ever learning, but never able to come to the knowledge of the truth.

6. Lack of discipline – not only in their own lives, but also in the lives of those they have the rule over.

7. Lack of love – Believing they give love but violates the ingredients of 1 Corinthians 13. Keep in mind, that the main office, and function of the Holy Spirit is to shed the Love of God in our hearts. Love is saying you're sorry, with a repentant heart to God, and others around you.

8. Lack of compassion – Believing themselves to be the epitome of compassion, but always seeing the faults of others instead of the needs of others.

9. Refusing instruction, and correction by the word – thinking they are wise in their own eyes instead of having knowledge of God, His word, His understanding, and wisdom to use it.

10. No admission of error – The attitude of always being right while everyone else is wrong. This is big time pride. Not realizing all the above pertain to them because they do not have knowledge of the truth, and their eyes of understanding have not been opened.

In general, pride of life, being their sole foundation in living. Pride comes before a fall (Proverbs 16:18). "Seven things God hates: Haughty eyes, a lying tongue, hands that shed innocent blood, a heart that devises wicked plans, feet that run rapidly to evil, a false witness who utters lies, and one who spreads strife among brothers (sisters) (Proverbs 6:16-19)".

Having these traits, and not being able to see them is due to a lack of knowledge of the truth. If the truth were known, it is as a mirror reflecting the flaws of our character. Without knowledge of the truth, blindness results, allowing Satan to take control of one's life.

Example: If you defend something of which you have no knowledge, you are defending something about which you know nothing. Does it make sense to defend something of which you have no knowledge? You be the judge. This is the way Satan gains control. You become stubborn in your own opinion of which you have no knowledge with which to be stubborn.

If the truth were known, you are only being stubborn to keep from giving in to the person trying to give you knowledge. In other words, and I say this with the utmost love, "You don't know what you are talking about", and it shows. Proverbs 10:14 reads, "Wise men layup knowledge, but the mouth of the foolish is near destruction". If most of us knew how much our words reveal about us, we would never talk, unless we are speaking the word of God.

While in this condition, you hear the truth, and the first thing you do is rebel against it. You do this because you don't understand it. You only know that it is different from what you believe to be the truth. You can't see the truth when you hear it because you are walking in blindness from lack of knowledge. If you are blind you can't see who is leading you. A prime example is: Do you get angry when someone recites a scripture to you, in trying to show you the truth in God's word about your situation? If you do, you are listening to the wrong voice, and reacting out of your ignorance to the truth. Think about it. Why would anyone get angry when hearing the word of God?

We need the Holy Spirit that He may teach us to hear the voice of God by teaching us the knowledge in truth. Jesus teaches that the Holy Spirit will bring to remembrance everything that He (Jesus) has ever said. If we don't study the scriptures daily, building upon our salvation experience, we can't build precept upon precept, precept upon precept, line upon line, here a little there a little, and learn to rightly divide the word of truth. If we stay at the altar of salvation, instead of the altar of daily forgiveness; renewing our minds daily; partaking of the manna daily; learning of what we need to forgive whether it be ourselves or someone else, we will never learn to hear God's voice, and what the Spirit is saying to us. In this, we will become undernourished, dried up, wells without water.

In partaking of the manna daily, we will receive God's wisdom, and learn to recognize God's word when spoken to us, either by people or by the voice of the Spirit. In this there will be no debate.

On the other hand, walking by our own opinion is a full proof sign that we don't have knowledge of the scriptures, and we are indeed, displaying our ignorance for all to see. 1 Kings, 18:21 reads, "How long will you halt between two opinions? If the Lord be God follow Him: but if Ba'al, then follow him." How can we hear what the Spirit saith, if we continue in the pride of our own opinion? Who are we that our opinion is worth anything?

Eve did not wander far from God to give place to Lucifer. She was still in the garden when she was deceived. Her mistake was listening to a voice other than God's voice. She knew it wasn't God speaking to her, yet she yielded to Lucifer all the same. Adam did the same when he listened to Eve. He knew that what she was saying was the opposite of what God had said, yet Adam also yielded to temptation.

Here the seed of destruction for all mankind was first planted. Adam and Eve were deceived and yielded to temptation. They knew God's voice and His word, yet in their knowledge to do right, they chose to disobey Him. They knew as soon as they had yielded to disobedience that they had listened to the wrong voice and had made the wrong choice. Just like us, when we disobey, they probably thought, "How can we justify this action to God?" When God approached them regarding their actions, repeating what He had told them, they immediately placed the blame on each other, and God. They knew God's voice yet listened to Satan, and then formed their own opinion as to the direction they would take. Never minding that God's word was the truth.

After they fell, knowledge of good and evil had entered their minds, or heart, but before they admitted to their mistake, they laid the blame on each other, the serpent, and on God. Therefore, voicing their opinion for the second time. They were trying to get out of their mistake by making it seem as if it were God's mistake that caused them to fall. They were working out of their own opinion and didn't know what they were talking about.

Believers, and nonbelievers alike do the same thing. They disobey God; someone reminds them what God's truth is and they say to them, "that's your opinion". By taking this attitude, the blame of our actions are being placed on God. Whether or not you know it, you are not receiving the truth, and you are denying the operation of truth in your life. We can walk in the garden all day long with God, but unless we receive His word as truth, we are walking in self-destruction, and disobedience. Disobedience is sin.

The goal is to become mature Christians, in accepting responsibility for our mistakes, admitting our wrong doings, and disobedience to God. Don't admit to being wrong, and then try to justify the wrong. That is what Adam, and Eve did. Wrong is wrong, and God knows our heart. Repent with a repentant heart, asking God to renew a right spirit within, and create in me a clean heart. Pride diminishes in daily confessing our faults.

One thought of which to take careful consideration is this: "If you don't like to retain God in your knowledge, God will give you over to a reprobate mind, to do those things which are not convenient." (Romans 1:28) By not retaining God in your thoughts, you will believe a lie. It's a spiritual law that automatically takes place.

God said to never cease praying. We don't do this by staying on our knees twenty-four sevens, but simply by keeping a praying state of mind, making the will of God our every thought in addition to our intimate prayer time. Staying in constant communication with God, disallows Satan entry to the spirit of our minds, disallowing us to hear the wrong voice.

It is our choice in what course of action we take when temptation is placed before us. In hearing the voice of God, we will choose the right action, and not what seems right. If God's word of truth continues to be rejected, you will be made to believe a lie. Thessalonians 2: 11 reads, "And for this cause God will send them strong delusion, that they should believe a lie." (Thess. 2:7-12)

I was in my 1st two years of college, and I wasn't living for the Lord. I hadn't lived for the Lord very much at all since I had been saved. I was living in an upstairs apartment. The backdoor lead to an outside staircase. The door itself was the kind with the nine little windows on the top half. The door was located off the Kitchen.

One day when hungry, I went to the refrigerator to get something to eat. I was standing in front of the refrigerator looking at what food was available when I heard a knock on the backdoor. The door was five feet away, and I could see no one there. I dismissed the knocking as a mistake and went about looking for food. I heard the knocking again, and still no one was there. I then thought it was a friend stooped down hiding behind the door pulling a prank. I went to the door, peeked down through the windows, and I saw no one. Puzzled I went back to the refrigerator, and I heard the knocking again, only this time, I heard a voice. "The voice identified Himself as the Lord, and said, "I stand at the door and knock, if you will open the door, and let me in, I will give you food to eat, and water to drink, that you will never hunger, nor thirst again." I immediately recognized this to be Jesus. I walked over, opened the door as an action and Jesus came in. He has never left me.

Revelation 3:20-22 Jesus said, "Behold I stand at the door and knock; if any man hears my voice, and open the door, I will come in and sup with him, and he with me. To Him that overcometh will I grant to sit with me in my throne, even as I also overcame, and am set down with my Father in His Throne? He that hath and ear let him hear what the Spirit saith unto the churches." Amen!

CHAPTER 7

Satan In Person, and The Blood of Jesus

Christians may be saved but will still be influenced by the rulers of darkness. Like many other Christians, I had unknowingly fallen into Satan's trap. Even as a Christian, for years, I walked in sin. I thought I was abiding in Jesus, but His word wasn't abiding in me. I thought myself to be a "good hearted" person but didn't realize I was cutting my own throat.

I wasn't a prostitute on the streets, but I committed spiritual adultery against God. I wasn't a drunkard, but I committed the sin of drunkenness (drunk on the things of the world). I wasn't a witch, but committed the act of witchcraft by manipulation, domination, daily horoscope readings, fortune cookies, and superstition. I wasn't a murderer but had killed with my tongue. I wasn't a sorcerer, but had committed sorcery in using drugs, on goes the list.

As is with most people, the way I saw myself did not reflect the corruption in which I lived. Though I was saved, I still lived a sinner's life. Areas of my life had not changed, and I was still living in the ways of the world, as it is with most Christians.

Without the word of God, a person can receive Jesus all day long, and by choice, still be in bondage. Unless a change takes place in the heart, a lifestyle of sin will continue. God said in Revelation 3:15-16, "I know thy works, that thou art neither cold, nor hot: I would thou wert cold, or hot. So then because thou art lukewarm, and neither cold, nor hot, I will spue (VOMIT) thee out of my mouth". God isn't saying you lost your salvation, He is saying you make me sick to my stomach.

My moment of decision came when it was discovered I had breast cancer. It was through this disease God got my attention. In receiving a miraculous healing from God, my life finally became His. Once I made a commitment to God, changes began to occur. I didn't change because I had to, but I wanted to change. The desire to change didn't occur until my encounter with the Father, after which I threw myself into extensive study of His word.

Linda L. Evans

The more I read the word of God, the more I desired to know Him. I hungered, and thirsted after His word, as though I had an addiction. For three years, God took me under His wings, and fed me, gave me drink, feeding my heart with His righteousness. The more I desired of Him, the more He gave of Himself. Then one day I woke up, and I knew Him as Father, Mother, Sister, Brother, Husband, and Lover of my Soul. He has met my every need, fulfilled my hearts desires, and continues to do so.

While sleeping, demons would attack me through nightmares. There was one who would come and push me down onto the floor. Like a very strong wrestler, she would pin me down. She was so evil I couldn't move from fear. I told this to a friend psychiatrist, and she instructed me to plead the Blood of Christ over myself before going to sleep. After applying the blood, I never had any more trouble from this she demon.

Having learned in part the power of the Blood of Jesus, I never went to sleep without pleading His blood over me, and my bedroom. Christians will have a difficult time accepting, not the blood, but in thinking it is necessary to plead the blood over, and over again. They believe Jesus' blood shed on the cross and received in salvation is once and for all time. They are right regarding salvation, but wrong in thinking the blood is never to be applied again as protection against evil. It is a warrior's weapon against Satan and his minions.

One night, like all other nights, I said my prayers, pleaded the blood over my bedroom, myself, and went to sleep. Something woke me up about 3:00 o'clock a.m. I opened my eyes and saw standing in my bedroom doorway a man dressed in a black suit, white shirt, black tie, and black patent leather shoes. He had no hair, (hair representing glory). His skin was a gruesome, powdery, scaly, white with red, and blue vessels, and veins marking his face, and hands like a road map. He looked as if he had been dead for centuries. I noticed his hands were overly large, and strong. His head was huge, with extremely large eyes. His nose was evidenced by two little holes, and a tiny horizontal slit represented his mouth. There were others with him, maybe two or three. They were behind him. I remember thinking this is Satan, or else the vilest, most wicked demon in all hell. He exuded evil.

I sat up on one arm in my bed and continued to watch. Then just before fear was about to take me, the demon tried to step inside my bedroom. When the toe of his shoe entered the space of my bedroom, he jerked back, and began clutching his throat, gagging, throwing his head back, and roaring like a lion. It was a gruesome scene to say the least. I didn't have a clue as to what was happening. I could only sit on my bed and watch in amazement while the demonic being tried to enter my bedchamber. He made the same attempt three times. In the third attempt, he loosened his tie, and unbuttoned the top button on his shirt. He was about to give his all. He charged like a raging bull, only this time was different. He experienced the same gagging, clutching his throat, and roaring, and I could see he was growing weak. Instead of stepping back, as in the previous two attempts, he became faint, and in stumbling, he nearly fell. He began grasping for breath, and his strength failed him. In anger, and utter disgust, he, and his friends, suddenly disappeared.

I mentioned earlier, I was just before fear. This visitation happened so much faster than I can tell it, that you must understand it was a thought process. Just as I was about to fear, I became completely mesmerized by the scene, and then I remembered the blood I had pleaded. In the midst of the encounter, I could see my room filled with a color of yellowish, topaz, clear liquid. It was liquid like water, but more like a dense fog. I want to label it as looking like clear gold. Imagine competing swimmers diving into a caramel filled swimming pool. They could only swim at a very slow pace, because the caramel is so thick. The blood was a shield like water, completely encompassing my room, and extremely thick. I could see the life in the blood, as well as I could see the death in the evil being. I didn't become afraid after seeing the shield of blood. I knew no evil could penetrate the thickness of its nature. I just sat and watched who I thought to be Satan torment himself with each attempt to enter my room.

Thinking back on that night makes me laugh a little. I was watching Satan beat himself up. While it was no laughing matter when it was happening, it humored me in later years. I wish every Christian could see, as I saw the blood that night. They would never fear again. I believe Satan made three attempts, hoping to penetrate me with his darts of fear. If I had feared Satan, the blood would have become defiled, and Satan would have succeeded in his attempt to destroy. Had I not seen the blood I would have been scared to death at seeing the devil standing in my home. The point is to plead the blood of Christ, and believe it is there whether you can see it or not. Believing without seeing activates faith and leaves no room for fear.

Soon after this demonic encounter people began reporting UFO sightings, and abductions. News of these UFO's seemed to fill the airways, on television, radio, and drawings of aliens were depicted in the local newspaper. People in several states were claiming to have been abducted by the aliens, with claims of being surgical Guiney pigs.

One day I happen to see like drawings, of the alien creatures, drawn by several abductees. In amazement I stared at a drawing submitted to the newspaper. It looked like the demonic being I had seen in my home. I began listening to as many alien-UFO broadcast as possible. I wanted to learn more about the abductions. All abductees drew nearly the same picture. The aliens all had large heads, large hands, large black eyes, and the gray, white scaly skin.

I believe I would have been an alien abduction statistic today had I not known how to apply the blood. I learned then that fallen angels a.k.a. aliens are real, they are demonic, and they can't cross the bloodline of Christ. I've seen many other demonic forces but have not had any more alien encounters. I have seen the UFO'S again, but not the fallen angels, thank God.

This experience taught me Satan can't encounter the blood of Christ without much pain and suffering. I believe it is why we should teach children to have faith. Faith is the exact opposite of fear. If faith abounds in us, we will not succumb to fear when the evils of the world come in like a flood.

The children of Israel experienced the covering of the blood when they lived in bondage in Egypt. God told them to take a young lamb and sprinkle its blood on the doorposts of their homes. He then said, "For I will pass through the land of Egypt this night, and will smite all the firstborn in Egypt, both man, and beast, and against all gods of Egypt (Fallen Angels) I will execute judgment: I am the Lord. And the blood shall be to you for a token upon the houses where you are: and when I see the blood, I will pass over you, and the plague shall not be upon you to destroy you when I smite the land of Egypt (Exodus 12:1-13".

Today when we plead, or apply the blood of Christ, it is done in a verbal way, while believing and trusting in its power. When God said, "I will pass over you," He was saying, "I will over-shadow you, and cover you in the shadow of my wings, and nothing by any means will harm you."

What would have happened had I not pleaded the blood, and believed? Had I become afraid the seal of protection, by the blood, would have broken? Fear is doubt, and unbelief. Where there is unbelief, there is lack of faith. "Without faith it is impossible to please God", thus being of a carnal mind, living not in the spirit. (1 Thess. 3:2-(5), Heb 11:6, Rom. 8:1-8) Allowing fear to enter one's heart is the same as walking in the flesh, for to be carnally minded is death, but to be spiritually minded is life, and peace (Rom. 8:6).

When we are children, we have the utmost faith. Growing into adulthood, we learn to doubt from having not learned how to use faith. Even the strongest of Christians in the most desperate circumstances waver in their faith. When a precious family member is on their deathbed, it is automatic for us to fear their death. It may be a fleeting thought, backed up with prayer, but in that moment the thought was there. The thought may not have completely materialized, but in the actuality of faith, should never have come.

Those who have lost loved ones please understand it wasn't your fault they died. Only God has the power to give life. In these life and death situations, we find out how much faith we have. Did you automatically believe the person would live without even thinking the possibility of death? God wants us to come to the place in our mind where our thoughts are so completely changed, and consumed by His word, that we will never consider anything other than by faith. The Bible says in Hebrews 11:1, "Now faith is the substance of things hoped for, and the evidence of things not seen", and 11:6, "But without faith it is impossible to please Him: <u>for he that cometh to God must believe that He is, and that He is a rewarder of them that diligently seek Him.</u>"

It is our nature after Christ to try and use the measure of faith He gave us. The problem with our faith is it must become in character like a little child's faith. If you tell your child something, the child believes you with his/her whole heart. There is no doubt. Not even a little. They just believe you because they trust you.

As adults, having a learned doubt behavior we live in unbelief. This learned thinking needs to be undone, restructured, and replaced with faith. It doesn't happen overnight. Unfortunately, we will walk through many wilderness experiences before we ever learn to replace our doubt with faith. Like all God's word, faith must become heart knowledge, not just head knowledge.

Now more than ever, people are searching for answers that will give them more power, and control over their life. For this reason, the rituals of Satanism, in form of witchcraft, demonology, new age, Islamic fascisms, Zionism, scientology, etc., are being sought after, and practiced. These rituals are not only practiced but have become the lifestyle of billions across the world. Until the last three decades, acts of Satanism in America were not only unbelievable, but also unmentionable. Now it is considered one of the most desired religions of our time. It is evident in our young people through their music, symbolism, clothes, jewelry, movies, literature, lust, and in general conversation, and ideas. Notice all the movies about vampires on television, and the cinema. Is it any wonder that Satan wants to defile the blood?

While forms of Satanism, (voo-doo), are common practice in some third world countries, it is no longer a closet religion in America. Twenty years ago, rarely did a day pass without some mention of random acts of Satanism, in the news media about ritual-site findings, and blood sacrifices whether animal or human. It is so widespread now, that we barely ever hear it mentioned. Now that there is an open church for Satan worshippers, this religion is an accepted contender of faith.

Abortion is one of the largest components of Satanism, in the shedding of innocent blood, while children are another source for satanic ritual subjects. In past years the news media and talk show host have interviewed children as young as two years, and older, who have taken part in satanic rituals. During these ritual ceremonies, children have been forced to commit heinous acts such as drinking blood, urine (mixed, and separate), sex acts with adults (sometimes with their own parents) and stabbing infants in a sacrificial offering to Satan. If the child was too young, and physically weak, the parent usually helped by placing a hand on the child's hand, forcing the blade of the knife to penetrate the sacrificial infant.

I personally have listened, and studied numerous Telecast exposing these ceremonies. I've watched the frightened, and disturbed children as they shared their experiences. They describe in detail sexual acts, and murders, in which they were personally involved. These children couldn't have known these kinds of details, unless they were participants as they claimed. It is the kind of religion Satan offers. He preys on the innocent, and unprotected, as well as the ignorant.

While I have never witnessed a ritual, I met a young teenage boy who claims to have seen one. He describes them as detestable acts of barbaric rituals. To prove they exist, he took me to a site in Rocky Mount, North Carolina, once used for satanic ritual. I saw the altar, the leftover rubbish of beer cans, liquor bottles, and the somewhat shack was partially burned to the ground.

Serial killings are another example of Satan's agenda. The "Night Stalker – Richard Remirez", a convicted serial killer, and rapist in California, admitted to the authorities that it was Satan who made him kill. His comment when asked why he had killed was, "You don't know Satan." The New York Times reported Remirez as saying, "Lucifer dwells within us all. You don't understand. You are not expected too. You are not capable of it. I am beyond your experience. I am beyond good and evil. Legions of the night; night breed. Repeat not the errors of the Night

Prowler and show no mercy: I will be avenged." His list of crimes included burglary, sodomy, and 30 other felonies, as reported by the New York Times in 1989. These kinds of crimes are evidence of the satanic forces in our world. But as, so called intellectuals, we disregard them as acts of Satan, and claim them as acts of the flesh, or self-will. The majority is in denial.

"America: The Sorcerer's New Apprentice," by authors Dave Hunt, and T. A. McMahon states, "Any attempt to understand the current worldwide revival of sorcery must candidly face the issue of spirit manifestations. Since the dawn of history, a belief in the existence of nonphysical beings that interact with mankind has been basic to all religions, and occultism. It is not surprising, then, that a belief in these mysterious entities (whether they are real or imagined) is also playing a key role in today's New Age movement. As we have already noted, an uncanny sense of the behind-the-scenes existence of the spirit world is so deeply embedded in the consciousness of every human being that nothing can uproot it. This is just as true to modern, sophisticated Westerners, who consider themselves too scientifically oriented to be religious, and who reject the possibility of psychic experience."

Most of us would rather dismiss acts of crime, and violence as issues of insanity, or drug abuse. When we do this, we are overlooking the cause, and relating to the condition, and/or the manifestation of the cause. Satan is extremely powerful in his influence over our lives and is a very real contender in the world today. He is out to destroy our children, you, and me. Until we face the fact that he is the adversary, he will continue to destroy all that we are, and have. If we don't know God, we are an open door to be used of Satan.

A person with the least bit of intelligence, compassion, and love, would realize, and recognize that the things I've mentioned deviate widely from what is right, and acceptable in human behavior. There must be a reason causing one's mind to allow pornography, adultery, child abuse, abortion, murder, and the like. If you are looking at, or buying pornography, you are encouraging the films, and books to continue being made, and the models to perform. Your money is financing the production of filth.

When you betray your spouse in sex outside the marriage bed, you are an adulterer. If you are a doctor performing an abortion, or the mother of the child being aborted, if done willingly, you are both murderers. If you are a supporter of the pro-abortion movement, you too are a murderer, etc. There needs to come a time when the eyes of the human race will open and see the corruption in which it lives. If you support these evils, your heart is full of deceit.

Through the evil of our times, we have learned to disguise sin. We no longer call sin, sin. The acts of sin listed above have new names. If adultery were called sin, instead of extra marital affair, if pro-choice were called murder, instead of abortion, we may be more apt to flee these acts. Sin by any other name is still sin, but by their new names, has become somewhat more acceptable. Instead of fleeing from it, we now justify it.

Immorality has seized the world, and has captivated the hearts, or minds of the people. We have profusely accepted sin until our hearts, or minds have become a mass of putty in the hands of Satan in giving him charge over our thoughts, and actions. Chapter 3:1-5 in 2

Timothy speaks of the times when the world will turn to evil. It reads, "This know also, that in the last days perilous times shall come. For men shall be lovers of their own selves, covetous, boasters, proud, blasphemers, disobedient to parents, unthankful, unholy, without natural affection, trucebreakers, false accusers, incontinent, fierce, despisers of those that are good, traitors, heady, high minded, lovers of pleasures more than lovers of God; having a form of godliness but denying the power thereof: from such turn away." One can easily see that these verses describe the evil that has swept the face of the earth today; and blind we are.

In chapter 4, "Who Is Your Mirror Image" I covered the topic of parents teaching and warning their children to beware of the drug trafficker, kidnappers, and the stranger with candy. We worry about our children's safety from the predators lurking in the streets. What about the spiritual predators lurking about in the shadows, and roaming freely throughout the world? Those are the real adversaries.

We send our children out into the world each day, unprotected from the rulers of darkness of this world, and spiritual wickedness in high places (Eph. 6:12). Our children's lives are in danger, not from the obvious, but by the unseen forces at work. While these forces follow them in their daily walk, they are oblivious to the evil because their minds are on the predators that can be seen. The following is a list, found in Texe Marrs' book, "Ravaged by the New Age." It is a New Age blueprint consisting of 13 bold pillars upon which Satan intends to build a new humanity, with our children as his sacrificial lambs.

1. The children of the future will serve a One World (Planetary) Government and live in a One World culture.
2. Patriotism to one's country must be abolished, and all national barriers destroyed in order to build a New One World Order.
3. Children will accept that Eastern mystical religion is to be married to the Christianity of the West to forge a new unified social, and religious order of "Universal Truths."
4. Teenagers, and youth will rebel, and revolt against their parents, and against authority to help usher in the New Age World Order.
5. Youth, and all of humanity must accept that the time will inevitably come when grown-ups who refuse to become part of the New Age will have to be killed. They are to be considered as lowly germs, an infection or blot on humanity that must be stamped out, and eradicated.
6. The traditional family unit is not desirable for the Aquarian, or New Ager. Children belong to the government, to the world, and the community—the human group— not to their parents. A new kind of family unit must inevitably come into existence.
7. Young people must be taught to believe in reincarnation, and karma (the law of rebirth) rather than the resurrection, and judgment teachings of the Bible. This belief must guide behavior, especially the sexual conduct.
8. Absurd, and immature notions of "sin", and "guilt", must not be imparted to children by parents, teachers, pastors, and other adults. A more permissive worldly, and attitude must be adopted.

9.   Children are to be taught that all religions - -Christianity, Witchcraft, Hinduism, Buddhism, Islam, Judaism, Paganism, etc, - - are equally worthwhile, and that it doesn't matter in which god one believes.

10. The new generation of youth must recognize that Jesus did not come to save or convert anyone: because no one is lost.

11. Christian doctrines, such as that of heaven, hell, and judgment, must be discarded, and the theology of the Old Testament must be repudiated.

12. A New Age World Religion must be established without Jesus Christ as Lord, and Savior. The Christian Church is dead and must be replaced.

13. The coming New Age World Religion will emphasize the unity of all religions while rejecting Jesus Christ's profound Biblical statement, "I am the way, the truth, and the life."

Marrs continues, "It is apparent from these thirteen foul doctrines that Satan's demon chieftain, Djwahl Khul, and his many New Age followers despise Jesus Christ. This leads them to seek to destroy our children by undermining Christian principles in all spheres of society. They plot to decompose, and destroy the family unit, subvert Bible doctrine, and promote a One World New Age Religion, and Government. Children are expected to rebel against their parents, do as they please without fear or guilt, and freely worship false gods without condemnation. Our children are, also taught by New Age leaders to picture themselves as gods, a blasphemous lie that leads to selfishness, and to destruction."

I don't know about you, but I see all the above working in the world today. The family unit for the most part is destroyed, Bible doctrine is no longer considered as truth, children rebel against their parents, and a one-world government is being established as I write.

Adults are not immune to the evil in high places, and are just as susceptible, and unprotected as are the children. We have been warned time, and again of the troubles we will face if God isn't part of our life. It seems some people never learn. They keep rejecting the knowledge of how to combat their enemy, then turn around and play with a poisonous viper. "Ever learning, never able to come to the knowledge of the truth (2 Tim. 3:7)." First one needs to recognize and learn who the enemy is. Without recognition of who he is, there is no chance of victory.

In some Christian circles, they won't admit, or accept the existence of the devil. Lack of acknowledgement is the same as America closing her eyes, and saying there were no Saddam Hussein, Hitler, or Osama Bin Laden. We can close our eyes to anything, but that doesn't make it go away. We must recognize our enemy, learn his strategy of warfare, and learn how to walk from under his influence before he destroys us.

Since the beginning of time, people have been warned of Satan, but instead of realizing the remotest possibility of his existence, they have closed their eyes, bowed their heads, and suffered his abuse. Worse still, a larger number of Christians are the quickest to deny Satan's existence. Many Christians may claim he exists, but they don't want to hear how he is influencing their lives.

Christians, above all, need to know their enemy, that they aren't immune to the forces of evil. The fact remains, Christians that walk the walk, and talk the talk, are more apt to encounter Satan more times than a nonbeliever. They, like anyone, need to know how to keep Satan from controlling their lives. If you aren't living for God you are living against God, and Satan has already taken you under his control. If you are under the control of Satan, you won't have to deal with him on a regular basis. With you under control, he can focus his attention to those Christians that live a Godly life, knowing the truth, in his attempt to drag them down.

David Wilkerson, a renowned New York pastor, a great man of God died this year in an automobile accident. He wrote a newsletter on June 15, 1992, entitled, "The Truth About Judas – Betrayer of Christ." He explained how Judas Iscariot is a prime example of one who walked with Jesus, and yet, he betrayed the Lord.

> Judas was a disciple of Christ, walking, and living with Jesus daily, yet he betrayed the Lord. At The Last Supper, Jesus told His disciples that one of them would betray Him. After Jesus washed the disciple's feet, showing them His love for them, He exposed His traitor in dipping the bread, and giving to Judas. Jesus had shone His great love for Judas in the foot washing before He exposed Judas as His enemy. This act was to demonstrate to His disciples how much they must love their enemies.
>
> Jesus had informed His disciples that after dipping, the one to whom He gave the bread, would be the traitor. In the moment Jesus dipped the bread, He was giving Judas the chance to repent. Judas didn't take the chance and ran into the night to betray Jesus.
>
> His running into the night is symbolic of running into darkness. Judas loved the ways of darkness more than the way of truth, and light. His deeds of darkness were manifested in when he told Jesus' adversaries where Jesus could be found. When the soldiers arrived at the place where Jesus had been praying, Judas was with them. Here again Jesus gave Judas a chance to repent when He said to Judas, "Friend, why have ye come?"
>
> In referring to Judas, a traitor, and enemy, as friend, Jesus was showing His great love for Judas in giving Judas the opportunity to be forgiven. Judas, instead, embraced Jesus, and kissed Him. Judas then went back to the ones to whom he had betrayed Jesus and told them he was sorry for what he had done. They told Judas that his sorrow was of no concern of theirs, and they threw thirty pieces of silver at Judas' feet. This was the price paid for the betrayal of Christ.
>
> Judas, realizing in that moment, what he had done, could not bear the sorrow he felt. He then went and hung himself on a tree. Judas had been completely given over to Satan, even in his walk with Christ. Judas

allowed Satan to control, and destroyed his life through his lust, greed, and love of money.

I believe, as did David Wilkerson, that this is where many Christians stand today. They go to church, professing kinder ship to Jesus, embracing Him, and kissing Him, but in their heart, they are traitors. When Judas saw his act of betrayal, he did not repent, though given more than one opportunity. He saw he had spilled innocent blood, yet he did not have the Godly sorrow of repentance. Godly sorrow will produce repentance, and repentance will produce a change. Judas, instead, was feeling sorry for himself (selfishness) and the pain it caused him. In his sorrow, instead of turning to God, Judas rejected Jesus, thus producing death, instead of life.

Whatever your status, believer, or nonbeliever, not living by God's word of standards in applying Biblical principles, and practices, Satan will overtake you. Unless you line up with the word of God, you will not recognize your sin, and you will not produce Godly repentance. You must examine your heart daily that your spiritual eyes will see sin, and your heart may become educated, and changed.

Until you look into the eyes of God, you are the mirror image of Satan. You will continue to love the ways of darkness more than the ways of truth, and light. This is what happened to Judas. His greed, and love of money caused him to betray an innocent man. It wasn't until it was too late that his eyes were opened, and he could see clearly what he had done. Had he not taken his eyes off Jesus, and ran out into the night, he would not have died a sinner's death.

Some people believe that Judas was not held responsible for his actions. It has been said that Judas was appointed to betray Jesus, that prophecy could be fulfilled. This may be true. Jesus could have hardened Judas' heart the same way Pharaohs heart was hardened against Moses in the deliverance of the children of Israel. Had Judas really loved Jesus, Judas could not have betrayed Jesus. Judas' walk had not become a personal walk, in coming to know Jesus in His Lordship. The greed in Judas' heart was like a mask that kept him from seeing whom Jesus really was, and from knowing whom his enemy was, and yet he walked with Jesus daily. Here we must remember some vessels are made to honor and some to dishonor.

Having a personal relationship with God is something most Christians don't have. The Bible tells us that if we know the truth, the truth will make us free. It does not say it will set us free. There is a marked difference between the word "make", and the word, "set". The word set means, "to place in a certain position." We are brought to a place of freedom, but to receive this freedom we must perform an act. The word "make" means, "To bring about, shape, fashion, mold, construct, to form, or create in the mind, as a plan, conclusion, or judgment." To be made free is to bring about a change to the thing that was set in a specific place. In the case of the truth, we are instructed to know the truth. It is the knowledge of the truth that will make us free. Therefore, if we don't have the knowledge of the truth, a change will not occur, and we will not become free in knowing who our enemy is, and from our bondage to sin.

In the moment of our salvation experience, we are set in a place of freedom. From there we must find the keys that will unlock the chains of the sin that binds us. Once these chains have been unlocked, we are then made free daily as the word of God is performed in us. It is a process of learning and applying the principles of God's word that we become free.

Until we come to know Jesus, the truth, we are not made free but are only in a place to accept freedom. In studying the Bible, the hidden truths are made manifest. We receive keys with each truth we discover in the Bible. Each key received, unlocks another truth, and so on, building upon the foundation of our salvation experience. Building precept upon precept.

As we learn to meditate upon scripture, praise, and worship God, and pray without ceasing, we come to know God as He is, and thus a personal relationship is established. By meditation, reciting, and committing scripture to memory, we come to know God in a personal way. He said that heaven, and earth shall pass away, but His word will never pass away. If we completely transform ourselves into God's word, we will never pass away.

In praise, and worship, we learn to be in the presence of God. In His presence we find His joy, and in His joy, we find His strength. His strength is needed to carry out the truths we learn. It is not an easy thing to walk in the way of truth. We have been trained in the way of darkness for so long that walking in the way of truth will seem to fight against our very nature. There will be times when the way seems easy, and other times will be like going through a fire as the sin, and dross are burned out of our lives. It is in these times that God's knowledge, wisdom, joy, and strength are needed. These are the times our faith needs to be strong. If we don't have God's strength in our trials, we will fall by the wayside, slipping into darkness.

In prayer we are allowed to talk with God, and He with us. In taking time to talk to God we are showing our love for Him, and our desire to spend time with Him. If we stay in constant communication with God, we will learn more of Him, and learn to hear His voice. When we hear His voice, we are not hearing the voice of Satan. Therefore, by never ceasing to pray, we stay in a constant state of the knowledge of God. Never ceasing to pray can be accomplished by the renewing of our mind, having the mind of Christ, which is a state of being rather than a kneeling position.

In performing the above Biblical principles, and practices, we can stay in constant communication with God. In doing so, we are recognizing His Lordship over our life, and we always dwell in His presence. If we don't know God in this way, we can fall by the wayside, from the way of truth, into darkness, giving Satan the chance to overtake us. If we are not filled with God's word, represented by a change in our lives, we can't walk in the way of righteousness, and truth. If we are not walking in truth, it is because the truth is not in us, and we will be like Judas, loving the things of darkness more than the things of truth, and light. The Bible tells us that it is better to have never known the truth than to know it and fall from its way; whose end is to be burned (Heb. 6:8). This doesn't mean we will be forgiven of having not learned the truth as it is given to all as guide to life.

In learning the truth, we must start with the blood of Christ, and knowledge of its cleansing power. Blood is a word with which most people can't identify. It has always been puzzling to me how some people can persecute Christians regarding, the applying of Christ blood, and in the same breath turn to Satan, and drink blood, or shed blood. Satan has caused people's eyes to be blinded when it comes to the blood of Christ.

In Satan's teaching of the blood, he uses it directly as a visual aid. Because we are a people that needs to see with our eyes to believe, Satan's tricks of spilled blood will deceive. When the blood of Christ is introduced as a verbal agreement, people reject it in disbelief, because it can't be seen with the natural eye. There are others turned off to Christianity because of the blood. This is a definite deception of Satan. How can we be turned off to the very thing that gives life? Blood flows through our veins, and is in the natural, our body's life source. The blood of Christ gives us everlasting life and is our atonement for sin.

The Bible tells us in 2nd Timothy 3:13, "But evil men, and seducers will wax worse, and worse, deceiving and being deceived." If you have been deceived into believing that the Bible isn't the truth, then you have no defense now, or in the evil times ahead. There is only one way to walk in perfect peace, and victory, and that is through the shed blood of Jesus Christ. Satan can't cross over the bloodline of Jesus. His blood is our protection against evil.

The scriptures tell us that the battle has already been fought, and won, and that the victory is ours. The battle has never been ours. The battle was between God, and Satan, and Satan lost. We are victorious through God, The Victor. If we don't reach out and receive the victory, we will be fighting a battle that ceased over two thousand years ago.

The battle Christians now fight is the good fight of faith (1 Timothy 6:12) This is a spiritual battle where our flesh wars against the spirit; a battle, in which, we fight against the rulers of darkness of this world, and against spiritual wickedness in high places (Eph. 6:12). By walking in the flesh, we are defeated foes, having no conscience, and are dead in our sins. The soul that sins shall die.

By accepting Jesus and being washed in the spiritual life-giving source of His blood, we are made free through the knowledge of His word. In performing this act, our eyes will be opened. We will see we are no longer a victim of the battle, but a partaker of its victory through Christ. In this knowledge, we can walk freely, in all confidence, assurance, and knowledge of the hope of eternal life. Free from the control of Satan, and his power to dominate our lives in any one capacity. Free in the knowledge that you are covered in the blood of Christ and having all power over the enemy and any evil thing that may come against you. Romans 1:6 tells that the Gospel is the power of God. Satan gets his power by using God's power and twisting it to his own use. This twisting is the power to deceive, which is the power to kill, steal, and destroy in our lack of knowledge of the word of God.

People are always looking for power and control, in all the wrong places. Yes, Satan has power, and yes, he does give power to his followers. However, the power he gives is temporal, and limited to this world, and those who give him power. Since his power is temporal, the things it gives are also temporal. The pleasures of the world, which are pleasing to the eye, will pass away with the passing away of the world (or this age). There is only one real power, and that is the power of the blood of Jesus. I saw with my own eyes, the devil defeated under the power of the blood of Christ. This power is the greatest weapon against evil and is an everlasting power.

Those who want to take control of their life must give control to God. Do this by tearing down all you have built on any foundation other than the foundation of God. Anything built on the foundation other than God will come tumbling down on its own.

We are surely living in perilous times. A time when all is crashing down around us. The economy in America is bankrupt, unemployment is higher than it's ever been, there is pestilence, famine, earthquakes, nations rising against nations, iniquity has abounded, and the love of many is cold. (Matt. 24) How far must we fall before we will believe the truth? How long will we allow all these horrible, hideous works of Satan to continue?

We can close our eyes, but the responsibility lies with us all. God gives us the answer and tells us what to do in 2 Chronicles 7:14, "If my people which are called by my name, shall humble themselves, and pray, and seek my face, and turn from their wicked ways; then will I hear from heaven, and will forgive their sin, and will heal their land." The reason all this iniquity exists and has abounded is the people of God have stopped praying.

Christians are always saying they don't know what they can do about any given situation, such as the problems of the world. The way Christians can do their part is to pray. When Christians stopped binding in the heavens, they permitted evil to flourish, and be loosed on the earth. Masses of Christians don't know how to pray. They can pray for five minutes, and they are out of something to say. Jesus said in the garden of Gethsemane to His disciples, "Could you not tarry for one hour?" Jesus had been praying and returned to see His disciples had fallen asleep.

There is coming a day of judgment when all will stand before God. In that day ignorance will not be an excuse, for God has given His word in the Bible for all to learn how to live life. God no longer winks at ignorance. The scriptures are our instructions to life. The blood is the life and is alive. In Leviticus 17:11 we read, "For the life of the flesh is in the blood." In the book of Genesis when Cain slew Abel, the Lord said, "What hast thou done? The voice of thy brother's blood crieth unto me from the ground (Gen. 4:10). It is obvious that after Abel's death, his blood spilled upon the ground, was still alive. God is telling us that shed blood cries out to Him for vengeance. Can you even imagine the cries that are ascending to God from the shed blood of countless numbers of souls on this earth, having been murdered (aborted)?

Jesus had risen from the dead and had come out of His tomb. He was standing nearby when Mary Magdalene saw Him. She had been to the tomb, had found it empty, and was afraid the soldiers had taken Jesus away. She began to weep. Jesus asked her why she was weeping, and for whom was she seeking? When she realized that He was Jesus, she reached for Him to touch Him. He said to her, "Touch me not for I have not yet ascended to my Father (John 20:11-17)." The reason He wouldn't allow her to touch Him was because He had not been to heaven to place His undefiled blood upon the Mercy Seat of God, as the atonement for our sin.

To understand we must go back to the Old Testament. The High Priest of a city could enter the Holy of Holies (a sort of temple where the priest met with God), to place the sacrificial blood offering for sin upon the altar. The offering of blood came from killing an animal, usually a lamb, as a sin offering for the people. Before the priest could enter the Holy of Holies, he had to wash his hands, and purify himself. Once he was purified no one was allowed to touch him, lest he, and the blood for atonement, became defiled. Much like surgeons before they go into surgery. They wash their hands, put on rubber gloves, and touch nothing but the patient, and sterilized instruments.

Jesus was on His way to heaven to sprinkle His own blood on the Mercy Seat. Had Mary touched Him the blood would have been defiled. Now, the blood of Jesus has been sprinkled on the Mercy Seat in heaven. When we plead the blood over our lives, and situations, His blood cries out to God for vengeance, or protection in our behalf.

To be used as a protection against Satan, the blood must be applied by a believer. The believer must keep himself covered by the blood, by confessing his sins continually. Un-confessed sin is never under the blood. Therefore, a non-believer has no protection against Satan. They have no covering without the blood. When a non-believer pleads the blood of Christ, he is bringing damnation upon himself because he is defiling the use of the blood by his own sins. There is only one way to benefit from the protection of the blood. That is to first accept it by faith, as atonement for sin, having a born, again experience in Christ Jesus. When faith is activated, the unseen things are made manifest and become the evidence of the things hoped for. Thus, your spiritual eyes have been opened.

Without the blood of Jesus Christ, you are powerless. Satan can enter your bedchamber while you sleep, and have his way with you, anytime he pleases. How can you rest in this knowledge? Where is your comfort, and peace?

Satan is a liar, and he doesn't want you to know the truth. If you follow him, you are deceiving yourself. You have become as a fool, being wise in your own eyes, rebellious (witchcraft), and stubborn (idolatry) with deceitful hearts, and an unteachable spirit. Just because you can't see these personality traits, and attitudes in your heart, doesn't mean they aren't there. Instead of searching for answers in Satan where there are no answers, turn to God, wherein lie all the answers.

If you are a Christian, and you are still doing the things you did before you were saved, having the same bad attitude, using the same foul language, thinking the same selfish thoughts, trying to control those around you, thinking your way is better, getting angry when someone doesn't agree with you, thinking yourself to be better than others, you need to examine yourselves, and learn to recognize your enemy. If these character traits are still present in your life the enemy is in you. Look in the mirror of God's word, to see whether you have spots or blemishes.

Accepting Jesus into our heart by faith is the first step in beginning a walk with God. When we accept Jesus, we are saying that we acknowledge our sin against God and believe there is a better way to live life through Him. Upon receiving Jesus as the Son of God, He in turn, sends the Holy Spirit to dwell in you. In John 14:26, Jesus told His disciples He would send them a Comforter, the Holy Ghost. The Comforter will teach you all things and will bring back to remembrance all that Jesus said before He left. In John 16:7, Jesus said, "It is expedient for you that I go away: for if I go not away, the Comforter will not come unto you: but if I depart, I will send Him unto you."

The Holy Spirit is our Comforter, Guide, teacher, and intercessor. In essence, He is the intermediary between us, and God. If Jesus were still here in the flesh, He could only be seen where his physical body was present. Through the Holy Spirit, Jesus can be where two or more are gathered in His name (Matt. 18:20) and can be seen with our heart instead of our eyes. Therefore, is why He said, "It is expedient for you", meaning us, that He go away. Because the Comforter is a Spirit, He can be in many places at once. Jesus in a physical body can only be seen with the natural eye and is limited to being in one place at one time, just like you, and me.

To receive the Holy Spirit, we have only to ask in the name of Jesus (Luke 11:13). The reason we ask in the name of Jesus is, Jesus is the one who forgave us, and He is to whom God gives. When we accept Jesus into our heart, we are taking on His likeness, and His character, and are cleansed by His blood. The Holy Spirit then comes to dwell in us. He will teach us Jesus, as we study the scriptures (John 14:26). Then, when God looks at us, He will see His son in us, thus becoming our Father, and we become His children. In order to communicate with God, this transformation must take place.

God once walked with man, but when sin entered the world, He could no longer allow man to dwell in His presence. This wasn't because God is a cruel God, but because He is Love. God is so pure, and holy that sin can't exist in His presence. He separated Himself from us for our protection. To dwell in the presence of God our sin must be washed away, that we may stand pure, and holy before Him. The blood of Jesus makes it possible for us to stand in the presence of God, in His likeness pure and holy without spot, or blemish, and without being consumed by God's glory.

Whether you choose to believe, or not believe, every person will someday stand in the presence of God. If you have not accepted Jesus into your life, being redeemed by His blood, you will still be covered in sin, and will perish in God's presence (Luke 13:3-9). "God is not willing that none should perish, but that all should come to repentance (2 Peter 3:9)".

I'm sure Christians automatically walk in the covering of the blood daily. We probably don't have to plead it over again. In this case it did no harm. I can't help but remember I applied the blood over my bedroom, no other room. Is that why the fallen angels were allowed to come into my home? The blood didn't cover the other rooms, allowing them entrance. However, the blood applied over my bedroom stopped them. I believe I will stick with the pleading, if for no other reason, I have done all to stand. There's power in The Shed Blood of Jesus.

CHAPTER 8

My Moment in Heaven

In 1977 I moved from Charlotte, North Carolina where I had grown up, to Glendale, California. This portion of my story begins in 1979, in Glendale, where I worked as a waitress in a little diner on main street.

Nothing was unusual as I performed my duties on this particular day. When the lunch rush was nearly over, I stopped to total the customer receipts. As I stood by the counter totaling the receipts, a miraculous, and extraordinary thing happened that changed my life. In a second, with no warning, my soul, and spirit were taken up into a portal of heaven. The portal wasn't far above the place my natural body was standing. My natural body was still standing at the counter though no life seemed to be there. My soul and spirit were both in the portal in another dimension above looking down at myself, and all the people eating lunch.

I wasn't in the portal long. I had entered the other side of eternity where time stood still, with no beginning and no end. Realizing I was in what I would call Heaven, I was in the bosom of God and could perceive heaven as my home. I knew I was where I belong and would live forever.

Human spirits are sent to earth for a specific reason. In heaven I experienced everlasting peace, tranquility, beauty, and completeness. Rest assured there is no need to fear going to heaven. There is life after we leave this world. I am an eyewitness. In fact, once you are there, you will have no recollection of the things you experienced on earth. You will be the person you are now, but without sin, in a glorified body.

In heaven you will have the abundant life you should have had on earth. Your life there will be as though you have always lived there, as though this life never happened. Imagine having the life you only dream of having now. Everything will be as it is here except it will be completed, and perfected, with no more tears, pain, or sorrow. Now that's heaven. (1 Corinthians 2:9)

Linda L. Evans

One amazing thing about this experience was the portal. It was like an opening into another plane, realm, or perimeter of this world almost as if it is a co-existing world with earth. I could look down and see my natural body. It was standing there, motionless, empty, void of life, yet still looking down at the receipts. My body in the earthly plane was still dressed in my uniform, and still looking like me. The only difference was, I wasn't there. My body was a shell, and all my senses had left, all but one, vision. The body in the earthly plane was dead for all practical purposes, but it could see myself in the portal. My natural body was looking down, not up, so this was amazing how it could see me above in the portal. Maybe it has something to do with the brain since it is said the brain lives up to 10 minutes after death in the body.

Inside the portal of heaven, my soul, and spirit had a new body, and was also dressed in a blue uniform just like my body below, yet different somehow. There was purity, unfamiliar to me. It reminds me of the scripture in Revelation 6:9-11 where it speaks of the souls under the altar. They had left this earth but had not yet received their white robes. They cried out, "How long oh Lord before you avenge our blood on them that dwell on the earth (paraphrased)?" I didn't know about this scripture in 1979, but after reading it later I applied it to my experience. It was Just like when I went to heaven, but I didn't get my white robe right away. I wasn't under an altar, and I wasn't martyred for Christ to get there, but I was there all the same. I wonder if the souls under the altar were wearing earthly attire, while waiting for their white robes? If the blue uniform I was wearing when I went to heaven, still wearing while in heaven is any indication, I would have to say yes.

The transformation from the earthly body to my new one in the portal took place during the transition between the earthly plane, and the heavenly perimeter. I wasn't aware of this transition until the transformation was complete. It happened so quickly, and without warning that there wasn't even a previous thought in my mind to constitute this action.

My new self-looked down from inside the portal, and I could see, and hear the customers eating, talking, and laughing, having no knowledge of my transition. As I observed the people, my thought was one of compassion for them in their ignorance. These people were some of the most influential people of our town. They were the presidents of corporations, insurance tycoons, doctors, lawyers, etc. The diner was their favorite breakfast, and lunch spot, and they all seemed very content, and happy. Yet, as I gazed around the room, I was able to see their spirit man. I could see into the depth of their soul, and I knew they didn't know the truth; that they were bound for an eternity of great pain. Sitting there in all their earthly riches with nothing to show for it but their outer garments.

Seeing, and knowing their destiny brought great pain to my heart. Not pain in the way we know pain here on earth, but a knowledge of pain that doesn't feel like the pain with which we are familiar. The knowledge of pain, and feeling pain are different. It was an all-knowing kind of pain of the ignorance of the human race in the concept of their integrity. A kind of seeing that allowed me to know how foolish we are in our feelings regarding the world, all that is in it, and the shame of it all. The knowledge of pain goes much deeper than feeling pain.

The feeling of pain is but for a moment, or a trace in the passage of time, but the knowledge of pain is everlasting. Everlasting in the sense it will never pass away because it is knowledge.

The portal appeared as a round opening, a kind of door in the atmosphere, leading to another dimension. I had heard others claim their spirit left their body during a near death experience, but I was very much alive, and awake when this happened to me. As I mentioned earlier, my natural body was empty, but it could still function to a point in vision. It was as if my vision in the natural was linked to my vision in the spiritual. My natural eyes could see myself in heaven without looking up, but my eyes in my spiritual body could see everything.

God revealed to me while writing this chapter that this experience was like an ordination or anointing in beginning a prophetic ministry. He has given me vision to see from the heavenly plane. What I see in the earthly God gives me heavenly meaning and understanding. My spiritual vision is my dominating vision. I no longer see the earthy explanation of a thing. I know what others see, and how they interpret it, but I can only interpret what they, or I see by spiritual understanding, given from the mouth of God. The worldly way of rationalization no longer computes, for we know in part. The answers, and solutions are in the word of God.

I say to you, that everything happening on this earth is but for a moment. The trials, and tribulations, are meaningless and are nothing more than stepping-stones to the Kingdom of heaven. I hesitate to say this because most will not understand it, and will think I am minimizing their pain, their problems, their troubles, and the like. I say this to let you know that the only thing that matters in this life on earth is to make it into the Kingdom of God. Everything else is vanity.

Learn by your errors, let Jesus be conformed in you, and don't anguish over the trivial matters of this life. Trust God in that all things work together for good to those who love God and are called according to His purpose. You are going to have to let go of the earthly way of thinking, and learn to hear from God, His thoughts. He wants to give you His thoughts, but if you don't prepare to receive them, you will not.

While I was in heaven, I had all my senses, but they operated in a different way. I could see, hear, smell, feel, and think. Talking was especially different. I was able to talk with my mind, so talking with the mouth really wasn't necessary. We may still have this function, but it won't be needed. The difference in our senses on earth compared to in heaven is in the way they function. They function entirely by the knowledge of God in the spirit of the mind.

In heaven, taste is the same as smell, smell is the same as hearing, hearing is the same as seeing, seeing is the same as feeling, and feeling is the same as thinking, in no certain order. All five senses are as one in the spirit of the mind, in the form of knowledge. For example: When I thought something, I not only thought it, but I could see it, smell it, taste it, feel it, and hear it, all at the same time, just by having the knowledge of it. Can you imagine eating an apple in heaven, and experiencing that apple to the fullest, with all five senses at the same time wrapped up in a blanket of knowledge in it? WOW! INCREDIBLE!

In heaven we will have knowledge of all things. There will be no secrets. In my moment in heaven, I knew God's infinite plan for mankind. Though I had all knowledge, I knew only one thing. I knew God. In knowing God, I knew all things. All mysteries had been revealed, but there are no words known to me allowing me to explain what these mysteries are. These mysteries are not mysteries in heaven, only on the earth. Actually, it was only one mystery, and it is only a mystery to those who don't know God. All I can really write is, I knew I was in a place I could identify as heaven, and God had spoken many things. He didn't announce them one by one, but by being in the kingdom, or presence of God, knowledge was automatic, and it came instantly. This is exciting news for the believer. HEAVEN EXIST, AND SO DOES GOD.

My transition from earth to heaven was the same as the rapture. It wasn't the rapture, but I was caught up the same way it will happen in the rapture. The only difference being, I didn't receive, neither my white robe, nor my rewards, and I didn't see Jesus. By this I know it wasn't THE RAPTURE at the end of the age. I knew Jesus was there, but I didn't get to see anyone, Him included. I wasn't there long enough. It seemed like I was there a long time, but it was only for a moment this side of eternity. When I came back, I didn't want to be back, and I have longed for the day when Jesus will come to take all of us home.

I was in a spiritual body, but it was only a taste of what is to come. I can tell you the Rapture of the Church will be so sudden you'll not even know it happened. Suddenly, without warning, you will be in heaven, all knowing, and oh so glad to be there. All your trials will be over, and you will be with the Lord forever. If people could really grasp what is waiting for them in heaven, they would never, want to delay going there. Truly we do "see through a glass darkly;" (in this time) "but then face to face; now I know in part; but then shall I know even as also I am known" (1 Corinthians 13:12).

God is in a real place called heaven, and is in fact heaven Himself, waiting for us. Jesus said in John 14:1-2, "Let not your heart be troubled: ye believe in God, believe also in me. In my father's house are many mansions: if it were not so, I would have told you. I go to prepare a place for you. And if I go and prepare a place for you, I will come again, and receive you unto myself: that where I am. There ye may be also."

Now that I am back in my natural body, I can't tell the things that were told to me in that day, but I have a blessed assurance of heaven. I have knowledge, some of which I can share, am going to share, and some of which I have tried to share. However, I can assure you of the blessed hope that is in Christ Jesus, our Lord, and Savior. I can assure you not to be concerned with the cares of this world, but to learn of Jesus, and strive with all your heart to be ready to meet God when the time comes. Luke 21:34-36 Jesus said, "And take heed to yourselves, lest at any time your hearts be overcharged with surfeiting, and drunkenness, and cares of this life, and so that day come upon you unawares for as a snare shall it come on all them that dwell on the face of the whole earth. Watch ye therefore, and pray always, that ye may be accounted worthy to escape all these things that shall come to pass, and to stand before the Son of Man (Jesus)."

The Bible tells us that Jesus will appear in the twinkling of an eye. A twinkling of an eye computed by people other than me is said to be 11/100th of a second. I don't know how fast that is but judging by my experience I think it is even faster. When I was caught up, I didn't glide up but was taken in a sudden fashion. Thinking back, I don't think the transition took enough time that it can be measured. I wrote about this in chapter 1, "A Timely Visit With Jesus". The 11/1000th of the 3rd day of which Hosea spoke, could very well be the faster equivalent to 11/100th of a second.

If you are reading this book after the year 2011, and a great disappearance of people in masses has happened, you will know the rapture happened. If the rapture has happened, all you can do now is give your heart to Jesus or be doomed to eternal damnation. Find other Christians, stay together, and don't take the mark of the beast, of the antichrist, by denying God.

While I was in heaven looking down on my natural body, it was like looking at a picture on a page, in a storybook, or an artist perception of a still life. The world isn't a permanent place, and it is only for an appointed time. It's like unto a model that an architect might build for a building project: a sort of prototype of the world to come. We are here to learn how to live in the world to come: a learning center, if you will, for the Kingdom of God. The life we live now is in preparation for the life to come. I'm not saying this world will end, but the world to come is going to be much different. It may be on this earth for a season, or not. I do know there is a place called heaven, and it is not on this earth.

I'm going to try and explain in mere words heavenly things. I pray the Holy Spirit will guide me as I attempt to do this. There is nothing on earth deserving the devotion of time, attention, and concern we lend ourselves to in our daily lives. Other than sharing the Gospel of Jesus Christ, leading others to Him, loving each other with the Agape love of God, growing in His grace and knowledge, and overcoming evil with good, we miss the mark in the doing of anything else. Anything outside of watching for the return of Christ, praying always, never ceasing is a waste of time. We humans are so caught up in the cares of this world that we spend way too much time striving for the worldly things, and not enough time striving for the spiritual things of God.

I encourage you to read this chapter closely, even though you will think you know most of what is being said. There are nuggets, and keys to help you understand. You must understand what I'm saying here. We have been conditioned by the world, to live in the world, by all the things in the world, making us of the world. Jesus said, "If you were of the world, the world would love his own: but because ye are not of the world, but I have chosen you out of the world, therefore the world hateth you." (John 15:19, and John 17) Jesus said, "A man's foes shall be they of his own household. He that loveth father or mother more than me is not worthy of me; and he that loveth son or daughter more than me is not worthy of me. And he that taketh not his cross, and followeth after me, is not worthy of me. He that findeth his life shall lose it; and he that loseth his life for my sake shall find it" (Matthew 10:36-39). "And everyone that hath forsaken houses, or brethren, or sisters, or father, or mother, or wife, or children, or lands, for my name's sake, shall receive a hundredfold, and shall inherit everlasting life." (Matthew 19:29)

Linda L. Evans

Don't be offended. This will make some people angry, but there is no other way to say it except just say it. We have made our families, homes, lands, etc., to be our god, our idols. Yes, it is true. Recall the story of Abram, and his son Isaac, and how God instructed Abram to offer Isaac as a sacrifice (Genesis 12:1-18).

If the truth be known, there are none, including me, that could possibly take our beautiful child to an altar, raise a knife in our hand, with intent to take our child's life. There are none that knows they hear God clear enough to follow through with such an act as this. Most would say, "Oh. I know God wouldn't have said that to me. That must be the devil."

It is true. We aren't required to give a blood sacrifice any longer, because God sacrificed His Son Jesus, as our ultimate sacrifice. His blood was and is the redemption for our souls. It is true, God would not ask you to take your child to a blazing altar and sacrifice your child: If you should hear a voice saying this, IT IS NOT GOD. However, Jesus IS asking you to give yourselves, a living sacrifice to God, in obedience without thought for your family, houses, lands, and yes, even your children and precious pets.

It isn't His intent for us to spend the time we spend on all the things in which our kids are involved, and all the things in which we are involved. There are entirely too many things taking us away from teaching our children about the Lord, and learning about Him for ourselves, "redeeming the time for the days are evil". (Eph. 5:12-21, vs. 16)

How many will put their child, or family before God in all things? You say you love God with all your heart, yet God is not first in your heart. He is not saying you are not to take care of your children, and family. He is saying, that in your heart He is not first.

Let's take a test. If the Father were to say, "Choose between Him and your little daughter, or son, or a family member". You look at your child whom you can see, you can't see God, and you weigh the choice. You have faith so you believe God is there. You believe He is who He says He is, but you just can't believe He would ask you to choose between Him and your child. So, you walk away with child in hand, saying I know that wasn't God.

Dear friend, this is exactly what Jesus has asked you to do: to choose Him over anything, anyone, and even over yourself. If you choose Him over all things in this world, you are losing your life, and in doing this you will find your life. God is asking for your willingness to walk in obedience, and to love Him before anything else. In fact, unless you love God first, you can't love anything, or anyone. Your true feelings without loving God first, will not be love, but lust, making what you lust after, an idol.

We are not to love our life unto death. I was sharing the Gospel with a young, professed Christian, family man recently. He is just beginning to write a series of books. He asked me where I think we are on God's timetable. I assured him I think Jesus is overdue in coming, and I believe He will be here soon. The young man responded by saying, "I hope not, I want to publish my books, and hopefully give my family some of the good life before Jesus comes".

Then there are those who want to go to heaven, but they don't want to die just yet. You know people like this, I'm sure. Does this sound like people who love Jesus' appearing? Does this sound like he who has this hope of Jesus appearing purifies himself? These people are so caught up in the cares of the world that they aren't even thinking about Christ coming back. We are to desire to go be with the Lord, and to always watch for His appearing in prayer, and supplication, before all things. To desire to stay here in this life is the same as saying, "I love my life". If you love your life, you will lose it.

A few years after this experience God led me in the reading of His word where Paul said, "I knew a man in Christ above fourteen years ago, (whether in the body, I cannot tell; or whether out of the body, I cannot tell: God knoweth) such an one was caught up to the third heaven. How that he was caught up into paradise, and heard unspeakable words, which it is not lawful for man to utter." (2 Corinthians12: 2-4)

Theologians have never been sure what Paul meant by this scripture. It has been said that Paul had a dream of heaven, that he was carried away in the spirit, or that he had had a vision of heaven. Based on my experience, I know Paul was raptured, or caught up into the phase of eternity that co-exist with earth. Until I read this scripture, I had nearly been made to believe that I'd had a New Age experience, and that it wasn't at all of God.

I was young in the Lord, and His ways when the experience occurred. I had gone to see a counselor at a one of the largest known churches in California. I didn't believe him when he told me my experience wasn't of God. Even in my youth as a Christian, I could see he didn't know about what he was talking. This counselor prayed I would never have this experience again. My spirit didn't bear witness with his counseling session. I went home, prayed to the Father, and He showed me the scripture about the Apostle Paul's third heaven experience. After finding, and reading the scripture about Paul's experience, I recognized it as the same experience I encountered.

I went back to that counselor and asked him why he didn't tell me about Paul going to the third heaven. He didn't even remember Paul's experience. This just goes to show, we need to know God's word for ourselves. If one is going to counsel by the scripture, one had best know them and have understanding of them.

In your Christian walk there will be people that will try to discourage you in your experiences with God. Many people think they are so close to God that if such experiences occur then why haven't they themselves experienced these phenomena? Each person has a different relationship with God. Not every person is going to experience the same things with Him. He loves us all the same but deals with everyone differently just like we do with our own children. I believe it all depends on our gifts and calling of God. In your mission you may not need the supernatural happenings about which I'm writing, but you have access to them.

God wants to deal with people in a supernatural way because that is who He is. He doesn't work this way with many people because they wouldn't see in their experiences His hand at work. I believe the average Christian has experienced God in the supernatural and has dismissed it as something that just happened without regarding God. If you don't give God the glory for it, He won't work with you in the supernatural. It is the same as the word of God falling on deaf ears or giving credit to the pizza, they ate the night before.

Do you recognize God's miracle of multiplication when you squeeze the flattened toothpaste tube, and toothpaste still comes out? What about the gas gage on your automobile registering empty, and you drive another 100 miles or more, when the norm is 30 to 40 miles? Then there is the time you broke the speed laws, speeding past a highway patrolman, and he didn't see you. How about the times you pull into the empty parking lot at the convenient store, and suddenly the parking lot fills up with other vehicles? In all these examples we see the hand of God, and His mercy, and goodness following us. However, most people chalk these examples up to coincidence, when it is the favor, and blessing of God in our life.

I would love to have that experience again, but God has not given me that right. While I was in heaven, God's bosom, I longed with all my heart to stay there. God said that wasn't possible, and He sent me back to tell of these things at the end of the age, which is now.

I have begged God to give me as much of Him as I can have, but I wouldn't suggest doing that unless you are serious and committed to the work of the ministry. To whom much is given much is required. One of the ladies in the Church made the comment, "Christianity is not for wimps." She is so right.

Our mission is to overcome evil with good, to love one another as we love ourselves, love Christ as He loves us, and to love God with our whole heart. This is the perfect will of God. When we come to know Jesus, and desire only Him in our lives, above all things, He will give us the hidden treasures of heaven. In Colossians 2:2-3 Paul writes, "That their hearts might be comforted, being knit together in love, and unto all riches of the full assurance of understanding, to the acknowledgement of the mystery of God, and of the Father, and of Christ. In whom are hid all treasures of wisdom, and knowledge".

"America Has Been Aborted. The Silent Scream"

Looking at the world, it appears the things of God have been aborted. Even in America where statistics say 91% (Perry Stone telecast 2007) of the people believe "one nation under God" should be in the pledge of allegiance. I wonder in what god do they believe: especially when it comes to abortion. The pro-abortion movement believes a fetus is not a living being until it has been born into the world. There are Christians who believe in pro-choice. This is unbelievable. If a person really knows God as Father, Jesus as Savior, and the Holy Spirit as Comforter, how in God's earth can they believe it is okay to have the choice of murdering babies.

This chapter is focused on educating people about their spirit man, where he came from, for what purpose, and where he will return. Abortion plays a large role in this chapter and is a main tactic of Satan in destroying God's creation. If Satan can destroy us before we are born into the world, he has destroyed our future. Abortion affects every person alive on the earth.

Maybe you haven't been concerned with abortion, but to God it is priority. Ask God to open your eyes to the truth, and as you read, search for the nuggets.

A fetus is not only flesh, and blood with a heartbeat, but is also a living soul, and spirit which God has created, and predestined before He placed the fetus into the womb of the woman. Some medical professions have established that a fetus is not a human being until it is born into the world. They, and many like them are convinced of this lie from Satan. (Romans 1:28)

They wouldn't even listen to Jesus Christ Himself if He were here to tell them the truth. They don't want to know the truth. If they did, they couldn't be self-serving. Here again is another example of being caught unawares, and concerned over the cares of this world, over charged with surfeiting, and drunkenness being drunk on the lies of Satan. People wouldn't listen to Jesus 2000 years ago, and they aren't going to listen to Him now. Rather than give up their selfish ways, and know the truth, they would rather condemn their souls to hell. It's a self-defense mechanism called selfishness.

I saw the film entitled, "The Silent Scream" in 1985. It is a film, filmed inside the womb while an actual abortion is being performed. When the suction tube entered the womb, the baby began to move frantically. As the tube explored the womb searching for the baby, the baby knew an intruder had entered his little world. It was obvious to the viewers; the baby was fighting for his life. The baby was confined to a small space and could not out- maneuver the tube. The tube, as it ripped the baby, limb by limb, with its powerful suction, ended the baby's life. It was a horrifying sight to witness and is etched in my memory as if it were yesterday.

Abortion is the shedding of innocent blood. The Father is not pleased, and there will be recompense. Some have tried to discredit this film, saying it was staged. I saw the film. I know it is real. Had it been staged the photographers did a good job reenacting what would happen in the womb during an actual abortion. It's the same spirit ancient Israel had in offering their children to the god Molech as sacrifice.

A couple of years ago, during a local political selection, I was speaking with a Republican candidate. I wanted to know her views on the issues. My priority at the time in voting for a candidate is where they stand on the abortion issue. This candidate, though Republican, was pro-abortion. Most people believe Republicans are pro-life, and most are. However, there are some who are not. That is why we need to know the candidate, and not just vote a straight ticket.

Her story was based on experience. She had been raped as a young woman, conceived, and had an abortion. Her defense for her actions was the psychological damage incurred from having been a rape victim and bearing a child under that duress. Folks, this is a lie from Satan. How could anyone endure the fact they murdered a baby, regardless of the circumstances involved, in the way that baby was conceived. What this woman did was choose her own way by aborting her baby. Then she didn't have to bear the pain of the rape. She said to me, "It isn't right to have to live the rape over again every time I would look at my child. I didn't want to put myself through that."

Apparently, she could live with herself having committed murder. She didn't want to bear the stigma of the shame attached to the rape and didn't want the inconvenience of a child at that time. She would be better off to admit that to herself and be healed.

It is a sad day in America, or any other country when we choose to kill a baby over enduring our own selfish ways. The woman is selfish, and she wasn't following God's way. God said, "Choose life that thou and thy seed may live". (Deuteronomy 30:1-20 (vs. 19). If this woman had known God, and His ways, she would have known He would, and will get us through these kinds of life changing problems. In this case, a precious little baby was conceived, and this woman chose her own feelings over the life of her baby. Had she known God, she would have bore the burden of her situation, and wouldn't have chosen abortion at any cost. (John 16:2-3)

You see; this is what I'm talking about. We have become a selfish nation of people going our own way and accepting the lies of Satan. He duped this woman into believing she was doing a service to herself by killing the baby. God does not accept ignorance, as an excuse to do as we please, using our liberty for an occasion of the flesh. In Satan's eyes, this baby is just one more soul that won't be around to conquer evil in the world. Ignorance is a sign of the times in which we live. Peter wrote in 2nd Peter 3:9, "That God would rather none should perish, but that all would come to the knowledge of the truth".

From my out-of-body experience, I have actual proof that a fetus is a life before it is conceived in the womb. Perhaps not the proof that will change the way the world thinks about abortion but will bear witness with those who will open their hearts to the truth. I hope the information I am supplying will cause people to re-examine their moral values concerning abortion, and perhaps have a change of heart.

Let us begin, for instance, with the invention of a product. Before an inventor can create, he must have a preconceived idea as to what he is inventing. First, there would have to be a reason, or need for the invention – second, an idea as to how the invention must operate to fulfill the need, and the assembly of the invention – third, a period of operation for testing its functioning skills – fourth, reconstituting where necessary to enhance its performance. Last, but not least, the fifth stage, deciding whether, or not the invention is worth keeping, or to be cast aside, and destroyed. If the invention, or creation does not fulfill the need, or meet the demands for which it was created, there is no purpose for its existence.

It is the world's belief that once a baby is born the pregnancy is over, and life begins. Like the invention, there are five stages to a pregnancy. These stages are not the law of nature, but an attempt to educate the ignorant of the spiritual side of pregnancy.

Stage One

Life begins before we are even conceived in our mother's womb and continues through out eternity. In Jeremiah 1:5, God spoke to Jeremiah, and said, "Before I formed thee in the belly,

I knew thee; and before thou camest forth out of the womb I sanctified thee, and I ordained thee a prophet unto the nations". Other scripture references about this are Ephesians 1:4-5, and Romans 8:29-30. These verses prove that we were someone before we were ever conceived, as we know conception. We were with God before we ever existed in this world. Tears fill my eyes when I think of the spirits sent by God to this earth to be born into the world, and someone kills them. They never got a chance to live and bring to this world their gifts God had given them to share with the world. This devastates my heart. The spirits return to heaven, but they never had a chance to live out their purpose.

First, God had a need to fulfill. His need was a longing for someone with whom to share His great love, someone in whom He could expand Himself. God is love, and love is not fulfilled until it is shared. With this thought came the formation of another thought, which transpired into you, and me. We were preconceived ideas conceived in the heart of God. Therefore, we came straight from the bosom, or heart of God. We were in His heart long before we were placed in the womb of our mothers. From His heart, He molded, and shaped us into His likeness, and laid plans for our future. Then He placed us in the womb, and thus our journey began. (Psalms 139:13-16)

Stage Two

When we were first placed in the womb of our mother, we were the heart of God from the beginning. We not only had a heart, but we were a heart even before the moment of conception. Not just any heart, I might add, but we were a piece of God's heart. Therefore, a fetus may not have any visible shape to the naked eye, but it is, nevertheless, a heart. There is no one who knows what God's heart looks like. Because we are made in the image of God, our image is spirit. A spirit can't be seen with the natural eye, or with microscopes. Therefore, when we are placed in the womb, our heart, the heart of God, can't be seen; yet, it is a heart already filled with a structured life, plans for a future, hope, and love – God's love.

One day I picked up an apple, and after examining it for worm holes, and found none, I took a bite. As I chewed, I was enjoying the deliciousness of the juice, and how sweet it tasted in my mouth. As I brought the apple toward my mouth to take another bite, I noticed something in the apple. Examining the apple closer to see what it was, I found it was a small worm. Thank goodness, it was a whole worm, and not a half worm. I had never in all my life seen anything like this before. There was a little worm; its head moving around, and half its body still inside the apple. It was wiggling, trying to get out of the hole it was in, and couldn't. I have a slight overbite, enough to keep my front upper, and bottom teeth from coming together when I bite into something. This is the only way that little worm survived, and I didn't eat him. For the first time in my life, I was glad I have an overbite. Praise God.

I shared this with a friend later, about how I examined the apple, for worm holes, and all, and found none. So how could the apple have a worm inside? I learned that day that the worm larva is on the apple blossom, and as the apple grows, the worm ends up growing inside the apple from the beginning. That means the worm has to eat its way out of the apple and doesn't come from outside in; just because your fruit doesn't have worm holes doesn't mean there are no worms in your fruit. I am willing to bet we have eaten lots of worms in our time. In the future, we should look for apples with a worm hole, meaning they have eaten their way out, and are no longer in the apple.

My point being this: Just like the apple has a worm that can't be seen, doesn't mean it isn't there. The baby in the womb that cannot be seen doesn't mean it isn't there. That is why God gave us certain signs in the body, so we could know when a child has been conceived. If a computer microchip, no larger than a quarter inch by a quarter inch can hold the entire contents of the Bible, don't you think a fetus can have its entire future programmed in it. That is what God is saying. He has programmed each one of us with a plan, hope, and a future. These are things that can't be seen with the natural eye. We must know by faith they are there, just like we can know a worm is in the apple. I like to say, "I know because God said so."

Once the heart of God is placed into the womb, the body, as we know it, begins to develop. Symbolically speaking, its development is much like that of a pearl as it develops inside the shell of an oyster. As a grain of sand embeds itself in the bed of the oyster, the oyster begins to form a crust around the particle of sand. This crust is made of a secretion from the body of the oyster. After the pearl forms, in all its beauty, it becomes a much sought-after treasure.

Inside the womb, the heart of God (which is the spirit, made in the image of God, who is spirit) becomes encased in a shell, which is the natural body. In the womb the fetus, God's heart, grows, and develops into functioning parts that will allow its intended purpose to be fulfilled. A spirit needs a body to manifest its deeds, whether good, or bad, thus the human body becomes a much desired, and sought-after treasure by Satan, and his demons. While in the womb, the breath of life, or spirit of God has become a living soul. In Genesis 2:7, it reads, "God breathed into the nostrils of man the breath of life, and man became a living soul."

In stage two, after the soul (the living, breathing, decision making part of man), and the spirit (God's heart), have been placed in the womb at conception. The womb acts symbolically as a cocoon for the body as it forms, and becomes a body of flesh, a shell if you will, in which the soul, and spirit will dwell. The shell is the body, and will shelter the soul, and spirit until the fifth stage of the pregnancy.

In the womb, the body will grow, and develop into a mechanism that will aid the soul, and spirit of that body, in fulfilling its intended purpose. The purpose of birth in the natural is to bring our spirit into the world to be tested, tried, and tempted, that we may be conformed to the perfect will of God. Had Satan, when he was in heaven with God, not fallen in iniquity, and had Adam, and Eve not fallen in disobedience, we wouldn't have to be tried and tested.

When we are born, we are born as children of wrath, and we need to be conformed to the image of Christ. God wants a people who can say, "I don't love you because I need you; I need you because I love you." Satan, Adam, and Eve went against God's commands, in following their own pernicious ways. They started out perfect in every way, until iniquity was found in them, and they were cast out of their perfect domains. Once God saw His creation had flaws in them, He made a way for us to be tested, tried, and able to make an informed decision in loving Him. He wants a people who will not rebel against Him: A people who will let Him love, and take care of them, making them perfect, and living in a perfect world. He wants us to love Him above any, and all things, not turning away from Him for idol worship.

That is the intended purpose for our soul, and spirit, to decide to come to God, through Jesus, because we love Him, and want to be with Him. He will not force you to love Him. Satan's iniquity, and Adam, and Eve's disobedience are the pathways to our souls, and spirits having a choice between life, and death. If we choose these paths, we will live in destruction, and death, which is sin. When sin enters, the protective glory of God departs.

There are teachings in the world claiming a man's soul isn't what leaves the body when a person dies. This teaching teaches that if a man became a living soul when God breathed into his nostrils, then when he dies, he becomes a dead soul. I must differ from this opinion based on my going to heaven experience. The part of me that left my natural body was the living, breathing, decision-making part of me in my spirit. The living, breathing, decision-making part of a person is the soul.

Soul is a one-word term used to describe the five senses of the body. The soul is a type of package that contains the five senses governed by the mind, which is the spirit part of man. When the soul leaves the body, the body becomes dead, having no life, but the soul is very much alive. If the soul were what God named the body, He would not have distinguished between "man", and a living soul".

First, we were a spirit sent from heaven, and then God created the body, and gave it a soul, the life of the body, and man became a living soul. Man had no soul before God breathed life into him, and he became a "living soul". Once the soul was alive, the spirit man having always been alive, had a place from which to perform an action. God breathed life into the nostrils of man, placing His spirit (God's heart) into man's natural body. His breath, or spirit became the life of the body, which gave the body movement, operating power, and the ability to reason. God called this mobility, the soul. Outside the natural body, we are spirit. Inside the natural body we are spirit, governed by a soul.

Stage Three

Once the body has been birthed from the womb the third stage begins. The natural body begins to grow and develop further. The major developments took place in the womb, but it has to learn to operate according to its construction, and characteristics. The brain functions much like a computer as a memory center commanding the body functions in reasoning, and physical activity. It is the instruction center for the body. Just as the computer is programmed to aid mankind, the brain, mind, or spirit serves as a communication, and memory system to aid the soul.

Linda L. Evans

During the third stage the spirit grows, but not in the way the body grows. The body gets larger in size from infancy to adulthood. Unlike the body, the spirit, or mind does not grow large in size, but develops in maturity by the knowledge it is fed. Paul in Romans 7:25 said, "I thank God through Jesus Christ our Lord. So then with the mind I serve the law of God; but with the flesh the law of sin." This verse explains that the mind, and the flesh can serve in two different capacities. The soul is a separate entity from the body, and the mind. It takes all three, body, soul, and spirit (mind) to operate in the natural realm. The mind, or spirit feeds the brain information needed for it to operate by passing along that information to the soul, and from the soul to the body. This is one explanation of why the vision in my natural body had limited vision when my soul was no longer present in my natural body. My soul, and spirit were in heaven, therefore, my five senses were in my body in heaven.

When I left my natural body, my body had not actually died, as we know death. For an instant the brain still functioned but had no soul, to carry out its commands. It is taught by science that the brain lives for about 10 minutes after a person passes. Therefore, my body stood motionless. Vision was the only sense my natural body had, and it could not function, as is the norm. It could only see the last thing it had the capability to see, and that was the departure of my soul, and spirit. The brain being a functioning part of the natural body allowed the last command of vision to be transmitted, but the actual sight of the eyes had been transported with my soul, and spirit, entering the spirit realm of heaven. I like to think of it as jet lag. It all happened so quickly that my brain did not have time to compute the command of death to my natural body. Therefore, my natural body was not dead in the sense that would cause it to collapse, but perhaps frozen in time. I say frozen because it had no temperature. With the life gone, the body has no heat. My life (soul and spirit), returned to my natural body so quickly that my body did not have time to die in the natural. Thus, the brain was still alive and operable.

We learn from Romans 7:9-25, that the flesh can serve, and has a will of its own in which it is governed by the powers of darkness in the world. If we reach out and partake of the tree of life, we will have the power to bring our flesh under subjection (Ephesians 6:7-18).

We must make the sole functioning performance of the body the will of God as the temple of God, or it will become Satan's abode, the temple of doom. If the bit of God's heart given to the body becomes tainted with the spots, and blemishes of sin, it is a haven for demon spirits. Demon spirits roam the earth looking for a home in which to take up residence. (Matt: 12:43-45, Luke 11:20-28)

As Christians we serve God, but in serving God, we still find our body serving the law of sin, in that the body will perform actions, influenced by the underworld, against the will of God if we allow. Christians, and unbelievers alike fall into the lust of the flesh, evidenced by the works of the flesh. This is a war between our body, and soul (Galatians 5:13-26, Ephesians 4:12-32, 2nd Corinthians 10:4-6, James 4:1-17). You've heard the goofy TV commercials, "Just say no"? There's your answer to the flesh problem. When your flesh wants to sin just say NO, and mean it, of course.

In giving Satan our will, he then has the power to work through our flesh. The demons, like vultures, are all around the body just waiting for a person to sin. They can attack the body and take up residence at the very moment God's power is denied by self-will. Vultures only feed on dead things. It stands to reason that the body, being dead in sin, will automatically attract the demon spirits. This is where oppression begins. Oppression, however, does not become possession unless a person does not repent of his sin and present his temple clean unto God. Through a genuine repentant heart, the body can again operate by God's Spirit. Just don't entertain a sinful thought. Repent of it, and cast it down immediately, or you will carry out the action of sin in your mind.

On the other hand, a similar thing occurs when a person dies. When the soul, and spirit leaves the body in death, the body is automatically empty, and void of God's Spirit. Only in death of the body, does the Spirit of God permanently depart from the body. Then God's Spirit doesn't return unless it is called back, as was in the case of Lazarus (John 12:17). Even then it is God's choice to give life. I might add here that I believe fornication causes God's Spirit to depart from the body: however, not a permanent departure. I discuss this in the chapter 9, "Sex the Devil's Advocate".

The seed is a form of life before it is planted in the ground, so is the flower once the seed has sprouted, and grown. If the seed were never planted it would be considered dead, even though it has the life of a flower dormant inside. If the seed never fulfills its purpose by becoming the flower it is the same as never having lived. Therefore, until it is planted it is dead even though it has life and will virtually, live in death for eternity. The same applies to our body.

The body is alive spiritually only by the Spirit of God dwelling inside it. If the Spirit of God is not allowed to fulfill its purpose through the body in which it dwells, the body though being dead in sin, still has life inside if the spirit is there, our purpose our seed. When the body ceases to live, the purpose (seed) will still be alive, but will not have fulfilled its intended end. If the Spirit of God departs, our spirit will never realize its purpose. Read the parable of the talents in Matthew 25.

The day my soul, and spirit left my natural body I could see through the eyes of my spiritual body. Until my soul, and spirit returned to my natural body, I could not further fulfill the purpose God placed in me. In this experience God allowed me to see through the eyes of the spirit by lifting the veil that once covered my understanding. I know that how much of our purpose we fulfill on the earth is the portion we will have in heaven. These fulfilled purposes will play a great role in the rewards we receive. You may want to stop here and reread the parable of the talents.

God intended the soul, and spirit part of man to be brought into His Kingdom to live with Him for eternity. Therefore, our major, and only objective should be, "How to get our soul, and spirit into the kingdom of God from whence it came".

As we are growing from infancy into adulthood we are fed, sheltered, and clothed by our parents as a means of survival in the world. We begin at birth, learning to satisfy the flesh in all its proposed needs, and desires. In this satisfaction, no thought is given to the soul, and spirit. While the soul, and spirit is a separate entity from the body, we cannot discount the body, in that it needs special care. The body is the womb for the soul, and spirit, and must be cared for properly. There are many ways to abuse the spirit, soul, and body. God teaches in the Bible the foods we are to eat, the cleansing of the flesh, and the laws we are to obey for our spirit, soul, and body to be pure, and holy, without spot or blemish.

Just as there is a set time of nine months in the womb during a pregnancy in the natural, God likewise, appointed man to live a certain number of days in the flesh. (Genesis 6:3, Psalms 90:10) A doctor once told my dad the human heart is constructed to last for eternity. We know, had sin not entered the world, man would have lived forever in the original body God created. Because of sin, man began to die in the flesh. Had God not sent Jesus as the Savior, man would forever be a lost species. Because sin had entered the world God had to teach us what to do in order to be saved from our sin. If man had continued, after sin, eating the foods God had supplied in the garden to Adam, and Eve, and obeying His commands, the body would still die, but would die a natural death after fulfilling God's intended purpose in us. We would just go to sleep and wake up in heaven.

As man would have it, he has abused his body by the foods he eats, and the worldly habits he has undertook in his flesh allowing sin, and corruption to abide. The combination of these elements causes a body to collapse before its time. If man abuses his body, the time of death in the natural body will come sooner than the appointed time. In this event the soul, and spirit, if saved, may not reach maturity, and will result in a premature birth into the kingdom.

Man was intended to live forever, but he partook of the tree of good, and evil. After being told by God not to touch it, or eat of it, man did it anyway, and thus, began to die. When Adam and Eve partook of the forbidden fruit, whatever it was, it was illustrative of mankind disobeying God, and partaking of the evil of the world. The apple was merely representative of the evil brought forth by Satan in his attempt to destroy the DNA of mankind – the heart of God.

Sin entered the body through the choice of the soul to serve the spirit of evil instead of the righteousness of God. Through this act of disobedience, the spirit, soul, and body began to die. Then God, who is rich in mercy, provided a way for the spirit, and soul to continue to live, and fulfill God's intended purpose, or will. Now through Jesus we can have a new body, and a renewed spirit, in place of the old, and continue to live forever.

As we grow in the natural, and are being taught the things of the world, the spirit, and soul are going to respond to these teachings. The spirit, or heart of God was placed inside the womb where God had already programmed it with its destiny. The Apostle Paul said in Romans 8:29, "For whom He (God) did foreknow, He, also did predestinate to be conformed to the image of His Son, that He might be the first born among many brethren". Although we are predestined, we still have a freedom of choice as to our destination: eternal life in death, or eternal death in life.

God in His infinite wisdom knows who will and will not accept His plan of salvation. He knows the intent of His heart in each, and every spirit that contains it, and whether, or not that spirit, after being exposed to the world, will reject Him or not. This doesn't mean that some people have a choice as to their destiny, and others don't. It means that God's plan of salvation came from the depths of His heart, and He has seen the end from the beginning for His Creation (Psalms 33:11, Isaiah 46:10, Revelation 22:13). God is the Alpha, and the Omega. Every soul that has ever lived or will live has equal opportunity to eternal life.

In Ephesians 6:12, the Apostle Paul said, "For we wrestle not against flesh, and blood, but against principalities, against powers, against the rulers of darkness of this world, against spiritual wickedness in high places." Paul is saying that when a soul, and spirit is born into the world, they, like the body, are influenced not only by food, and the environment, but also by a world we can't see with the natural eye.

If a child grows up in a lifestyle of crime, and violence, the child is likely to continue in this lifestyle throughout adulthood, whereas a child that is raised on the word of God will continue in a lifestyle of fearing (reverence, or respect) God. This is not a rule of thumb and can vary with each circumstance. Although, God did say, "Train up a child in the way he should go; and when he is old, he will not depart from it." (Proverbs 22:6) Once a child is introduced to a certain lifestyle, though he may leave the environment that produced it, a higher power can set in, and take control. This higher power is the motivating force that determines the type of person the child is to become. It is the higher powers, and principalities of which Paul spoke.

When a child has been taught the way to go, either the spirit of God, or the spirit of antichrist will lead him throughout his life (Prov. 22:6). Notice in this verse, God said, "Train up a child in the way he SHOULD go, and when he is old, he will not depart from it". If we are taught to serve God, we will not depart from that service, whereas, if we are taught to serve the world, or Satan, we will most likely continue in that service. Unless we turn from the world and accept Jesus as Savior we will not depart from evil.

After we are born into the world Satan knows he must destroy us before we learn who we are in Christ Jesus – that we are an extension of God's heart. Satan will use any device, trickery, lies, and deceit, to destroy us. He is our enemy, the thief. He is coming to steal your spirit, soul, and body: your life, God's heart. Satan doesn't want us to spend eternity with God, and since he was cast down from heaven, he wants to try, and destroy God through us. What better way to get to the Father, than through His children?

Satan was once in control of the world, until he was cast out of heaven, and man was created. God then gave dominion over the world to man, and Satan has hated man, and has been jealous over him since. Man is the very heart of God – something Satan never was, and never can be. When Satan was cast out of heaven, his main goal was to repossess the world, by destroying mankind. He did this by causing man to sin, which means to die. When man disobeyed God by listening to Satan, Satan again gained control of the world.

Being born into the world, we are born into the hands of Satan. Unless we are taught to serve God instead, we will automatically serve Satan. Adam proved that man's nature was to disobey God by making a choice to listen to Satan instead of God. Man spoiled his own heart, the heart of God, by turning to the evils of Satan through his wife Eve. In man's disobedience to God by listening to Satan, and partaking of the forbidden fruit, man exalted himself above God, the same as Satan had done before his fall.

We learn by Adams example that man's nature is to walk after the lust of the flesh, serving the master of this world. Unless the spirit, and soul of man feeds on righteousness, and the law of God, His love, creating a clean heart, and renewing a right spirit within, he will be led by the spirit of anti-Christ, eternally lost. The soul of the unsaved will be cast into the lake of fire along with his unclean spirit, to burn for eternity, with no hope of salvation, and never to receive a new body, and a life of righteousness.

Stage Four

How many times have you heard someone say, "I wish I could start over, and know what I know now?" If we continue in sin, we can start over as many times as we like, and our end will forever be the same – death. Without the knowledge, and wisdom of God, man cannot do anything right, but will do everything wrong, and evil.

It may appear that man is progressing in life through technology, knowledge, etc., but man is blinded to the truth, and can't see his failure. However, there is a way to start over, and fulfill the desire of success.

The children of Israel disobeyed the Lord, and death was to be their end, but God, who is rich in mercy, for His great love wherewith He loved them (us), made a new covenant with them (us). This covenant wiped away the sin in them (us) and gave them (us) a chance to start over giving them great success. (Ephesians 2:4, Isaiah 1:18)

Jesus is the new covenant. By accepting Him as such, we invite the Spirit of God to dwell in us, and we begin a new life. Through His forgiveness, His love, our slates are wiped clean of our disobedience to God. His forgiveness provides a way for our soul, and spirit to receive a new body, and enter God's Kingdom. Our natural bodies, dead in sin, can no longer dwell with God, but our soul still has a choice. In order to receive His forgiveness, we must be born again, or we cannot see the kingdom of God (John 3:3). When we become born again, we take on the life of Christ, by being renewed in the spirit of our minds (Eph.4: 23). In the heart of our minds (soul) is where the Spirit of God, or the spirit of anti-Christ dwells. Being born again simply put: to receive Jesus as the open door allowing us to commune with God instead of being set apart from Him.

In taking on the life, and mind of Christ, we must prepare the spirit by giving it the proper care, that it may be transformed to live in a new spiritual body and enter the kingdom of God. We cannot feed our spirits with natural food because our spirits are spiritual entities, and no flesh, and blood will enter the kingdom of God. Therefore, we must step out of the natural, and into the spiritual to find food for the spirit. To learn how to step into the spirit we must go to the word of God. In the Bible, God has provided all the information needed to learn to walk in the spirit, and not in the natural fulfilling the lust of the flesh.

I find believers, and nonbelievers alike are far too concerned with the fleshly habits of man. It is right to be cautious, but not all habits will send a soul to hell. Funk and Wagnall's' definition of habit is: An act or practice so frequently repeated as to become almost automatic: a tendency, or disposition to act consistently, or to repeat. Most believers, and nonbelievers alike get habits mixed up with lust, and they are not at all the same. Funk and Wagnall's' definition of lust is: "Sexual appetite; Excessive sexual appetite, esp., that seeking immediate or ruthless satisfaction; an overwhelming desire; a lust for power." Lust begins as a thought. Lust means desiring the wrong things.

A habit is a repeated practice. If a person, regardless of his, or her beliefs, has a habit of smoking, it doesn't mean he does not know Jesus, and is going to hell. It doesn't mean the person is not holy. Some of the finest believers I know have a smoking problem, but their Christian walk is dedicated, and sincere. I can tell you from experience that smoking has nothing to do with salvation, no more than does an excessive appetite for food.

The church is always saying a Christian should be transparent. Meaning, don't try to hide what you do in secret. The problem with this is most Christians don't know the difference in what sin is and what it isn't. If someone sees a person from the Church smoking, they are automatically labeled as having sin in their life. We don't label a fat person as having sin in their life. The reason we don't is because we are all likely to have exuberant appetites. If you don't believe me, just go to what is called "an eating" at one of the local churches, and you will see what I mean, or in some cases, you can look in the pulpit of the church. Look, I am not trying to be a Christian basher. I am trying to get the church to wake up and see sin for what it is, and what it is not. I am writing these things with the utmost love in my heart for the people of God. We are not where we should be in our Christian Walk. We all need to hear the truth. Amen?

Habits play a significant role in our testimony for Christ, but they have nothing to do with our salvation. It is why Jesus came to save our souls and spirit from death. The body is dead in sin, even in the salvation of our soul, and spirit. There is nothing we can further do, to the natural body, to cause it more harm than that which was done in the Garden of Eden when man sinned. This natural body is dead. It is only a shell encasing the soul, and spirit. However, there is one way that man can sin against his own body and cause it to be defiled. Fornication is the sin against our own body. Fornication is sexual immorality. It is lust. Lust can be an addiction too, but it's the lust in the addiction that is sin.

Habits can be detrimental to the body, in causing heart attacks, cancer, diabetes, arthritis, and most of our health issues. We have been told the foods we eat, the things we drink, and the other habits like smoking can send us to an early grave. This is the real issue to me. If we go to an early grave, we are cutting our days in fulfilling our purpose, short. Then on the other hand, can a life be cut short, or is God in control of when we leave this world? God knows when each person is departing this world. Our days are numbered.

These worldly habits can be detrimental to the body, but not to the soul, and spirit. However, Satan uses these habits as a distraction from the truth, and way to salvation. Most believers, and nonbelievers spend so much time trying to clean up the flesh, that they overlook cleaning up the spirit. Many Christians think because they don't indulge in certain habits they are sanctified, and holy. Some of these same Christians are usually lacking in the fruits of the spirit to the point of sending their own souls, and spirits to hell through condemnation, and judgment of the brethren (Matt: 23:27-33).

Christians need to realize that, by focusing their attention on the worldly habits of the flesh, they are neglecting the real problem of lust. This is another trick of Satan. Satan knows the average Bible reader is not going to take time to check the dictionary, and/or commentary for the meaning of words in the scriptures they don't understand. Words that will make them free, and will enlighten them to their spiritual condition, and knowledge of the truth. By not knowing the meaning of scripture in its entirety from the Greek, and the Hebrew a person does not learn the whole truth. This ignorance is an open door for Satan, and his demons to move in and work through a person.

The work of Satan is to control the body by works of the flesh in saturating the spirit of the mind with sin. Living in a half-truth is worse than not knowing any truth at all. In little, or no understanding of what the truth is, one can get into error, and wrong judgment, condemning oneself. It is like going to 1ˢᵗ grade and staying there.

A child learns to read, and write, maybe add, and subtract, and then tries to live their whole life with this little bit of information. It can't be done. One can't add, and subtract a multiplication problem, and one can't start a thesis with, "Dick and Jane ran up the hill. See Jane run". Give a Christian salvation, and they think they have arrived, and will not listen to wise counsel.

People need to get their minds off the flesh and concentrate on renewing the spirit of their mind. The flesh will never be cleansed before it returns to the dust of the earth. There are more people calling themselves Christians, yet spending more time praising themselves for having no habits than they spend in reading the Bible, praying, and getting right with God.

There was a man in a church I attended for, who complained about what people were wearing. I agreed with this man that women shouldn't wear revealing clothes, especially to church. However, the complaints brought by this man revealed his lust problem, and he didn't even know it was showing. This is what I'm talking about. (Matt. 7:3-5)

People who really give me the willies are the ones who say, "I'm a good person." All the while they are full of gossip, wrath, malice, un-forgiveness, selfishness, and on goes the list. Most of these people look on the people with habits, and judge them by the works of the flesh, and then labeling these habits sin. The works of the flesh will manifest the acts of sin, but these sins are without the body (Galatians 5:19-20, Matthew 25:22-28

Sin manifested itself through Adam, but sin originated from God. God didn't sin but sin was an option long before Satan used the serpent to tempt and beguile Eve. Sin is ever present but needs self-will to be empowered to operate. The soul, and spirit are what will enter heaven, not the flesh. So, clean up the heart, or mind of your spirit. The flesh is merely a component for the manifestation of sin. Paul writes in 1 Corinthians, "Every sin that a man doeth is without the body." If sin is without the body, then sin must come from within the body, or can be performed without using the body. Jesus said, "If a man looks upon a woman to lust after her he has committed adultery already in his heart (Matt. 5:28). This verse can be applied with any one of the works of the flesh. "The works of the flesh" is simply the label given to the spirit of our bad thoughts, intents of the heart. Think about what it is saying. Say the words slowly, THE 'WORKS' OF THE FLESH.

If a person's flesh appears to be clean, without habits, but his tongue is unruly, he is still in sin. The Bible tells us that if a man can tame the tongue, then he is a perfect man, and can bridle the whole body. Therefore, taming the tongue tames the body. God said, "The tongue cannot be tamed (James3:8)". Jesus' tongue was tamed. He tamed His tongue because He knew we couldn't tame ours. We are all guilty of tongue bashing.

I was talking with a woman one day who is in the holiness movement. She wears dresses, not pants, wears her hair in a bun, does not wear makeup, or jewelry, and her household does not watch TV. I think this is marvelous, and commendable. However, when I disagreed with her about clothing for women, she went off on me with such anger, and malice, I couldn't believe what I was hearing. No cursing, just extreme wrath: and the expression on her face, well, if looks could kill, I'd be dead. Poor woman couldn't see the sin in her anger, and condemnation of others. God judges the intents of the heart, not what the body is wearing. Wonder what would happen if this woman had to wear fig leaves? We expect women to dress modestly but that doesn't mean covered from the neck to the ankles. God will honor holiness but that has nothing to do with what the body is wearing.

The flesh will never come into complete subjection and is why Jesus came. We cannot keep the whole law, but we are still governed by the law. Everyone preaches grace, but still lives under law. Jesus came to teach us that keeping the law is not done through the flesh but through the spirit, or heart of man under the New Covenant, that you love one another as Christ has loved you, and love God with your whole heart. Jesus looked down from the cross and saw all the imperfections in every human who ever lived, and is going to live, and He died for us all (Romans 8). He took every sin known to mankind, unto Himself. Does anyone really have any idea how unbearable this would be? No one life can have enough pain to even come close to the suffering Jesus suffered for you, and me.

Jesus asked the Pharisees why they were so concerned with washing the outside of the dish when the inside of the dish was so filthy? He told them to first cleanse the inside, and the outside would take care of itself. By this we know that the flesh can't become clean until the spirit is cleansed.

Likewise, the tongue cannot come under subjection until the spirit is cleansed. If your flesh seems to be clean but you have an unruly tongue then your spirit is not right, and your flesh is still capable of manifesting the works of the flesh at any given moment. It is the same as being an accident just waiting to happen. You are not free from the works of the flesh they just haven't manifested themselves for a time. This lack of manifestation tricks you into thinking you are free from them, when all the while you are full of them. He who has eyes to see, and ears to hear, let him see, and hear what the Spirit is saying. Its human nature that fails us.

There are some church organizations that state in their bylaws, that people who smoke or use tobacco in any form can't become a member of the church, yet they built their entire organization on tobacco farming funds. Friends, this is condemnation, hypocrisy, and compromise. Jesus did not come to condemn, but that we may have life (John 3:17). When the spirit of God draws an individual, that person becomes a member of The Church of Jesus Christ, not an organization. Jesus came for the sinner, not the righteous.

LUST, on the other hand, is a desire that can manifest itself in the works of the flesh. In Galatians 5:17, Paul writes, "For the flesh lusteth against the spirit, and the spirit against the flesh: and these are contrary the one to the other, so that you cannot do the things that you would." Lust of the flesh affects the soul, and spirit of the mind.

Paul continues in Galatians 5:19-21 to list the works of the flesh. "Now the works of the flesh are manifest which are these; Adultery, fornication, uncleanness, lasciviousness, idolatry, witchcraft, hatred, variance, emulations, wrath, strife, seditions, heresies, envying, murders, drunkenness, revellings, and such like; of the which I tell you before as I also told you in time past, that they which do such things shall not inherit the Kingdom of God."

Anything that puts you at enmity with God is a work of the flesh, which is lust"? Notice all the above-mentioned works are things conceived in the mind. They all produce an action however the action isn't necessary in fulfilling the act. These sins are without the body. In other words, these things are sin while in the mind, and don't have to be followed by the action for it to be sin.

The familiar saying, "You are what you eat best describes this next section. Paul writes in Romans 14:23, "And he that doubteth is damned if he eats, because he eats not of faith; for whatsoever is not of faith is sin." If we walk in the lust of the flesh, we are partakers of unbelief, and doubt because we are not walking by faith in God. Sin is anything that is not of faith.

If we are not walking by faith in God, the anti-Christ spirit is still leading the spirit of our mind. If we are walking in doubt, and unbelief, we are walking in disobedience to God. Our spirits will be undernourished; a right spirit will not be formed within us, and we shall die instead of inheriting everlasting life. We perish from lack of knowledge, and without faith we cannot please God.

Before nourishing a thought, always ask yourself, "is this faith?" If it isn't, then don't think it, and don't manifest the action in your flesh.

The lusts of the flesh are foods that will feed our spirit man. If we dabble in witchcraft, commit adultery, live in hatred, and drunkenness, to name a few, the flesh will war against the spirit of our minds disallowing our spirits to mature and fulfill its intended purpose.

Whereas, if we would take hold of the tree of life and eat of the fruits of the spirit of truth, we shall live. In Galatians 5:22, Paul continues, "But the fruits of the Spirit are love, Joy, Peace, long suffering, Gentleness, Goodness, Faith, Meekness, and Temperance." When we become born again, we are to desire the fruits of the spirit, for in them happiness, and life is found. Always compare what you are thinking, saying, and doing to the fruits of the spirit. It your intentions don't line up with them, repent, and sin no more.

The tempter, that ole Satan came, and caused man to sin. Man relinquished his happiness, his life, and his place in paradise with God. Since then, man has been searching for his happiness, purpose, and life. The sorrow in it is that man will keep searching for his place never to find it unless he turns to Jesus.

Man has become what he eats. Instead of eating the fruits of the spirit in obedience to God, and being restored to the Garden, he is feeding on the lust of the flesh leading to eternal damnation for his soul, and spirit. "Dearly beloved, I beseech you as strangers, and pilgrims, abstain from fleshly lusts, which war against the soul (1 Peter 2:11". It is the desire, or lust of our hearts that either sanctify, or condemn us.

Man had strayed so far from God that there was no hope without Jesus. To be born again is to accept Jesus into ones' life by faith. This is the beginning of death for the old man, and life for the new man. By becoming born again you are acknowledging God and allowing Him to retrain your mind in the way you should go. In this you can start over, and do things the right way, God's way, the only way. It is the New Covenant, a new hope, and salvation. Salvation justifies us to receive sanctification which is a daily renewal, or process of cleansing our soul, and spirit.

To get the fruits of the spirit, food for the spirit, you must study the Bible, and desire God's Kingdom, and His righteousness before all things (Matt. 6:31-34). When one is born again one begins a new life in the spirit, and by the reading of God's word this change from the natural to the spiritual will take place. Jesus will manifest Himself to you, reprogram you, and change you into the person you were created to be. He will change you from a natural person of a carnal mind to a spiritual person having the mind of Christ, or a spirit of righteousness, if we will put into practice the new covenant. This change will not occur overnight, and some people never achieve it. They stay in first grade.

It all may seem frightening to some of you, because you may not want, or see the need to change. That is why reading the Bible is so important. As God begins to unfold the hidden treasures of the truth, found only in the scriptures, you will begin to see yourself, and others in the spiritual realm. Your eyes of understanding will be opened, and you will see yourselves as God, and everyone else sees you. As you begin to take on new understanding, your mind, or spirit will grow, and increase in God's wisdom, and knowledge. The spiritual realm is the realm we are to live in eternally. It stands to reason we want something better for ourselves there than what we have in this world. This is why we must be born again, that we can become the righteousness of Christ, and receive an inheritance in heaven, not in hell.

Jesus said in John 3:5-7, "Verily, verily, I say unto thee, except a man be born again of water, and of the spirit, he cannot enter the kingdom of God. That which is born of the flesh is flesh; and that which is born of the spirit is spirit. Marvel not that I said unto thee, ye must be born again."

Stage Five

Once one's body dies the soul, and spirit leaves the body, and by the Rapture is birthed into the kingdom of God, or hell, and damnation (2 Corinthians 5:6-10). God's Kingdom is a wonderful place where we will function spiritually in a spiritual body that can never die. The changes made in our spirit man while on earth will form the right spirit of truth that will never die. Paul writes in 1 Corinthians 15 how corruption will put on incorruption before we can enter God's Kingdom. In this chapter of Corinthians, Paul explains the resurrection of Christ, the natural body, and the spiritual body. In verses 45-46, Paul writes, "And so it is written, the first man Adam was made a living soul; the last Adam (Jesus) was made a quickening spirit. Howbeit that was not first which is spiritual, but that which was natural; and afterward that which is spiritual?"

Because of the carnal nature of man, man was destined to die. Because of Jesus, and through His righteousness, man was given another chance to live. Instead of living in ease, as was Adam's beginning, we must now live by trials, and tribulations in this natural body to learn how to live in the spirit. Living in the spirit is returning to the life of ease before the fall of man. This can only happen by learning to desire the spiritual over the natural things. Then, and only then can we know to choose life over death?

Adam was the example of death, and Jesus is the example of life. It is our duty to learn the difference and make a choice. We cannot make the right choice without knowing the truth, which is Jesus. If we continue in the natural without knowledge of the truth, we have already made the decision to die, and not live.

In the first Adam, we were made corruptible, to live in corruptible bodies of sin and death. When this body dies it is buried in the ground from whence it came. It is, in a sense being planted like the seed, that it may bring forth fruit. Jesus is the last Adam. When He returns these bodies (those who are born again) and were buried will be raised from the ground a spiritual body of flesh and bone and not flesh and blood.

In the spirit realm, as spiritual bodies having been sown in corruption, and raised in incorruption this mortality puts on Immortality. The natural body won't be raised, the spiritual body will. Just as the first natural bodies were formed from the dust of the earth, the spiritual body will come from the spiritual earth as a new, and fresh creation, changed from this present vile body into a glorious spiritual body. The natural body must die for the spiritual body to be birthed. It is like planting the seed we mentioned earlier. When the seed springs forth from the ground there is a beautiful flower in its stead full of life.

The Bible tells us that when Jesus returns, we will see Him as He is, and we will be like Him. Jesus has a spiritual, or glorified body, for flesh, and blood cannot enter the Kingdom of heaven. By this, we know, that when the dead in Christ rise at His return in the Rapture 1 Thessalonians 4:15-18, they will have glorified bodies as well as those that are alive and remain will be caught up. Those that are alive and remain will not be changed by way of the grave. They will be changed in a moment, in a twinkling of an eye, at the sound of the last trump, after the dead in Christ have risen (1 Corinthians 15:52-54).

This body will go from mortality to immortality, and the grave is swallowed up in victory. O Death where is thy sting? Death once held the dead in Christ like prisoners, but now has lost its power to sting. O grave where is thy victory? The grave has opened like doors unchained, and bursting forth the release of the sons, and daughters of God forever to dwell in the presence of God (1 Corinth. 15:55).

You now have the five stages of the birthing process, beginning with the natural, and ending with the spiritual.

When sin entered the world, God would no longer commune with man in the natural, but would only commune with him in the spirit. "But the hour cometh, and now is when the true worshippers shall worship the Father in spirit, and truth: for the Father seeketh such to worship Him. God is a Spirit, and they that worship Him must worship Him in spirit, and in truth". (John 4:23-24)

In Genesis 3:21-22, God made coats of skin, and clothed Adam, and Eve. And the Lord God said, "Behold, the man has become as one of us, to know good, and evil: and now, lest he put forth his hand, and take also of the tree of life, and eat, and live forever." Because man put forth his hand and partook of the evil in this world, he must put forth his hand and take hold of the good before he can be restored. To have the heart of God and live forever we must be retrained to overcome evil with good, having a desire to dwell with God for eternity.

God gave us a covering for our sin in the Garden made of coats of skin. Under the new covenant our covering is the grace of God by the shed blood of Jesus Christ, which isn't just a covering, but a cleanser, God's forgiveness, making our sin as though it never were. His Blood is the ATONEMENT for our sins, once and for all. We are to abide in God's grace until we are caught up to be with Him. In Philippians 3:20-21, Paul writes, "For our conversation is in heaven; from whence also we look for the Savior, the Lord Jesus Christ; Who shall change our vile body, that it may be fashioned like unto His glorious body, according to the working whereby He is able even to subdue all things unto Himself."

After the soul, and spirit is birthed into God's Kingdom life begins. Know that every time a baby is born into this world the pregnancy is not over, but just beginning. Remember the five stages of the pregnancy one must go through in order to be born into the Kingdom of God. Will you give birth to your soul, and spirit by becoming born again, and taking your place in the kingdom, or will you allow your soul, and spirit to live eternally in the lake of fire which is set aside for those who rejected their salvation in disobedience to God? The choice is yours. Your soul, and spirit is your only valuable possession, and your only means to life. Possess ye your souls, your life depends on it.

I leave you with this thought: Every man, woman, and child that has breathed the breath of life knows deep within their heart, which is the heart of God, that there is a God, and that one day the end will come. Even Satan knows this. When Jesus comes, for His own, how will you feel if you are left behind? How will you feel when you learn the truth, and there is no longer a hope or choice to be made? Right now, it doesn't register with you because you may not believe there is a choice. But when Jesus comes you will know, and then it will be too late. What will you do with your most prized possession? Will you sell it to Satan, or will you let Jesus take it to heaven where it came from, and rightfully belongs?

Your soul, and spirit is your life waiting to be birthed, and you shall be judged according to your decision. Committing your soul, and spirit to hell is aborting your own life, whereas excepting Christ is life, and birthing of the soul, and spirit. If the bit of God's heart that He gave you does not come back to Him pure, and holy, and without blemish, or spot, it will be worthless to Him, and will be cast aside, and destroyed. What works of righteousness you may have done, will be given to another because you didn't yield your members to the effectual working of righteousness. After finishing this chapter read Romans chapter 6.

This is the trump of warning for believers, and nonbelievers alike. We are living in the end of the Church age or age of Grace. According to the signs of the times, there is little time left. "Examine yourselves, whether ye be in the faith (2 Corinthians 13:5). Choose life, and look up for your redemption, Jesus Christ, draweth nigh, and is even at the door. Amen!

In my moment in Heaven the Father spoke to me that there is nothing He esteems higher than the LOVE OF LIFE. Not the love of the earthly life but our life in the Kingdom of Heaven. If we would ponder this in our heart, we would see this is who God is. He created life. He is Love, and He is Life.

CHAPTER 9

Sex, The Devil's Advocate

Above all other acts of sin, sex is the most controversial to people. We know that murder, theft, and the like are wrong, but sex has been labeled wrong, and right. The question is, "How, and when is sex wrong, and when is it right?"

Like you, in my youth I was told from as far back as I can remember not to have sex before marriage. In my mind, I always held the question, "why do we have to wait until marriage?" No one had an answer, not even the Biblical answer. When I would ask why, the answer was always the same, "If a boy really loves you, he won't ask you to have sex."

First, when we are young, the word love in the sex act didn't compute. What kids were asking was, "Why is it wrong?" Once puberty sets in, hormones raging, kids don't care if it is love, or not. They only care if they get to experience intercourse or not. So, the question of "Why is it wrong to have sex before marriage", for me, and most others, was never answered.

After becoming a committed adult Christian, I studied and prayed about this subject. The Holy Spirit began to teach me the answer to "Why we need to stay pure until marriage. Until the late 1960's, sex was a subject considered taboo in conversation. The act of sex outside of marriage was concealed. This doesn't mean it wasn't happening, it just wasn't a conversation piece the way it is today. The sexual revolution of the sixties in most societies, abolished chastity and promoted the sanction of sex outside marriage. The beautiful union between a husband, and wife has been marred by the act and idea of 'Free Love'.

The use of drugs since the early sixties has increased at an alarming rate, and its use has become widely associated with the sex act. Unwanted pregnancy has skyrocketed, and venereal diseases, leading to AIDS, and other have become incurable diseases. The moral issue of sex is no longer questioned, but is an accepted, and expected practice outside the marriage bed. It is no longer a private, intimate act between a man, and wife, but has become popular for all to do, and see. It has become filth on the pages of literature, movie screens, magazines, and television. Sex has been vicariously adopted as a free immoral agent in advertising, while nudity is widely considered an art form.

It is no wonder people are confused about the issue of sex. Teenaged girls, and boys are hopefully being told by parents not to engage in premarital affairs, but in society today there's no moral evidence encouraging chastity. Everything, it seems, encourages promiscuity. There is no rhyme, or reason given why one should practice chastity.

On the other hand, premarital relationships are encouraged, and employed on a trial basis as a test of success, or failure in future marriage. Birth control, and condoms have taken the fear out of premarital, and extramarital affairs, encouraging safe sex. With the fear of unwanted pregnancy, and disease almost eliminated, increased sexual activity is automatic, indiscriminate in age, and gender.

The general question in society today is "With the fears eliminated, wherein lays the harm in having multiple sex partners, whether heterosexual, same sex, or race?" There are no boundaries in sex where the general populous of the world is concerned.

Looking back to the fifties, and early sixties, America had stability in the workplace, home, and Church. People knew what they wanted, and were in general, satisfied in living a lifestyle of holiness. There were people that lived outside the guidelines of the Bible, but for the most part, God was a central foundation in the family. The big dusty white Bible full of colored pictures laying undisturbed on the coffee table will attest to that. We may not have opened it very much, but it was always there in plain view as a reminder of the Holiness of God.

Seriously, there was an order that doesn't exist in today's majority populace, not just an order in obeying the laws of the land, but also in obeying the laws of God's love in commitment to each other. People adhered to the holy order of the family set forth by God. Christ as head of the man, man the head of the woman, and children obeyed their parents (Ephesians chapters 5, & 6). Perhaps not total compliance, but as a rule, in most cases, commitment was practiced.

Today the world is walking in disorder, and confusion due to a lack of God's divine order of the family. In this chapter I am going to discuss:

"How, and when the devil uses sex to destroy lives"

1. Where in it is the harm
2. How, and when sex is permissible
3. Spare the rod, and spoil the child

Ezekiel 16, and 17 lays a foundation and tells the story of Jerusalem in her adultery, and fornication against God. God took Israel and fashioned her into a great Nation. She became as a beautiful chaste woman in God's eyes. He cleansed her, swaddled her, dressed her in beautiful clothes, and jewels. He made a covenant with her to love her, and she became His. In all her beauty there was none arrayed like her. Then came the day when she, in all her beauty, thought she could get along without God. She came to trust in her beauty and began to give herself out to the neighboring nations like a prostitute to every man who came along. She took the resources God had given her and used them as aids in her adultery against God.

In her adultery, not the physical sex act, but spiritual adultery, she broke her covenant with God, and began whoring after other nations. She committed fornication with the Philistines, who hated her, and were ashamed of her; with the Assyrians by making them her allies, and worshipping their gods (even then, she wasn't satisfied); and with Babylon by living by their laws and worshipping their gods. Through her fornication, she gave herself away little by little, bit by bit, until she utterly, destroyed herself. She became lonely, poor in spirit, and riches, and her people were scattered throughout the Nations of the world.

God likened her unto an adulterous wife who lives with other men instead of her own husband. He told her that she was worse than a prostitute because she did not charge for her services, but gave gifts to her lovers, bribing them to come to her. God continued to tell her that, because of her sin, she would be given to her lovers, many nations, to destroy her. But even in this, God never ceased to love Israel, and desired to save her. God told her He would see that she cease her adulteries and His fury against her would die away, then He would not be angry anymore. Because of her fornication, God allowed her lovers to use her by taking all she had. They then cast her aside to lie in her own ruins, and destruction, having nothing left of her.

In Ezekiel 18, God explains to Israel that if she would come back to Him and discontinue her fornication that He would forgive her, and she would be restored, and live. Though her forefathers had sinned, if she would obey God's laws, she would surely live. It is for man's own sins that he will die. "What", you may ask. "Doesn't the son pay for the father's sins?" No! For if the son does what is right and keeps God's laws, he shall surely live. The one who keeps God's laws; or rather walks in obedience to God's word will be rewarded for his goodness, and the wicked person for his wickedness. But if a wicked person turns away from all his sin, and begins to obey God's laws, and do what is just and right, his past sin will be forgiven, and forgotten. He shall live because of God's goodness. (Living Bible translation)

The Church today is like Israel. God made us in His image (Gen.1: 26-27), and we are one with God. He fashioned us, dressed us in fine linen, made us beautiful, made a covenant with us, and we became His. He gave us everything we need to maintain a relationship with Him and be happy. Then along comes Satan and causes us to reject God in following other gods (our own pernicious ways). We are committing spiritual adultery against God when we yield to the temptations of evil, especially in following our selfish and prideful will.

In the beginning, when God made Eve from one of Adam's ribs, He fashioned her into a helpmeet (suitable help) for Adam. God said, "Therefore, shall a man leave his father, and mother, and shall cleave unto his wife, and they shall become one flesh (Gen. 2:22)." God created man for Himself, in His image, and made woman for the man. They both were one in God, because God had made the woman from the rib of the man, which was one with God from the beginning. Here we have a three in one concept, showing how three separate things can unite becoming as one (building a triune spirit with God the Father, and Jesus the Son, by allowing the Holy Spirit to dwell in us, and orchestrate our lives.

It wasn't until after the fall of man (sin) that Adam knew his wife in the biblical sense (intercourse), and begat, or had son's and daughter's. Therefore, we know from this that sex wasn't a part of man's lifestyle before sin entered the world. Man, and woman were one in spirit with God without the act of sex. They were joined together in the Spirit of God, with God. When sin entered the world, man, and woman were cast out of the garden, separated from God in spirit. This was the first account of adultery against God. Here we see that through man's disobedience to God, he gave himself over to Satan, in spirit, soul, and body, bringing destruction upon himself, and alienating himself from God, just as Israel later did when she worshipped other gods.

Through sin, man was no longer one with God. He had given himself over to Satan through the lust of the flesh (man's desire to follow his own way, or rather Satan instead of God). After sin, sons and daughters were born into sin (Psalms 51:5). They were born into a world that had been corrupted by sin rather than a world, in the state of holiness, as it was before sin began in the Garden of Eden.

From the generations of old until this present time, sin has destroyed humanity little by little. It has become a cancer that has eaten away the memory of our oneness with God. Our minds no longer serve the Spirit of God but are controlled by the spirit of antichrist, or Satan. Satan has turned us from the selfless love of God to the me-centered, selfish love of the world. The world seeks a love that will make it happy, and secure, whereas the love of God seeks what one can do for others to make them happy, and secure.

People are always looking for happiness, moving from one relationship to another. They are searching for emotional satisfaction instead of a love rooted in commitment. In this search, they give themselves out in fornication to everyone that comes along. What they don't realize is they are becoming one flesh with each person with whom they have sexual intercourse.

Whether there is one, two, or three sex partners, they are all becoming one flesh with each of them, giving themselves away little by little, bit by bit. While giving away a part of themselves they are also receiving a part of the persons to whom they gave themselves. After multiple sex partners have been engaged, the once single, individual spirit is no longer the person they were before fornication began but is now a person of multiple spirits.

It is the reason many people are confused and disoriented in their lives. It is like multiple personalities, only these personalities have names like depression, delusions, unmerited fear, withdrawal, and in general is noted by conflicting emotions, and could be compared to schizophrenia.

According to the National Institute of Mental Health (NIMH), "Schizophrenia is a chronic, severe, and disabling brain disorder that has affected people throughout history. About one percent of Americans have this illness.

People with schizophrenia may not make sense when they talk. They may sit for hours without moving or talking. They may think they hear voices, or that others are reading their minds. Sometimes people with schizophrenia seem perfectly fine until they talk about what they are really thinking.

Families, and society are affected by schizophrenia too. Many people with schizophrenia have difficulty holding a job, or caring for themselves, so they rely on others for help.

Treatment helps relieve many symptoms of schizophrenia, but most people who have the disorder cope with symptoms throughout their lives. However, many people with schizophrenia can lead rewarding, and meaningful lives in their communities. Researchers are developing more effective medications and using new research tools to understand the causes of schizophrenia. In the years to come, this work may help prevent, and better treat the illness. (NIMH report April 2011, Internet)

Most people will not admit to having the above, mentioned personality traits, because they are usually not aware that this psychotic disorder has invaded their lives. It can act like a disease having no symptoms. It slowly invades and takes a person captive a little at a time. Then one day the original person is gone, and in their stead is a state of confusion, and having multiple spirits. Who wouldn't be confused if they were completely taken over by multiple personalities; hearing voices (the voices of the enemy), waking up one morning to find they don't know who they are, why they exist, and where they are going in life?

These are the people who often stand across a crowded room thinking everyone in the room are talking about them, assuming everyone is against them, that no one wants them, and everyone is plotting against them. Most people have experienced these emotions at least once. This is an identity crisis that has cultivated the earth and is now the onslaught in the battle between life and death, and the medical field doesn't know what causes it, how to treat it, or if it can be cured.

Since the sexual revolution of the sixties, we have seen a higher increase in psychic disorders, like ADHD in adults, Schizophrenia, Bipolar and Depression. Could it be because of the increased sexual activity, and multiple sex partners we are seeing in the masses? I believe so. Multiple spirits are being housed in one body, (remember the spirit Jesus cast into the swine? His name was legion)

According to the U S Centers for Disease Control and Prevention in the year 2007, 35% of U S high School students were currently sexually active, and 47% of U S high school students reported having had sexual intercourse.

Initial Sexual Intercourse

The average age of first sexual intercourse in the United States is 17.0 for males and 17.3 for females.[13] By the time they are high school seniors, 66% of girls and nearly 63% of boys report they have had intercourse.[14] Among younger teens, the majority claim to be virgins, and this percentage has risen over time.[15]

Surveys indicate that the majority of American teens who have had sex wish they had waited. The number of teens who waited, but wish they had not, has not been studied. Among sexually active girls, two-thirds say they didn't want to lose their virginity when they did or that they had mixed feelings about it.[16]

Sixteen percent of adults first had sex before age 15, while 15 percent abstained from sex until at least age 21.[17] The proportion of adults who first had sex before age 15 was highest for non-Hispanic blacks (28 percent) compared to 14 percent for both Mexican-Americans and non-Hispanic whites.[17] Six percent of blacks abstained from sex until age 21 or older, fewer than Mexican-Americans (17 percent) or non-Hispanic whites (15 percent).[17]

Girls will most likely lose their virginity to a boy who is 1 to 3 years older than they are. [16] According to one study, almost 14 percent of teens lose their virginity in June, the most common month.[18] The teen's home, their partner's home or a friend's house is the most common place for virginity to be lost, with 68% of teens losing their virginity in one of those three places.[18] The same study found that "the likelihood of a first sexual experience happening will increase with the number of hours a day teens spend unsupervised."[18] Other research has found that teens from non-intact homes are more than 50% more likely to have had sexual intercourse.[4][16]

Factors that correlate with teen sexual activity include:

- "Individual—having a history of sexual abuse, depression, heavy alcohol or drug use.
- Family—living in a single parent or stepparent household, living in a poor household, having parents with permissive values about sexual activity, having little supervision from parents, having siblings who are sexually active, feeling unloved, unwanted, or not respected by parents.
- Community—having friends who are sexually active, having few positive experiences at school, living in a neighborhood with poor neighborhood monitoring."[19]

Depression and emotional distress

Longitudinal research has shown a significant association between teenage sexual abstinence and mental health."[61] In a broad analysis of data from the National Longitudinal Study of Adolescent Health, researchers found that engaging in sex leaves adolescents, and especially girls, with higher levels of stress and depression.[62] "Depression, anxiety and increased stress accompany the abuse of alcohol and drugs also observed in sexually promiscuous teens."[60]

Research has found "a dramatic relationship" between sexual activity among adolescents and "multiple indicators of adolescent mental health. Compared to abstainers, membership in any of the risk clusters was associated with increased odds of depression, serious thoughts about suicide, and suicide attempts."[163] Sexually active girls are more vulnerable to depression, suicidal ideation (thinking), and suicide attempt than sexually active boys, but there is little difference between boys and girls who are not sexually active.[163] Risk for depression is "clearly elevated" for the sexually active of either gender.[163]

Doctor of adolescent medicine Meg Meeker writes, "Teenage sexual activity routinely leads to emotional turmoil and psychological distress. [Sexual permissiveness leads] to empty relationships, to feelings of self-contempt and worthlessness. All, of course, precursors to depression."[164]

This tidbit of information gives a small overview of the sexual activity beginning early in life, and that mental stability is affected by early on sexual intercourse. The above is just a portion of the research and study. You can find more information about sexual activity, at U.S. Center for Disease and Control on the Web.

I did not include homosexuality in this study though its rank will probably be on the incline in coming years among young people.

"How and When the Devil Uses Sex to Destroy Lives"

As we are growing up, our minds develop along with our bodies. If we begin to take drugs in the early teenage years, or younger, our minds are going to become impaired. By the time we reach our twenties, with continued drug use, we will have become depressed, and confused, prone to do the wrong from not caring about the right. Drugs can alter the pattern of thinking in such a way that wrong becomes right, and right becomes wrong.

While under the influence of drugs, things that we normally would not do, we will now do. For these reasons, the teen suicide rate is on the increase. Teenage drug users reach the age of adulthood, and their minds have not grown along with their bodies. Instead, their minds have become stunted. Brain cells are killed as soon as they form, and others before they form.

The mind literally begins to deteriorate with each use of a drug, or alcohol. As adults, the confused teens feel as depressed, and confused as they did when they were teens. They can't understand in their limited capacity to reason that drugs are the primary cause for their lives being miserable. Their minds have not matured, and they know of no other way of life with which to compare their adult personality.

Had they waited until they were thirty or more years old to try the drugs (not to encourage drug use, but for demonstration only) they would have known their adult personality and would have been able to see the effect that the extended use of drugs had on them. To my knowledge this is not a medical decision. I base my theory on studies from my dealings with people during years in ministry, personal experience, and spiritual revelation of scripture knowledge.

By starting the use of drugs early in life, teenagers have not yet become the person they are going to be. In their impaired way of thinking from the drugs, things will never change. Had they waited until they were grown, chances are they would have had better sense than to try drugs, though this isn't a full proof conclusion.

Assuming they do turn to drugs as an adult they would be able to see the drastic changes from drug use occurring over an extended period. They would see definite personality changes, and mood swings, whereas in their youth, their personality wasn't developed enough to see the effects, or changes between the before and after of drug use.

Sexual sin plays on one's mind in the same manner. If young people begin to have sex before they can understand the sexual relationship in a marriage, they begin in fornication to give themselves away little by little, bit by bit. Sex plays on the emotions of a person in the areas of acceptance or rejection. Premarital or extramarital sex usually ends in a state of rejection leaving a person feeling empty. This emptiness is caused by the part of themselves they gave away in that relationship, or affair. The part they gave away was their affection, and what they identify as love. When their love is rejected, and/or abused the victims feel inadequate. They suffer great loss in their lack of understanding of what love is, their ability to give love, and to receive love. It then becomes a matter of low self-esteem.

In the case of child molestation, the abuser tells the children they are loved. This love develops into a distortion of what love really is, and the child grows up believing love is the sexual act. Love cannot be found through sex, and by the time children reach adulthood they have scattered themselves in so many directions looking for love that they have nothing left of themselves.

They have given a part of themselves away with each affair until all that is left is a confused mind; they feel used up, unloved, and despondent (dejected in spirit); they become mistrusting of the opposite sex, and don't know the real value of the sexual act, or of love. This mistrust often leads to homosexual relationships.

To fulfill the need for closeness, or touch the sexual act becomes a fleshly desire which serves as an act of love, but is never complete, or fulfilling as a result. Therefore, the need for love becomes part of the sexual act instead of the sexual act becoming a part of love.

It is evident not only in the case of child abuse, but in people who come from a family that doesn't express love and caring for each other. Because family order is no longer the fashion of today's world, sex has become the number one antidote for love. It is the bodily contact, in the way of touch, that is needed to secure a feeling of love and caring in one's life. Touch is a very important part of showing love for one another, but now it goes beyond a hug, or pat on the back. Everyone is looking for approval, but few are giving that approval anymore.

Instead of hugs, and pats on the back, fathers are molesting their daughters, mothers are molesting their sons, and children are seeking approval in the bedroom, the backseat of automobiles, motels, and anywhere that it is convenient to engage in the physical contact of sexual activity. Through sex, the words of love can be expressed, and a general acceptance of each other is found. This is the beginning of destruction in the lives of millions.

I was a volunteer for eight years in a women's minimum, security prison. I met with the inmates twice a week, and conducted a program of ministry for young girls, up to elderly women. I counseled with them at length, and the stories of their childhoods would break your heart. One girl in her twenties microwaved her baby. Another girl in her early twenties came from a home where her father, and mother pimped her out in prostitution as far back as she could remember. Neither of these girls had any idea what love was all about. If they weren't being abused, or abusing, they didn't know how to function. These are only two examples of people coming from a background of drug use, and physical, sexual abuse.

In the prisons the inmates turn to each other of the same sex much of the time for affection. Some are driven to homosexuality by force, and fear, while others because they need the touch, and caressing of another human being. The one who acts the strongest are usually the most fearful. They try to cover their fear through domination, intimidation, and manipulation. If they can be in control of others, they feel strong and don't need to face their weaknesses. They don't know how to love because they never had love, so in the absence of love they harbor great fear, low self-esteem, and rejection.

By making others fear them, they do not need to face their own fears, and usually don't know they live in fear. Homosexuality results in cases like these. It doesn't mean the person, or persons are homosexual, but they turn to this lifestyle for lack of anything else, and more often than not, for the protection factor against inmate bullies.

The mind is tricky and can lead you astray if it isn't trained to do the right thing. It can make you think you are right when you are very wrong. The mind is the devil's playground.

The devil has turned love into sex in the hearts, or minds of dysfunctional children, lasting throughout their entire lives. Lives are being destroyed a little at a time in their search for love. This search will never end as long as love is being sought in all the wrong places. As the search for love in the wrong places continues fulfillment will not result. Love will become a label for attraction, passion, and self- fulfillment. Thus, love becomes a part of the sexual act of fulfilling one's own desires of the flesh, a me-centered love of selfishness. Fearful thinking leads to the need to fulfill one's own desires of love, and security, through the sex act. This is the kind of thinking Satan instills in the minds of those seeking the love they so desperately need.

When a person is starved for attention, or love Satan uses sex to destroy the correct way of rational thinking. In a lack of security, caused by a loss of the right kind of love, love becomes overbearing, jealous, mistrusting, and selfish. While harboring these kinds of personality disorders it is impossible to lead a full, productive, confident, secure life having a moral spirit, free from fear. This is how Satan uses sex to destroy lives.

"Where In It is the Harm?"

The sexual act as a part of love, on the other hand, is a selfless love, and has nothing to do with how the flesh reacts to stimulation caused by attraction, or passion for another person. This is not to say that sexual desire is not relevant to a real love relationship, but in a real love relationship it is not the predominant factor. True love for a person is based solely on "What can I do for you," instead of, "What can you do for me?" When feelings are triggered by sexual attraction, it isn't love at all, but a work of the flesh posing as love. It is a trick of Satan that causes a person to sin against his own body in fornication (premarital sex, and adultery).

The Apostle Paul tells us in 1st Corinthians 6:13, 18, and 19, "Now, the body is not for fornication, but is for the Lord, and the Lord for the body. Flee fornication, every sin that a man doeth is without the body; but he that committeth fornication, sinneth against his own body. What, know ye not that your body is the temple of the Holy Ghost, which is in you, which ye have of God, and ye are not your own?"

God made our bodies for Himself as a dwelling place for His Spirit. God being all love, can give bits of Himself (each bit containing His love), to all people, and still be all love Himself. He gives His love by His Spirit when His Spirit comes to dwell in a person. Each person, upon receiving God's love, will become complete in Him. God, being all love, gives out bits of love, and everyone including Himself remains as one whole in Him.

Through fornication a person, even in a small bit, is no longer whole, or one with God, but instead has become in part with God, or separated from God, as in a little leaven leaveneth the whole lump. Therefore, as a person sins in fornication, he/she gives away what love of God he has (the Holy Spirit), and replaces that space or emptiness, where God's love was, with fear. If sin continues, the person will eventually be filled with fear, having all manner of evil, with no love of God in the spirit of their mind, or heart.

The Bible tells us that God's prefect love casteth out all fear. Therefore, when God's perfect love no longer dwells in one's heart, the heart becomes separate, and set apart from God in Fear. The same thing happened to Adam, and Eve after they had sinned. They heard God calling them, and were afraid, and in their nakedness, hid themselves from Him. Likewise, when a person commits sexual sin, they mentally try to hide themselves from God.

This is what happens to the body when we indulge in sex sin. The love of God in us, not the love God for us, leaves us, and is replaced with fear that automatically abides in darkness, bringing with it guilt, and shame. When the love of God has departed from our hearts, evil can, and will enter our spirit through the fear. The fear turns our thinking around, and we automatically think the things of darkness, or evil instead of that which is in the light, or good. If not constrained by repentance the sin enters the mind, and separation from God and deterioration begins.

I believe this is what has happened to the people involved in pornography, and the like. They are so far removed from knowing the love of God, and the love that God has for them, that they are filled with darkness, and fear, the worldly kind of love made manifest by the lust of the flesh. This is how sex becomes the devil's advocate.

Fear produces lust, a desire, or need to fulfill the flesh, and destroys the love of God in a person, (not God's love for the person), and keeps that person from being one with God in the spirit of his, or her mind. When people are in bondage to fear, it becomes doubt, and unbelief. In this condition it is impossible to believe God. In this unbelief the person instantly becomes captive to Satan's false love through their lack of faith, which is unbelief. Without faith it is impossible to please God (Hebrews 11:6). Faith works by love. Therefore, if love is absent from the heart, so is the Holy Spirit, and so is faith. The opposite of love, and faith is fear.

A young woman having been saved after years of promiscuity once told me how she was about to engage in sex sin after salvation, and actually saw the spirit of fear. The spirit was standing next to the bed waiting, and ready to enter her body. The spirit of fear is a black entity with no physical form. This same spirit of fear is visible in any case where faith, and love is lacking. It is also the spirit present in people who are shy; bashful, angry, jealous, lonely, insecure, low self-esteem, and the like. Not all people will have second sight but just know the devil is ready and waiting by the bedside to take you over.

The harm in premarital sex, and adultery allows Satan to destroy one's faith. Without faith it is impossible to come to know God. The Bible teaches, "Everything that is not of faith is sin". If one's life is void of faith, sin is an automatic replacement. Without faith the mind comes to serve Satan through the lust of the flesh, which is a desire to do wrong instead of doing what is right. This is a spiritual law that automatically takes over when we separate ourselves from the Spirit of God. In this desire to do wrong, or lack of faith, the understanding of the mind becomes blinded to the truth of what is right, making the wrong seemingly right in our own justification process.

Because God's will to overcome evil with good, the mind becomes frustrated, and confused in its lust for doing wrong. The reason for why the confusion is there is not apparent to the recipient. The lack of knowledge in why the confusion is there and is the cause of the frustration. Though man is naturally a child of wrath, or prone to disobedience, he was not created to do wrong. It is why the mind becomes confused. In committing an act of wrong, man is going against that for which he was created. Having been created in the image of God, who can do no wrong, man was also created to do right, to fear (reverence) God, and keep His commandments. Therefore, doing wrong goes against one's created purpose, and thus causes a conflict in his, or her spirit.

Satan's job is easy, in that, he causes man to destroy himself when man chooses to separate himself from God through the act of immoral sex, or fornication. When in sex sin, a person is no longer the dwelling place, or temple of God, and therefore causes destruction to his own body by harboring a wrong spirit, a spirit of fear. God will not become one with harlots, and whoremongers, unless they turn from their wickedness, repent, return unto Him, and go and sin no more. Spiritual adultery happens today in humans the same as it did to Israel.

Most Christians will not agree with what I'm about to write, but nonetheless it is truth. When a person is young (nothing to do with age) in the Lord and has not learned the importance of serving God in all truth, and purity, the Holy Spirit still strives (contends, fights, make earnest effort) with them. He doesn't condone their sin and does not inhabit (make His home) them but doesn't leave them in it alone.

There is a point, and time in which the Spirit of God will not tolerate sin to continue without recompense. The time of reckoning is different for each person depending on where the person is in his, or her walk with the Lord. I know of people who God deals with in visions, dreams, prophecy, etc., and they are still engaged in some acts of sin. Not intentionally, but through ignorance. However, their day is coming when God will not wink at ignorance, and they will have to put away childish things.

Fornication is the way a person sins against his own body. The natural body being dead in sin has only one function, and that is to house the Spirit of God while on this earth, and perform the good, and perfect will of God. There is only one way to defile the natural body, and that is to house the filthy spirit of Satan instead of the Holy Spirit of God. Rejecting the Holy Spirit is the only unforgiveable sin and disallowing the Holy Spirit to dwell in one's body is bordering blasphemy.

If you reject the one who can save you, there is no hope for you. If you have no hope, you have no faith, and if you have no faith, you have no love. If you have no love, the Holy Spirit is not present in your heart. Therefore, fornication causes the body to be unclean by becoming one with spirits other than the Spirit of God. Thereby making the body a den for devils rather than a temple for God. In this void of the Spirit of God, the body is harmed in that it is not only dead in sin, but one's spirit is unclean as well. Fornication is the only sin against the body. The issues of the heart which comes out of the mouth is what defiles a man/woman. Defilement is not the same as fornication.

The spirit becomes defiled when it is no longer one whole spirit with God but has become one spirit with the many diverse spirits of darkness, which are present in sex sin. If the spirit becomes unclean, there will be nothing left of a person to live eternally with God. For one's spirit to be found spotless, blameless, and without wrinkle it must be filled with the Holy Spirit of God.

There is nothing else that can defile the body but that of a perverse spirit, in which case, the spirit, soul, and body is unclean, and instead of being raised incorruptible, and glorified they remain in corruption, and become fuel for the lake of fire (1 Corinthians 15).

In our search for love as a fornicator we begin to feel like a failure. Feelings of inadequacy, and rejection fill our spirit. We begin to ask ourselves, "What is wrong with me?" It appears that we have given, and given, and all anyone seems to do is take, and take. In a relationship of fornication that doesn't work out, we feel we gave our love, our most prized possession.

The problem is we gave our body as a sign of love, but real love wasn't present at all. After the affair falls through, we feel cheated, and robbed. Our body was used, our spirit was wounded, and broken, and we became hurt, and despondent, lacking God's Spirit the same as Israel when she played the harlot. We found we were left with our grief, and broken heart, having lost everything, and gained nothing, all by the giving of our body through the lust of the flesh. With each failure of romance, we begin to feel no one loves us. This is exactly what Satan wants.

As long as we feel unloved, unwanted, and looking for love in each other we will not look to God where love is found. The devil can keep us in his control this way. At the end of our search for love, we have given so much of ourselves away, that we have little of our original self- left. Our mind has now become confused, and a form of mental breakdown is evident (possibly a form of schizophrenia). In this condition people feel the need to "Find themselves." There is only one place you can find yourself, and that is in the love of God.

There are multitudes of people who believe they are reincarnated. This is just another step in the ripple effect of demon possession. There are those who believe this because under hypnosis they have regressed into what they believe to be past lives in which they have lived. They don't realize that demon spirits have lived since the beginning of time.

These same demonic spirits lived before and after the flood of Noah in the fallen angels in Genesis 6, and in their offspring after that. After the flood those drowned offspring came back as Nephilim (Giants) demon spirits. They were here in the days of the Old Testament, New Testament, and during each age, or era taken place on planet earth. All demon spirits know the time periods in which they have lived, and experienced. These demonic spirits can dominate a person, by dwelling inside them, through the open door of sin in one's life.

When a person thinks they remember living a past life, it is the demon in them that remembers. It is the demon's memories the person is experiencing. There is no such thing as reincarnation. Our minds when filled with evil, or sin are controlled by Satan. He can make a person believe just about anything if that person is yielded to him in sin. The harm in this is, without our mind having the right spirit of truth we can't serve the law of God. With our mind distorted, and nothing of ourselves left, we serve the law of sin by the lust of our flesh. In the absence of God, a person can't see the truth, and will believe a lie, wherein is the harm.

"How, and When Sex is Permissible"

God tells us in His word how to reverse the process of lust and replace it with His love. He said to be renewed in the spirit of our mind, from the washing of water, by the word. We have only to ask God to create in us a clean heart, and renew a right spirit within us, then go, and sin no more (Psalms 51). If we will come to God asking for restoration, He will restore us.

God said in Isaiah 1:18, "Though your sins be as scarlet, they shall be white as snow, though they be red like crimson, they shall be as wool."

In our state of deterioration, God begins to renew in us His love. For restoration to begin there are five categories to be viewed depending on our marital status. Keep in mind how He loved Israel in her whoredoms with the nations. He asked her to come back and let Him love her and clean her up again.

1. The Duty of the Single Person
2. The Duty of the Woman in Marriage
3. The Duty of the Man in Marriage
4. The Sex Act in Marriage
5. A Three-Fold Cord

"The Duty of the Single Person"

As we grow in God, His love begins to replace the evils of the flesh by His knowledge, and wisdom. We can't attempt to love another person until we are restored by, and to God. We must first learn how to love others with the love of God before we can love in the right way. To learn God's love, we make God the center of our life and become one in spirit with Him before we can become one with another person.

If we fall in love before the lust in our flesh is replaced with the love of God, we will be in LUST, NOT LOVE, and needing what a person can give, or satisfy in us instead of what we can give and satisfy in them. Falling in love means exactly what it implies. If we FALL in love, then we have engaged ourselves in the wrong kind of love.

It is not possible to "fall" in a case of true Agape love. Agape love will be a right, and uplifting experience, and not a fallen condition. If there is a falling action present it is a sure sign, we have fallen in lust, not love. You may think this play on words is a bit far out, and it is in a way, however it serves to make a point between a fallen condition, and an uplifting experience.

There are three questions we can ask ourselves to see if we have the love of God in us. Jesus said, (1) Do you "Love your neighbor as you love yourself; (2) Do you Love your enemy; (3) Do you hate anyone? "If you hate your brother, the love of God is not in you." If the love of God is not in you, you can't possibly love anyone including yourself; but if the love of God is in you, you are ready to love another. In loving another there are guidelines to follow. Paul writes in Ephesians the rules for holy living, and duties by which a follower of God must live. When you have learned to live by these rules, as a first nature, not a second nature, then you are ready, and free to love.

Since the beginning of time God has sealed His covenants with man by blood. The first animal sacrifice slain to clothe Adam, and Eve was the first blood sacrifice for sin. After that it became a way of life that lambs, doves, and other animals were slain, and burnt on an altar as an offering to God for the sins of mankind. The last and final sacrifice was Jesus the Lamb of God. Without the shedding of blood there is no remission for sin (Hebrews 9:22).

All through the Old Testament God uses blood to make covenants with His people. Remember when you were children, and it was customary to cut your finger, and mingle it with the blood of your friend to become blood brothers? This action constituted a covenant with your friend and was a form of a blood covenant.

God does not take His blood covenants lightly. He considers a blood covenant sacred, holy, and final. Let us look at another blood covenant that is never mentioned. It is found in the body of a female. Being a virgin when a girl marries is extremely important. Read Ezekiel chapter 16, and chapter 23 to see how important it is to God.

God has designed the female body to be able to make a blood covenant with the man she is to marry. If the female is a virgin, she will shed a small amount of blood on her wedding night as she becomes one with her husband. It is not taboo to speak of these things, for God fashioned, and designed us this way. In the shedding of blood, a covenant is made between the virgin, and her husband, and should endure until death separates them, and God blesses this union.

They have become one flesh, and it is unlawful for them to depart one from the other. In 1 Corinthians 7:2 Paul explains how God has said for a woman not to leave her husband, but if she does, she is to remain unmarried, or be reconciled to her husband. The only way God accepts divorce is in the case of adultery. Otherwise, if a man puts his wife out, he is causing her to commit adultery if she marries another while he is still alive.

In the case of a second marriage, the woman's body isn't designed to make a blood covenant twice. Based on this, one may ask, "Since God only allows a second marriage in the case of one spouse committing adultery, are multiple marriages right in the sight of the Lord?" I will address this later in the chapter, but in keeping with the blood covenant, one can see how God views the sanctity of the first marriage, and how it is to be honored with purity in the woman, and the man. Men are also to be virgins when they enter the blood covenant with their wives.

In the marriage covenant, the two espoused individuals enter a covenant with God, and with each other. The marriage covenant is binding, sacred, and holy because God is in the center of the covenant with the husband, and wife.

God's Spirit comes to dwell in the marriage, and by the union of holy matrimony, man, and wife are allowed to engage in sex, and still remain in holiness. God's Spirit abiding in the marriage of two pure individuals fills the marriage with His love by the Holy Spirit through the blood covenant. Once the blood covenant has been made, there are guidelines that must be followed if a right relationship with God is to continue. Each person in a marriage has a role, or duty to perform. The duty of the single person is to keep your body pure for the sanctity of marriage.

Linda L. Evans

"The Duty of the Woman in Marriage"

Paul writes in Ephesians 5:22, "Wives submit yourselves unto your own husbands as unto the Lord." If a woman has not learned how to be submissive unto God before she marries, she will not be submissive to her husband. "For the husband is the head of the wife, even as Christ is the head of the Church; and He is the savior of the body." In Genesis 3:16 because of Eve's sin God said to her, "I will greatly multiply thy sorrow, and thy conception; in sorrow thou shalt bring forth children, and thy desire shall be to thy husband, and he shall rule over thee (Genesis 3:16)".

Woman's punishment for sin is not only pain in childbearing but that her husband will rule (not control or possess but have the authority) over her. This is not man's rule but is God's rule (authority over mankind). In being submissive to her husband, she is still under the authority of Christ first. Wives are to submit to the husband when the two cannot reach an agreement over a matter.

If the wife, and husband are not submitted to one another in an agreement, their prayers will be hindered (1 Peter 3:7). When the wife submits to her husband, has reverence, and respect for the husband with a willing attitude, wanting to make peace, and being in submission to God, she receives honor, and power from God. In submitting to her husband, she is submitting to God through her husband. Obedience is better than sacrifice, for God honors obedience.

The head of the wife is the husband. This doesn't mean the husband is above his wife, and that she is under his feet. It means the husband has the authority in the home. This holds true whether the husband is in Christ, or not. In being submitted to an ungodly man, doesn't mean a wife has to follow her husband into sin. It means she must realize it is God to whom she is in submission. Wives are to stand beside their husband as a partner, being one flesh. Being in submission to your husband doesn't mean you have to surrender to abuse by your husband or that you can't make any decisions. Paul says in 1 Corinthians 7:11, "But if she (the wife) leaves her husband let her remain unmarried or be reconciled to her husband."

If a woman is a virgin when she marries, this makes a special bond between her, and her mate. If she is a virgin, the man holds his bride in high esteem. It is a spiritual law that can only be seen with spiritual eyes. When the blood covenant between the husband, and virgin is made the husband will always cherish his wife. Even if the marriage ends in divorce, the man will always feel a certain responsibility toward his first wife if she were a virgin when they married. If they stay together the man will forever cherish the wife and treat her as a precious gift from God. He will respect her, protect her, love her, and will lay down his life for her. It is a spiritual law put into effect by God through the blood covenant between the man and his wife when they recited their wedding vows. They vowed to love, and cherish one another, till death do they part. Then the vows are sealed by the blood covenant on their wedding night, honored, and blessed by God. This couple will live, not without trials, in blessing and happiness in the Lord.

"The Duty of the Man in Marriage"

"Likewise," as Paul continues in Ephesians 5:25, "Husbands, love your wives, even as Christ loved the church, and gave Himself for it." If a man doesn't love his wife enough to lay down his life for her, he isn't ready to be married. Laying down his life for her not only means protecting her from harm, but loving her unselfishly, unconditionally, and making her feel secure. An unselfish love is seeking what he can do for his wife to make her happy, in laying aside (or laying down his life) his ways. In laying aside his ways the husband is trusting God for the fulfillment of his own needs. The husband, in doing this, is saying, "Lord, let this cup pass from me, but nevertheless, thy will be done, not mine." 1 Peter 3:7 reads, "Likewise, ye husbands, dwell with them according to knowledge, giving honor unto the wife, as unto the weaker vessel, and as being heirs together of the grace of life that your prayers be not hindered".

Laying down his life for his wife will not be a difficult task if the man marries a virgin. When the wife is a virgin upon entering the blood covenant with the man, she will instinctively allow the man to be her head, or spiritual leader, giving the rule over her to her husband. This is a spiritual law. Spiritual laws are laws of God that supernaturally happen with no natural understanding. The only way to understand them is for the Holy Spirit to reveal them. It doesn't mean Satan can't attack this marriage, but if this couple lives by the laws of God's love, and grace, they will defeat the devil. It takes this partnership to have agreement in receiving anything of the Lord in a marriage.

It is the will of God for the husband to love the wife as Christ loved the Church, and this is how Christ loved the Church; He laid down His life for her in submitting to the will of God that the Church could be presented spotless, and without blemish.

Having the rule over the wife doesn't mean the wife is always wrong, and the husband is always right. In the case of Abraham, and Sarah, Abraham gave Sarah her way in sending Hagar, and Ismael out of the camp. Abraham did not want to do this, but he let Sarah have her way, and God upheld Sarah in this decision. God will always uphold the right, not the wrong. If the husband insists on having his way in all things, God is only going to honor him if he is right.

The reason God gave man a wife was to help man. God took Eve from Adam's side, to stand beside him, not from his feet to be trodden underfoot having no right to her own individuality in the Lord. There are many instances in the Bible where the wife was right in the sight of God, and God justified her. Man having the rule over the wife has been severally abused, and God is not pleased.

The husband must, also love his wife enough to be a spiritual leader, studying to show himself approved unto God, a workman that needeth not to be ashamed, rightly dividing the word of truth; teaching her the word of God; being an example of the Lord Jesus Christ, in all wisdom that she may be presented to God without spot, or blemish. Isn't this what Jesus did for the Church? A husband must love his wife as he loves his own body, for the way he loves her reflects how he loves himself, and God.

I knew a man once who worked the third shift. He hated working nights and would always get out of bed in a grumpy mood. He would come out of his room with a frown on his face, and a bad attitude. This man was setting the mood for his family. He was the priest of his home, and the way he presented himself was the way the family would respond. He made everyone in the household afraid to speak. Through this fear the door for Satan to enter was opened. There were always grumpy, moody, angry people in that family. Nothing ever seemed to work out for them. The atmosphere in their home was one of walking on eggshells, no peace, no happiness, no love, and having all the problems this condition brought to them.

The wife, and children are a reflection of the kind of man the husband is. If the husband is a God fearing, man, in submission to Christ, having the love of God in his heart, fulfilling his role as the head of his house, loving his wife as Christ loved the church, a balanced holy order will be established. If the husband is not in submission to God, making Christ his head, the entire family will be out of order, as the gates of hell will prevail against it. Satan, and all his demons will invade this family, and destroy it. (Matthew 12:25). Here, again a spiritual law comes into effect.

I have heard in times past a spouse will say "I love my mate, but I still need extramarital affairs, because my mate just doesn't understand me. My mate doesn't love me in the way I need to be loved." First of all, if you are one of these people, the love of God is not in you, and you are living in adultery; second, you do not even love yourself, much less your mate. How can your mate love you in the way you need if you do not know how to love yourself? If you love yourself, you are not going to sin against your own body in adultery causing your separation from the Spirit of God. How can your mate love you if you don't love your mate the way he, or she needs to be loved? It is impossible to expect from another person what you can't give to yourself, or them; it is impossible to expect from another what only God can give. How does love exist if one doesn't know how to love? Therefore, one must learn the Agape love of God before love can exist between two people, because God Is Love.

Applying the guidelines listed in Ephesians is not something learned over night. It can't be read, and laid aside, but must be studied, nurtured, and applied to one's everyday life. When this kind of love has been established in one's heart, then, and only then can there be a marriage. A marriage doesn't take place through a ceremony of flowers, people, and a church, but begins, and transpires in the hearts of the two people getting married. Paul sums it up in Ephesians 5:33, "Nevertheless, let everyone of you in particular so love his wife even as himself, and the wife see she reverence her husband."

A wife can't very well reverence her husband if he doesn't love her, as Christ loved the Church, in laying down his life for her. What woman is going to come under submission to a man that physically, and/or verbally abuses her? If a husband treats his wife as a possession instead of a partner, she is not going to be submissive. Satan came to possess. Jesus came to make the captive free. If either spouse is trying to possess the other, he, or she is the one possessed. Possession, manipulation, and control are witchcraft. A woman will not submit her body, soul, and spirit to a man she can't trust to keep her safe, respect her, and love her.

If a man tries to rule his house by his own way instead of God's way the entire family unit will collapse. A man must rule his house by the saying, "As for me and my house we will serve the Lord." If a man is following God's way, the woman should reverence the man as her head, as this is right in the Lord. In doing this she is being submissive to God just as the husband is being submissive to God when he loves his wife as Christ loved the Church. By being in submission to God, they become submitted to each other. It is not in the submitting to each other's will that sets one in God's will, but it is in the submitting to God's will that sets one in submission to the other. If both husband, and wife are following the will of God then each one's will, will be the same as God's will, and in turn the same as each other's. In this case there will be unity, and a right spirit will be formed, becoming one spirit with each other, and one with God.

"The Sex Act in Marriage"

I feel much empathy for the men, and women of today. Men don't know how to treat women, and women don't know how to treat men. There was a time when everyone knew his, or her place in a relationship. Now, a man doesn't know if he should pick up the check at dinner, and the woman doesn't know whether, or not she is to call a man for a date. Things are all mixed up, and no one seems to realize that there is a problem. Of course, if the problem were realized publicly, someone would be at fault, and would have to plead admission to guilt as to how this mix-up happened.

The problem is, the men are blaming the women, and the women are blaming the men, when in fact they both are at fault, but the man is the one who God will hold responsible. This is not to say that women will not face judgment for their sins, but that men will face a greater judgment for not taking their rightful place as a leader, and his God given responsibility as the priest of the home in submission to Christ.

When man fell from the authority of God over him, this caused a chain reaction; woman fell from her authority, which is man, and children became disobedient to parents. This simply means, when man stopped serving God, woman stopped serving man, and children stopped obeying parents. God's holy order of the family is broken, and people no longer know their place, and position in life. I believe this is why there is so much confusion in the world. Man has sold his right to reverence by the woman in giving her authority over him In this, men, and women are walking in total disobedience to God.

Man giving his authority to the woman happens in various ways, but the most common is through sex. In most cases the man will easily give his rule away to get sex. It has always been that way, is that way today, and will probably be that way tomorrow. Here again it is not the rule of thumb but is common.

It started with Adam when he was tempted by Eve to partake of the forbidden fruit. He disobeyed God and obeyed his wife. Not only did Eve yield herself to Lucifer, but also Adam gave Eve the rule over him when he went against God and gave in to her. The same happened to Samson in giving his rule to Delilah, and King David gave his rule to Bathsheba. Man is still giving his rule away to the woman. He is disobeying God by obeying his wife. Women on the other hand are doing the same thing. They are still trying to entice and take away from men the rule God has given them.

God made a woman as a helpmeet (suitable help for man) to compass a man, not to usurp authority over him. There are women in the world who consider themselves more intellectual, and more capable than men in everything. In many cases, women have come to handle the responsibilities meant for men, but this does not make them more intelligent, or superior to men. It proves that women can do exactly what God made them to do, be a helpmeet for man. God gave women a different intellect than He gave man, but not one that will make them superior to man.

If men, and women could organize their intellects, which God has given them, and use their intellect together, much would be accomplished. As it is, the battle of competition between the sexes is causing most of the problems. If the men of the world would let the women use their God given qualities in helping them, and the women would stop trying to rob men of their God given character, and responsibilities in taking care of the women, by not letting the men take care of them, the world would be a better place.

Why should a man love a woman as Christ loved the church if she is going to continue to tempt him and try to take his God given place in the world. Part of the curse that women are under is to desire the place of men; but God said that the head of the woman is the man, not the head of the man is the woman. Jesus broke the curse of the law, but He didn't do away with the holy order of the family God set forth in the beginning.

Don't get the curse of the law mixed up with the curse from original sin. Jesus fulfilled the Law of Moses, but the fact there is still pain in childbearing, snakes don't walk upright, and we still work by the sweat of our brow proves the curse from original sin still exists in the natural.

Jesus redeemed us from the curse of the law on the cross at Calvary, overcoming death, and restoring all things from death to life. He reversed the curse of original sin, but for now sin still abounds on the earth. We are made free by grace, but we won't see its fulfillment until we go to live in God's kingdom where everything will be restored back to the original state before sin. Jesus said He goes to prepare a place for us. Man has reached out, and taken of the tree of life, choosing to live and reign with Christ. Jesus is setting everything in order in heaven to receive His bride, and there will be no sin there.

God made a blood covenant with Adam, and Eve when they sinned, by killing the first animal, taking its skin, and covering Adam, and Eve's naked body. The second part of that covenant was that women would desire to rule over the man, or the place of the man. Paul is addressing this in Ephesians 5, thus more proof that the original covenant God made in the Garden is still in force.

If women were as intelligent as they think they would let the men rule. It is his God given responsibility, and nature to take care of the woman. Women have believed a lie in thinking something is wrong with a husband taking care of them. The women's lib movement consists of rebellious renegades that turned the world upside down and caused an unnatural imbalance in the Holy order of God. I believe it is right, and comely for women to work outside the home under certain circumstances, but the scales have tipped too far to the left on this one. We are now experiencing a dysfunctional world caused in part by trying to balance career, family, and marriage. I'm saddened to say, the Eves of today have, once again, fallen for the forbidden fruit trick. And they said they were different!

There will be some women who will say I'm wrong, and that's okay. They will say the devil didn't make them do it, but I beg to differ. They were offered the things of the world, and the women went to work compromising their family in order to gain material wealth.

I can only look around and see that since women joined the ranks of the employed as a means of gaining more in material wealth, alongside their husbands, the cost of living has skyrocketed from supply, and demand. Now that the women are working, two cars, a larger, nicer house, and childcare are needed, etc. Had women stayed out of the work force the cost of living would have been set on a scale of a one-income family instead of a two-income family? Perhaps then when a single mom needs to work, she could still afford to feed her family.

Once there were two-incomes, credit cards became a way to buy now, pay later, increasing the pricing index even more. Now nearly everyone needs a credit card to buy anything, and most of America, and other countries are in a pattern of robbing Peter to pay Paul. It is a matter of having good sense, or common sense. If you don't believe me just look at the American government: they are in debt up to over fourteen trillion dollars. America is bankrupt. Good sense wouldn't have allowed this to happen; however common sense may have.

While I'm talking about good sense, I remember the cliché, "At least I have common sense". People seem to be so proud to have common sense. As Christians, we shouldn't be willing to settle for common sense. Christians are children of the King, a royal priesthood, and common sense is not becoming royalty. The people living in a commonwealth, or kingdom, have towns people referred to as commoners. I believe common sense belongs to the commoners, while integrity, and good sense belong to those who govern themselves by godly integrity.

Those living in the palace should have a higher degree of intelligence from better education in God's word. God's word is filled with the highest form of knowledge, understanding, and wisdom. His word is royal sense. The next time you want to say, "At least I have common sense", don't say it too proudly. Anyone can have common sense. Of course, if you don't have the knowledge found in the word of God, with understanding, and the wisdom in how to use it, then common sense is better than no sense at all.

This is strictly an analogy used to show the way Christians should be divinely intelligent. There is no excuse for being ignorant, or common. The word of God has all the Wisdom anyone needs. Unfortunately, the governments of the world have been led by common sense and look where we are today.

What do cliché's have to do with sex? Nothing. I only used it as an example of how things can become so run of the mill common that we miss the big picture. Sometimes we need to remove ourselves from the forefront, take a few steps back, and take a good look at what is really happening. The world has progressed in technology far beyond most people's imagination of fifty years ago. It has happened so fast and is accelerating at such a pace of which no one can keep up. On this fast, moving, track we have lost sight of the moral values God has given us, and the integrity in His word. The world, Christians included, have fallen so far from God, that sin is no longer recognized.

Another cliché is, "Stop the world, I want to get off." No explanation necessary. Rapture anyone???

The way for man to have the rule (authority) God gave him is to take back what rightfully belongs to him, by developing good sense, royal sense. The way to do this is to get right with God and establish once again God's holy order of the family. If the holy order were to be established again, the entire world would fall back into order, including nature (This should make the environmentalist happy; here is their answer to preservation). This dumps a big responsibility on the men, but it is the only way out short of the return of Christ from the confusion in which the world of today lives.

If the world were in God's Holy order again marriages would begin to work instead of ending in divorce; children would begin to obey their parents instead of living in rebellion, and good would begin to overcome evil, which is the will of God. Here again is a spiritual law that must be practiced for good results. The way to get this holy order back is to pray to God. He said, "If my people who are called by my name, will humble themselves and pray, and seek my face, and turn from their wicked ways, then will I hear from heaven, and will forgive their sin, and will heal their land (2 Chronicles 7:14)". We can use this as a pattern prayer, but things have fallen too far in the world to change it. The end times are here and the falling away has begun.

When a man has established God as his head, and marries a true woman of God, they are allowed to engage in a sexual relationship. Through marriage, God allows a sexual relationship to be active in the right way. However, the Apostle Paul writes in 1 Corinthians, 7:37, "Nevertheless, he that standeth steadfast in his heart having no necessity, but hath power over his own will, and hath so decreed in his heart that he will keep his virgin, doeth well." He explains in 1 Corinthians 7:34, "There is a difference between a wife, and a virgin. The unmarried woman careth for the things of the Lord, that she may be holy both in body, and in spirit, but she that is married careth for the things of the world, how she may please her husband." Paul's statement clearly states that sex before marriage is unholy and causes the body to be unholy. (Applied to the body of Christ, spiritual adultery is unholy.)

It is better not to marry, and not to engage in sexual activity because one can serve the Lord in a better, and more efficient way than if one is married. This simply means that a single person has more time to give to serving God without distractions, whereas married people take time to consider their spouse, and how to please them. Paul continues, "Nevertheless, to avoid fornication, let every man have his own wife, and let every woman have her own husband. Let the husband render unto the wife due benevolence, and likewise also the wife unto the husband. The wife hath not power of her own body, but the husband; and likewise, also the husband hath not power of his own body, but the wife." (1 Corinthians 7:2-4)

If a person doesn't want to be married or doesn't really feel the need to have a mate it is perfectly all right. However, most people can't understand a person who is completely happy in serving the Lord without a mate. If a person is secure in their relationship with the Lord, and they don't have a necessity for anyone else in their life, leave them alone. It is natural for a person living close to the Lord, having a personal relationship, to have no need for a relationship with the opposite sex. A right relationship with God will fulfill every need.

In brief, Paul is saying that, if we can't keep from engaging in sexual activity, we must be married for sex to be in right standing with God, and for our children to be holy. If we can contain ourselves, having no need, it is better to abstain from marriage, and sex, because we can keep our minds focused on the things of God, in serving Him better, without distractions in how to please our mates. God did say in Proverbs 18:22, he that findeth a wife, findeth a good thing, and in Genesis 2:18 God said, "It is not good for man to be alone".

Next, Paul explains that the reason for marriage is to keep from committing the sin of fornication; but after marriage, the body belongs to the spouse, to do as the spouse wills. In doing so, it must be done in the right way, as not to abuse one another, but to love one another with the love of God. I believe therefore one must know the love of God before he, or she can love another. Without the love of God, it is easy to abuse the body of our mates. Without the love of God in our hearts a selfish attempt for self-gratification, which is lust, instead of love, may prevail. Always remember, that once two people become one flesh, what one does to his, or her spouse, he is doing to himself, because they are now one flesh. Don't forget that how one loves his spouse reflects how he loves himself, and God; and don't think that it isn't obvious to others how you love each other. People try to hide their faults, but it is impossible to hide ungodliness.

The act of sex joins two people together, and they become one flesh; but to experience the bonding of committed love comes through many years of marriage having a committed love for, and of God. The main goal, in life, is to stay in one spirit with God. Sex cannot bond two people with the Spirit of God. If it could, there would be no need for marriage, and fornication would not be a sin. On the other hand, sex without marriage, is a sin, and the bonding of an evil spirit is manifested in this kind of relationship. If a person is in sin, he, or she is at enmity with God. There are two kinds of spirits, right, and good, and wrong, and evil. Being at enmity with God is dwelling on the other side of right, which is wrong.

In the sex act, outside of marriage, when two people are joined together, becoming one in the flesh, there are two spirits being joined. If the one spirit is good (in the case of a Christian), and the other is evil (a sinner), the one spirit that will manifest will be that of the evil. The reason for this is God will not dwell where there is sin, and fornication is sin. If a Christian, and sinner engage in sex outside of marriage, becoming one flesh, the sin in it (adultery against God) causes the Spirit of God to depart, leaving the Christian naked of God's glory, and separated from God. To be restored the fornicator must confess his, or her sin, come to full repentance in Godly sorrow, and go, and sin no more (John 8). God still loves the fallen one, but can't commune with him, or her, because God's presence will not dwell where sin is. God's Spirit will not leave you anymore than God left Israel, but He will separate Himself from you until you realize you have become naked.

Even in marriage, a believer should not be unequally yoked together with a non-believer. In this kind of relationship one spirit will war against the other spirit, and the relationship will be a constant battle. This happens because one will be the spirit of good, the other the spirit of evil, having unlike characteristics, and being adversaries one to the other. This relationship will most likely end in divorce or result in the evil spirit reigning in both individuals. It will take a strong Christian, devoted to God, filled with the word of God to overcome the evil spirit of an unbelieving spouse. It can be done, but with much tribulation, and prayer.

Paul said in 1 Corinthians 7 that if the believer has an unbelieving spouse, and is pleased to stay with the believer, let them remain married. Paul believed the unsaved wife, or husband is sanctified through the believer, otherwise their children would be unholy, or unclean. He also believed that an unbelieving spouse is saved through the believing spouse. Paul does explain however, this is his belief based on his knowledge of God, and not something the Lord said. I believe Paul thought the unbelieving spouse is saved through the believing spouse because they are one flesh in marriage. I believe, one flesh or not, every man, woman, and child will stand before God to give an account.

To become one with another, we must become a whole within ourselves, by being united with the Spirit of God. Because God is complete, and we are in part, we must receive His Spirit to become complete. Otherwise, we are still in part, and cannot become a whole with another person. However, after marriage, if one partner does become saved, and the other does not, refer to 1 Corinthians 7 and find there is a chance that the unsaved spouse is sanctified through the one saved, because good overcomes evil. Paul said the saved women could win unsaved husbands by their upright conversation, and actions. Be encouraged, I have seen this happen.

The main fruit of the Spirit a believing spouse needs when married to an unbeliever is unconditional, sacrificial, Agape love. Being unequally yoked will bring much conflict, affliction, and need of spiritual warfare. Just remember that unconditional love cannot be hurt. In dealing with an unbeliever, the believer must keep their eyes on Jesus, and what He did on the cross for all. He was abused, afflicted, spit on, beaten, smitten, but He was able to look beyond our faults, and see our need. In Him we find the love we need, and salvation.

A believer married to an unbeliever will encounter these kinds of sorrows. In this sorrow ask yourself one question, "How can I think of myself any higher, or any better than they?" Jesus saw no difference in you before you were saved than He does the unbelieving spouse. You must do the same. You must see yourself in the condition you were when you were unsaved. By looking at your own faults, you will see you are no more deserving God's grace than the unbelieving spouse. Jesus has no respect of persons. Rather than take a chance that the unsaved spouse is sanctified through another, it would be better for the unbelieving spouse to come to God making their election sure.

In order to stay in one spirit with God, and have a sexual relationship, one must be married. This is the way God allows sex to be right and holy. In a relationship where there are two believers, joined together in holy matrimony, God's spirit blesses that marriage. In the joining together of two Godly spirits, the two become one flesh, and one spirit in God. In this kind of relationship bits of oneself is given away, but also receives back that which is given. This action forms a triune spirit, which links the two partners with the Spirit of God, thus becoming one spirit with God by the committed love of God. When one right spirit is joined to another right spirit there are no longer two separate spirits, but instead are one complete spirit with the Spirit of God. Then the couple becomes a whole, a complete unit in love with God.

In Ecclesiastes 4:9-12 the preacher is saying, "Two are better than one; because they have a good reward for their labor: for if they fall, the one will lift up his fellow; but woe to him that is alone when he falleth; for he hath not another to help him up. Again, if two lie together, then they have heat: but how can one be warm alone? And if one prevails against him, two shall withstand him; and a threefold cord is not quickly broken."

The cliché, "Two heads are better than one" is true. If men, and women could get the understanding of this, there would be less fighting among husbands, and wives, over who is going to rule. If the man has a problem, he may not be able to come up with the solution. If he shares the matter with his wife, now they have two heads working together to find a solution. This is what God wants. He wants man, and woman to work together in making decisions, and solving issues in their life's journey together. In many cases the man, and the woman have a problem with working together, and accepting the solutions each provide. This ought not to be. If the two heads joined together with the Godhead, there would be no question over finding a right solution. Then there is no battle over who is right, or wrong. With both following the Godhead all things work together for good to those who love God, in Christ Jesus, and there will only be one absolute solution to all things.

In becoming one in Spirit with God and forming a triune Spirit with God and each other a threefold cord is made. If one part of the cord becomes frayed (worn by friction) the cord loses its strength, and the frayed part will break loose. This is what happens when one of the partners in a marriage falls into sin or breaks covenant with God. The breaking of covenant can be done in any number of ways, and not just by the act of adultery in the flesh, or heart, by the husband, or wife.

Friction is caused when one marriage partner does not comply with the commandment of God in loving each other as God loves, walking in His statutes (falling into sin). For instance: If a person, married, or unmarried has an unruly tongue, and says things to purposely hurt another person, he, or she is committing murder with their tongue.

The Bible says out of the abundance of the heart the mouth speaks. If unkind, and unholy words come out of the mouth, this reflects the condition of the speaker's heart. If this heart doesn't get right with God, the person is going to continue to murder with the tongue. The sin is the friction that breaks the cord. If friction persists the cord will become frayed. With every abusive word spoken the cord becomes more frayed.

If the cord is never mended one-third part of the three-fold cord is going to snap and break away. The scripture reads that the three-fold cord is not quickly broken, depicting the longsuffering of God. It does not say it can't be broken. If, and when this strand breaks, the remaining two strands will still be intact. The only strand that cannot break is the God part of the triune cord, or spirit.

If, and when a strand breaks, the covenant relationship made with God is broken, and the marriage is defiled. The breaking of covenant is spiritual adultery against God, and against the spouse with whom the marriage covenant was made. It is the same way Israel committed adultery against God. Israel did not continue to serve God but became self-serving in serving other nations. Likewise, a spouse breaks covenant directly with God, and indirectly with the spouse when the sin of self-service (Selfishness, Pride) is committed.

Satan however uses sex as a covenant breaker, and as a diversion from God's love. The flesh is very weak when it comes to sex. Sex is a natural desire between men, and women, given by God, but to be used in the right way. Through people God's love can be multiplied in abundance. That is why He said to Noah to be fruitful, and multiply, and replenish the earth. Because sex is a natural, not spiritual desire, Satan can, very easily, persuade us to engage in sex in the wrong way if we don't know the right way. If he can get us to participate in sex without the presence of God's love, he can succeed in destroying God's love in our spirit. God did not make the body for sex. God's intended purpose for sex was to give us a way to multiply and remain in one spirit with Him outside of sin.

God made the body for Himself, a dwelling place for His Spirit. If we join ourselves together with a wrong spirit in, or out of marriage, we are making our body an unholy, and defiled temple void of a dwelling place for God. Paul said in 1 Corinthians 6, "What? Know ye not that he that is joined to a harlot is one body? For two saith he, shall be one flesh. But he that is joined to the Lord is one Spirit. What? Know ye not that your body is the temple of the Holy Ghost, which is in you, which ye have of God, and ye are not your own."

I, not the Lord, though I have the Spirit of God working in me, believe that in a marriage where both partners are believers, but one is not abiding in Christ the sex act should not be performed. First, the one who is out of fellowship with Christ, in not keeping God's commandment of love has committed spiritual adultery against God and causing the covenant breaker to become a harlot. I for one do not want to become one flesh with a harlot. Secondly, the covenant breaker would not have broken covenant with God had the love of God been in his, or her heart.

If God's love isn't present the covenant breaker will have no love present in his, or her heart for another. When the love of God is not in the heart the sex act will be performed from the lust of the flesh, which is sin. If someone does not love God, they can't possibly love anyone else. In this case, I do not feel that persons are bound to each other by marriage vows previously spoken.

If the three-fold cord is broken, it was the covenant breaker that broke away. The remaining spouse is still in covenant with God with, or without the covenant breaker. I believe this is a form of adultery overlooked by Christians. Jesus said that he allows divorce on one condition, fornication (meaning immorality of any kind), I believe this, also includes spiritual adultery. He did not say only adultery in the flesh constitutes a divorce. Spiritual adultery is spiritual death.

When a three-fold cord is broken the covenant relationship with God has been severed, and the covenant breaker is out of fellowship with God, which in turn places him, or her in spiritual adultery. I believe when a spouse commits spiritual adultery, and their marriage ends in divorce, a person is free to marry again without consequence of being in sin. Committing adultery is as easy as looking upon a woman, or man to lust after them in one's heart (Matthew 5:28). On the other hand, if the covenant breaker repents, and gets right with God, I see no reason why a marriage can't be restored when two agree touching the matter.

Being in God's will, whether single, or married should be the singular motive, and reason for our lives. It is the bond of God's love that joins us in the Spirit with Him, and with each other. It is through Jesus that we all are made one spirit with God. In loving Him and committing our lives to Him we grow in His love, and righteousness.

In His love we find committed love instead of a selfish love. Committed love is the kind of love for which everyone is looking and cannot be found in the love of the world. It can only be found in God. That is why infidelity can surface in a marriage without God. The love of God isn't there to keep Satan from causing one to fall in the lust of adultery.

Like marriage, adultery is not only committed by the act but is committed by the thought of it in the heart (Matthew 5:28). A marriage that isn't built on the foundation of God's love cannot be void of lustful thoughts. If God's love isn't in one's heart, fear, and evil are there, and where fear, and evil are, lust abides. Therefore, sex is only permitted in a marriage by staying in one Spirit with God, having a committed selfless Agape love of God established in one's heart.

"Spare the Rod, Spoil the Child"

Let us reverse the curse of the sex stronghold Satan has used to destroy the love of God in mankind. To do this we must reestablish the solid foundation of moral character by returning to the adage of "spare the rod spoil the child (Proverbs 13:23)." The problems of spiritual seduction are surfacing because parents have failed in teaching children obedience to God's laws.

A committed love will never manifest in our hearts if the word of God has not been taught and applied to our lives. I believe that is why it is important to bring our children up in the admonition of the Lord correcting them by His word with a rod. THE ROD IS THE RULES AND REGULATIONS OF GOD'S LAWS ADMINISTERED TO THE BUTTOCKS WHEN CHILDREN DO NOT WANT TO LISTEN TO THEM. However, we cannot discipline our children if we cannot discipline ourselves.

Therefore, we are to be Godly parents, and are to set rules, and regulations in the home that will comply with the laws of God. Parents be careful when administering correction. Parents untrained in the word of God, without the love of God in their heart can abuse their children by using the rod of correction in the wrong way. This kind of correction in the long run will prove to be harmful to the child's mental development.

Children will not want to come under subjection to rules, therefore disciplinary action must be taken. If children are not made to learn the laws of God, bringing their body, soul, and spirit, into subjection, they will walk in disobedience, not only to their parents, but also to God; being unruly in all manner of evil. Adam, and Eve broke God's rule, the one and only rule they were to obey, and God disciplined them by doing exactly what He said He would do. He told them, because of their disobedience, He would cast them out of the Garden, and He did.

If we love our children, we will set a standard for them according to the standards of God, seeing to it that they abide by the rules of these standards. If we do not set these standards in our homes, we are sending our children's soul to hell (Proverbs 23:13-14), and we will be accountable for them before God. In not correcting our children we are saying to them, "I DON'T LOVE YOU ENOUGH TO TEACH YOU HOW TO OBTAIN ETERNAL LIFE".

Unless we learn obedience, and bring our spirit, soul, and body into subjection by the renewing of our minds, we will die a sinner's death. That is why our children are lacking in love and seeking love in the things of the world.

God wrote His laws in our hearts. If we are not admonished when we go against these laws something happens in our spirits that causes us to feel unloved, and unwanted. We have God's laws in our hearts as a reference for our spirits. When the laws, or feelings of our spirits do not match up with the laws in our hearts our hearts become wounded or confused. We may not know the word of God in the sense that we remember it word for word, but it is there written in our hearts as a spiritual guide for our lives. When these laws are violated, our heart becomes confused even though the awareness of "Why" is not evident. In this confusion is where Satan begins to work.

A child knows in their heart when they are loved or cared for by another person. When someone says, "I love you", this love will be shown by loving deeds. For instance: If a child becomes involved in a situation that most parents are against, the first thing their peers asked is, "What will your parents say?" If the child's response is "Oh, they don't care" it's a sure sign the parents really don't care. The child may say this with a tone of aloofness, but his heart knows that his parents really don't care; for if they cared they would correct him, and discipline him in the way he should go. In this lack of caring, and correction the child's spirit knows that his parent's lack of concern is really a lack of love for him. Then in the knowledge of his parents not loving him he begins to search for love, and care in all the wrong places; trying anything that will fill the void of love in his life. In his search for love, he doesn't realize it is love for which he is searching. He only knows that he is dissatisfied with life, and begins searching for satisfaction in anything, or anyone.

Here is where Satan gets a stronghold in one's life. Usually resulting in the practice of, fornication, alcohol, drug abuse, materialism, self-centeredness (selfishness), slothfulness, all the things of the world, and having, in general, no respect for parents, others, or themselves. If love is not taught, shown, and practiced, how can one know that it is the lack of love that is causing all the problems?

In many cases people use the term, "I love you', very lightly. It is said with the mouth to mean, "I love you", but really means, "I need you for what you can do for me" (this is selfish lust, not love). Love is, needing someone because you love him or her. This is where many fail the test of true love. To love the correct way can only be learned through the discipline of God's word.

For example, I know a woman who does not love her children equally. She confesses love according to what her children do for her. She doesn't realize that a love relationship isn't based on what one can do for her. She doesn't give to her children loving words of encouragement, tenderness, caring, and a mother's sacrificial love. She is only proud of the one who is doing something for her at the time, or when one excels in something about which she can brag to her friends.

The love of God is found through the disciplinary actions of God's laws of love. If a child is not taught to respect God's laws of love, he will not learn to love, and respect others, or himself. The lack of respect is spiritual suicide, and is a natural breeding ground for confusion, and sin. A lack of respect goes against the very nature of God, in whose image we are created. Though we are created in His image, respect (reverence) does not come naturally. Jesus is that image, and if we alienate ourselves from Him, by not reading, and studying the Bible, which is the life of Christ, we are seducing our own spirit.

The mother that doesn't love her children equally, has a lack of respect for herself. Her parents did not raise her in respect, and love, and now she is walking in confusion, lack of respect for herself, and everyone else. She expects piety, but doesn't understand the spiritual law of sowing, and reaping. Since she did not sow into the lives of her children when they were young, the children in adulthood don't have the fruits to give her.

If we allow our children to do as they please, in word, and deed they are by nature going to do, and say all the wrong things, because they are by nature inclined to choose the wrong. In not correcting our children we are causing them to grow up, living a lifestyle of abusing others in word, and in deed to get their own way, fulfilling their own selfish desires, or lust of the flesh. If one does not love himself, he is going to abuse his own spirit, defiling it with sin. One of God's commandments is to love others as you love yourself. If you do not love yourselves you are going to sin against, not only yourself, but also against others, and God. The penalty for sin is death, not eternal life.

In allowing our children to disobey us, and/or commit acts of sin without taking disciplinary action, we are saying to them, "I don't know how to love myself, much less love you, or teach you how to love". If we do not discipline ourselves, and our children by the word of God, we do not know how to love, and if we do not know how to love, we do not know God; for God is love, and He corrects the ones He loves (Revelation 3:19). God's correction gives Eternal Life.

Without correction in our lives, we are going to automatically commit spiritual adultery, like Israel did, against ourselves, and God. Without knowledge of the love of God we are going to look for love in all the wrong places following Israel's example. Without the disciplinary action of God's word, we are going to sin against our own body through our natural desire for affection, and love, giving ourselves over to our lovers (Satan), and becoming harlots.

As much as possible we should desire God to restore His divine, and holy order of the family. People must learn to desire the law of God's love in their heart and strive to walk by nature in obedience to God's law of love. Once the law of God's love is rooted into the heart the person is no longer in bondage to the law but is walking in the liberty of God's grace by nature. This nature can only be found in the mind of Christ because He is the only one that has ever fulfilled the law. When the new nature is developed there will be no problem in laying down, for others, one's life. Whether husband, wife, father, mother, sister, brother, children, friend, or foe, without the nature of God's love in the heart the commandment for love can't be fulfilled. In sparing the rod of correction, the child becomes spoiled, and his soul is bound for hell.

Sex isn't the only way a body can harbor evil spirits. By engaging in sex sin, we are taking the beautiful gift God gave us, and are destroying ourselves bit by bit by scattering this gift in every direction becoming one flesh with many. This includes marriage that isn't sanctified by God, such as homosexuality. Love not for what one can do for you but love because God loved you first. Let God give back all that you have given away of yourself. Learn of His love so that you can have the right spirit working in you. Loving unconditionally is the perfect will of God.

Measuring love by anything other than by God's word, you have fallen in love with the world, which is enmity against God. Love is not accusing, abusing, or using, but the fusing together, becoming one with God, and each other. Sex can be performed without love, and love can be performed without sex, but sex without the love of God is lust and is the devil's advocate.

CHAPTER 10

The Enemy's Camp of Fallen Angels

There are many things that border on our lack of knowledge, determining the status of our health, finances, destiny, and our way in this life. God said His people parish from lack of knowledge. In this chapter, we will explore one of the major ways people can be destroyed by lack of knowledge.

No matter how long a person has been a Christian, Satan's aim is still the same. He targets you with his arrows of deception and is relentless in not giving up on you. His intent is to kill, steal, and destroy. He will attack you in your health, finances, family members, and anywhere you will allow him a stronghold in your life.

This chapter is dealing with discerning of spirits. It is a true story. It is a story that continues to happen in many churches across America and needs to be addressed. Several of the characters in this story have passed on, but there are those who are alive and remain, and will recognize the contents, and characters in this writing. The names have been omitted to protect the innocent.

The Holy Spirit spoke one evening and told me to prepare myself for moving. I didn't know exactly what he had in mind, but I did as He said. I can't remember exactly when I had the vision of New Jerusalem, but I believe it was in the late part of 1986, or the early part of 1987. It was because of this vision that I made my decision to give my all to God. I had made a prior commitment to serve God, but my decision now was to say, "Here I am Lord, send me." God had given me a choice to either serve Him to the fullest or stay where I was and limit Him. 2 Kings 7:3 came to mind, "Why sit we here until we die?"

In February 1987, I sold all my belongings, and moved in with a friend. I kept enough belongings, and furniture to aid me, if I were to set up house somewhere else. At all costs I had chosen to serve God. and was willing to go wherever He would send me. Yet, He had not told me where He would be sending me. I just wanted to be ready to go as soon as He let me know my destination.

On March 31st, 1987, God told me to attend a Women's Aglow meeting being held the following Saturday, April 4th. I had been invited by a friend to attend these meetings several times before, but I wasn't interested. I had never had much interest in getting involved with women's organizations, and I didn't plan to start now. When my friend invited me to attend the April 4th meeting, I declined. After declining I was instructed by Father God to accept the invitation.

In that meeting, I learned when, and where God wanted to send me. The speaker was a lady evangelist from North Carolina. Ironically, I thought, God had sent a speaker from the state in which I had lived most of my life. Having never seen a female preacher before in person, I listened with enthusiasm. As she began to speak, she told how God had awakened her at 5:30 a.m. that morning and changed her sermon. When she began to deliver her message, she spoke on 1 Kings 16 and 17; the exact scriptures God had spoken to me a few days prior. This was confirmation.

The evangelist continued to speak. She spoke everything that God had spoken to me, nothing left out, and I began to weep uncontrollably. My spirit was pouring out tears of amazement, cleansing, and complete surrender. For the first time in my life, I knew who I was, and understood the transformation that was occurring in my spirit. In that meeting God's mercy and love became a revelation to me by the knowledge of His magnificence and greatness filling my heart.

God had told me previously, and in this hour that no matter where He would send me, if necessary, He would send the ravens to feed me. He told me that as I remained faithful, and true His hand would guide me and care for me in supplying all my needs, and He would never reject me. He has remained true to His word and continues to this day to fulfill His promises to me.

After the meeting, I went home, and began immediately to prepare myself for moving. I had to sell the remainder of my possessions because God was sending me 2500 miles away to begin my full-time service for Him. My friends, the few I had left, thought I was crazy and had lost my mind. They weren't Christians, and most of them couldn't understand what had happened to me. They had known me through many situations, as a friend, business owner, mother, wife, and someone that liked to have fun in the beggarly elements of the world. They knew me when I was part of the world and knew that God had made a change in my life, but to them it seemed a change for the worse. They couldn't understand that I had come to love God more than life itself; that He had become my reason for living, and my reason for everything; that He had become the lover of my soul. I had come to know God as the joy of my life, and my salvation.

I planned a garage sale to finish selling the things I couldn't take with me on my journey. The only thing I had left at the end of the sale was a sofa, and a loveseat. That night I had a dream. In the dream I was at my grandmother's house in South Carolina. The house had not been in my family since the death of my grandparents many years before, but in the dream, I was in that house. Suddenly a fierce, and mighty wind arose, and began to fill the house. I knew a terrible storm was brewing, so I ran to close the windows. One window in the back room would not close. It seemed to be stuck. Seeing my effort to close it was futile, I ran to close the backdoor. As I tried to close the door, the wind became so fierce that it ripped the backdoor off its hinges and carried it away.

When this happened, I grabbed hold of the doorframe to keep myself steady. The wind was violent as it whipped through my long hair. I was hesitant in letting go of the doorframe for fear I would be blown away like the door. While fighting to hang on I looked across the way and saw the most powerful tornado ever known. It was so large that it covered the entire sky. Then in front of the storm, I saw what appeared as swords of fire falling from heaven. Only the fire never touched the ground but stayed in a huddle in midair as it moved in front of the storm. The whirlwind of fire was a pillar of fire. I know now this was God going before the storm. After seeing all this, I breathed a breath of hopelessness.

Letting go of my support, I hurried to get away. It was such a great storm that I knew there was no hope of survival. Feelings of fear were unnecessary. In a storm of this size, hope was the only factor, and hope was lost. Nothing could live through a storm of this magnitude. There was no place to go for safety, but to take shelter under the house. There I found a sofa, on which I laid down, and covered myself with a comforter I had found. In waiting for the storm to hit, I fell asleep in my dream.

When I woke up, in my dream, much to my surprise, the storm had blown over, and I had not been harmed. Under the house with me, were other people who had sought safety. Among these was a girl who had long dark hair, and she was holding a baby girl, about the age of six months old. She held the baby in a way that allowed the baby to face me. I could see her face clearly. I recognized the baby though I had not seen her before. Walking over to the girl, and pointing at the baby, I said, "Oh, you're the baby." Why I had said this, I didn't know. It was all very strange.

The next morning, I woke up early, and I remembered my dream from the night before. It was a dream in which I knew God had given me. I couldn't explain it, but I knew it was prophetic somehow. Not all dreams are from God, but the ones that are, leave no doubt.

Later that day, someone phoned to see if I still had my sofa set for sale. I told them yes and made arrangement for them to come and see it again. They had seen it at the garage sale but had not yet decided to purchase it. In selling my belongings, I had let God guide me in pricing them. In the case of the sofa set, I had priced it $325.00. When the young couple that wanted to see the set arrived, I went out to meet them.

They got out of the car and walked into the yard. The man was carrying a baby. I saw the child and asked if I could hold her. The man gave the baby to his wife, and I thought by this action, they didn't really want a stranger holding their child. The wife turned the baby toward me and held her out for me to take. In that moment, I looked at the baby, pointed at her and said, "Oh, you're the baby." To my surprise the girl, and the baby were the same as in my dream. The girl had long, dark hair, and the baby was a girl six months of age. It was the same baby. I had seen her face clearly in my dream, and I was looking at her now in real time.

I told them about my dream and witnessed to them of the Lord Jesus. They offered me $275.00 for the sofa set, and I knew this was God's way of telling me to accept the offer. They were young and didn't have much money. I helped them move the sofa to their home and visited with them for a little while. They felt they were blessed to get the furniture because they knew it came from God. This is how the Holy Spirit guides people to help one another. He will always send help in time of need. I needed to sell the furniture, and the couple needed it.

The other part of my dream held another significance. After the storm in my dream had passed, there were houses that had been destroyed on the same street as my grandmother's house. The Lord spoke to me to go and tell of the dream.

On May 17th, 1987, having said my good-byes, I set out on my journey across America. Little did I know what the future would hold? I traveled through fourteen states and claimed everyone for the Lord. He had told me that wherever my feet shall tread, I should possess the land. I believed Him and did just that. I got out of my car in every state and claimed it for Jesus.

Having arrived on the East coast, I went first to South Carolina to warn the people in my hometown about the dream and coming storm. These were God's instructions. I was afraid to go and tell the people but was more afraid of what might happen if I didn't. I recalled the story of Jonah at this point. On the other hand, I wanted to be obedient to God.

The Holy Spirit told me the people would not listen, but to be not dismayed. "Oh, this really made things better." Not only did I have to go and see people I had not seen for twenty-five years, but I had to tell them to repent, and prepare for a storm. As if this wasn't a difficult enough task, God said they would not listen.

He was right. I was not received, and neither was the prophecy. I couldn't help but feel sad for what was about to come. I knew from the dream that homes, and lives would be destroyed. I had seen all this in a vision and had traveled 2500 miles to sound the trump of warning. It was two years later that hurricane Hugo passed through this little town, and homes were destroyed. It was the worst storm that had ever come that far inland, and many were caught off guard, and overtaken as a thief in the night.

I later had a dream of one of the houses I had seen destroyed. It had been rebuilt having a different siding than before the storm. Months after Hugo had passed through this town, I drove down the street where the house was located. It had been rebuilt, and the new siding was as I had seen in my dream.

God works through dreams, visions, prophecy, His word, and His voice. He is looking for obedience in His people. This dream illustrates the goodness of God, in how He goes before the storms in life, and protects us in our obedience to Him. He is gentle in His approach, and never gives us a task we can't perform.

Continuing to travel I at last arrived at my destination. I was on fire with enthusiasm, and ready to do a great work for God. I drove into the once dirt driveway that led to a summer camp. The camp holds two and one half, months of summer camp meetings annually. That year, they were starting a one-year Bible School. The courses of study were Old Testament Survey, New Testament Survey, Homiletics, Foreign Missionary training, and church ministry in music, teaching, and other administrations of the church. Bible School was to start at the end of October that year.

The camp held three services daily, seven days a week, from June, and ending the first week of September. The first summer of camp meeting was great in many ways. It was exciting, and new. The praise, and worship services taught freedom in spiritual praise, and worship as well as dancing before the Lord. Unless you have experienced hundreds of people singing, dancing, and praising God under the same roof, you can't imagine the spiritual lift it gives.

Having a zeal for God, making new friends with people who came from all over the world, and literally caught up in the joy of this new experience, I let questionable things slide by; I didn't forget them, I just put them on the shelf for safekeeping. The first thing I noticed was how miserable the camp family worker's and staff seemed to be. These people lived at camp, year-round maintaining the grounds, tape ministry, administrative duties, and worked foreign missions. During camp meeting, the camp family all sat together on the large platform front and center facing the congregation in a large tabernacle. The tabernacle was where worship services were held.

The leaders of the camp, and the laborers that sat on the platform wore expressions of bleakness, dismay, discouragement, weariness, and altogether, unhappiness. I didn't understand where their joy was. I thought Christians were happy, peace loving creatures of God. I hadn't known many Christians before, but I knew the joy I felt, and I assumed all Christians felt the same: especially in this place, where thousands came to be ministered too. This camp should have been the epitome of Joy.

The next thing that stood out to me was one of the owners of the camp. In the first evening service he made the statement, "The first thing the devil will do is say you shouldn't be here." For some reason, this sounded odd to me. I didn't think it was wrong to say it, but discernment pricked my spirit. Rather than dwell on this, I pushed it aside, and continued to enjoy the service. You must understand. This was my first real encounter with The Church, other Christians, after knowing the one true God in a personal relationship.

Next, I noticed how the services were conducted. In all the services, trash cans nearly two feet high, were used to collect the evening offerings. There was nothing wrong with this either, for the crowd attending was quite large. However, the hour and a half, collections disturbed my spirit. During the offering the spokesman would say, "God has told me there are a certain number of people here to give a certain amount of money." The number of people, and the amount of money varied from night to night. I have since learned this is not uncommon during camp meetings. Here, again I wasn't sure what was wrong, but my spirit discerned a wrong. I just couldn't see it clearly, so again, I pushed it aside, and continued in my excitement.

After a few weeks, I noticed how badly the staff, camp family, and the owners were treating the visitors. There was jealously, strife, anger, malice, wrath, and bitterness, directed toward me, and the others. It was difficult for me to understand what was happening. There we were, financial supporters, and we were being treated like the enemy. It was like biting the hand that feeds you. There were women on the platform that glared at us while we were praising the Lord during worship services. If looks could have killed, we would have died on the spot. Rather than concentrate on them, I closed my eyes, and continued to bask in the glory of worship to my God.

Summer camp came to an end, and Bible classes were to begin one month later. There were approximately sixty bible students enrolled. The Bible classes were fun, and it was wonderful to live each day in the word of God. To attend classes, students were not allowed to work off campus. We had dormitory style dwelling, which was crowed. There was barely enough space in one room for two people, and we were being housed at three, and four to a room.

Assuming this was a part of the foreign mission training, we all accepted the limited space of our living quarters without much complaining. Out meals were supplied by the camp as part of our tuition agreement. We had to work on camp with no pay as a supplementary payback for food, and shelter. Our entire lives were spent on the campground except going into town to buy personal items from time to time. Even then permission had to be given to leave the grounds. Most of the students didn't own a car and were stranded. They had no way to town unless they rode with someone who owned a vehicle. I was blessed to have a car.

I knew God had sent me to this camp, and I knew He had gone before me to prepare the way. I had no doubt He would tell me when it was time to leave. I had hoped to be leaving soon, because things were beginning to get rough, and the devil began to manifest regularly. Though, I had a car, and with permission could go and come as I pleased, I felt I was a prisoner held captive. There were things in this camp that just didn't add up to the Christian walk. At this point, I couldn't help, but wonder why God had sent me to this den of devils, however I don't question God about His direction for my life.

Christmas vacation came, and went, and we were back into our studies again. We were discouraged from leaving camp for vacation, but not prohibited. Most students stayed at camp for fear of creating tension by leaving. Some of the camp family had gone to foreign mission fields, and trips, leaving the Bible students to run the camp. There were chores such as cleaning bathrooms, unstopping sewers, enormous amounts of yard work, washing camp linens, washing dishes, preparing meals, and whatever else it took to keep the camp operating, and clean. We didn't mind the work, but it was the attitude of the staff over us that was so demeaning. They treated most of the students like slaves.

Meals had to be prepared three times a day for nearly 100 people, except on Wednesdays, Fridays, and Sundays. These were fast days, and only two meals were provided, consisting of broth. Fasting days were observed by the students, and some staff members, while the owners, camp family, and leaders would eat in their homes. On occasion, they could be seen dining out on fast days. Fasting is supposed to be a personal decision between God, and the person fasting. However, at camp, it was a mandatory practice for the workers, and Bible students.

Some of us believed it to be a way of saving money for the camp (a food for thought). It obviously wasn't for spiritual reasons in most of the cases. If it were for spiritual subjection, the owners would have, also participated. Of course, the Bible students, and the uneducated camp family weren't supposed to be spiritual enough to discern this. Discernment was thought to be a gift only the owners, and leaders possessed.

Along with the everyday chores and Bible classes we also attended church four times a week, Wednesday, Friday, and twice on Sunday. Church did not provide much teaching. The foundation of the services consisted of subjects on submission, and the flesh coming under subjection, with the all-time favorite topic being "The Potter's House." The camp owned the church, and the owners delivered the sermons.

The sermons birthed fear in the hearts of those present: not the fear of God, but fear of the camp leaders. The fear was caused in such a subdued way that it wasn't obvious without having lived at camp. Going to church on a regular basis was like going to regular brain washing seminars. No one was allowed to miss any one service. Wednesday night, Friday night, Sunday school, Sunday morning worship and Sunday night worship were our regular meeting days, along with the ministry times at camp. I didn't mind going to church. What I did mind was the lack of teaching from the scriptures, and the constant teaching on the flesh. I later understood why all the teaching on the flesh.

I had learned many things in my first year at camp, some good, and some bad, but nothing like what was to come. One of the good things I learned was how to walk in the gift of prophecy. I knew that, as I testified of Jesus, God would sometimes speak through me. I knew it was God, because the things I spoke were things of which I had no prior knowledge. Plus, they lined up with scripture, and was confirmed by the recipient. Learning to give the prophetic word to individuals was fascinating. I had not yet learned how to give congregational prophecy, but I knew it would come.

I remember the first time the Holy Spirit took me in the spirit during a church service. We were in church, and all were standing for the opening prayer, praise, and worship. While everyone was praying, I went to Texas. Eighteen-month-old Jessica McClure had fallen into an eight inch well 2 days prior. Some of you will remember the story. She had fallen 22 feet down, and it had taken 58 hours to get her out. The whole world was watching, waiting, and following the News.

I was in the Spirit, in the well in Texas, and my body was standing in church. I was in the spirit inside the well coming up with the paramedic that was holding Jessica. I heard the echoing sounds inside the well, and then the cheers of the people as Jessica was brought to the surface. Afterwards, I told my friend that Jessica had just been brought up out of the well. I could have prophesied that in church right then, but at that time I didn't know how to give congregational prophecy and I was afraid to give it. After getting in the car after church to go home we heard on the car radio that Jessica had been rescued at the exact time I was in the Spirit.

After I had started sitting on the platform, singing, and helping to lead worship, I was told I had better prophesy during the camp meetings. I couldn't understand how I could prophesy unless God wanted to speak. I later learned that people attend this camp mainly to hear from God, have and encounter with God, and to get individual prophecy. People came expecting to hear the prophetic word, and we were to give it. However, we weren't allowed to use scripture in prophecy.

Prophecy is the main drawing card for the camp and brings in flocks of people from all over the world. Looking back, it all resembles fortune telling more than hearing from God. There were scheduled times for people to come and get a word from the camp Mother. I believe she was a true prophet of God. I also believe that for the most part the prophetic word from some of the leaders were God given words. However, I have my doubts about some others. There were a few words spoken over me that I did not receive.

Though prophecy is from God, the fact that false prophets exist cannot be overlooked. (Ezekiel 34) I never prophesied falsely. I feared God too much to speak from my flesh. Besides, I didn't know how to speak from my flesh. The word tells us not to think about what we will say, and the Holy Spirit will speak expressly through us. I listened for the Lord to give me the word and spoke what I heard Him say. I finally did get enough courage to start giving congregational prophecy, but only if I heard from God.

There was a newly married young couple living at the camp. One morning during prayer the Lord gave me a word for them. He said they would have a son and continued to say they should name the child Joshua. The Lord said the child would be a special child, etc. The couple had just found out they were going to have a baby, but they had not yet announced this news. I didn't know it either. They were excited when I prophesied over them about having a son. Of course, they thought the word was for the child they were going to have then. Years later I met someone who knows the couple, and they told me the couple has 4 girls. They probably think I'm a false prophet, but I know I heard from God. It could be that the Lord gave them that word so they wouldn't become discouraged waiting to have a son. I still believe the son will come if he hasn't already. I've never given a word that hasn't come to pass. If a word given has conditions attached to it, unless those conditions are not met, the word will come to pass.

I, also, learned the importance of prayer. Each morning from 8:00 a.m. until 9:00 a.m., the entire camp gathered and prayed. The first thirty minutes were devoted to individual, private prayer. The last thirty minutes was given to songs of praise, and worship, and praying for the nation of Israel, America, finances, and leaders. This was very good for me and taught me discipline in my prayer life. I, however, had one problem with this hour of prayer. I couldn't understand how the camp leaders, and owners could spend an hour in prayer each morning and come out having attitudes worse than before they prayed. Prayer changes things, but they weren't changed, and most of them had been practicing prayer for fifteen to thirty years, or longer. This was even more puzzling, but I did as before, and laid it on the shelf.

I learned about people, and that not everyone professing Jesus is a Christian. They may call themselves believers, but the spirit of God isn't evident in their lives. I saw on more than one occasion, the male owner, the camp pastor, evangelist, teacher, and leader of the camp, throw fits of anger, acting like a wild man. I saw him come so close to striking a female Bible student, over nothing, that he pushed her with his body, clenching his fist, and teeth, while yelling at her. A girl who had been associated with the camp for twenty years took the student by the arm and led her outside. She told me later that he would have struck the girl had she not pulled her away. I knew this to be the truth, for I had seen with my eyes that he could barely restrain himself. I believe he restrained himself because so many others were watching him. Had I not seen this with my own eyes, I wouldn't have believed it.

The Twenty-year vet to the camp said she had seen him worse than this, and then told me stories of how people when they were younger were beaten (herself included), and at times were restrained by tying them. After seeing him lose his temper, and publicly embarrass the Bible student before her peers, I could now believe anything about this man.

I had heard other stories of warning that verified the ones about which I had been told. On more than one occasion, I saw him lose his temper, and yell uncontrollably at his then seventy-four-year-old mother. This man was supposed to be my spiritual leader, but I couldn't accept his vicious conduct. If he would abuse his mother, what would he do to me?

There were treasures the male owner, and his family stored up in their homes from the foreign mission trips to China, Egypt, Israel, Tibet, and various other countries. I saw the nice homes that the camp owners and leaders lived in and compared them to the slums in which their workers, and prayer warriors were made to live. I saw the food that the owners put on their table and compared it to the food served to the camp family, and Bible students. The difference was the difference between a pauper, and a king.

I experienced times of no heat in 16-degree weather from lack of oil, while finances were being spent to purchase a motel, radio station, TV airtime, and radio time for Sunday services to be aired. Understanding that advertising is necessary for raising finances, building an empire for self-gain, and power is beyond my comprehension. The tuition paid by the Bible students was supposed to cover our heat in the dorms during snowy winter months.

The camp, of course had the right to spend finances any way they liked, but it was at the expense of the residence health. I don't mind ministry growing but neglecting those for whom one is responsible is going a bit far. There were elderly women working and living on camp that got sick with pneumonia during the cold of winter, and no medical help was available. We lived by faith alone, and God did heal many of these people.

The living conditions were so bad that I can't even begin to describe them. There are no words to paint a picture of how it really was. These conditions were spruced up for summer, and winter camp meetings when the public was invited to come in. The visitors were not to know just how badly conditions were normally. People from all over the world, mostly from India, attended this camp during summer, and winter meetings, and donated thousands of dollars each year. These supporters want to see their money at work; therefore, a big front is put up as an eye pleaser. After camp meeting ends, everything would go back to the poverty-stricken level of environment it really was, presenting unclean conditions for daily living, a regular health hazard.

There was a wealthy woman who built a lavish two-story house on camp property as her permanent residents. She donated a considerable amount of funds to repair the sewage system that always seemed to be broken. After at least one and a half years had passed, the sewers were still in need of repair. The woman said to me one day, "I can't understand why the sewage problem hasn't been repaired. I donated more than enough money to complete the work." She knew the lack of attention to this problem wasn't due to a lack of finances but couldn't understand why the work had not been done.

There were many other financial misconceptions that appeared fraudulent. These are the things to which the supporters of the camp closed their eyes. If there were no misappropriation of funds, why did the living conditions remain so unsanitary, and poverty-stricken? I know for a fact the finances were plentiful.

These conditions, however, never touched the owners, and some leaders. Most of them lived on the hill, so to speak, in luxury. Compared to the living conditions in the sewer pits where the workers were housed in cinder block buildings having cement floors with no rugs, or carpet. The owners and special leaders lived like royalty. Many times, we the lower class, went without water because our water well would run dry. Going without daily baths presents a problem, especially in cramped living quarters. I was blessed in getting to live in one of the better quarters near where the cafeteria, and school was located. We still suffered in the cold, and lack of water, but we had wooden floors, and decent rooms, though still cramped.

I watched as the ignorant, unstable, uneducated, and weaker humans used not as servants of God, but used as slaves to the owners, and leaders. These slaves were overworked, verbally abused, persecuted, and belittled. The men were made to serve the women. This is completely against God's law of divine, and holy order of male, and female. Women were lifted, and turned into power-seeking, domineering heathen jezebels, while the men were cast down, and made lower than dirt and ashamed of their gender. The Bible says woman was made not to usurp authority over the man (Gen. 2:18, and 1 Tim. 2:12)

The reason camp raised up women was because they are more easily deceived (like Eve) than are the men. These women are brainwashed into doing the bidding of the owners. They became rude, unloving, inconsiderate, uncaring, jealous, power-driven false prophetesses. They were made to do the work of men, and they considered this a privilege. The women leaders had a perverse spirit like the owners, and the few male leaders. They all had the appearance of holiness, but inside were ravening wolves seeking to devour anyone that got in their way (Matt. 7:15-18). They sought to destroy instead of buildup and were out to satisfy self at the expense of someone under their leadership.

These women walked in the deception of Satan and were as much his servants as are his fallen angels. Not only did they walk in deception they went about deceiving. They displayed a loving, and kind spirit to unsuspecting souls. It was not easy to detect the demonic spirits that possessed them unless they became angry. The women dressed, and presented a state of holiness to the public, but in their natural environment, and their spirit the true demonic personalities would surface in hostility, rage, and lies. "Satan is a liar, and the father of it (John 8:44)." The sad part was, they didn't see themselves as they really were. They believed they were God-fearing women, but instead feared the owners not God.

It is one thing to be obedient, but to live in constant fear of man is not of God. This was a Pentecostal camp. It was my first encounter with that angry, mean spirited, religious spirit that seems to harbor in Pentecostals. The long uncut hair in buns and clothed from neck to ankles were their calling cards to holiness. Many of these women were in foreign missions, and I often wondered what spirits they were imparting to people around the world, and what spirits were being imparted to them? I realize not all Pentecostals are like this.

I knew a few women there that really believed and wanted to serve God. However, if they can stay there in that environment, they must also, have a like spirit. There was one girl, married, with two small daughters that had lived at camp for many years. Her husband was one of the trusted male leaders. He had seen the things of which I am writing, and even told me things in secret concerning the camp. I knew that as soon as they could get finances enough to leave, and an open door to carry on their ministry, they would go, and so they did, Praise God.

There was one among them, a female owner, a worldwide evangelist, and leader that had made her home in a foreign country. She was a sort of queen bee under her mother (head of Camp) and resided at the camp during the time I lived there. She was grotesquely overweight having unnatural affections for her own kind and was a tyrant. Stories told by missionaries who had served under her and lived in her house are horror stories. Stories of starvation as disciplinary action, fits of anger, and beatings for no apparent reason, homosexual advances toward her female servants, and verbal abuse to such extent that one's soul, and spirit was ripped apart (Rom. 1:26).

These accusations are difficult to believe, and had I not lived in, and around it for nearly two years, I wouldn't believe it either. I was never physically abused, but the verbal abuse touched everyone. Because I was somewhat educated, and knowing who I was in Christ, many things were hidden from me. I wasn't the typical uneducated, nowhere to go, person that was common to residents.

The camp's token widow informed me that I didn't belong there. She told this to me in a jealous rage and fit of anger because I didn't show up at her house after one of the camp meeting services to meet prospective supporters. They always wanted prospective supporters to see the ones of us who could present a well-balanced and educated front. I didn't receive an invitation to her house, but she had looked for me after the service, and couldn't find me. I had gone with some of the others to get something to eat. Apparently, this was ground for her yelling, and screaming, that I wasn't there for her beck, and call.

She told me she would see that I wouldn't go on any mission trips. Later I found out that camp leaders were keeping an eye on me for fear I would find out the things about which I am writing. I had long since made this camp venture a research for my book, unknown to them of course.

I needed to talk with someone at the camp that would know some answers to my questions. I asked God to show me who I could trust. That night I had a dream, and in my dream was a girl who had lived at camp for five years. The next day I mentioned to her I needed to talk with her. She knew exactly what I was doing. She told me later, God had come to her in the middle of the night on the same night told her to talk with me.

We planned to meet at 2:00 a.m., in a secret place in the dark. She opened up about the corruption she experienced while living with the female owner in the foreign country. We sat there in the dark because we were afraid of being caught. She told me that while she lived in the foreign country with the female owner, she was beaten because she would not commit homosexual acts. I knew this to be true because others had related this same information to me. In fact, that is what prompted me to want to talk with someone I could trust. I wanted to know the truth.

I had been planning a trip to this female owner's house and to live with her for about a year, as a missionary in the foreign country. She told me to purchase a one-way ticket, and to prepare to stay at least a year. I considered this trip to be the beginning of my foreign mission training on foreign soil.

When knowledge of my trip was noised throughout the camp, I received warnings such as, "Once you get over there, and have no money to get home you will be stuck and will fall prey to her demands. She will subject you to beatings, and starvation, literally becoming a slave to this great-white-goddess." Numerous others who had lived with her, and knew her nature, warned me against going to stay with her.

Another twenty-year veteran of camp had also warned me not to go. She said, "I will not let you go, and live with that woman, and return in a spiritually dead condition." It was statements like this that led me to believe that these people knew they were in bondage but felt they had no choice but to comply with the demands of the owners.

The token widow for example: She had used all her finances twenty years earlier to build a house at camp. She fell in love with the male owner and could not leave him. What was she going to do when she entered her elderly years, or if he would die, were questions that came to my mind? As it was, she continued to stay and abuse, while being abused. One sad thing, she didn't even get the man.

After hearing accusations about the female owner from the foreign country, I wanted to see for myself if these things were true. I knew in my heart they probably were, but I didn't want to go by hearsay. I could discern the spirits whenever I was in the presence of this woman, but I wanted to find out what she believed. There were times that she was very nice and even fun to be around, but her spirit was one of pride, arrogance, and lover of self. She was overbearing and demanded power over others.

On one occasion I was talking with her about the soon coming of Jesus. I asked what her feelings were about it and she replied, "I believe the Christian way is just a way of life." This proved her true colors after thirty-four years of ministry, with a following you wouldn't believe. I'm talking about heads of states, governments local, and foreign, and you name it. I knew for myself right then of what spirit she was. How she could have deceived so many people for so long, I don't know. I believe she must have been on the right path at one time, at least long enough to gain trust from those around her. I have said this before; you don't know someone until you live with them.

I prayed for direction from God concerning my trip. I had already paid for my ticket and wasn't sure what to do. I could have gone with the missionary tour group, and returned instead of staying in the foreign country, and living with this woman. I wasn't sure what God wanted me to do, so I just waited for His answer. I had a problem of jumping ahead of God and didn't want that to happen at that time.

After a few days God spoke to me and told me not to go on the trip at all. I was a little disappointed at not going on the tour, but nevertheless wanted to stay in God's perfect time, and will. Therefore, I delayed my trip, and stayed behind.

Had God not taken me aside for three years, and trained me in His word, I would have fallen into diverse temptations in this den of devils, and darkness. There were sins of adultery, fornication, homosexuality, drunkenness, witchcraft, lasciviousness, jealousy, theft, gossip, filthy conversation, and completely perverse, and familiar spirits at work. Using God's word as a tool for bringing in finances, touring the world, and living in sin was a main ambition of the camp. I am not saying everyone was engaging in these sins, but it was happening.

The casting out of devils by any other than the owners, and leaders, was forbidden. I never saw them casting out devils except during camp meetings, and ministry. I can understand why. Evil can't cast out evil for in that Satan works against himself if he does (Matt. 12:26). If the Bible students were to cast out devils, they were told to stop. Jesus said to His disciples in Mark 9:38-40, that if devils were being cast out in His name, even though it is being done with some irregularity, "Forbid them not." I believe the camp owners were afraid of losing some of their devils.

I wrote about the man with the limping spirit in chapter 2, but merits repeating. I witnessed the male owner praying for a man that had a limping spirit. When the man went to the altar to be healed, he limped all the way down the aisle. While being prayed over, I saw a demon that looked like a skeleton jump from the man, and into the male owner as he began to pray for the man. The male owner began to limp. I approached him asking if the limping spirit could have jumped on him? The male owner assured me the spirit couldn't have jumped into him. I didn't tell him I saw the spirit jump on him. He would have taken that as an insult and may have yelled at me or worse.

It is difficult to believe that a place like this really exist in modern day America, but the Bible clearly warns us against them, and says that they do exist. We have only one way to measure, and discern the spirits, and that is by the fruits of the Spirit, and works of the flesh. If the fruits are not being produced in our lives, we are not God's children. In Matthew 7:15-18, Jesus said, "Beware of false prophets, which come to you in sheep's clothing, but inwardly they are ravening wolves. Ye shall know them by their fruits. A good tree cannot bring forth evil fruit, neither can a corrupt tree bring forth good fruit."

There will be many people in the world that profess Christianity, in saying, and practicing all the right things (bearing green leaves), but upon closer examination of their lives, no fruit will be found. In the example of the fig tree, Jesus was showing the disciples how easily they could be led astray. He showed them that they couldn't go to just any tree, because it looks good, and find food, or fruit. Jesus cursed the fig tree, and it died. He cursed it, because it represented something it was not, and could easily draw men to it by its false appearance.

The camp wasn't necessarily a remake of the Jim Jones, and Waco but the same blood was coursing its veins. I believe in the beginning of their ministry, the motive was to serve God, and do his will, given the benefit of the doubt. But somewhere in their service of forty years, new family members taking over, error entered, and they lost sight of their first love. They owned the camp, and couldn't be voted out, and without accountability they slid into error.

Through the years they became power driven, and the love of God in their hearts was replaced by the love of money. Many great Evangelists have entered this camp with warnings of their error, but they didn't listen. (Ezekiel 33:31, Titus 1:16, 1 Tim. 6:10)

The people that visit the camp came seeking an encounter with God. Many of them are unlearned, and uneducated, but they love God. The camp presents a false appearance of paradise for the believer and lures them into a state of oblivion through praise, and worship. The people are raised to heights of joy during the praise, and worship, and they become cheerful givers. It works on the same principle as alcohol. The drunker one becomes, the more one spends to buy more strong drink.

During praise, and worship, the people would become so drunk in the Spirit they would give away houses, lands, jewelry, automobiles, and money. The poor were guilt driven into giving. The camp owners, and leaders knew that the poor would give their last dime to save souls.

The elderly was being preyed upon for the purpose of obtaining their social security checks, as well as any other property they might own. While the giver, in this circumstance will be blessed in giving from their heart, and through ignorance, the camp was strictly after personal gain, and will be cursed.

When we give to God, regardless of the organization to which we give, we will be blessed. However, if we give to an organization with knowledge of their error, we will not be blessed for giving, and most likely will be cursed. When giving, we should never give to man, but only to God. If we give to man, and then find our money was used for wrong, we will lose our reward. On the other hand, if we give to God from our heart, and find our money was wrongly used, we will still be blessed by our motive being right.

The average visitor to the camp spent two, to three days there, and never saw the underlying deceitfulness at work. Whereas, living there day to day, week to week, and month to month, a person's eyes will be opened, unless that person is of a like spirit. The devil can hide for a while, but eventually will show his true self. His true nature will surface from time to time, but rarely, if at all, when visitors are present.

Those who frequented the camp from year to year, and knew the owners personally, were, also in need of deliverance, or couldn't discern spirits very well. Many of them had eyes to see but would turn their heads away from the many things they saw. It was much easier for them to keep their eyes closed. I don't know if they really understood that God knew their heart, and they were as responsible for their actions whether they closed their eyes, or not. Most knew the camp was in error but chose to support them anyway. They were wells without water reserved for the mist of darkness. They were being held in bondage by their own lust. Their desire to be recognized by man consumed them in their lust.

One of the major ways the camp workers were held in bondage was through a lack of joy. Nehemiah 8:10 reads; "The joy of the Lord is our strength." A fulltime resident was not allowed to work outside the camp; therefore, they had no way of earning money. The camp provided the bare necessities for living, and money became scarce until one had no money. Having no money, and no place to go, one couldn't easily leave the camp. Most became stuck and could not leave. They then considered it a blessing to at least have food, and shelter. Once they had no resources, and the owners were aware of this, the owners began to put the pressure on by verbal abuse. If they tried to stand up for their rights, they were threatened by the owner's favorite saying, "The road that leads in, also leads out." By this saying, the owners began to manipulate the workers, leaders, and anyone living at the camp. The owners knew once you had no money, no place to go, your dependence on them was sealed.

Most residents eventually came under subjection, and thus began their life as slave labor. Eventually, any joy in the Lord they had was replaced with fear, and loss of strength. In fear, and lack of strength the devil held them captive. They became like walking zombies with no reason to care anymore. Thus, the unsuspecting, servant's heart would fall back into the defensive mode from which it was before coming to know Christ. Without the right kind of servant's heart, one can't, and will not serve God effectively, having a right attitude, and spirit.

Promises of overseas ministry, and missionary work became a thing of the past as potential ministers were stripped of their joy, and spirits of fear, and degradation were placed in its stead. There were opportunities to go on mission trips, but only if you were trusted as a like spirit. The mission tour trips were mostly to raise money for the camp. Some of the camp preachers (women) did go to China, and other places, but I'm sure it was to bring back some of the marketable trinkets like jade for the camp and other treasures for selling.

If one is not well versed in the word of God, they will not see the evil schemes of the devil. They will be caught in the devil's snare before they know what has happened, having no strength to get out. Without the knowledge of God's word in them they will never get out. "For such are false prophets, deceitful workers transforming themselves into apostles of Christ. And no marvel; for Satan himself is transformed into an angel of light." (2 Corinthians 11:13-14)

I wasn't afraid of the enemy, even in the lack of finances. I knew that my God could and would supply all my needs. While I was there, I was determined not to lose my joy. I knew this was the only way to survive. Had I not known God's word I could not have stood in victory against the fiery darts of the devil.

The owners, and leaders, hated me and others like me. The more we sang and praised God the more the old devil flared up in them. Their eyes shot arrows of evil when they looked at us, but in most part, they kept their distance. They even tried to drive us away at first, but God wasn't ready for us to leave. God had sent us there to learn.

After I had stayed long enough to see what was really happening, they wanted to keep me as a prisoner. I was watched constantly, and was told by the twenty-year veteran that they had instructed her not to tell me things of the past (about the beatings, etc.) God had allowed me to go to this camp to learn. He instructed Joseph, and Mary to take baby Jesus into Egypt, a city filled with idolatry, where they would be safe until Herod Antipas died. God used a bad situation to bring about good, as was the case with me going to camp.

Then the day arrived when God told me it was time to leave. All the while I was in this camp, many things that weren't of God were revealed to me. During the time I lived at camp, from time to time a camp member (a slave, not a leader) would leave to go out to preach, but never returned. I wondered and inquired of others what had happened to them. No one ever knew. I couldn't understand why they would just leave, never to be heard from again.

Bible school was over, graduation ceremonies ended, and it was time for me to leave. When I went to tell the head Mother that I was leaving, I found out why others left quietly without telling anyone.

After making my announcement of departure, I was verbally attacked by three she devils, the head Mother, her daughter (the female owner from the foreign country), and the head mother's granddaughter. I was firmly ordered to unpack, and to get myself back to my room where I belonged and stay there. I was accused of lying, cheating, and the like, and was literally under assault by three demonic spirits. I couldn't believe what I was seeing, and hearing. I thought the daughter to head mother was going to physically harm me as she had others. She was outraged because I wouldn't obey her command in going back to my room.

When their scare-tactics did not change my mind, I was literally thrown out in disgrace, as if I were the one in the wrong. Of course, they had to make concession for the camp, and make it look as if I had wronged them. The camp's reputation was at stake. It would have looked bad on the camp, if I had left, and exposed the horror stories about which I'm writing, validating the stories of others who left.

I was even told by the female owner from the foreign country that she would disgrace me and see to it that I would never come back to camp and would never preach again. Didn't she get it? I was leaving because I didn't want to be there anymore. Why would I want to come back? This kind of remark proved her state of confusion, and the confusion she was trying to instill in me. Her twisted way of thinking was full proof of her using Satan's fear tactics, and strategies.

I had done no harm to anyone, but when I realized what a fraud this organization was, I couldn't support it any longer. The public who supports the camp with finances are deceived, and don't know the work that is really performed there. There were donations given for different things, but those things never got done.

In leaving, I wasn't going to give my reasons, but was trying to leave in peace. I wasn't sure at that point if I would get out or not. There was another lady with me. She had been affiliated with the camp for at least twenty years. She was very young when she first got tangled up with them, and she grew up in their deception. Once she saw the light, she was going to leave with me.

To uphold the camp's reputation, we were made to appear the culprits. There were people that supported this camp who lived in the same town to where I moved. I have told a few what I saw while at there, but they can't believe it, and continued to support the enemy's camp. I can half-way understand their disbelief because I lived among the corruption, and still find it hard to believe. It is no wonder that passers-by can't see it. Although, some of my supporters came to visit me at camp, and they discerned the deception, but I assured them nothing was wrong. That was in the early days of my stay before my eyes were opened.

Most of the camp supporters were ignorant women that have fallen under the seductive light of the male owner/pastor. I call it seductive because he was able, under the powers of Satan to seduce with his eyes. It is a sort of hypnotic gleam, and glitter of light that induces a trance of attraction toward him, whether male or female. He was very likable. I saw this happen with numerous of people. They became enamored over the man.

When I left camp, I felt my life was in danger. As ludicrous as this may sound, I know it to be the truth. I had been at camp long enough to see the evil spirit there, and this knowledge wasn't to be made known. When I wasn't allowed to leave, I informed the male owner in a letter of what his sister was doing to me, and the other girl. This really brought out the demons. My friend, and I were taken aside by the male owner, and he yelled at us for at least an hour.

I stayed in a motel for a few weeks until I could gather enough money to leave the town. The camp owned the motel, but I knew the workers there. They helped me by hiding me in a room, along with my friend who was leaving with me. We took jobs with the 1989 Census and made enough money to sustain us while trying to decide where we were going, and how we would get there. I still had the car, but cars need gas, and it takes money to buy gas. Catch 22.

I knew my life was in danger because of the hostility displayed toward others who had tried to leave. During my stay at camp, I was treated with comforts others didn't have. I was considered a handmaiden for the female owner, and this gave me special privileges. So it wasn't that I suffered so much, but I found it difficult to bear the abuse I saw happening to the uneducated, unsuspecting souls around me.

Now, as I sat in my motel room, reflecting over the last 18 months I reviewed in my mind the events that had taken place. I marveled at the memory of what I had been through.

I had left camp without a penny in my pocket. I needed finances in a big way. I had met a preacher, and his wife during camp meeting that knew about the spirit over this camp. I knew if I could find them, they would help me. In fact, they had said if I ever needed them, I could call.

Someone had given me enough money to move into the motel, but I had nothing left. I didn't know how to contact the preacher because they lived out of town. Praying for God's help, He heard my prayers. The next day there was a knock at my door. Not sure if I should answer, I tried looking through the peephole to see who was there, but I couldn't see.

Taking a chance, I finally asked, "Who's there", the voices I heard replying was a great blessing to hear. It was the preacher, and his wife. They told me how the Holy Spirit had sent them to see me, but found I wasn't at the camp. There were people at the camp that had found out where I was staying but wouldn't tell my friends. My friends sensed something was wrong, and finally found someone who told them where I was. The Preacher, and his wife gave me enough money to help me escape.

There were many things that happened at camp that wasn't of God. I want to emphasize how easily Satan can take you if you don't know God's word. Some of you will probably think you would have done differently and wouldn't have gotten tangled up in this web of deceit. Must I remind you that many of you, saved, or unsaved are living in the enemy's camp right where you are? He is offering you the world, and you are so blind that you can't see beyond the surface of his underlying schemes. Through the glitter, and glamour of the world you are held in bondage to Satan, and one day you will have no strength left, and no way out of his grip. If you don't have joy, and peace like a river, it is a clue you are in bondage.

Money can bring a certain joy, and peace, but not without fear, worry, confusion, restlessness, problems, and the like. I am not saying believers can't have money; but to have money, and to not know its limitations, in that it can give nothing, but physical pleasures, is the downfall. The only satisfaction in having riches comes in using those riches for God's service.

Here, again, is a mystery that can only be solved through the practice, and experience of demonstration.

There are believers in bondage as much as nonbelievers. The church you attend may not be a true church. If your church does not teach Jesus or teaches any other Jesus than the gospel of Jesus Christ, and if you receive another spirit, other than the Holy Spirit, you are walking in deception (2 Corinthians 11:3-4) This scripture clearly teaches that if we don't know the real Jesus, and the true Spirit, believers can be deceived as easily as nonbelievers.

The Jesus that the camp professes in not the Jesus I know. The Jesus I know came to serve, to love, and to save. He is the light of the world, and full of love for all mankind. During the two years I was there, I saw no love at the camp.

I challenge believers, and nonbelievers. Invite Jesus into your heart, begin to study the word of God, and the Holy Spirit will begin to reveal your captivity. If you are as intelligent, educated, and civilized as you think, and if you are not in bondage to the world, you have nothing to lose, and everything to gain.

Always remember that there is good, and bad in everything. Jesus said the tares, and wheat will grow together until the time of the harvest. Then will the tares be rooted up, and burned, and the wheat would be gathered into His barn (Matt. 13:24-30). The Church is no exception. It has good as well as bad. There are professed Christians proclaiming the gospel who are, in fact, not Christians at all. They are false prophets, and familiar spirits, trying to profit by the name of the Lord Jesus Christ.

It is no wonder people fall away from the church because Satan has nearly destroyed the credibility of the church. However, just as one person's actions can't be judged by another's actions, neither should one church be judged by the actions of other churches. Go to a church that teaches the truth found only in the Bible. Don't judge the church body by the people attending, but by what the pastor is teaching. If his, or her teaching is not word for word, God's word, find another church. If the actions of the pastor, the church leaders, and the congregation are not lining up with the word of God, find another church. Don't think that you are the one that will turn the church around if it appears to be teaching wrong doctrine. You will not. Just get out, and go somewhere else, lest you become defiled.

If we are true Christians, with renewed spirits, we will begin to walk in that newness of spirit. We must stop supporting the devil's work and begin to support the true church. Using our gifts of discerning of spirits, and praying is exercising our authority over evil. By binding and loosing, the powers of evil we can overcome Satan. This is what the true church is supposed to practice.

A true Christian will walk in humility, and love, not in rebellion, and haughtiness. It is the true believer's responsibility to be his brother's keeper. When a brother, or sister is taken in a fault, or found to be in error, we the church are not to forsake them but love them and if they are teachable teach them the right way to go. We are to take them under the shadow of our wings the same way God hides us under the shadow of His wings. Because the church has come to trust in her beauty, and riches, more than trusting in the word of God, we have left our brethren out to die.

The purpose of the Church is to proclaim liberty to the captive by the Gospel of Jesus Christ. This is the law of God's love. Instead, the Church has become so much like the world that there is no significant difference between them. While today's Church is truly the Laodicean Church, God has a remnant that has not revolted, nor defiled their garments. However, many are falling from the faith, and their blood is on the hands of the Church. It is the responsibility of the Church to know the state of the sinner, and believer in the church, whether Jew, or Gentile. When we see our brethren overtaken by the enemy, or in need, we must stop, and take the time to help him, or her. This help will not always be received, but at least plant, or water the seed. The Holy Spirit will do the rest.

There are many Christians that have forsaken their first Love, Jesus Christ. I have ministered on Face Book to multitudes of people who were once in the body of Christ. They have either been hurt by the Church, led astray by the Church, or didn't find the love of God in the Church when they did belong. These people are now in the world, testifying against Jesus, and have rejected the only one that can save them. The Church did this to them.

Church, the blood of these dear children is on our hands. Had I not known the word of God while I was at camp, based on what I saw the presumed Church doing, I could have easily rejected the Church. Thank God for His word, and that I knew it well enough to escape the enemy's camp.

In early 1987, I had a vision in which I saw people laying on the ground in masses. They were crawling and grasping their way to a small church building that had been boarded up and condemned. They were reaching their hands toward the church in a feeble attempt to reach out for God. But God was no longer there because the people of God were not there. The Spirit of God had never been in the church building, but in the earthen vessels of His saints.

Then the Spirit of God spoke to me and said, "There is coming a day when the Church buildings will be closed and condemned. In that day the true worshippers will have to be led by the Holy Spirit to individual homes for worship. At this time America, and parts of the world will be under a type of martial law that will abolish the written word of God, and forbid it being taught. America is on the brink of seeing this happen very soon. It will be as soon as the establishment of the one world order, or government, which will deceive the very elect."

We are seeing this happen today. The devil's mission is to destroy souls before they come to the knowledge of who they are in Christ. To do this, he will profane the name of the Christian, and will use any device necessary to drive people from the truth of God's word. His goal is to lead you away from God, not closer to Him.

For these reasons, it is of utmost importance to literally learn the voice of God, eat the word of God, study it, live it, teach it, and make it the abundance of our hearts. If we don't, we will become as silly women being led away captive in our own lust (men also), just like the people of the camp. (2 Tim. 2:5-6)

Another phase of being led astray in our own lust is in the leadership of a Church. There are many occasions where one, two, or three persons, (numbers vary) who seem to do all the work. This is found in many churches around the world. The pastor is always crying for help, but the ones in charge won't give up a job so others can help. I have been in many church bodies where there are numerous people in the congregation having the ability to lead but are never given the chance to lead. The one's in charge feel like others can't do the job as effectively as they, so they continue to stress themselves out doing more jobs than they can perform effectively. This kind of thinking is selfish. The one's in charge, I'm sure didn't do their best the first time they performed a job. They had to learn, and develop, just like we all.

I know churches that claim they are "raising up leaders, educating them, and preparing them", but then they are left out to dry. There are people in many of these same churches having gifts to exercise but are never allowed to exercise them. Who cares if the timing isn't just right when a new prophet of God stands up and gives a prophecy? God will make it right, and He will make the time right. The point is this: Let people exercise their gifts. If the Holy Spirit is in charge, the gifts will bring fruit. Make the way comfortable for people to stand up and exercise their gifts. If the church doesn't start letting the Holy Spirit have His way during Sunday services, and in all phases of the church work, the church will die. A church is to teach others how to operate in the gifts of the ministry, and Spirit. If your church claims to be training up workers, don't just teach them from a book, but help them exercise their gifts. They need hands on training.

I know of a church that has great potential in being used in these end times. The church body consists of previous, evangelist, pastors, teachers, prophets, and people having so many gifts to offer, but are never asked to do anything. Just like other churches, the same people are doing the work of the ministry. This type of church is close to getting into error, blinded by their lust for power. They don't even realize this is happening, and this is what leads to places like the camp the same people doing the same jobs, under the same leadership, under no supervision, having no accountability. Sure, they have board members, but the board members are overruled many times by the pastor. If the board members are men, and women of God, they need to be heard, and received. If they have been chosen to govern let them govern. Isn't this the kind of problem we have in the Congress, and Senate of America, and the government of other countries in the world. These things must be guarded against.

The Church is supposed to help workers get established in their office and calling. When the same people do the same job over, and over, they get into error. This is how dictatorships begin. That is why most businesses have hands on training programs after the schooling is over. First work in the mailroom and go up from there. If the business hires a vice president with experience, they don't need to work in the mailroom first. They have already been there, done that. If a church wants to be a resource for ministry, begin by using the resources available. A Church can't be a business ran like the businesses of the world. It can be a business but must be operated by the Holy Spirit.

"You are not to keep company with anyone who claims to be a brother Christian, but indulges in sexual sins, or is greedy, or is a swindler, or worships idols, or is a drunkard, or abusive. Don't even eat lunch with such a person. It isn't our job to judge outsiders: but it certainly is our job to judge and deal strongly with those who are members of the church and are sinning in these ways. God alone is the Judge of those on the outside, but you yourselves must deal with this man, and put him out of your church." (1 Corinthians 5:11-13, Living Bible translation) This verse of scripture alone makes me somewhat skeptical of a church that has a pastor that can't be voted out. I hesitate in supporting a church where the Pastor can't be voted out. There is too much room for error in this type of organization. However, I do, and will support a church if the Holy Spirit is in it.

The Holy Spirit is a gentleman, and He will not be out of order. More churches need to rely on the leading of the Holy Spirit in their services. Church has become a business, of raising money for overseas missions, building projects, television ministry, feeding the hungry, etc. While this is fantastic, if it is not done under the anointing of God, it is labor in vain.

Church is a hospital for the people. It is to bind up the broken spirit, heal the sick, and cause the lame to walk, open the blind eyes, and make the captive free. If your church doesn't practice these gifts, your church is a false church. Get out and find a true church.

Don't judge every church by the bad ones. I would be lost today had I judged all Christians by the experience I had at camp. My experience has taught me that not every spirit that professes God is of God. This is why we are to try the spirits and see what spirits they are. 2 Peter 2:1-22 reveals what a false prophet is, and his pernicious way. I am going to give a few scriptures found in 2 Peter, but I urge you to read the entire chapter yourself. In it you will learn what to look for when you come face to face with the angel of light, that ole Satan.

2 Peter 2:1, "But there shall be false prophets among you, having EYES FULL OF ADULTERY, and that cannot cease from sin; BEGUILING UNSTABLE SOULS: a heart they have exercised with covetous practices; CURSED children. Which have forsaken the right way, and are gone astray, following the way of Balaam (Satan), who LOVED the WAGES of unrighteousness. These are WELLS WITHOUT WATER, CLOUDS that are carried with a tempest: to whom the MIST OF DARKNESS is reserved forever. For when they speak great swelling words of vanity, they ALLURE THROUGH THE LUST OF THE FLESH, through much wantonness, those that were clean escaped from them who live in error. WHILE THEY PROMISE THEM LIBERTY, THEY THEMSELVES ARE THE SERVANTS OF CORRUPTION: FOR OF WHOM A MAN IS OVERCOME, OF THE SAME IS HE BROUGHT IN BONDAGE." (Emphasis mine).

I have been involved in many ministries where the anointing was there when it started, but after man got through instilling their rules, and regulations, and leading in the way that seemed right, the anointing left, and the ministry became unfruitful. It had green leaves but no fruit, and it didn't get this way overnight. It happens slowly one error at a time.

In my case, I remained at the camp, living there as a worker, and Bible student. I didn't know for some time just how bad things were. Once I did know, I completed my research, and I tried to leave. At that point, I knew too much, and the owners didn't want me to leave. Besides, I was told they had invested too much time in me to let me leave now. Thank God His time invested in me didn't come back void, and I was allowed to leave by His hand. Thank God I knew the scriptures well enough that my life didn't get into error before I realized the error was there.

This camp is still in operation today, under a different leader. The original family have all passed on. I don't know if this camp has the same spirit or not. From all appearances it does. I went on their web site while writing this book, and they are still using the sewer system to generate funds.

I realize that plumbing for a camp must be maintained, and probably breaks down more than most. However, there are only at best 49 staff living there year-round. The summer camp meetings have a few thousand people come through, but winter camp meeting, the preacher's convention, women's convention, and the few other events, during the year probably generates a few hundred people at best.

Judging by their video's the crowds are much smaller than those of the past, so I suspect the sewers shouldn't have need of repair as often. I have learned that all the leaders present when I lived there have all left the camp, and God has restored them to ministries of their own. I am glad to know that most of them are still in the ministry, and I hope the best for them. Some have written books, and others are still traveling as Missionaries, and some are pastors.

The original owner's granddaughter wasn't as fortunate. She was born, grew up, married, raised her children, and lived most of her adult life at camp. Camp is all she knows. She had never had a job outside the camp, didn't know how to earn money, and take care of herself. When her last relative was on their deathbed, they signed the camp over to the current director. Now the granddaughter is no longer permitted to live at the camp. She is in the world trying to make her way with God's help. I feel such empathy for this woman. It is sad to watch as she struggles through trying to work a job for the first time in her life. This information should shed light on the type of spirit the original camp owners had. They didn't even look after their own blood.

Once Satan has staked his claim on you, you can get away, but you must let Jesus take you away, by submitting to His way. Learn to recognize the enemy's camp in yourselves and discern the spirits that are not of God in you, and around you that you may be made free by the knowledge in the Word of God.

A friend of mine in California, once I had left camp, told me he had a dream about me. In the dream he saw me staying in a motel, and my life was in danger. He prayed for me and asked God to protect me. Since he didn't know where I was, there was nothing else he could do. The time God gave him this dream was at the same time I was staying in the motel praying for God to send help.

God is faithful, and true, and wants you to know Him as your Father. He will always protect you, and take care of you, if you will trust Him. Take your eyes off man and look into the eyes of Christ. Receive the Love of God by the Holy Spirit.

God's love is the greatest weapon we can possess in our arsenal for performing spiritual warfare. Even if you are a slave in the Enemy's camp, become a servant to Jesus Christ, having His love in you, and for you. When you have the Agape Love of God working in you, no demon in hell can come against you and win.

CHAPTER 11

Will You Sparkle in the Presence of God, or Burn?

A friend came to visit one evening, and we began talking about what Jesus means to us. As we talked, my friend's countenance became aloof, and distant. Just as I noticed this I was suddenly caught up in the Spirit, and carried away to another place, and time. I found myself standing in front of a gigantic mountain. It wasn't until much later I discovered I had been standing in front of Mt. Horeb, or Sinai, the Mountain of God.

While in the Spirit, I saw a multitude of people standing below the mountain dressed in brown, hooded robes that hung to the ground. Only their faces were exposed. The crowd consisted of what appeared to be millions and reached as far as I could see. The top of the mountain was arrayed with the Glory of God. His light of glory appeared like that of the earth's sun, only much brighter and pure white. I couldn't see the similitude of God, but I knew He was in the light. The light appeared mostly white, with a hint of amber in its beams. There was no doubt that I was in the presence of Jehovah God. I was standing on a high cliff on the outskirts of the multitude of people. The light of glory reached far, and wide, and there wasn't anyone, or anything that couldn't see the light.

I don't know what I was wearing, but I wasn't wearing a robe. My apparel, cosmetics, and jewelry didn't make a difference to God. It was my heart that mattered to Him. Had I been wearing the strongest suit of armor, made of steel, or wearing nothing at all, God's eyes could still have seen through me. The light of God's glory targeted me, and pierced my body like a laser beam, or torch of fire. It shone completely through me, and in that moment, I knew I was naked.

I wasn't naked in the sense that I wasn't wearing clothes, but naked in the sense that God could see all of me, inside, and out. He was examining my heart of hearts. Most importantly He was revealing my hearts intent to me. I saw my life flash before my eyes, and how I had excluded God. My embarrassment, and shame, of how I had wronged God felt worse than if I were naked, wearing no clothes. His glory was like a light that lit up my entire being, leaving no part of me untouched.

My chest was pounding, and I began to feel pain. I could see a fire had begun to burn inside my chest. It was a fire started by the light. The fire spread quickly. Pain began to engulf my body like a wildfire engulfs a forest. The pain wasn't the same as felt by a burn to the flesh in the natural, it was much worse. It was a fire I couldn't escape.

As the fire spread, it became a consuming pain, tormenting my entire being. The pain was the pain of shame. It was the shame of my spirit that kindled the fire. I was burning like the burning bush Moses saw; my flesh was not being consumed. Had I stayed in God's light much longer I felt it would consume me, leaving nothing. I later learned this fire wouldn't consume in the way we know consume. The fire will ignite all those things unlike its nature, and those things will burn for all eternity. God was purging me.

The light of God's glory is a light that shines brighter than any light known to man. It is a light that can't be looked upon, not because of its brightness, but because of its nature, and all it reveals. No one can stand in the presence of God in the natural body without feeling great pain and burning. I was in the Spirit, and only in God's presence for a moment, but seemed like an eternity.

In that moment, I saw the goodness, greatness, excellence, and love of God, and how much He loves his creation. I saw and felt the very nature of God though I couldn't see His being. I saw the evil state of humanity and had to look away while covering my eyes with my hands. I could not bear the things I saw, and the pain of my shame for more than a moment. Thank God I was in the Spirit. My first thought was to scream out for the mountains to fall on me and hide me from God.

John the Revelator saw a vision in which the people of the end times will cry out for the mountains, and rocks to fall on them. This will be at the end of the tribulation, when Jesus returns, and the truth is made known to all. The cries will come from the pain of their shame in not accepting Jesus as Messiah, and in not serving God when given the chance. The pain of knowing what one could have had by accepting Christ, and not receiving Him, will be far greater than one can bear. Revelation 6:16-17 reads, "And said to the mountains, and rocks, fall on us, and hide us from the face of Him that sitteth on the throne, and from the wrath of the Lamb. For the great day of His wrath is come: and who shall be able to stand?" This is how I know John the Revelator saw and heard the things he revealed in the book of Revelation. As I stood before God, my exact thoughts were as written in Revelation 6:16-17.

To the understanding of the natural man, the rocks, and mountains are the only things our minds can conceive of possibly hiding us from God. They are the only things we can identify with that could rid us of the pain we will feel in that day if we haven't accepted Jesus Christ as our personal Savior.

The intensity from the pain of shame for how I had wronged God, and myself, was more than any human in the natural, or spiritual can take. If I had been in God's presence any longer, I would have been totally consumed by the shame of my guilt, and the torment over my loss in not serving God my whole life, though I thought I had.

Having returned to the natural, my visitor could see something had happened, and inquired of me, "What's wrong?" I told him of the experience, and to my surprise, he laughed. I couldn't believe he was laughing. He claimed to be a Christian, so I expected more of an attitude of belief. As I looked deeper into his eyes, I saw evil, and a mocking grin lurking back at me. My spirit recognized the evil immediately, and I said to him, "I know who you are, and you have no ground here." This was all very new, and strange to me, but by the Holy Spirit, I understood it well.

In the Spirit the things seen are the supernatural forces at work. Whether they be good, or evil the supernatural is an entire world about which most people have none, or little knowledge. Satan had acted through this visitor of mine, and I had seen him in this man. I have since seen the eyes of Satan, and they always look the same. His eyes are very enticing, alluring, and beautiful. They shine like crystal, yet his stare is very distant, and deceptive, piercing the very soul of his intended victims with darts of evil. His stare is tantalizing, mesmerizing, and paralyzing, all at the same time. The only thing that stops his influence when looking into his eyes is the light in the eyes of Christ. That is why Jesus said the eyes are the light of the soul. The light of Jesus in your eyes conquers Satan.

Another example of this experience was with the preacher from camp. This preacher had credibility in international religious circles. I attended a dinner of ministry sponsors where the preacher was the host. He stood up from the table to make an announcement, and I saw a twinkle of light coming from one of his eyes. It was an exaggerated twinkle, bright, illuminating, and noticeable. I had an uneasy feeling about it.

It was like in the movie Cocoon. The aliens would peel off their outer suit of flesh, and inside they had glowing bodies. The glow would shine out of any part of them that wasn't covered by the suit. In the case of the preacher, it was more of a hypnotic twinkle of light, probably not noticed by the others. I am sensitive to supernatural figures, and am accustomed to seeing angels, demons, ghost, and the like. I knew after a short time this preacher was trying to deceive the dinner guest into giving more funds to the ministry. Upon closer examination one can see the true darkness that lurks in the eyes of Satan.

Getting back to my visitor, although, he claimed to be saved; he was oblivious to the tricks of Satan. Being completely naïve in the spiritual things of God, I told my visitor he was the devil. He responded with a wicked laughter. This was getting too weird for me. As he continued the mocking laughter, I was astonished, and amazed at what was happening. My spirit man suddenly took over, and I commanded my visitor to leave.

After he had gone, I evaluated what had just happened, realized it wasn't him, and me in this conversation but it was a conversation between God, and Satan. I couldn't believe I had just told a friend of mine he was Satan. He must have thought I was out of my mind. At that moment even I wasn't sure I was in my right mind. After all, I wasn't sure at that point what had just happened to me. I had encountered spiritual travel before, but had never been hurt, or felt pain the way I did in this experience.

For example, in the late 60's, a friend of mine worked on the pipeline. He was going to take me the next day to see the site where he would be working. That night I had, I thought, a dream. In my sleep, I was driving down a dirt road lined with a few trees. I came to a gate, got out of my car, opened the gate, and continued down the road. I came to a large rock query, filled with water. The landscape consisted of large mounds of tiny rocks, and some backhoes along with other equipment were there. That was the end of my dream.

The next day, my friend and I drove out to the site. We turned onto a dirt road, and I immediately recognized my surroundings. As we drove down the dirt road I told my friend about the bridge, query, mounds of rocks, trees, and all, before we got to them. This frightened him, and me. Sure enough, everything was just as I had seen in my dream. Only now, I know it wasn't a dream. My spirit man had been there. This wasn't a first for me, but one of many pleasant ventures. I didn't know then that God was teaching me about my future in Him.

The next time I saw my visitor from this present experience, he acted as though nothing had happened. He told me that in one minute he was listening to me, and the next minute he was leaving. This was the strangest, and most unusual experience I had ever had in the Lord. It was my first of many to come, real encounters with Satan in the flesh. I didn't know then spirits need a body in which to manifest their good, or evil deeds. They don't need a body to influence the mind, but to carry out the action of sin. I learned from this experience that truly is a spiritual war being fought that cannot be seen with the naked eye. The difference a moment in the presence of God made in my life is extraordinary, and was life changing.

Immediately after the incidents of that night, I began to cry, going over, and over in my mind the events I had witnessed. My emotions were running wild with happiness, love, sorrow, pain, and a bit of confusion, and fear until I read Exodus 24: 15 –17, and Deuteronomy 4:15 about God being on the mountain, and the children of Israel below. They paint a picture of exactly what I had seen. Then confusion, and fear left me, and astonishment, and confidence replaced them.

All this was very new to me. Supernatural experiences weren't new but knowing what they are was new to me. Part of me understood, and yet part of me did not. I know now why Jeremiah, aside from mourning for Israel, is called the weeping prophet. Experiences with God are so over whelming, that tears just naturally flow.

After this encounter my first thoughts were those of uselessness, and unworthiness. I saw for the first time how God views His creation of man, and how disgustingly filthy man has become. There really is nothing good in man. I can understand now why God said in Isaiah 64:6, "Our righteousness is as filthy rags." I couldn't help but ask myself, "what's the use in serving God?" From what I had just seen, none are good enough to make it to God's Kingdom.

No matter how good I become, I still can't stand in God's presence, and live. He is the epitome of goodness, pureness, holiness, and love. I am the exact opposite in self- righteousness. I had never felt so helpless, and alone in my life. I felt hopeless, and wanted to die, only then I was afraid to die for fear of being in God's presence again. I nearly gave up hope in that moment.

The experience came at a time when I had made a commitment to serve God with my whole heart. I had grown in His word, and felt secure in my hope of eternal salvation, but was still a babe in Christ. Sitting there after this experience, I was ready to give up. I was dismayed and discouraged over the condition of my spirit. I had thought I was righteous but found that I wasn't. I was disappointed in myself, and the condition of the intents of my heart. I thought I was a good person, but in the light of God I found I wasn't even near good. There is none good but God (Matthew 19:17).

In my dismay, God spoke to me. He told me to be strong, and not to be afraid, or discouraged. He assured me He would be with me wherever I go, and that His love for me will carry me through. I'll never forget these words He spoke, "Even in the fallen state of humanity, my love for man will never cease to be, for love is what I AM." He continued to explain that I, in myself, could not be righteous, and that it is the righteousness of Jesus that has saved me. He told me that He had given me this experience not to discourage, but to encourage me. He said Satan had come to plant seeds of discouragement in my mind. What better time for Satan to come than just after I had stood in the light of God's glory?

Satan had tried to rob me of what God was trying to give me. This is how fast Satan works. He was there with me before God ever took me into the Spirit. Satan was there to steal this experience by causing confusion and doubt as to the real nature of this encounter. Satan tried to make me believe that it was him that had allowed me to stand in God's presence. He nearly had me convinced that I could never be good enough to stand in God's presence, and how useless it would be to serve God. Had God not been there to tell me the truth, Satan would have stolen from me my most valuable possession. He would have stolen the very essence of God from my heart and replaced it with a lie that would have cost me my salvation – my life eternal with God.

Feeling much better and relieved, I was able to rejoice in the Lord. I began to give thanks that my understanding had been opened. Now residing in a space once void of hope, a sense of security I had never known filled the very depths of my spirit. I was grateful to be alive, and that God was giving me more time to grow in His grace, and knowledge. I know I'll never be pure enough by myself to stand before God, but through Jesus Christ I can become pure, because it is Jesus in me that is pure. I never want to stand in God's presence again in the same spiritual condition as that first time.

Since that night I have pondered in my heart this experience with God, while waiting for the revelation to come. The following is a brief interpretation, as well as is the entire chapter:

> The sea of people represented God's people on earth past, present, and future. The brown hooded robes hanging to the ground are coats

representing our sin, and the spiritual condition we are in before receiving Jesus as our Savior. Brown is the exact opposite of the white robes we are to receive in the Kingdom. It was a covering, however giving some protection from the light of God's glory. This robe was only a covering and would not allow them to stand in the presence of God.

Only Moses was allowed to go up on the Mount of God and live to tell it. There wasn't a white robe among them, meaning there is none who can stand before God in their sinful nature, and live life in eternity with God. The fire that nearly consumed me is what each person, dead or alive is facing on Judgment Day.

One of my friends got offended when I told her that there isn't a white robe among us. She took this as an attack against her personal spiritual condition. First of all we will not receive a white robe until we leave this world. Second, if we think we are righteous, think again. There are none righteous but God, no not one." (Romans 3:10) Until our spirit is changed from glory to glory, it will remain in these vile bodies of flesh, prone to sin covered in brown hooded robes that hang to the ground. These robes looked like the robes we have seen Monk's wear. This is just a visual for the writing. There is no read between the lines about the Monks intended. It's just how the robes looked.

We can be made righteous through Christ, but we will not be arrayed in a white robe until we are absent from this vile body, and completely purified. This can only happen at the return of Jesus, in the rapture. Until then we must continue to live in these brown robes of sin while choosing the righteousness of God that we may receive our white robes at Jesus' appearing in the air.

As I have said before, our nature is not changed once we receive Christ as Savior, although a change does occur. Once Salvation has been received, we are set in a place to be sanctified. Sanctification is a process over much time. While there should be evidence in a person of their salvation experience, they will not display complete holiness in the works of their flesh.

This leads me to mention what I call the holiness movement. I know people who think they are holy, yet they judge others based on their own personal convictions. For example: I know people who walk with God and have been changed from their old nature to the righteousness of Christ, who still drink wine on occasion, smoke cigarettes, and some overeat. The holiness movement degrades these people, and show anger, and hostility toward them. The holiness people think they are holy, because they don't wear makeup, jewelry, don't cut their hair, and women don't wear pants. I don't know if that is how holiness looks. It tells in Ezekiel 16 how God dressed the people in jewels, and precious ornaments, and made them rich. I lived for over three years under this bondage to manmade laws, until I read 1 Samuel 16:7. It is completely all right for a woman to wear long hair tied in a bun, to not wear makeup, pants, etc., but it is not necessary in the eyes of God.

There is no amount of washing or cleansing that can be done while we are in these vile garments that can make them white. Only the washing of water by the word, and the blood of Jesus can change these filthy garments into the glorious white garments of praise. Even then we have to take off the old and put on the new. This physical change will not occur until He appears.

We do have the promise, "though your sins be as scarlet, they shall be white as snow." (Isaiah 1:18) This doesn't mean we can't walk in the righteousness of Christ in the here and now. It simply means our conversion will not be complete until we receive our white robes. Once we receive Jesus and are saved, we can walk in His righteousness now. In our salvation, we have been made righteous. It is all about Him, not us. He is the one righteous, not us. Even after we receive Him as Savior, He is still the righteous one, not us.

While I was in God's presence, I didn't begin to burn because God is evil, but because He is good, and all love. It was I, that was evil, and the shame of my sin (disobedience to God) is what began to burn. Sin is evil and sin cannot stand in the presence of God without igniting into flames of fire. It is the same as striking a match and holding a piece of paper over the flame. The paper is going to burn. It doesn't burn because it is bad but because it contains flammable elements. The flame from the match isn't bad either. It burns because that is what fire does. If it didn't burn it wouldn't be fire.

This same principle applies when a person stands before God. God is pure Love. Love is what He is. He can't help what pure love does to evil, or sin. Pure love will totally consume sin. If people have sin in them when they stand in the light of God's presence, they will automatically begin to burn from the shame of their disobedience to God. This is reason we must receive Jesus as our Savior. He gave His life so that we can know the truth, and live.

A person can do good deeds all day long, but unless Jesus is in their heart, they are still in sin. Good works is not a ticket to enter heaven.

When God's light of glory touches the heart, it lights up the intents of the heart. If the intents of the heart have been committed unto good works, the heart will be changed to glory. This glory will appear as a prism of light that reflects God's glory and will return to Him in an array of beautiful colors.

An illustration of this is done with a diamond, and sunlight. When sunlight penetrates a flawless diamond, the diamond sends out an array of beautiful colors from each point of its perfect cut facets. If the diamond has a flaw in it, the light will not reflect from that spot, or blemish. These spots are usually black, and light will not reflect from a black surface. It will instead be absorbed. Imagine if you were to absorb the consuming fire of God. (Deuteronomy 4:24)

If spots of sin, or bad intents of the heart, having works committed unto evil, black flaws, are found in the heart, the light of God's glory will not be refracted back to Him. Instead, the spots will absorb the light, and the light will then ignite these spots, or blemishes upon contact. These spots are the decaying of the soul, and spirit, like leprosy is the decaying of the natural body. When God's light of glory shines upon these spots, the shame from having them will burst forth as a flaming fire, engulfing the very depths of the soul, and spirit.

It may seem difficult to understand how shame can burn. It will become flame in chest of the body, or heart of man, that will begin to consume his very nature. If you remember the TV show Bonanza, you will remember the map of the Ponderosa at the beginning of the show. As the theme song played a branding iron branded the middle of the map, and a fire began to burn, spreading from the middle to the ends. That's the way the fire in my chest began. The worst is: The flame never dies because the shame never ceases. Shame is a spirit and will ignite into an infinite flame that will feed upon itself for eternity. This fire will burn continuously, and there will be no escaping the pain once it begins to burn.

Have you ever done something you feel bad about? Remember the feeling of remorse you had in the moment you realized what you had done? This remorse is shame. It isn't a good feeling. In fact, it is a spirit that takes up residence in your heart to torment you forever, or until you rectify its cause. God placed this feeling of shame in us as a check- point for our intents. When we feel shame, and know we have done wrong, it is the spiritual law of God at work in us, is therefore why Jesus came. He knew we could not stand in God's presence in our pre salvation condition. He came to show us the way to prepare for God's Kingdom. He didn't come to keep us from having the life we like or want. He came to show us how to live life, have it more abundantly, and how to obtain eternal life with Him.

The words to a song come to mind, "Turn your eyes upon Jesus, look full in His wonderful face, and the things of earth will grow strangely dim, in the light of His glory and grace." The things of this world are temporal. Jesus was in the wilderness, and Satan offered Him the kingdoms of the world if Jesus would bow down and worship Satan. Satan was offering Jesus the shopping malls full of trinkets, clothes, automobiles, diamonds, and houses, with all the lights, and alluring display. Jesus already had all this, and He left the splendor of all these things, and more to die on a cross for us. Satan was trying to give Jesus what Jesus already owns. It was the same trick Satan used on Eve in the Garden of Eden. She was already like God, but he caused her to think otherwise. Jesus didn't fall for his trick.

It's odd the way Satan works. Think about it. Jesus is the light of the world. When He shines His light on us, do we sparkle? The jewelry stores, car lots, and the like all use light as a thing to make their product look better. Have you ever noticed how a diamond ring, a car, or a motorcycle, once it leaves the store, doesn't glitter like it did in the showroom? These things need the light to show how they really look. We are no different. We need the light to see how we really look too. When the light of Jesus shines on us, we either light up the world with His love, glory, and grace, or we stay dull, and lifeless like a piece of charcoal. When the light of Jesus shines on us, if He is not in us, His light will not refract back to God. Without Him we will not glow in the light of God's glory.

When the showroom light falls on a diamond, the facets reflect the light. The diamond shines, and is beautiful, except where there is a flaw. The flaw is made of carbon and is black. Black does not reflect light but absorbs it. If we are not in Christ, we are like carbon. Then when the light of Christ falls on us, we do not reflect the light of Christ, but we absorb it. When this happens it's like holding a lighted match to a piece of coal. The coal is going to ignite.

Sin in us is like carbon. It absorbs the light of Christ and reacts the same as lighting the carbon on fire. Sin is a flaw in a person, the same as carbon is a flaw in a diamond.

Jesus is the light (John 1). We must become born again to even see His light, and to see the flaws in ourselves. Without the light of Christ, we can't know the benefits of what Jesus is offering, nor for what He stands. John 3:3, Jesus said to Nicodemus, "except a man be born again, he cannot see the kingdom of God." In verse 5 Jesus said, "except a man be born of water and of the Spirit he cannot enter the kingdom of God."

There are people who call on God, but do not know Him, and have never been born again. They don't know that God doesn't even hear them if they are not born again and are outside repentance. There is only one way to God, and that is through Jesus Christ. You can't get there any other way, and you are not in Jesus if you are not born again.

In this day, and time people want to believe they can live in immorality, and the like, and that God is going to bless them anyway. God does not bless sin. If one is living a life of sin, you will not receive the blessings of God. Don't deceive yourselves into believing a lie. "Study to show yourselves approved unto God a Workman that needeth not to be ashamed, rightly dividing the word of truth" 2ⁿᵈ Timothy 15:1.

Don't be fooled into thinking all the things in this world is the gold in life. Jesus owns it all, and it is all yours if you let Him give it to you. If you let Satan give it to you, you will perish with the taking. Satan has nothing real to give. He doesn't have access to the spiritual blessings Jesus came to give. Satan gives all the things that will rust, and decay, be eaten by moths, and will vanish away one day. Jesus gives the things that are eternal. He blesses with all spiritual blessings. These will make you happy, satisfied, and will not vanish away.

Receive Jesus, that you may be able to make an informed decision on everything. Without Him, you can't see the truth. Without the light of Christ, you aren't seeing the true picture of a thing. Unless you look through the eyes of Christ, you are only going to see the glitter of what Satan wants you to see. He couldn't deceive Jesus, and Jesus died for us, so we too, can escape Satan's deception.

We only must receive Jesus by faith, for who He is, the Son of God, before our eyes will be opened.

Adam and Eve in the garden lived in paradise before Satan deceived Eve. When they partook of the forbidden fruit, their eyes were opened to all the bad in the world. Their new sight took them into another spiritual dimension where they could only see the earthly things. Once they knew the evil, they were no longer immune from evil. They now had to live with the knowledge of good and evil. They disobeyed God in what He told them not to do, and now we are all paying for that disobedience. You and I are no different. If we disobey God's word, we are going to pay for it with our lives.

God does not accept ignorance. His word is here for all to see and learn. There are no excuses that will hold up as to why we continue to live in sin. God is serious. He loves us and wants us to live a wonderful life, but He will not go back on His word. We can trust Him, for that very reason. Once He has said a thing, He doesn't change it for anyone. Sometimes He will delay it, but He never changes it.

Now, to see Jesus, we must receive Him by faith, by becoming born again of water and of the Spirit, that our spiritual eyes will be opened. Otherwise, we can't see the Kingdom of God, and the paradise in which we can live. Jesus is our way back to paradise. Don't delude yourself into thinking you can get there another way. There is no other way, and unless you can see this, you will live in constant turmoil your entire life. With Jesus, no matter what one goes through, it is bearable. It is bearable because the things of this world will grow strangely dim in the light of God's glory and grace. Amen!

Exodus 3:1-6 tells of Moses, and the burning bush. God was in the bush, and the bush was on fire. As the bush burned it wasn't consumed. It just continued to burn until God left the bush, after which, there was no change in the bush from its original appearance. It was left unharmed. The difference in the burning bush, and the way shame burns is, shame will always be there in the unrepentant heart. God will not inhabit the shame, but His knowledge of truth will be there, never to leave. Unlike the heart of man, the bush wasn't consumed because it was an inanimate object.

I'm sure Moses had a difficult time conversing with God while God was in the bush. The Bible doesn't tell us how Moses felt, but it does say God instructed Moses to take off his shoes, because he was standing on Holy Ground. Maybe Moses' bare feet on the ground acted as an electrical ground to the fire of God's glory. The light of God's glory is an electrical light. I do know after that experience Moses did God's bidding. After my experience I did God's bidding too. I know this is Wisdom. After an experience with God, you will do God's bidding. If you don't then you had an experience with something or someone else.

Some people don't believe there is a hell. I know there is a hell, and in hell the knowledge of the truth will cause one to burn because it was not received during the acceptable period of God's grace on earth. Hell is a place without God's presence. This is what being saved means. To be saved from the fire of God's love. If one has been saved through accepting Jesus as Lord, and Savior, he will not be consumed but will remain like as did the burning bush becoming part of God's consuming fire without harm. If one has not been saved, he will burn for eternity, and will feel the pain, and anguish in knowing the truth, but having not been transformed by it, that he may stand in God's presence, and live.

Hell is being eternally separated from God by our own choice, and then learning we made the wrong decision. Isn't that what Adam and Eve did? They banished themselves from Paradise through their disobedience to God's word. They knew the truth but didn't trust God enough to stand on the truth, and they fell.

What is the Truth? The truth is this. God is a loving God. Love is what He is. He knows we can't stand in His presence without automatically being consumed. He made a way for us to live with Him, commune with Him, and once again be in His presence without being consumed. If we do not take that way, we can't stand in the presence of God. Our elements must be changed.

When I stood before God that night, I knew Jesus as my Savior. I was testifying of Him when I was carried away in the spirit. I learned from this experience that saved, or unsaved we will burn to some degree in God's presence, unless we walk in obedience to Christ.

If our nature is in the process of change, and the intent of our heart is to be more like Christ the fire will not be a consuming fire but will be a purging fire filtrating our very being. Therefore, we must be purified, and our bodies changed before we stand in God's presence. When purity stands in the presence of purity, there is no conflict. There is unity, and completeness. Purity plus purity equals ONE WHOLE.

1 John 3:2-3, "Beloved, now are we the sons of God, and it doth not yet appear what we shall be, but we know that, when He shall appear, we shall be like Him; for we shall see Him as He is. And every man that hath this hope in Him purifieth himself, even as He is pure."

God later showed me a vision of a large vat. He often speaks by vision to enhance the understanding of His message. A picture is worth a thousand words. Visions are not always given in the literal sense but are likely to be symbolic in their meanings. In this vision of the vat, God is symbolically demonstrating the purifying process of the spirit. The vat appeared like that of a large, black, cast iron cooking pot. It was sitting over a fire. The contents, or intents of our hearts appeared in the form of a liquid (Isaiah 13:7). It would behoove you to read all of Isaiah 13. God then poured the liquid containing all the goods, and evils of our natures into the vat to burn away the sin, and dross; cleansing us of our unrighteousness; completing the purification process. Because sin cannot enter the kingdom of God, it must be destroyed.

The goods represent confessed sins of the saved, and our evils represent un-confessed sins of the sinner, and believer. In the vat, un-confessed sin is burned, and does not escape the vat. It now becomes weight, and lies in the bottom of the vat, continuing to burn, never evaporating. Whereas the hearts containing good intents when poured into the vat, burns, but are changed into steam, and rises out of the vat in the form of a vapor cloud. The vapor cloud, when it rises, is alive with a type of energy glowing as a white light. The cloud of energy, and light represent the now spiritual body. The size of the cloud, whether small, or large, is determined by the deeds that were performed by those persons while on the earth in their natural bodies (Heb. 4:12-13). The spiritual bodies I've seen are all different sizes. I've seen angels as small as infants (not cupids with bow and arrow), and as large as 8 or 9 feet tall. The times I saw Jesus, He was so tall I can't even begin to guess His height, another time I saw Him He was average height compared to us. Spiritual bodies can change in size, depending on the task it is performing, where it is, and in what dimension of earth, or heaven it is.

Therefore, when your nature (intent of the heart) is poured into the vat, or goes through the fire, your size when you come out, will be determined according to how much of your deeds, or works, are burned, and how much of them rises from the vat.

This reminds me of the scripture in 1 Corinthians 4:5, "Therefore judge nothing before the time, until the Lord come, who both will bring to light the hidden things of darkness and will make manifest the counsels of the hearts: and then shall every man have praise of God."

Once I was praying for a teenaged girl while washing dishes, when suddenly the spirit of intercession, and spiritual warfare came upon me. I stopped washing dishes and began to command Satan, and his demons to leave this girl. As I prayed with all my might, and God's Spirit, I saw myself growing in height. I was as tall as my ceiling of 8 feet when I realized my size in the Spirit. Just as quickly as I had grown, I came back to normal size. The Lord showed me that when we pray with authority we are like spiritual giants. The more we linger in prayer, the larger our Spirit man grows. In the light of this size transformation, Satan appears as an ant.

If you are a nonbeliever without Jesus in your life, there will be no good thing found in you, and your entire being, and nature will be burned in the presence of God, only leaving your shame to lay in the bottom of the vat to stew or burn (2 Thess. 2:7-17). On the other hand, if you have made Jesus your life, confessed your sins, and are washed by His blood, all of you will have been made good by the Christ in you, the hope of glory. (Col. 1:27)

The God part of your nature depending on the intent of your heart will be raised up as a vapor cloud (which is your eternal spirit, seen as a cloud of energy, and light). It will be completely illuminated, revealing your standing in God, and your service to Him while you were on the earth, for all to see. The things to be revealed will be your works, and whether they are of good works committed unto God, or built upon foundations of gold, silver, precious stones, wood, hay, or stubble.

If you performed the works for personal gain, or personal gratification, or for any other reasons than for the love of God, your works will be consumed. If the love of God is not found in them, they become fuel for the fire; being unlike God, therefore not being able to stand in His presence. If your works are burned, what rewards have you for your labor? Your works will be burned, but you will be saved if you accepted Jesus as your Savior. (1 Cor. 3)

If good is the intent of your heart, and your works were committed unto God, they will not be burned, and you will receive rewards for them. If you have done much good you will be great in the Kingdom, but if you have done little, you will be the least in the Kingdom (Rev. 20:12-13) it is, however, better to be the least in the kingdom than to not be there at all. You won't receive any crowns, if you have no works unto God to place at the feet of Jesus with exception the crown of life. (Luke 7:28).

When the vapor cloud rises, it rises in the appearance of a character, or personality trait revealing your works. As I have said previously, the spiritual eye can see things that can't be seen with the natural eye. For example: Let us assume that while on earth, your heart cried out for mercy on the world, and this was the greatest intent of your heart in your works. When the intent of your heart is poured into the vat, a vapor cloud of mercy will emerge, and this will be your new character, personality, and name in glory. Everyone will know you as Mercy. You will be known for the intent of your heart just as you will know others for the intents of their heart. It will be wonderful to spend eternity with names like, Merciful, Faithful, Joyful, Peacemaker, Poor in Spirit, Meekness, Gentleness, Kindness, etc. Others will know your works, because you don't only receive a certain crown for these works but works have an appearance that depicts the name. Mercy will look like Mercy, etc. I don't know what appearance Mercy will have, but it will be beautiful, I'm sure.

God has many names. Jehovah Shalom (God is our peace), Jehovah Nissi (God is our Banner), Jehovah Tsidkenu (God is our righteousness), Jehovah Rapha (God is our health/healer), Jehovah Jireh (God is our supplier/provider), Jehovah Rohi (God is our Sheppard), and Jehovah Shamah (God is there). He has more names, but I'll use these seven.

In each name of God, a part of His character is revealed. The body of Christ, or The Church is made up of many members, each having a part, which supplies the body (Church) with a measure of God's love. God is a spirit, and the character traits found in His names are also spirit (the seven Spirits of God). When we go to heaven, we will become complete in God by the intents of our hearts being made manifest. When God created us from His heart, we each became a bit, or part of His heart, containing His names along with the power, and wisdom in them. He gives us His names, and once saved, He begins to mold, and shape our personalities, and characters into the character of these names, and into the effectual working measure of that part that would make increase in His body (The Church, Eph. 2:23), edifying itself in love.

Therefore, each person in the world is predestined to become a part of God's body in a measure of His character. As we grow in Christ God's names in us will develop in the requirements necessary to represent that name. If a person shows mercy more than they show longsuffering, they will have the name of mercy. However, there will be those who don't respond, or accept the calling, and will never receive their new name written in glory.

So as the natural body has arms, legs, feet, etc., the body of Christ has, mercy, faith, joy, and all the names of God. When God's character, or God's nature has been established in His Church, The Church may be united with God in the unblemished, spotless form from which we came (God's Heart). If Jesus comes back before the Church has reached its potential, God help us. The question is will He come back if we are not ready? I think He will. He has been preparing us for over 6000 years. Somehow, I think that is ample time to get it right. Jesus said in Matt: 18:9, "if your eye offends thee pluck it out, for it is better to enter into life with one eye, rather than having two eyes to be cast into hell fire." This verse is saying to get rid of anything that may stop you from entering the Kingdom.

Another level of meaning in this scripture is Jesus saying, there will be some who will not be ready when He comes back: That it is better for the remnant to make it in than no one at all. I believe Jesus is referring to the rapture here. He will come back for His Church, even though many won't be ready. He will take His Church, so that this remnant will not have to endure the tribulation period. The eye that offends is a part of the body that would not supply his, or her part to the body. They chose to remain offended, rather than to forgive, and receive, thereby being turned over to a reprobate mind.

Our mission on earth is to come together in unity, having built, or raised up the same characteristics of God's heart, in our hearts, becoming a counter part for Christ, and to be united in marriage as one spirit with Him. We can't do this without Jesus. Unlike marriage on the earth, having one mate with many qualities, the bride of Christ will be many, each having qualities, or a measure of God's heart (nature) in its fullness, to complete the bride. Therefore, there will be neither male, nor female in heaven. In heaven we will have been transformed into spiritual bodies that portray the likeness, and image of Christ in His nature, or glory: joined together with Him in marriage, no longer being in part, but made whole, and glorified by God, becoming one spirit with Him. (Rom. 8:29-30)

Unlike marriage in the natural, becoming one flesh with our mates, we will become one whole with Jesus in the Spirit. We start that process here on earth when we receive Jesus as Savior. In accepting Jesus as Savior, He becomes our betrothed. Until we get to heaven, we are only engaged to Him. In Heaven we will marry Him at which time we become complete in Him.

Theologians can't seem to agree on who the bride of Christ will be. Some say the bride is the new city Jerusalem, and others say the bride is the Church. According to scripture the bride is both the city, and the Church. Like the Church is a building, but the people in the Church are the Church.

1. Revelation 21:9 reads, one of the angels having the seven vials appeared to John. He said to John, "Come up hither, I will show thee the bride, the Lamb's wife." Then the angel carried John away in the spirit, and showed him that great city, the holy Jerusalem descending out of heaven. According to this scripture the wife, and the bride of Christ is the city.

2. Revelation 21:12, 14 tells us that the new city Jerusalem has twelve gates made of pearl and written upon the gates are the names of the twelve tribes of the children of Israel. Verse 14 continues that the city has twelve foundations, and on them are the names of the twelve Apostles of the Lamb. Each foundational wall is garnished with precious stones, a different stone representing each foundation.

I believe the twelve gates of pearl represents the tribes of the children of Israel in the sense that God is no respecter of persons; that each tribe of people are God's children regardless of the tribe from which they come; represented by one kind of stone. Because the tribes of Israel represent the entrance to the city, I believe this is symbolic as follows: entrance to the city, for the Gentiles, is gained through the Jews. Not Jews as a whole, but through Jesus, the Jew.

Because all the gates were seen as made of pearls, there is no other entrance to the city, the pearl of great price (Matt.13: 46), but through Jesus. There are some who say the Pearl of great price isn't referring to Jesus. I believe it is.

However, the Church is to provoke the Jews to jealousy that they might come to see Jesus as their entrance to the new city Jerusalem. For the most part, the Church has failed in this duty. In this failure to go to the Jew first, entrance to the city will be denied to those who turn against the Jewish people (Israel). The Bible tells us that those who bless Israel will be blessed, and those who curse Israel will be cursed.

The twelve different stones in the foundational walls represent the Apostles whose name is written on that wall. I believe these stones (figuratively speaking) are the Apostles themselves, as I will continue to explain.

In constructing a building, the most important part of its construction is the foundation. If the structures foundation isn't strong, and sturdy, made of excellent materials, the entire structure will collapse. The Apostles are the foundation of the Church, and the rock, or stone upon which it was built. (Matt. 16:18)

> 3. In Revelation 2:17, Jesus said to the Church of Pergamos that if they would repent, and overcome, He will give them a white stone; and in the stone a new name written, which no man knows except he that receives it.

In the ancient days of old, there was a custom of giving a white stone at a trial if the defendant was acquitted, and a black stone if found guilty. Many scholars acquaint Revelation 2:17 with this custom, adding that the name written on the stone is one of acquittal, or guilty in the sense that each person knows whether they are saved, or not; that no one else can know what is in another person's heart, only he that receives it. I believe this is true. However, I believe that the white stone is a pearl representing those who will receive salvation through Jesus. These pearls (white stones), represents the over-comers, and the tribe of Israel from which they came. Meaning God's chosen – the Jew by blood. When Gentiles accept salvation, they do not become a Jew as most think. On the other hand, the Gentile, and the Jew do become one in spirit with God. Instead of two separate peoples, there are only one people in the spirit by the circumcision of the heart. Everyone receiving salvation through Christ becomes part of the Church and is allowed to enter the new city Jerusalem.

The new name written on the pearl that no one knows except he that receives it will be the same as the new name of Jesus, "The Word of God", showing that the over-comer is His whether Jew, or Gentile. One can't know Jesus if he does not know the word of God. The only way to know if salvation has been received is to know Jesus, who is the Word of God; and only he that receives it

Linda L. Evans

can know it. In knowing the Word of God, one becomes a part of the remnant of God's chosen people and is symbolized by a pearl (white stone), in the gates of the city new Jerusalem.

By knowing the Word of God, Jesus, the white stone, or pearl is Jesus, and all who receive this stone is acquitted.

The Word of God being the only thing that will not pass away, when the heavens, and earth pass away, will remain forever with God. John 1:1 reads, "In the beginning was the word, and the word was with God, and the word was God." The believer being transformed into the word of God, by the washing of water by the word, will not pass away but will become one spirit with the word (Jesus) to forever be with God. Having come from God's heart to begin with, the believer always was with God from the beginning. Entrance back into the city – God, must be gained through Jesus, the Messiah.

In Revelation 3:4 Jesus told the Church of Sardis, "Thou hast a few names even in Sardis which have not defiled their garments; and they shall walk with me in white: for they are worthy." Sardis was a city that was first converted by the Gospel from the preaching of John. It is said that they also became the first city to revolt from Christianity. The few names in Sardis that had not defiled their garments were a small remnant of believers that remained faithful to the Gospel of Jesus Christ during this revolt. Jesus said this remnant should walk with Him in white for they are worthy. The white represents the purity in the wedding garments of the believers that have not turned away from Christ and will walk with Him as a part of His bride.

No matter how evil the world becomes, there will be a remnant of God's people who will attend the marriage supper of the Lamb as His bride.

4. (a) In Revelation 3:12 Jesus told the Church of Philadelphia (the perfect Church of whom Christ will return to receive unto Himself), "Him that overcometh will I make a pillar in the temple of my God, and he shall no more go out, and I will write upon him the name of my God, and the name of the city of my God, which is new Jerusalem, which cometh down out of heaven from my God; and I will write upon Him my new name." From this scripture we see that if we overcome the natural, by the circumcision of the heart, becoming one spirit with Christ, we (whether Jew, or Gentile) will be made pillars in the temple of God. A pillar is a large column made of stone and is a supporting structural column for the building. In the new city Jerusalem, there is no temple in it according to Revelation 21:22; and John said, "And I saw no temple therein: for the Lord God almighty, and the Lamb are the temple of it." Therefore, we will become one spirit with Christ, and be made like unto precious stones, and placed in the bosom of God, and the Lamb (John 1:18, 3:13), who are the temple of the city, abiding in the temple to go no more out.

210

(b) Revelation 3:12 Jesus continues, "And I will write upon him the name of my God. According to Ephesians 4:30, and Revelation 7:3, the name of God is the Holy Spirit, of whom the servants (the believers) of God are sealed (pledged) or betrothed unto the day of redemption (the day the pledge is made good, or wedding day). Revelation 3:1 tells us that Jesus has the seven Spirits of God, which are the various names, and administrations of the Holy Spirit with His wisdom, and powers. For example: the seven names of Jehovah God, each one representing power, and wisdom of the Spirit, and its administrative duties.

I believe the Church of Sardis who had a few names, and had not defiled their garments is, also representative of a believer who bears the many names of God by His Spirit. Because the believer will not have reached perfection until the return of Christ, he will not have reached spiritual maturity in the fullness of God's names, and in the administration of their wisdom, and power. The believer who walks in the Spirit, though having not perfected his walk, but has been steadfast in Christ, will walk with Him in white; for they are worthy. They will receive all the names of God.

c) "And the name of the city of my God, which is New Jerusalem which cometh down out of heaven from my God." Galatians 4:26 tell us that Jerusalem is Mother of us all. In Revelation 21:2, 10, and 11 John said, "I saw the holy city New Jerusalem coming down out of heaven from God adorned as a bride prepared for her husband; having the glory of God (God's glory is the light of the city); and her light was like unto a stone most precious, even like a jasper stone, clear as crystal." (Think of how the body is formed, like a pearl, in the womb of a woman) New Jerusalem is Mother of us all. The body (the Church), having been formed, and fashioned, as part of the city, the same as a child is a part of his or her mother in her womb, will remain in the womb, or city forever. Entering the city will be like going back to the womb of our mother (figuratively speaking); a place of safety, warmth, serenity, peace, purity, security, a walled city of love; only, instead of being prenatal, we will be postnatal. Nevertheless, having been birthed back into the womb of our mother, New Jerusalem. "Ye must be born again." (John 3).

(d) Jesus concludes the verse with, "And I will write upon him my new name." Revelation 19:13 tell us that His name is "The Word of God". Jesus will write upon the believers His new name, signifying that they are His. We will receive His new name the same as a bride receives the name of her husband in marriage.

According as I have written, and the scriptures I've written, I believe as follow:

To enter God's Kingdom, we must have a pure heart before we can see God. (Matt. 5:8) We can be made pure by the hope of Christ coming. (John 3:2-3) We must have a renewed spirit, which bears the fruits of the Spirit. (Gal. 5:22:23) By these fruits we will be transformed, and sealed, having the nature of God, and all that is good in the sight of God. In bearing His names, by His Spirit, we become one with God. Jesus, who also bears the Spirit (and/or seven spirits of God), and the name, "The Word of God", is one with God in the same Holy Spirit; having always been with God from the beginning. The over comer who is sealed unto God by the Spirit with Jesus, is the same as becoming one by adoption, or salvation.

Having come from the heart of God as God's preconceived idea, we will return to the heart of God as a pillar in the temple; like as unto a precious stone – white pearl, placed back into the womb (a place where everything is brought into life), the bosom of God, as God, and the Lamb are the temple of the New City Jerusalem.

Having become a part of the temple, God's body, we become the bride of Christ, joined to Him by the Holy Spirit of God in matrimony. As a baby is the new life in the womb of a woman, so shall the saved be the new life, or spirit of the city (mother), New Jerusalem, in the bosom of God. A city without the spirit of it is like the spirit without a body in which to dwell; it accomplishes nothing.

Having been gathered in one all things in Christ, unto God from whence we came; to abide in the womb of the city, our mother, God's bosom, we will have been changed from glory to glory; from God's heart back to His heart. When we stand in the light of God, the Father of lights (we will be light also, as God is our Father), the colors of light produced from the precious, and flawless stones (the saints – us) in the city, which is the spirit of the city (the cloud of energy, and light); the sons, and daughters of God (us) will have been made manifest; His glory (us), of whom He is the Father; the adoption having been made complete, and we shall see God.

We will be arrayed like a spectrum (white light) in the likeness of a prism (a body having many facets – becoming part of the trinity, not as a God head, but by becoming one with the Spirit (Genesis 1:27 - God created man in His own image, Genesis 3:22, man has become as one of us). God's light will penetrate the prism (us). We will be wearing white robes of purity. Any artist knows white is the presence of all color. We arrive at this conclusion from the rainbow. White is not considered a color, but it is represented in the rainbow by the colors of the rainbow. Because Black is the absence of all color, then white must be the presence of all color, and if white is the presence of all color, then white is in the rainbow. Is this why paint stores use a base of white to get the color you want? Based on this theory, our white robes of righteousness will consist of all colors.

In ancient times the Hebrew Priest wore white robes with precious stones sown on them. These stones were of multiple kinds, and colors. Since we are considered as being a royal priesthood, then stands to reason we will have precious stones in our white robes. These stones can't be seen until the light of God's glory shines on our robes. Remember in the beginning of this chapter when I stood in the light of God's glory, and my first thought was for the rocks to fall on me? The rocks are the only thing man can identify with that could possibly hide us from the light of God and protect us from the pain of our shame. The rocks falling on us wouldn't hurt as badly as standing in the presence of God without the proper attire (righteousness). Good news is our white robes will be made with a breastplate of colorful stones, as reflectors of God's light.

Recall the coat of many colors Jacob gave to Joseph. Joseph was highly favored by Jacob above all his sons. The coat of many colors was representative of the love of the father: a gift of blessing, and favor. The stones in our robes will be a light conductor for the light of God. This is our coat of many colors. Our white robes will allow us to stand in the presence of God, in His likeness, without being harmed by His light. His light will reflect on the stones in our robes and refract back to God. That is how God lights up the city. As His light shines upon us, and refracts back to Him, we will be seen as we really are. Just like the diamonds in the showroom. The light that refracts back to God from the stones in us will light up the Spirit of God that we may see Him as He is.

God's light is an electrical current, that can devastate anything it touches that isn't a like component. I believe that is why, when a person touched the Ark of the Covenant, they would die. The same thing applied when the high priest would go into the holy of holies. If the priest weren't cleansed of sin, and pure, he would die in the presence of God where God sat on the Mercy seat on the Ark of the Covenant.

The veil acted as a conductor of the electricity that came from God, and so did the walls of the Holy of Holies. God instructed the children of Israel to build the Holy of Holies with specific instructions, walls inside lined with gold, strong, and sturdy, and the eight-inch thick, veil that touched the ground. These components were safety measures for the people outside the Holy of Holies to protect them from the light of God. If the priest that entered the Holy of Holies were impure, he would die. The bell he wore would signal the people, as he fell to the ground, to pull him out by the rope tied to him.

When we stand in God's presence in heaven, even though we will be like Him, and purified, we will not be God. Our spiritual bodies will have all the necessary elements to allow us to remain in the presence of God. We will have no shame, and will have been made righteous, and pure. We no longer need to hide from God, for now we will be arrayed in the glory of God. Our white robes of righteousness will allow us to stand in God's presence without consequence, and we will be like Him.

God our father has graced us with love, and favor. He has given us a coat of many colors; every precious stone is our covering. Isn't this what Lucifer had before his banishment from the presence of God? Ezekiel 28:12-22 in the King James Bible gives a description of Satan before his fall. Satan (then Lucifer) was in the Garden of Eden with God. He was arrayed with every precious stone as his covering; he was the anointed cherub that covereth; he was upon the holy mountain of God, and walked up, and down, amid the stones of fire. Satan was perfect until iniquity was found in him. His heart was lifted because of his beauty and his wisdom was corrupted by reason of his brightness.

Is this why Satan's hatred for the Church is so vile, and wicked? He not only lost his place with God, but the Church has been adopted to live in his stead; and will be arrayed with all the precious stones once belonging to him as his covering; and the Church being made perfect will, also inherit the mountain of God – God's Kingdom. It's our Birthright.

God's light will penetrate the prism (us) of stones in our robes, and the precious stones of our covering will refract God's light back to Him in beams of beautiful colored lights; causing a rainbow of colors to fill the temple – God, and the Lamb (Rev.4: 3); thus, having been transformed back into a pure spirit, which is light, by the power of God's names (His Spirit), becoming members of His body, the Godhead, filling all in all, with Christ as the head; in whom is the fullness of God, and the bride of Christ. Therefore, the Church is the Bride of Christ because we are the Spirit of the City New Jerusalem. We the church make up the city just as we make up the Church here on earth. The Church is seen, also as a building having no spirit until the people go inside. Amen!

I attended the 1992, east coast, Women's Aglow Spring Retreat in Rocky Mount, North Carolina. In one of the Worship sessions there was a demonstration of Esther being united in marriage to the King. It was representative of the Church being presented to Christ as His Bride. While I admired the dance, I was ushered to the throne room of God by the Spirit. I stood there and watched as the Church came together like cells in the natural body come together, uniting to form the Bride of Christ. In the natural the girl representing Esther in the dance was dressed in a beautiful wedding gown, and on bended knee. The King in his finest array of armor, was standing, and held out his scepter to her. As she took hold of the Scepter, the king took her hand in his, and raised her up from the floor. As she rose, I saw in the spirit, the body of the Church being raised up as the perfect female counterpart for Jesus.

Just as the natural body has arms, legs, etc., so does the members of the Church become a functioning part of the body of the bride. Each member of the Church will represent a characteristic of the bride's nature. Just as the arm is called an arm, and a leg is called a leg, so shall each member of the bride's body be called by a new name. Because we will have been made spirit, our names, and functions of the names will also be spirit, such as: the spirit of Mercy, the spirit of Faith, the spirit of Joy, and on goes the list.

In this vision of the Bride, all that was in heaven was God, and His Bride, surrounded by angelic host; like Adam, and Eve were in the beginning; but the Bride was made up of the Church; bearing the names of God, which is His nature; thus, becoming the nature of the Bride; being like God; but God, and the Bride were neither male, nor female, for they were one in the Spirit; I AM THAT I AM. In the beginning when God created Adam, and made Eve, He called 'THEM' Adam (Genesis 5:2). It was the most beautiful sight I have ever seen, and mere words cannot describe the real beauty of its essence. The bride of Christ will take her husband's name I AM with God the I AM OF ALL THINGS. I AM I AM. DO WE BECOME 'I AM' 'I AM' with God AS IN 'THEM'?

DNA: And the Spirit, and Bride say "COME"

In James 4:14-17 it is written, "Whereas ye know not what shall be on the morrow. For what is your life? It is even a vapor that appeareth for a little time, and then vanisheth away. For that ye ought to say, if the Lord will, we shall live, and do this or that. But now ye rejoice in your boastings: all such rejoicing is evil. Therefore, to him that knoweth to do good, and doeth it not, to him it is a sin." In this verse of scripture, James refers to this present life as a vapor that appears for a little time, and then vanisheth away. When this vapor vanishes where does it go? Is the vapor the soul, and spirit of man that leaves his body when the body dies? How do we become transformed from this earthly body to the spiritual body of the perfect Bride, arrayed in white, and adorned in brilliance?

When steam rises from a boiling pot of water it escapes into the air and can no longer be seen in its original form. Therefore, when the soul, and spirit leaves the natural body it will be changed from its original form, however present it is. There must be a process that occurs in which this change can be made.

Through the illustration of the vat discussed earlier, God is saying that our life on earth is but for a season, and that it will vanish away some day. He wants us to know that it is what we do now that determines our destiny, and that it is our choice. God will never change. We must change. The natural body cannot stand in God's presence. Without Jesus we cannot be changed from our present form into the renewed spirit of the bride. If we are not changed our lives will become like dried up hay, or stubble, fuel for the fire. We must begin to walk according to the law of the Spirit. The law of the Spirit is simply God's law of love, written in our hearts, and revealed when we receive Jesus as Messiah. Jesus did not come to destroy the law, but to fulfill the law. This doesn't mean we do not obey the law, but that we can keep the law in the spirit through Christ. We do not become righteous by our works. Only by the Spirit do we become righteous if Christ is in us (Rom. 7, and 8). There is no other way to enter the Kingdom of God (John 3:5).

James 4:7-10 reads, "Submit yourselves to God, resist the devil, and he will flee from you. Draw nigh to God, and He will draw nigh to you. Cleanse your hands, ye sinners; and purify your hearts, ye double minded. Be afflicted, and mourn, and weep: let your laughter be turned to mourning, and your joy to heaviness. Humble yourselves in the sight of the Lord, and He will lift you up." Jesus, the King of Kings, will stretch forth His hand, His scepter, and will raise you up unto Himself to be His Bride (Rapture).

This lifting up is the rising of our souls, and spirits having been perfected by the fire having our new nature and bearing our new name. When the vapor rises out of the vat, or vanishes away, it will have been changed into a cloud of water in the form of a white light that will glow as the glory of God; arrayed in brilliance, like as unto a precious stone, having been made pure, and flawless, perfected in size, and shape; as in a perfect, uncut flawless diamond. When John saw the stones on the wall of New Jerusalem, he was seeing the Apostles arrayed in the glory of God with every precious stone as a covering, and their names written in the walls (Isaiah 56:5, Isaiah 62:1-5, and Malachi 3:16-17)

Unlike robes in the natural, made of cloth, our white robes will be our new bodies made of water having been washed of water by the Word (Proverbs 30:4). Not water the way we know water in the natural, but like the dew that watered the earth before God made it to rain. The dew could not be seen until it covered the ground. When our new bodies are raised incorruptible, they will appear in the form of water, or a cloud from having been washed clean by the blood of Jesus; the dew of the Word of God; they will be solid as a stone, yet as clear as crystal.

The people of ancient times regarded the crystal as a permanently solidified form of water. Just as Moses dipped the sacred rod into the waters of Egypt, and defiled the water, to become red like blood, and poison, Jesus cleanses the water of our new body, and soul by His red blood to become white like snow (Isaiah 1:18). This explains why some of the angelic Host, I've seen, appeared as transparent. They are fresh, pure, and clear like natural spring water, yet they are solidified like crystal making them translucent.

When I lived in Los Angeles, California, some friends, and I would visit a place in the mountains, where natural hot springs were located. I always took plastic bottles back home filled with the spring water. It flowed down the sides of the mountains made of rock, and had no impurities, not even the smallest grain of sand. I believe this is why Jesus is called the Day Spring on High; He is even more pure than the purest of all spring water.

Water is the only thing that can stand in a fire, and not be consumed. I believe it is why God commanded us to be washed of water by the Word. The more of His word that abides in us, the more water we are supplying to our spirit. The Word, as it is applied to our lives, will become rivers of living water that will wash away the shame of our spirits; thus, allowing us to live in the presence of the all-consuming fire of God; a new Spirit made pure. We must be born of water and of the Spirit.

Bible Scholars teach that being born of water mentioned in John 3 is the natural birthing of our flesh. This may be so. However, from what the Father has revealed is: Jesus, the Word of God, must be born again in us, not as a baby, but as the Lion of the Tribe of Judah: washing us by the water of God's Word, that our eyes may be opened, that we may see God's Kingdom (just like washing a newborn baby's eyes so they may open. A baby doesn't have vision right away. Its vision comes a few days after birth). After this washing, we can see the Kingdom of God, by the light of His Word. After this washing, our eyes open, and we can see Jesus that He is the Son of God. We, also become born again, but it is our spirit man that is quickened (made alive), so that our spirit may be allowed into the Kingdom of God.

When the Holy Spirit came upon Mary, the mother of Jesus, she conceived a child. This child was Jesus. It was through her obedience to the word of God that she conceived. When the angel visited her, and said, "Mary you have found favor with God, and the Holy Spirit will come upon you, and you shall conceive a son. He shall be called Jesus". Mary answered, and said, "But Lord, how can this be? I know not a man. Behold the handmaid of the Lord, be it according to thy word". She agreed with the angel and received the Holy Spirit. She knew the consequences of being pregnant without being married. The custom in those days, if a girl betrothed was suspected having been with another man, she was to be stoned to death. Mary was obedient to the end. She knew she had the Messiah, Jesus inside her womb, and she was confident in that knowledge. She knew nothing bad would happen to her, because God had a plan, and she was part of that plan.

When we accept Jesus in our life, we are to be as confident, even in the face of death, as was Mary. After our eyes are open, and we have Jesus living inside of us, we must know, by faith, we are a part of God's plan, and trust in that knowledge. Never doubting God has a plan. This is the whole point. God loves His creation, and His plan is to raise us up to forever live again with Him in paradise. Faith is the substance of things hoped for and the evidence of things not seen (Hebrews 11:1). We have evidence of God if we want to see it.

Have you ever been to a foot washing? The transition that takes place as you look down at the person washing your feet opens your eyes to the servitude of Christ undying love for mankind. Watching someone kneel before you, and washing your feet, brings you into the very essence of humility. I'm not sure we can grasp the nature of being a servant as deeply as Jesus would like, without a foot washing experience. I believe that is one reason why Jesus washed His disciples' feet.

After being washed by the water of the Word (Jesus), we will be born (again) of the Spirit by faith that we may enter the Kingdom of God. Being born of the Spirit is allowing the Spirit of God to come and live inside of us. Without the Holy Spirit, our spirit would never know that we came down from God. We would never know that we are purged from our sins to go back to heaven. The Holy Spirit quickens (makes alive) our spirit (Eph. 2:1) and gives us the power to become the sons of God by the washing of water by the Word (Jesus).

While Jesus was on the cross the soldier pierced his side. Blood, and water spilled on the ground (John 19:34). Water is a sign of death to the Jewish people, therefore when they saw the water, and the blood spilled on the ground, they knew Jesus was truly dead; giving soundness to His resurrection when it occurred (2 Samuel 14:14). However, there is another meaning for the blood, and the water spilled on the ground. This was a sign the life of the natural body (the blood) had been dissolved, and the life of the spirit man had been birthed; for the water spilled on the ground meant the spirit made of water had left the natural body and will be birthed into the kingdom of God. Thus, the spirit is born again.

If we go to our graves as a sinner, there will be no washing of water by the word, to give us life. In this condition, we will have become wells without water, reserved for the mist of darkness. A mist is hardly enough water to stand in the presence of a consuming fire.

The demonic spirit I spoke of in chapter 7 whom I took to be Satan, appeared to have white, scaly, dried, decaying skin. There was no fountain of living water, or blood (the life source) in him to keep him from perishing. There was no water of the Word to preserve him blameless.

Just as the streets in the city of New Jerusalem are declared as being gold, though appearing as transparent glass; just as the blood of Jesus we plead is clear, not red (see chapter on Satan in the Flesh), so is the water – the blood of the spirit man, and of the resurrected Christ, that washes away sin. These are the pure forms of the thing before sin defiled them, and the form to which they will return in heaven. The resurrected Jesus was flesh and bone.

Without salvation, the flesh, being dead in sin, without the water of the Word, will begin to decay as rottenness to the bones, attracting the scavengers of the dirt, such as worms, to feast upon its dried stench. Because sin is corruption, and filth, these worms will never die. They will feast for eternity on the shame of sin, which is the spirit of the sinner never made righteous. Decay draws maggots. These maggots, and the spirit of the sinner never saved will burn for eternity. These are worms made of spirit, like a computer has a virus, or a worm. The spirit will never die, and the shame in the spirit will fuel the eternal fire.

There is a doctrine which teaches God is a merciful God, and will not allow a soul, or spirit to burn for eternity. They arrive at this conclusion based on the valley of Hinnom in the Greek, and Gehenna in the Hebrew. Gehenna was a valley to the south of Jerusalem where sacrificial offerings were made to the god of Moloch (a false god).

Later, this valley became a garbage dump where sacrificed dead bodies, trash, and all that defiled the city were disposed, and set on fire. The ever-burning fires made Gehenna the image of ever-lasting punishment, or hell. This doctrine teaches that hell is like Gehenna, only if no fuel is added to the fire the fire will burn out. They are saying that when all the souls, or spirits bound for hell, have been consumed, the fire of hell will cease to burn from lack of fuel. That is not Biblical. The Bible plainly states that sinners will have their place in the lake of fire for eternity. Their worm (DNA) shall not die, and their fire shall not be quenched (Isaiah 66:24).

What this doctrine does not teach is that the natural body isn't the fuel for the fire. The worm that never dies is a representation of the spirit, or soul that lives in sin. The spirit of a sinner becomes as a worm in the likeness of the serpent, that old Satan. The soul, or spirit that sins against God, never coming to repentance, is a worm in that it is disgusting, and filthy. A scavenger feeding on the stench of corruption, the rottenness of the world, and all that is against God. The filth, and corruption of the worm - the spirit, will continue to burn, fueled by the spirit of shame, and its fire shall not be quenched. It's the DNA of Satan that will burn for attorney.

The spirit that came down from God, but was born into the world corruptible is everlasting, and will be the spirit that will burn for eternity. The flame will be kindled by the shame of the spirit when it realizes the Word of God is the truth, and that Jesus is Messiah; thus, is hell formed. All people are spirit, housed in a body of flesh. The flesh of the natural body is not who a person is. Their spirit man is the essence of who they are.

There are many doctrines having false concepts that will send masses of souls to burn in hell. If one can live a life of sin, which is pleasurable for a season (Hebrews 11:25), die, go to hell, be burned to ashes, as though having never lived, then many would have no justifiable reason to accept Jesus, as Savior. In the eyes of a sinner, if there were no recompense for sin, then there would be no reason for rewards for works, and victories over the trials, and tribulations of one's life on earth. It is like the laws of Moses. The people didn't even know they were sinning until the law was given. They just enjoyed sin like there was no tomorrow.

Likewise, how will the sinner know there is a heaven, unless they know there is a hell? What purpose would a sinner see in laying his life down on the earth, and serving Christ as a servant unto death, if he can see there is no recompense for his denying Christ? The law was given to bring sin to the light. The children of Israel didn't know they had come down from God and were to go back to God one day. They only knew there was a God, and He was the fullness of power. Once the law was written, and they entered a covenant with God to abide by the law, was their sin made manifest to them.

It has been over 6000 years, and mankind, still denies there is a God, and that our mission is to live in obedience to Him. Can you imagine trying to teach your children to walk in obedience for 6000 years? Most parents won't even correct their children. Many that do correct will stop correcting when they see it is too difficult in the face of adversity and convenience. It is difficult enough to correct our kids for a mere 18 years, much less longer. It is a wonder God didn't give up on us.

If this doctrine of Gehenna were true, I would say live today, and die tomorrow. Who cares what state I might find myself, in righteousness, or sin? I wouldn't care about the after-life Christ promises if there were no recompense for sin. Who would? Why should someone go through the fiery trials that try us on this earth if we could just die and make it go away?

As for God's mercy, He has warned us time, and again, through the scriptures what will happen if we do not obey Him. He has been extremely merciful, and long suffering, by His warnings, and in giving us a chance for redemption. He has sent His son Jesus to conquer death.

We, the spirit man, are not going to die, but will live forever somewhere. I think the problem is that people of the earth don't believe there is life eternal. They don't understand that Jesus conquered death, and there is no death for the spirit and soul of mankind. Our soul and spirit, the essence of man, are not going to die. We have a choice as to where we will live for eternity, but how can we get mankind to know there is an eternity. "For whosoever shall call upon the name of the Lord, shall be saved." "How shall they call on Him whom they have not believed? How can they believe if they have not heard? How can they hear without a preacher? How can they preach if they are not sent?" (Romans 10: 13-4).

While your life is but a vapor it will someday become a pillar in the temple of God if you submit yourself to Him now through Jesus Christ. Without submission to God your life will become "a well without water, clouds that are carried with a tempest; to whom the mist of darkness is reserved forever (2 Peter 2:17)". Your life without God will not even become a vapor but will be carried away, as clouds without water, to burn, and stew in its shame for eternity.

While we are on this earth in a natural body it is impossible to rid ourselves of sin. People have the wrong conception of what sin is. Most think sin is an action, when, in fact, the action is only the result of sin. Sin is a nature, a heart condition. It is disobedience to God. The body is only capable of one sin (not to be confused with the only unforgivable sin of Matthew of 12:31). That is the sin of fornication. Fornication is a sin against our body because you are becoming one with another person, outside of the guidelines of marriage. Fornication allows the spirit of lust to live in you because you are going against God's word concerning this. If a bad spirit dwells in your body, it brings sin into the temple of God. Your body is the temple of God, and God can't dwell where there is sin. The body was made for the Lord, and not for fornication. So, if you are a fornicator, the presence of God will not dwell with you. I addressed this in depth in the chapter, "Sex the Devil's Advocate".

Jesus came to rid us of sin. If we could cleanse ourselves, we would have had no need for Jesus. While we are here, we can only accept Him by faith, and let His blood cleanse us through His forgiveness. When we accept Jesus, we become justified which is a legal protection that takes place at the (marriage) altar, where we become betrothed to Christ, by receiving salvation. We can't grow in justification. It is a one -time gift.

However, sanctification means to be set apart from the world unto God for sacred use and is a daily process of growing in God's grace, and knowledge, to become the perfect Bride. The Spirit of God sends that perfect nature of Christ to live in us, which is to grow in holiness by the law of God's love.

Because sin is ever present in the world, sanctification is a daily renewing of the mind. We can be sealed with our new names, and walk in their power, and wisdom now, if we will set ourselves apart from the world, and learn to walk in the Spirit of Holiness. The only way we can do that is by the Holy Spirit of God dwelling in us by grace through faith.

There are nonbelievers, and believers that think they have no sin. I feel much compassion for these, because they don't know what they are going to face in that day when they stand face to face with God. When we think we have no sin, we deceive ourselves, and are blind, and cannot see afar off. If we can't see sin, it will be un-confessed sin, and this is the part of a person that will burn.

What if we think we have no sin, and all the while we are full of sin? Then what? When we go through the fire, it will be too late. Our entire natures will burn, and nothing will be left to live with God. But 1 John 1:9 reads, "If we confess our sins God is faithful, and just to forgive us our sins, and to cleanse us from all unrighteousness."

Confessing our sins does not mean we have no sin, but that God, who is rich in mercy, has forgiven us our sins. It is a daily asking for forgiveness. Some people think that once they have received Christ as Savior there is no need to ask forgiveness again, and again. If they never sinned again, I would agree with them. (1 John 1:8-10, and 2:1-5)

I was visiting a friend in the Mountains of Virginia in the fall of 1987. She, her brother, and I went for a walk through the woods to pray and seek the Lord. It was a beautiful day, and the scenery was extraordinary. The mountain air was fresh, and brisk. The leaves of the trees glittered from the brightness of the fall colors, and the sky was a Carolina blue with white velvety clouds gliding softly in the gentle breeze. The sun was at full strength, adding a warm glow to all God's creation.

I found a huge bed of rocks, the kind that are smooth, and large enough to lie down on, and look up to heaven. I lay down, and the warmth of the rocks, from the heat of the sun, felt good to my back. While I was lying there praying, God gave me a vision. I saw people in their spiritual body ascending to heaven. They appeared transparent, but were a hazy white, but I could not see through them. They were in the shape of the natural body, wearing long cloud like robes. God said in that moment, "If people had no sin, they would automatically be changed, and would instantly ascend to heaven (Hebrews 11:5-6)".

When we look around, and see each other, it means we are here on earth because sin has us bound inside a vile corruptible body of skin (flesh). This skin is a covering which God Gave Adam, and Eve to cover their sin.

I recalled a vision I had earlier that same day, while reading psalms 25. I saw spiritual chains cuffed around the wrist, and ankles of the earth bound, or natural body. These chains are weights of sin that have bound the natural body to the earth and held captive by Satan until the sin nature is changed. When the sin nature is changed, the natural body, or the will of the flesh will still be dead in sin, but the spirit, and the soul will have been made free. It is the flesh that is dead in sin and bound by Satan. If the body were not dead in sin, and bound, there would be nothing to hold the soul, and spirit to the earth, assuming the new nature of the spirit of God has been born in each of us.

However, the soul, and spirit, even after the new nature is born is still inside the natural body. It is free to leave but cannot leave until the death of the natural body, or until Jesus comes to receive it unto Himself. Paul said, "I have a desire to depart and be with the Christ, which is far better: nevertheless, to abide in the flesh is more needful for you (Philippians 1:23-24).

Because the flesh of the natural body is only a covering for sin, God sent Jesus to teach the world that it is not the flesh in need of change. The flesh of the natural body is dead, and will not be changed, but will return to the dust of the earth. The world had become so far removed from the knowledge of God since the days of Adam that it began to live according to the sinful, or fleshly things of the world. If people of the world would remember that they were made spirit, in the image of God, and be transformed back into the spirit of God, through Jesus, God would draw the world unto Himself. Lifting it up, forever to be with Him as he did with Enoch. This will be the finale.

There is a doctrine that teaches the new glorified body will be made flesh. This is contrary to the teaching of Paul according to 1 Corinthians 15. The spiritual body will be arrayed in glory, for flesh and blood cannot inherit the Kingdom of God.

Upon acceptance of Jesus, He will unlock these chains of bondage, giving us a new nature, and freeing our souls, and spirits. This new nature will free us from our bodies of sin, allowing us to ascend to meet Him when He comes. The spots, and blemishes in our sprits

(The old man) will have been washed away.

The unbeliever, or sinner, on the other hand, who has not received Jesus as Lord, will still be bound to the earth by these chains when Jesus comes for His Church in the gathering up, great snatch, rapture. The spots, and blemishes in their sprits, caused by living according to the flesh – sin (disobedience to God), will still be evident. The spirit will not have been made clean and will be held captive in the flesh of the natural body to suffer the consequences of being unsaved. When the catching away of the saints happens, known as the rapture, they will still be earth bound, and will not be able to leave. They will remain on earth through the tribulation, and until Jesus comes back in the Second Advent with us, His saints to rule the earth.

I am an eye - witness that Jesus is alive. He has come to me in visions bringing revelation, after revelation of His Word, and His message. He has shown me things to come, some of which have already happened. In this chapter I have told of the time I was in the presence of God our Father, though I couldn't see the similitude. I know without any doubt that, Satanism, witchcraft, the new age doctrine, Islam, Catholicism, and many other religions are false doctrines. Any religion other than the Gospel of Jesus Christ of Nazareth, is a false religion, and a road to hell in the fast lane. Isaiah 47:13-14 reads, "The astrologers, the stargazers, and the monthly prognosticators shall be as stubble; the fire shall burn them; they shall not deliver themselves from the power of the flame." Even horoscope fans are not going to escape the flame. Of course, this will not appear in a reader's daily forecast.

Many people who claim Christianity, and still dabble in the occult, horoscope reading, and the like, are classified as neither cold or hot. God said, "since you are lukewarm, and neither cold nor hot I will spue (vomit) thee out of my mouth (Rev. 3:15-17). Dabbling in these things allows an open door to Satan to enter your thoughts and direct your paths. It may seem harmless, but you are allowing Satan a foothold in your life. Even in knowing this, the eyes of many will continue in blindness. For they have not eyes to see, nor ears to hear. The day shall come when they shall see their shame, and it shall burn them up: they will be cast into outer darkness where, "Their worm shall never die, and their fire shall not be quenched (Isaiah 66:24)

Ezekiel 28:18-19, we are told what is going to happen to Satan. "Thou hast defiled thy sanctuaries by the multitude of thine iniquities, by the iniquity of thy traffic; therefore, will I bring a fire from the midst of thee: it shall devour thee, and I will bring thee to ashes upon the earth in the sight of all, them that behold thee. All they that know thee among the people shall be astonished at thee: thou shalt be a terror, and never shalt thou be any more." Does this sound like a leader to be followed? If you follow Satan, this is your heritage. When you stand in the presence of God on judgment day, Satan cannot save you. He, himself, will have been cast into the lake of fire, and brimstone that is set-aside for him, and all those who believe, and follow him (Rev. 20:10-15), (Malachi 3:16-18, 4:1-6).

God the Father of lights, Mother Jerusalem (came out from God), (see Rev. 4:3, 21:11,18, and Gen. 1:27), Jesus – the Son (came out from God), and the saints (the Church – us- came out from God), are all united in marriage to the Christ Spirit of God; who is the Word, that was with God from the beginning, and "IS GOD". By the Spirit of God, who is the Spirit of glory, and of God (1 Peter 4:14), all are made one to be the Bride of Christ. "And the Spirit, and Bride say "COME". (Rev. 22:17, Eph. 2,3, and 4)

Reach forth your hand and partake of the Tree of Life that you may live. You are bought with a price, and you are not your own. You are Spirit come down from God and are going back to God. You don't know whom you are except through Jesus Christ. Receive Him that

you will sparkle in the light, and not burn.

I leave you with this, thought. God Himself is Love, and He is the creator of life. So, stands to reason, He is the Love of Life. We are His counterpart, so I guess you could say: "God is the Love of our Life, and we are the Love of His Life", so stop searching for love.

Love has been found.

CHAPTER 12

Another Visit With Jesus

On November 29th, 1986, I was at home doing my daily Bible study. The time was 11:30 p.m. As I studied, I was suddenly caught away in the Spirit to another time, and place. For the record, you don't have to be slain in the Spirit, lying on the floor, to be taken by the Spirit on a journey.

The Holy Spirit took me to a forest far into the wilderness. In the forest, among the trees was a small clearing. In this clearing was a small flock of sheep. Even I, myself, was a sheep. I was seeing through the sheep's eyes, but it was still I. Though, I was myself, I was neither male, nor female. This was not a reincarnation experience, but a venture God had allowed. He had allowed my spirit to experience why He compares humans to sheep. I'm sure this will raise some eyebrows, but if God can make a donkey speak, He can surely take my spirit to where He wants.

While my spirit was in the sheep's body, I was busy running in, and out of the forest. Each time I returned to the clearing I brought with me another sheep to join the flock. These were sheep that had strayed, and I was bringing them back to the fold.

On one of my return trips from the forest to the clearing, I heard a rustling in the trees. As I looked toward from where the noise came, there stood Jesus. I began to leap for joy. It was the happiest feeling I had ever experienced. There is nothing in this world that can bring happiness the way I felt in that moment when I saw Jesus, face to face. Jesus had returned to the flock. I was leaping for joy and shouting, "Jesus is back, Jesus is back."

Here again He was extremely tall. I would say He was approximately 700, to 900 feet tall. He looked the same as when I had seen Him in the past, but this time He was closer to me. His skin was like I've never seen in this world. It was white, but it was a white that doesn't exist on earth. It appeared soft as a cloud, satin or silk, and had sheen as reflected by small feathers of a bird. If we could see "purity", His face is what it looks like.

Linda L. Evans

He looked down at me, and He smiled. In His smile was everything good anyone could ever want or need. It was the kind of smile that could melt a heart by its warmth, and goodness. If we could see "pure love", it would look like His smile.

Next, He made a gesture toward me with His righthand index finger, to single me out. Upon doing this, He spoke these words while smiling the prettiest smile I have ever seen, "You have done a good job." When He spoke, His lips did not move, nor did I hear His voice with my ears. He spoke from His heart, and I heard from mine. Our hearts were not the one inside our natural body, but the heart of our spirit, in our mind. The words He spoke was like receiving the grandest reward ever made. There is nothing in this world that can be compared to hearing Jesus say, "Well done thou good, and faithful servant."

As He lingered, I knew that Jesus, the flock, and me were all one being. I wish I could explain the beauty, happiness, purity, holiness, and oneness of that moment. I knew I had become a whole, whereas, before I was in part. Now that Jesus was with me, I had been made complete in Him. In that moment, I saw the beginning from the end in the plan of God.

Jesus continued to explain the three times I had seen Him when He had made me His bell sheep. He said, "I heard you call out to me, and I picked you up, and placed you at my feet. Now follow closely behind me, and I will train you in the way you should go. Then you shall go out, and bring back to the flock, those who have lost their way." After saying this, He left, and I was suddenly returned to my natural body, in the present. I could do nothing for a while except ponder in my heart what had happened. I wept like a baby, tears of exultation, and tears of longing to be with Him again. I didn't want to be back in the natural, but I had to accept that I was. There is nothing to compare to being in the presence of Jesus.

Wiping the tears from my eyes I continued in my Bible sturdy. While I was reading, I heard God say the words, "Sheep eyes". Trying to understand why He said that I pondered it over, and over in my mind. I even called a friend and related to him what God had said. It made no more sense to him than it had to me. I knew it must be important.

The next day I went to the library to do research on sheep. The library was a large one, but only had one book about sheep. The book was small, and after searching diligently I could find nothing pertaining to a sheep's eyes. I prayed a silent prayer asking God to help me understand. He told me to check the index one more time. As I read the chapters one seemed to jump out at me. It was titled, "How to buy, and sell (market)". I began to read, and one paragraph listed the top five things to check when buying sheep. Third on the list stated, "check for blindness." Smiling I said, "Praise God, I finally found something about the eyes."

I went home, and should have been happy about my find, but I wasn't. These three little words of information just weren't enough. Enough for what, I didn't know. I guess I thought I would find the answer to what God was trying to tell me. When I didn't, I became a little disappointed.

Days went by, and I still didn't know what God wanted me to know. Late one evening while studying my Bible God spoke to me again. He began telling me about the sheep in the flock and took me into a vision where a flock of sheep was grazing in a pasture. The shepherd was standing at the head of the flock. When the shepherd began to walk the sheep followed. Continuing to walk, the sheep spread out in a pyramid pattern behind the shepherd. There were two bell sheep directly behind the shepherd, then three behind the two, and so on. The triangular pattern must continue each row of sheep in order for each to have a lead sheep and stay as close to the shepherd as possible. If one sheep too many is in a row the odd one out will have no lead directly in front of it. In this position the odd sheep out won't be able to stay in line. If the odd sheep out has no lead, it and those following him will fall away causing the flock to fall out of order.

This illustration can be used for the Church as well. To be close to the shepherd (Jesus), we as believers must stay close to each other behind Christ so that we don't fall away and become lost. It only takes one believer to get out of order, and many will follow. For instance: If the pastor is out of order in his teaching his entire flock will be out of order. Lucifer is an example of this kind of falling away. When Lucifer exalted himself above God, and fell from heaven, many angels under his authority fell with him. God is saying to us that we must stay in line with Christ, our shepherd, assembling ourselves together in fellowship, and worship. We are to stay close to each other that we will not stray in a time of temptation. If one believer falls out of order the flock is no longer in complete unity, and many members will suffer from the fall. Paul explained it accurately in 1 Corinthians 5:6 saying, "Know ye not that a little leaven leaveneth the whole lump?" Leaven in the Bible, and to the Jews is a type for sin.

Continuing to speak God explained that "a sheep's vision is very near-sighted. That is why they huddle close to one another in a flock. Sheep tend to be blind and that is why some sheep fall away from the flock. In the flock the two most likely to fall away are the sheep the most distance away from the shepherd on the ends of the last row. The sheep in these two end positions are open to the outside, and no sheep behind them to nudge them along. They only have a partial connection to the lead sheep in front of them, and none to the side to keep them in line. Sheep are naturally dumb and need to be lead. They have no sense of direction without a leader.

The sheep inside the flock are secure and are not apt to fall away. They are surrounded on both sides front and back by other sheep in the flock. They have leads all around them. The only sheep that do not have two leads are the outside sheep. These sheep are, also exposed to the outside world around them, and can be easily distracted, causing them to be more inclined to stray off on their own. The outside sheep in front of the two ends are not as likely to be distracted as the two ends on the last row. They still have some from behind nudging them should they begin to stray. These are also closer to the shepherd which also helps them stay in line. If the two-end sheep stop to rest, graze, or are distracted, there is none behind them to nudge them on, or to keep them in line.

Linda L. Evans

<pre>
Outside sheep are leads   *   Shepherd

                    *   *   Bell sheep

              *   *   *

       End - *   *   *   * - End
</pre>

God is saying that some in the flock are apt to fall away most often because of their exposure to the outside world. He is speaking about all who fall away from Him. When a man falls from the flock, it doesn't mean he is no longer a part of the flock, it simply means he has become lost from the flock, and now has become a lost sheep, not lost in the sense of never having been saved. This example illustrates how a believer can be distracted by the world when he is not in constant communion with fellow believers. If believers do not always keep their eyes directly on Jesus they can be distracted by the worldly things, and temptation to follow these things can lead them astray.

If a believer is not one to attend church often, the other members are not going to know when this one believer is in trouble, or in a fallen condition. When a person is faithful in his attendance, and suddenly stops attending church, hopefully fellow members are going to visit him, and find out what is the problem. Then, if a fallen condition is found in the absentee, the members can lead him back to the flock to regain his position as a believer.

In our journey as a Christian, before being weaned from the milk of the word, temptations by the worldly things are great. When we become saved, and a part of the Church body, we often stop to graze, or stop coming to church as often as we should. While we are grazing, there may be none to nudge us, or to encourage us to continue our walk in Christ. For this reason, it is important to have a church home in which to become a member.

In a church home, the members will become like family, and will be there to encourage our faith in God. As a new babe in Christ, and in the church family, we are like the end sheep, apt to stray often. Therefore, the church body is to help nourish the new baby in Christ, and teach him how to stay in the flock, and not be distracted by the world. The church is to do this by teaching the new member the right way to go and guarding him as if it were their own child. Age is not a factor in being a new member to the body of Christ.

When the end sheep falls away, and there is no one to help him back to the flock, he cannot return on his own. When he stops to graze, the flock continues to move forward, and becomes further, and further away. The lost sheep is left wandering in the outside world, and because of distractions, and blindness, doesn't realize he is lost. While he wanders around in the world, doing his own thing, he is chased by wild animals (enemies). He can't find lush green grazing like his shepherd provided; he misses the unity, and love he once experienced in the flock, and he has no direction. His lack of direction, and purpose becomes more evident with each passing day.

Upon remembrance of his shepherd, the lost sheep begins to run in a feeble attempt to catch up with the flock. After running in every direction, he becomes tired and stops to rest, putting even more distance between him, and the flock. Now he will have to work twice as hard to catch up, assuming the flock has moved on without stopping. As his search continues, his remembrance of the flock becomes dim, and is fading away. While trying to survive in the world, he becomes uncaring, bitter, and blind. Not blind in the usual sense, but blind in the eyes of his memory. He continues to search for he knows not what, and in his blindness, he is truly lost. "All we like sheep have gone astray: We have turned everyone to his own way (Isaiah 53:6)." The sheep is an excellent example of the fall of man.

Each person in the world is a sheep in God's flock. When Adam fell, he brought disorder to the flock causing all future people to wander aimlessly without a shepherd. We, like lost sheep are out wandering on our own trying to do our own thing and find our place in the world. Like the lost sheep, we are running a race to we know not where, completely blinded of the memory of who we are in Jesus.

Instead of remembrance we experience feelings of emptiness, loneliness, lack of purpose, and weariness from running an endless race to reach a goal we cannot see. We don't know that we are looking for our flock, and our shepherd. We only know that we are looking for whatever we can find that will give us unity, security, a purpose, a place, direction, happiness, and love.

When the lost sheep was in the flock, closely knit together with the other sheep, and his shepherd, the shepherd supplied all his needs. He had the best pastures to graze, water was plentiful, he got plenty of rest, and most of all he had love, and security. Out in the world he must struggle to get his needs met, and because of his blindness he can't distinguish between his enemies, and his friends.

Having wandered a long time, he becomes hungry, thirsty, and weary. One day he wanders into a pack of wild beast (foxes, bears, lions, etc.). The sheep, being rundown, and puny, from lack of food is very thin, and frail. When the wild beast of the field sees the sheep, the beast has visions of lamb chops. Instead of attacking the sheep, the wild pack takes him in, and begins to fatten him up.

The beasts feed the sheep, provides shelter from the weather, they play with him, and they make him feel part of the pack. He is kept so busy by their affection, and attention that he becomes drunk with deception for all he has come to possess. He doesn't know he is being fattened up for the kill, and that it is only a matter of time before he will be eaten. All he knows is his needs are being met, and he SEEMS to have all he desires. There is a way that seems right, but the end thereof is death (proverbs 14:12).

We, like the lost sheep, have become drunk on deception. We can't distinguish between our enemy, and our friend. Our enemy-Satan, and our friend-Jesus are our only enemy, and friend. Man became lost when he fell into the hands of his enemy Satan. By our distance from God, we are become blind, and Satan has lied to us, by professing to be our friend. Satan's lies have led us further, and further away from God. His lies have made us totally dependent on him.

Under his lead, we have fallen into deceit, wickedness, evil, and iniquity. It is a plot against our lives, and we can't see it because Satan has deceived us in giving us the world. We have become drunk on all we possess. If we look back to the beginning of the fall of man, we can see man's goal clearly, a goal of obtaining more, and more in material possessions. All we can think about is how to get what we want, how to get more, and how to maintain, and keep it.

The story of the lost sheep continues as we find him being fattened up for the kill, but he is oblivious to the scheme of his enemies. The pack is just waiting for the day when food supplies will be low. They have all the food they need for the moment. Besides, the sheep works as hard as they do, and he takes care of himself for the most part. All they must do is pay him attention and include him in their lives. Being careful they don't lose the sheep they follow him everywhere he goes. The sheep thinks this is wonderful. He can go anywhere, and do anything, and his friends follow him, never leaving his side. He thinks this is true love.

One day when the sheep is out grazing, he meets his original flock. Of course, he doesn't recognize them, for too much time has lapsed since he last saw them. They tell him he is lost, and they have come to show him the way home. He thinks they are preaching to him and tells them they are crazy as he runs to join the pack waiting nearby. Unable to convince the lost sheep that he is one of them, the flock moves on once again.

As time moves from summer to fall, and then to winter, food supplies begin to get quite low. The pack is getting hungry, and the sheep is looking good. One day, the awaited time arrives. The pack decides the time is right, and they begin to chase the unsuspecting little lost sheep. He flees for his life. While he is running in fear, he is frantic wondering what has happened. Everything has fallen apart. His peaceful life has been turned upside down; his false friends have become as ravenous beasts, seeking to kill, and devour him. "He cries out, "What has happened? Someone please, help me."

Finding a place to hide, and rest, the lost sheep remembers the day when he met the sheep from the flock. They had told him things he couldn't believe at that time. They had told him they too were once lost, but they had cried out to the shepherd, and he had found them, and taken them home. They told the lost sheep that when the day comes, and it will, that you get tired of running, and want to come home, you should just call out, and the shepherd will find you.

In his desperation, he found this hard to believe, but would try anything now. He had lost all he had, and there was nothing else to lose, but everything to gain. There in his little hiding place, he began to cry. He was afraid to cry too loudly, for fear his enemies would hear, and find him. So, he quietly whispered in his heart, "I'm ready to come home shepherd please come and get me." As soon as he had spoken those words, the shepherd was there. The shepherd retrieved the lost sheep, nestled him in his bosom, and returned him to the flock.

After a few days he couldn't imagine having ever left the flock. He had everything here. All his needs were supplied, and everything was better than when he was in the pack. In the flock he knew he was home because here, he looked in appearance like the rest of the flock. When he was in the pack, he didn't know he was different from them because they all were different in appearance from each other. No two looked alike. Now that he was home, he could see clearly, and he had missed the love, and care of his shepherd most of all. His eyes, once blind, could now see, and he could now remember that this is where he belongs. He was home.

Like the lost sheep, we come to a place in life when all is going well. Then one day a believer (Christian) begins to tell us about Jesus. For the most part we do not want to listen. The reason we don't want to listen is because the character of Jesus sounds too good to be true. It sounds like a fairy tale. His character is so much the opposite of our own that it is hard to believe that this kind of goodness exists. But like the sheep there is coming a day when the devil will require payment for all he has given us. He is fattening us up for the kill as he pampers us, gives us affection, attention, and supplies all our wants. We can't see what is happening because our wants are being fulfilled. We can't believe there is a life we can lead that will supply all our needs, and at the same time give us life more abundant, and eternal.

The pasture we are grazing SEEMS to be sufficient, in that, it supplies all our needs. The difference is, we are grazing with our enemy instead of our friend that sticks closer than a brother, Jesus. In the end, an enemy will turn against us, and will seek to take all we have accomplished, and will take our lives too. When this happens, and it will, what are we going to do? Where will we turn? In 1 Peter 5:8 we read, "Be sober, and be vigilant, because your adversary the devil, as a roaring lion, walketh about seeking whom he may devour."

Because the devil's crowd has many faces, none looking alike, you can be easily distracted, and led astray by them. When you become a believer, you can know your friends by their fruit, and the light in their eyes. True believers all look alike. Like a tree bearing fruit, one true believer bears the same fruit as the next. The Bible declares that you shall know them by their fruit. This is the way that God gives you to distinguish between your enemy, and your friend. Do your friends possess the fruits of the Spirit? Do they all look like Jesus?

When the lost sheep called out for his shepherd, he called out from his heart in fear. His shepherd heard him because he had been there all along. He had been calling out to the sheep, but the sheep was so distracted by the world, and beast of the field that he couldn't hear his shepherd calling. He was so busy doing his own thing that he had turned a deaf ear to the voice once so familiar to him. He had become accustomed to the voice of his enemy, and when the shepherd called out to him, he became as dumb to the sound of the shepherd's voice. He had not only become dumb, but he was, also blind. He could not see his shepherd was standing nearby. The shepherd had even sent other sheep from the flock to lead the lost sheep home. The shepherd thought the lost sheep might listen to them, but to no avail.

As the shepherd continued to call out, the lost sheep continued to ignore him. The shepherd knew the path of destruction on which the lost sheep would travel. Feeling sad for the state of this little lost one, the shepherd just waited for the day that the lost sheep would call out to him. That's why, when the sheep called out from his heart, the shepherd heard him, and knew he was ready to come home. Before the sheep could realize he needed his shepherd, he had to come to a place where he faced death, and disaster; a place where he had lost all he had; a place where his friends (enemies) turned, and sought to take his life, and a place where he had nowhere to go. When he hid from his enemies, he had stopped running long enough to consider his place in the world. He had run as far as he could run. Having reached his end, he had to stop, and consider his way.

Jesus is our shepherd. He is by our side every moment of our lives. He would rather we come to Him before our lives are turned up-side-down; but like the lost sheep, we will not stop running long enough to hear Him calling us. Because we are blinded to who Jesus is (the truth), we can't see Him standing nearby. We like the sheep, are near-sighted, and cannot see afar off. We cannot see what lies in the future for us in a life without Jesus. We can only see that which surrounds us in our everyday lives. Because our surroundings SEEM to be right, we cannot see the lost condition in which we walk, nor can we hear the voice of our Lord when He calls us. There is none that isn't called, for Jesus said, "All are called."

Jesus sees the path of destruction we are on, and what is ahead in our lives. Unless we take a chance, and trust Him, we will fall prey to our enemy, and he will devour us. There is coming a day when all men shall know that the Lord, He is God. "For it is written, as I live saith the Lord, every knee shall bow to me, and every tongue shall confess to God." (Romans 14:11, Philippians 2:10)

If you don't call out to Jesus your shepherd, then you will not know you are lost. This story is not a story made up as an example. Word for word, it is a true story; for we all are that lost sheep. Each of us is the one, for whom He left the ninety and nine, and found. God allowed me, in His Spirit to see through the eyes of the lost sheep, and to experience his lost condition. Through this experience, God revealed to me the true state of being lost from Him in a way I could never have otherwise known.

Living in the wilderness as an animal is exactly how we live when we are lost. We are animals running wild; but we don't see it in our blindness. When I came home, God told me it didn't matter what I had done while I was lost. He told me there is no amount of evil that the blood of His son couldn't cleanse. He took me just as I was. I was once lost, but Jesus found me when I called out to Him. I once was blind, but now I see.

Though you have become deaf to the sound of His voice, you will not only hear Him calling, but you can also see Him if you will allow yourself to believe He is there. If you will come to Him by the measure of faith He planted in you in the beginning, you can know Jesus.

"O come let us worship and bow down: Let us kneel before the Lord God our maker: for He is our God; and we are the people of His pasture, and the sheep of His hand. Today, if you will hear His voice, harden not your heart as in the provocation, and as in the day of temptation in the wilderness: when your fathers tempted Me, proved Me, and saw My work. Forty years long was I grieved with this generation, and said, it is a people that do ere in their hearts, and they have not known My ways: unto who I swear in My wrath they should not enter into my rest." (Psalms 95.6-11)

You are part of God's flock, and Jesus is calling you. He wants to open your eyes that you may see your lost state in living without Him. Come home, that there may be unity in the flock. Without you, the body is incomplete. If you will, whisper His name from your heart, He will hear you, and you'll not be turned away. He will come, and find you, bring you home where you belong, and you will be made complete in Him.

I'm not sure of the exact year, but it was July 16th around the year 1990 when the Lord spoke to me saying, "It is time to lay all aside, and come home; for the church is on the rise; God is restoring His people. Today is the day of salvation. The work of the ministry is growing, prophecy is going forth, and the revival in the heart has begun."

Then the Lord took me into a vision. In the vision a friend, and I were taking food from the stovetop, and placing it on the table (there were masses of people there). The table was set for a mighty feast.

As we were busy taking the food to the table the Lord spoke again saying, "It is time to begin to do what I have called you to do; to fulfill that purpose for which I created in you. Let nothing, and no one hinder you from your purpose. My people have been waiting on me to perform that which I have called them to do, and the time is now. Just as the food for a meal must be prepared that each dish might be placed on the table at the same time, so I prepare my people to come out at the same time. Many have tried to run ahead of me, but have failed, and wondered why they could not do what I called them to do. Many have become confused and saying, perhaps I did not hear from God after all. It is time to recognize that YES, I have called you, but the time was not yet right. I had to prepare each one for a different length of time that all could come together at the same time to do that which I have purposed for each life. It is the same as the meal: one dish to be cooked a little longer than another but must come to the table together for the meal to be served right. If one dish to be served hot were placed on the table before the others the first would be cold, and unfit for the feast before the other foods are served. For all the food to be served at its best, it must be timed to be served at just the right time."

By this vision we can know why our loved ones aren't always saved at the time we think they should be. If all people were saved at the same time, some would mature before others, and some would still be on milk when they needed to be on meat, and so forth. For the fullness of the gentiles to come in, preparation must begin in stages. Keep praying for those you love, that have not yet seen the light of salvation. Praying gives them supernatural strength. When the time is right, they will be saved, we will all complete our purpose, and then we can all go to the marriage supper of the Lamb.

I had another vision shortly after this. I saw Christians lying on the ground face down, and very much persecuted. Then I saw them one, by one began to stand upright, like soldiers standing at attention. The Lord spoke to me saying, "My people are like seeds that have been planted in the ground. When a flower seed is planted it does not spring forth immediately as the flower it is going to be. It first must be watered, sprout roots taking root in the soil, and then began to grow. Even in all this, the time to break through the crust of the earth into the world is not yet. As you go, and look for the flower each day, and water the spot in which you know the seed is planted, you keep the hope of its appearing. As your hope grows, so does the flower. One day when you have grown weary of waiting and watching and you go to water the spot, behold the new life has burst forth from the earth. The key here is to never stop watering, or you will lose your hope/faith.

Thus, the Christians that have taken root, and grounded themselves in the hope of their calling, and the appearing of the Lord Jesus Christ, will now break forth into the life, and purpose for which they were called. Many have stopped watering and have given up hope. The life in their seed lies dormant, which is their measure of faith, I planted in them. For these the time has come, and that part which was to be supplied by them has been taken away, and given to another, that measure of faith which gives the strength necessary for breaking through the crust of the earth. You did run well; who has hindered thee that you should not obey the truth? (Galatians 5:7) But I have a remnant that has not forsaken the truth but has continued in the hope of their calling: forsaking all else to stand firm upon my word, and in the face of their adversary. The time is now that thy calling, and purpose shall be revealed. There are many that do not even know what their calling, and purpose is, but have stood steadfast in the faith, and have not faltered. They have continued to sow, water, wait, and watch, and now is their time to reap. Now is the time for the coming together for the feast that has been prepared. The table is set, and the meal is about to be served. Whosoever will, come and dine", saith the Lord of Host.

Won't you give your heart to Jesus, so you too can live in the light of God's truth? Just say, "Jesus come into my heart and be my Savior from the lies of Satan. I give you my heart, and I believe you are the Son of God. I believe you came to save me from my sins, and that you died for me, and rose again, the third day that I may live." If you say this and really mean it with all your heart, Jesus will manifest Himself to you. There will be no question of whether, or not, Jesus is real. You will see the truth as the light of Christ shines on you, in you, and through you. Just remember the light of the soul is in the eyes. Turn your eyes upon Jesus, then you too Will SPARKLE in the LIGHT.

THE END

THANKS TO GOD

I give honor and glory to my Father who in the day of my nativity picked me up, cleansed me, clothed me, swaddled me, and made a covenant with me, and I became His. Ezekiel 16

My Father God never gave up on me, and He has loved me unconditionally, showing me the sure mercies of King David, and dealing with me as He did with Moses.

This book is a success story in the transformation of life, from Glory to Glory. I give Father God all the glory for His longsuffering, gentleness, His Holy Spirit striving with me, molding me, and loving me unconditionally. I thank Him for the many trials, and tribulations that have brought me into His Kingdom as His daughter. Most of all I thank Him for Jesus who gave His life that I may know Him and live.

I give Praise, Honor, Glory, and Thanksgiving to God in all things. I ask the Father to do the same, for all who read this book, as He has done for me, in the name of our Lord, and Savior, Jesus Christ. Peace.

Acknowledgments

Thanks to Jan, for the word of prophecy during blessing Sunday, 2009. The word from the Lord was, "Get the writings from the attic, and begin to write those things He has and will give you." (paraphrased).

A special thank you to Bill for taking time to share with me his knowledge, and experience in wheat farming.

Cover Layout by Graphic Designer Lisa Latham.

Cover Picture of Open Eye Vision on August 21st, 2009, captured on canvas "The Glory of God", by author Linda L. Evans

* To schedule speaking engagements direct correspondence to evanslinda7@gmail.com

NOTES

a. A book by a single author, Cumbey, Constance E., "The Hidden Dangers of the Rainbow", revised edition, 1983 Huntington House, Inc.

b. A book by a single author Randal N. Baer, "Inside The new Age NIGHTMARE", Huntington House, Inc., Lafayette, Louisiana 70505

c. A book by two authors, Hunt, Dave, and McMahon, T. A., "America: The Sorcerer's New Apprentice". Harvest House Publishers, Eugene, Oregon 97402 (reported statements on Oprah Winfrey show on 2/17/88)

d. Abortion (videotape) – produced by Peg Yorkin of Los Angeles, Ca., - Author: Simpson, P., refutes the antiabortion film – Silent Scream, Source; MS, Aug. 89, p79, ½ p, issn: 0047-8318, Item No: 8909040723 reported in Time Magazine 1985 Issue.

e. Adolescent Sexuality in the United States, website April 2011

f. Comments, and Information from Jack Van Impe Presents. Jack Van Impe television host, Christian news anchor, World Events, and Prophecy Teacher, and Evangelist, 2010-2011.

g. Comment by John Hagee Televison Host of John Hagee Ministries, Leader of COIF, Author, and Pastor, Cornerstone Church, San Antonio Texas.

h. Comments by Larry Bates, Banker, Economist, United Nations speaker, guest speaker on many Christian Television Broadcast. Comments from 2008, on God TV.

i.   Comment by Miles Monroe television Evangelist, and Author

j.   Comments by Perry Stone of Manna Fest, Pastor, Evangelist, Prophet, Teacher 2010- 2011.

k.   Funk & Wagnall's standard desk dictionary, copyright 1980 by Lippincott & Crowell, Publishers.

l.   Living Bible (paraphrased) Tyndale House Publishers, Wheaton, Illinois.

m.   Matthew Henry Commentary, Marshall, Morgan & Scott, Limited, copyright 1961 by Zondervan publishing House, Grand Rapids, Michigan 49506.

n.   National Institute of Mental Health, Schizophrenia, website April 2011

o.   New Age Lies To Women by Wanda Marrs, wife of Author Texe Marrs, listed above.

p.   Oprah Winfrey statements on her television show in 2010, and 2011 noted on Face Book

q.   "Out On A Limb," author Shirley McClain, actress

r.   Richard Ramirez, "Nightstalker" – New York Times, national Wednesday, 11-18-89, Pg. A18, Column 5, 8-16-89 pg., A16. Col. 1, and 8-17-89 Pg., A20, Col, 1.

s.   Silent Scream – (The Motion Picture) do not have the information on who made this film.

t.   Silent Scream – (antiabortion film) article in Time Magazine dated 3/25/85 p62 2/3 page, issn; 0040-781X – item No; 8500009888.

u.   The Holy Bible, King James Version, and verse reference edition, A. J. Holman Company, Philadelphia.

v.   Three books by a single author, Marrs, Texe, "Mystery Mark Of The New Age", "Dark Secrets Of The New Age', Crossway Books, Westchester, Illinois, and "Ravaged By The New Age", Living Truth Publishers, Austin, Texas.

w.   Turn Your Eyes Upon Jesus, song – score, and lyrics by Helen H. Lemmel

x.   U.S. Centers For Disease Control And Prevention, website April 2011

y.   Unger's Bible Dictionary, by Merrill F. Unger – Moody Press, Chicago – third edition copyright 1985.

z.   Watchman Fellowship 2001, index of cults, and religions, a Mormon expositor of nearly every religion from A-Z on the web.

aa. Wikapedia, Jessica McClure

ab. Wilkerson, David, Times Square Church Pulpit Series – Newsletter, 6-15-92; The Truth About Judas – Betrayer of Christ.

ac. Grant Jeffrey Bible Prophecy Teacher and Author